the *Apologist's*
TOOL KIT

the Apologist's TOOL KIT

RESOURCES TO HELP YOU DEFEND
the Christian Faith

ROB PHILLIPS

TABLE OF CONTENTS

MORMONISM

JEHOVAH'S WITNESSES

ROMAN CATHOLICISM

THE WORD OF FAITH MOVEMENT

SNAKE-HANDLING PENTECOSTALS

VI. OTHER APOLOGETICS TOPICS

EVANGELISM AND THE EXCLUSIVITY OF CHRISTIANITY

THE UNSEEN REALM, THE AFTERLIFE, AND THE END OF THE WORLD

TOUGH QUESTIONS ABOUT GOD

SCIENCE AND RELIGION

RELATIVISM AND UNBELIEF

HOMOSEXUALITY

STEWARDSHIP

FOREWORD

I was embarrassed into Christian apologetics.

It happened one bright Saturday morning when two ladies from the local Kingdom Hall knocked on my front door. A new believer, eager to share my faith, I invited the Jehovah's Witnesses in while my wife eavesdropped from another room. It didn't take long for the pleasantries to spiral downward into a series of pointed questions directed at me concerning the deity of Christ and other biblical doctrines Jehovah's Witnesses deny. After several agonizing moments in which I stammered, stalled, and flipped aimlessly through my Bible, the ladies stood and smiled. One of them said, "We'll come back when you're better prepared." Ouch.

As I watched them leave, a sick feeling descended to the pit of my stomach. I knew that what Jehovah's Witnesses teach about the person and work of Christ is wrong, but I was ill equipped to present a positive case for historic Christianity. For the next several days I found it difficult to eat or sleep. The Lord used that humbling experience to develop in me a passion to more successfully defend Christianity. That's what apologetics is: a reasonable defense of the Christian faith.

Followers of Jesus always have faced withering attacks from those outside the church – from worshipers in the cult of Caesar to militant Muslims. But potentially more damaging are threats from *within* – from false teachers who tickle our ears (2 Tim. 4:3) to false prophets who come to us with "cleverly contrived myths" (2 Peter 1:16). The apostle Peter urges us to "always be ready to give a defense to anyone who asks you for a reason for the hope that is in you," and to do so "with gentleness and respect" (1 Peter 3:15-16).

The Apologist's Tool Kit 3rd Edition equips you to defend the Christian faith in just this way. The pages that follow address some of the most commonly challenged Christian doctrines, from the existence of God to the authority of Scripture. Each chapter concludes with probing questions, talking points, and references for further reading, making this a handy resource for personal or group study.

My prayer is that these pages equip you with the basics of Christian doctrine and provide you with enough information about popular false belief systems so you can engage your lost friends in meaningful conversation – and perhaps even avoid humiliating experiences in your own living room.

Rob Phillips
February 2016

I.

APOLOGETICS AND WORLDVIEW

1
WHAT IS CHRISTIAN APOLOGETICS?

Christian apologetics is the field of study concerned with the systematic defense of the Christian faith. Stated more simply, it is a reasonable defense of Christianity. The term "apologetics" is derived from the Greek word *apologia* and was used in a legal sense: The prosecution delivered the *kategoria* and the defendant replied with an *apologia*, or a formal speech to counter the charges. The verb form, *apologeomai*, means "to make a defense." The Christian apologist is engaged in defending Christianity's claims to the truth.

In Scripture, the apostle Paul uses the term *apologia* in his speech to Agrippa when he says, "I consider myself fortunate ... that today I am going to make a *defense* before you" (Acts 26:2). Paul uses a similar term in his letter to the Philippians to describe his role as a defender of the gospel (Phil. 1:7, 16). Peter tells believers they should be ready to give a *defense* of their faith, with gentleness and respect, in 1 Peter 3:15-16. The term is used in a negative sense in Romans 1:20, where Paul says those who reject the revelation of God in creation are "without *excuse*."

Why Christianity is reasonable

Christian apologists throughout the centuries have appealed to eyewitness accounts (specifically having to do with the person and work of Christ), as well as to Scripture, history, philosophy, archaeology and other scientific disciplines. Many have suffered martyrs' deaths, not because they clung foolishly to a blind faith, but because they were fully convinced of the truth of Christianity based on careful examination of the evidence.

Consider how these passages of Scripture exhort Christians to defend their faith:

2 Cor. 10:4-5: ...*since the weapons of our warfare are not fleshly, but are powerful through God for the demolition of strongholds. We demolish arguments and every high-minded thing that is raised up against the knowledge of God, taking every thought captive to the obedience of Christ.* **Christianity is powerful.**

1 Thess. 5:21: *…but test all things. Hold on to what is good.* **Christianity is testable.**

Titus 1:9: *…holding to the faithful message as taught, so that he will be able both to encourage with sound teaching and to refute those who contradict it.* **Christianity is practical.**

1 Peter 3:15: *…but set apart the Messiah as Lord in your hearts, and always be ready to give a defense to anyone who asks you for a reason for the hope that is in you.* **Christianity is rational.**

Jude 3: *Dear friends, although I was eager to write you about our common salvation, I found it necessary to write and exhort you to contend for the faith that was delivered to the saints once for all.* **Christianity is durable.**

Why apologetics matters

There are at least three reasons apologetics is essential to Christians:

Our faith depends on it. William A. Dembski, research professor in philosophy at Southwestern Baptist Theological Seminary and author of *The Design Revolution*, comments: "It's worth remembering that until two centuries ago, most people in the West saw the Resurrection of Jesus in historically the same light as other events of antiquity, such as the murder of Julius Caesar. The Resurrection and Caesar's murder were both regarded as equally factual and historical. Unfortunately, in the two hundred years since the Enlightenment, Christians have steadily retreated from seeing their faith as rationally compelling. Instead of being apologists for the faith, we have become apologetic about it."[1]

The Bible tells us to love God with all our minds (Matt. 22:37). Emotions and experiences are important gifts of God, but they are not compelling reasons for trusting in Christ, Muhammad, the Buddha, Krishna, Joseph Smith, or anyone else. We should be as the Bereans, who, upon hearing of Christ's death, burial and resurrection, "welcomed the message (of Paul and Silas) with eagerness and examined the Scriptures daily to see if these things were so…. Consequently, many of them believed" (Acts 17:11-12).

Our witness depends on it. Major world religions and cults of Christianity have high views of Jesus, yet they fail to properly answer the question Jesus asked in Matt. 16:15: "Who do you say that I am?"

Muslims, for example, teach that Jesus was a prophet, but they deny His deity and substitutionary death on the cross. Many Hindus readily accept Jesus into their pantheon of 330 million gods yet refuse to accept His uniqueness as the eternal Son of God. Mormons insist that Jesus earned His deity in a pre-mortal existence. If we truly believe, as Peter did, that Jesus is the Christ, the Son of the living God (Matt. 16:16), we need to know what that means and why it's true.

Our future depends on it. Christianity is under attack on many fronts – from atheists who mock it (*The God Delusion* by Richard Dawkins; *God is Not Great* by Christopher Hitchens) to charlatans who fleece the flock rather than feed it (see 1 Peter 5:2-3; 2 Peter 2). The apostle Paul warns that in the days before Christ's return people will "depart from the faith, paying attention to deceitful spirits and the teachings of demons" (1 Tim. 4:1).

He further warns that a time is coming when people will "not tolerate sound doctrine, but according to their own desires, will accumulate teachers for themselves because they have an itch to hear something new. They will turn away from hearing the truth and will turn aside to myths" (2 Tim. 4:3-4). In fact, Paul says there will be widespread apostasy (a standing apart from the truth) before the return of the Lord (2 Thess. 2:3).

People of all religious stripes hope for a better future. But as Douglas Groothuis writes in *Christian Apologetics*, "In the end, hope without truth is pointless.... Truth is what matters most, particularly truth concerning our human condition in the world – its origin, its nature, its purpose (if any) and its destiny.... Only our knowledge of truth – our awareness of reality, no matter how sketchy or partial – can help resolve the inner bickering between the claims of hope and the fears of despair."[2]

THINK *Questions for personal or group study*

Our Muslim friends reject the doctrine of original sin and therefore generally are not persuaded by a guilt-innocence presentation of the gospel. More likely they embrace honor-shame or fear-power. How might you change your presentation of the gospel – without changing the gospel itself – to incorporate the consequences of sin (shame, fear) and God's work of redemption (honor, power)?

If apologetics is a reasonable defense of the Christian faith, how would you share the gospel with someone who argues that we can't know anything for certain?

Why are emotions and experiences untrustworthy ways to know the truth?

What types of evidence lead you to believe in the resurrection of Jesus?

Why is it important to know the core doctrines of the Christian faith?

SHARE *Talking points for Christian apologetics*

Christian apologetics is a reasonable defense of the Christian faith, offered with gentleness and respect.

Scripture shows us that Christianity is powerful, testable, practical, rational, and durable.

Apologetics matters because our faith depends on it; our witness depends on it; and our future depends on it.

DIVE *Go deeper in your study with these resources*

The Big Book of Christian Apologetics by Norman Geisler

The Case for Faith by Lee Strobel

Christian Apologetics: A Comprehensive Case for Biblical Faith by Douglas Groothuis

Reasonable Faith by William Lane Craig

2
WHAT GOOD IS CHRISTIAN APOLOGETICS?

Apologetics is a reasonable defense of the Christian faith. The word is derived from the Greek noun *apologia* and means "a defense." *Apologia* and its verb form *apologeomai* are used nearly 20 times in the New Testament, often in the classic legal sense, but more importantly to describe the call of God to all believers to defend the Christian faith with gentleness and respect (1 Peter 3:15-16).

But how is sound doctrine applied practically? Put another way, what good is Christian apologetics?

Four practical applications

Apologetics has at least four practical applications. We may use apologetics to:

Build. There is a positive case to be made for Christianity, and apologetics helps us get there. The Bible, history, archaeology, and other sources help establish that a real person named Jesus burst onto the scene 2,000 years ago. He claimed deity, performed miracles, spoke the truth, modeled compassion, died on a Roman cross, was buried and rose physically on the third day. His coming to earth was the most important event in human history.

Further, apologetics helps us know who God is; who we are; why there is purpose in life; how we can be restored to a right relationship with our Creator; why we can face death without fear; and what God is doing about evil in the world.

Defend. Christianity is under attack on many fronts, from moral relativists to radical Islamists to angry atheists. Many times they misrepresent Christianity, so we can go a long way in defending the faith by clarifying the Christian position on matters of faith, answering objections, and clearing away difficulties.

For example, Jehovah's Witness leaders historically have claimed that orthodox Christians worship a "freakish-looking three-headed god." While we may not be able to convince our Jehovah's Witness friends of the truth of the Trinity – their New World Translation of the Bible and their official publications have stripped this biblical truth from JW doctrine – we may at least provide biblical clarity.

The Bible teaches that there is one true and living God who exists as three distinct, co-equal, co-eternal persons: Father, Son, and Holy Spirit. We do not worship a three-headed god, or three separate gods, or even one God who shows up sometimes as Father, Son, or Holy Spirit. Defending the faith against mischaracterizations of Christian doctrines is an important function of apologetics.

Challenge. Sometimes Christians must go on the offensive by challenging critics to provide evidence for their unbiblical beliefs. For example, when a moral relativist boldly declares, "There is no absolute truth," a good response is, "Are you absolutely certain about that?"

When our Muslim friends tell us that Jews and Christians have corrupted the Bible, it's only fair to ask them how they came to that conclusion.

We have significant documentary evidence that the Scriptures have been carefully copied and faithfully preserved. Further, the Qur'an states in several places that the sacred writings of the Jews and Christians faithfully attested to the truth of Islam. If Muhammad believed the Scriptures were intact in the 7th century, what happened since then to make them corrupt?

Sometimes the best defense of the Christian faith is to hold critics accountable for their unbiblical views.

Persuade. Ultimately, Christian apologetics finds its greatest application as an effective means of evangelism. When we build a positive case for Christianity, defend Christianity from attacks, and challenge critics to defend their views, we can bring them to a point of commitment to Christ.

We should never coerce another person to trust in Jesus. Conviction is the work of the Holy Spirit (see John 16:7-11). But we should eagerly invite our unbelieving friends to receive Christ and thus pass from death into life (John 5:24).

In his book *Tactics: A Game Plan for Discussing Your Christian Convictions*, Gregory Koukl writes, "It may surprise you to hear this, but I never set out to convert anyone.... I have a more modest goal, one you might consider adopting as your own. All I want to do is put a stone in someone's shoe. I want to give him something worth thinking about, something he can't ignore because it continues to poke at him in a good way."[1]

May all of us be Christian apologists that gently and respectfully place stones in the shoes of our lost friends.

Jesus: the ultimate apologist

In *Christian Apologetics*, Douglas Groothuis illustrates how Jesus blunts the Sadducees' assault on the resurrection (Matt. 22:23-33). Leaders of this religious sect not only deny the bodily resurrection of the dead but the existence of angels as well. They appeal to the Law of Moses and then pose a hypothetical situation.

"Teacher," they say, "Moses said, if a man dies, having no children, his brother is to marry his wife and raise up offspring for his brother. Now there were seven brothers among us. The first got married and died. Having no offspring, he left his wife to his brother. The same happened to the second also, and the third, and so to all seven. Then last of all the woman died. Therefore, in the resurrection, whose wife will she be of the seven?" (vv. 24-28a).

The Sadducees think they have an ironclad argument. Jesus must either refute the Law of Moses or deny the afterlife. But Groothuis notes Jesus' four-part apologetic response:

1. He challenges their assumption that belief in the resurrection means we are committed to believing that all earthly institutions, such as marriage, are retained in the afterlife. None of the Hebrew Scriptures teaches this, nor did Jesus believe it (vv. 29-30).

2. He compares the resurrected state of men and women to that of angels, which the Sadducees denied (v. 30). Not that we become angels at death, but that the physical realm does not account for all reality.

3. He cites a text from the Sadducees' own esteemed Scriptures: Exodus 3:6. He could have cited Job 19:25-27 or Dan. 12:2. but instead He quotes a passage from the Torah (vv. 31-32).

4. He emphasizes the verb tense. God **IS** the God of Abraham, Isaac and Jacob (v. 32).

The Sadducees are not necessarily convinced, but Jesus silences them while those with open minds are "astonished at His teaching" (v. 33).[2]

THINK *Questions for personal or group study*

What are some ways to build a positive case for the Christian faith?

When a Muslim or a Mormon tells you the Bible can't be trusted, how could you respectfully challenge that assertion?

What's a realistic goal for having a first conversation with a Jehovah's Witness?

Why do you think Jesus so often responded to questions with questions of His own?

What role does the Holy Spirit play in Christian apologetics?

SHARE *Talking points for applying Christian apologetics*

Apologetics is a reasonable defense of the Christian faith.

Apologetics helps us answer life's most important questions: Is there a God? Does my life have meaning? Is there life beyond the grave? And many others.

We may practically apply apologetics to build a positive case for Christianity; defend our beliefs; challenge critics; and persuade the lost to consider Jesus.

One goal of apologetics is to "put a stone in the shoe" of unbelievers – that is, to leave them with a biblical truth to think about.

DIVE *Go deeper in your study with these resources*

Know Why You Believe by Paul E. Little

Tactics: A Game Plan for Discussing Your Christian Convictions by Gregory Koukl

What's So Great about Christianity by Dinesh D'Souza

3
WHAT'S YOUR WORLDVIEW?

Alex Rosenberg, a professor and chair of the philosophy department at Duke University, released a book in 2011 entitled *The Atheist's Guide to Reality: Enjoying Life without Illusions*. He writes:

"Is there a God? No.

What is the nature of reality? What physics says it is.

What is the purpose of the universe? There is none.

What is the meaning of life? Ditto.

Why am I here? Just dumb luck.

Is there a soul? Is it immortal? Are you kidding?

Is there free will? Not a chance!

What is the difference between right and wrong, good and bad? There is no moral difference between them.

Why should I be moral? Because it makes you feel better than being immoral.

Is abortion, euthanasia, suicide, paying taxes, foreign aid, or anything else you don't like forbidden, permissible, or sometimes obligatory? Anything goes.

What is love, and how can I find it? Love is the solution to a strategic interaction problem. Don't look for it; it will find you when you need it.

Does history have any meaning or purpose? It's full of sound and fury, but signifies nothing.

Does the human past have any lessons for our future? Fewer and fewer, if it ever had any to begin with."[1]

Rosenberg's text illustrates a naturalistic worldview. A worldview shapes our thoughts. It guides our words and deeds. It is the lens through which we view reality. And it says everything about us. It is important for Christians to have a biblical worldview – and to understand the worldviews of those with whom we share our faith.

A worldview defined

Simply put, a worldview is how we view reality and make sense of life from a specific standpoint. As Christian apologist Freddy Davis puts it in Marketfaith.org, "A worldview is like a pair of glasses ... your belief glasses. It is what you believe about God, the universe, mankind, life after death, knowledge, morality and human history."[2]

James N. Anderson, author of *What's Your Worldview: An Interactive Approach to Life's Big Questions*, writes that a worldview is an overall philosophical view of the world – not just our planet, but of all reality. A worldview is an all-encompassing perspective on everything that exists and matters to us.

He goes on: "Your worldview represents your most fundamental beliefs and assumptions about the universe you inhabit. It reflects how you would answer all the 'big questions' of human existence, the fundamental questions we ask about life, the universe, and everything."[3]

Anderson lists 21 different worldviews, from atheistic dualism to Pelagianism to Unitarianism. Like spectacles with colored lenses, your worldview affects what you see and how you see it. Depending on the "color" of the lenses, you see some things more easily, while other things are de-emphasized or distorted. In some cases, you don't see things at all.

A worldview is not a religion. Everyone has a worldview, but not everyone embraces a religion.

Put another way, a worldview is an all-encompassing perspective on everything that exists and matters to us. It shapes what we believe and what we're willing to believe, how we interpret our experiences, how we behave in response to those experiences, and how we relate to others.

A religion, on the other hand, is a set of fundamental beliefs and practices concerned with ultimate issues such as the nature of the divine, the origins of the universe, whether there is life after death, what it means to be "saved," and so on.

For example, an atheist has no religion but sees the world through the lens of naturalism, believing the material world is all that exists. A Hindu may see the material universe as an illusion, not as a reality. And a Christian sees the natural world as created by God for our enjoyment and as a means of bearing testimony to His existence and divine attributes.

In any case, it's important to keep in mind that a worldview is comprehensive. That is, it impacts every area of life, from religion to relationships and from morality to money.

Basic worldviews

While authors like Anderson list many different worldviews, others insist that there are just two: a biblical worldview and a non-biblical worldview. Freddy Davis acknowledges the diversity of worldviews, and the necessity of a biblical worldview, while listing four general ways people understand reality:

Naturalism. This is the belief that only material reality exists.[4] There is no God or spiritual experience. Mankind is the only known being in the universe capable of making moral distinctions and must decide for himself how to structure life. Naturalistic belief systems include secular humanism, atheism, existentialism, and much of postmodernism.

Animism. Animism sees reality as having separate material and spiritual parts that interact. Spiritual gods manifest themselves in nature and can cause good or evil to happen to people. Therefore, people must perform certain rites and ceremonies to keep the gods appeased. Animistic belief systems include Shinto, Wicca, and Voodoo.

Far Eastern Thought. This group understands reality to be a totally impersonal cosmos moving toward unity. Everything is understood to be a part of everything else: god is all and all is god. Far Eastern belief systems include Hinduism, Buddhism, and elements of the New Age.

Theism. This is the belief that there is a God, who may be personal or impersonal. Theistic belief systems generally rely on some kind of revelation – such as the Bible or the Qur'an – that acts as a source of authority. Theistic belief systems include Christianity, Islam, Judaism, Mormonism, and the Jehovah's Witnesses.

Key questions

In the 5th Edition of *The Universe Next Door*, James W. Sire offers eight questions that help us identify the worldview assumptions of any person or belief system:

1. **What is prime reality – the really real?** Is there a God or not? Is so, what is God like? If not, what is the origin of material reality?

2. **What is the nature of external reality, that is, the world around us?** Is it created or uncreated? Orderly or chaotic? Objective or subjective? Real or an illusion? Eternal or temporal?

3. **What is a human being?** A person made in the image of God? A highly evolved biological machine? A god or potential god?

4. **What happens to a person at death?** Does the person cease to exist? Is he/she reincarnated? Transformed into a higher state of existence? Does the person enter a spiritual realm like heaven or hell?

5. **Why is it possible to know anything at all?** Is consciousness the product of a long process of evolution? Is knowledge an illusion? Are people made in the image of God, who has knowledge and imparts it to us?

6. **How do we know what is right and wrong?** Are right and wrong products of human choice? Do they depend on feelings? Are they survival mechanisms? Did God reveal right and wrong to us?

7. **What is the meaning of human history?** Is there no true meaning other than what people give it? Is time an illusion? Does meaning result from discovering and fulfilling the purpose of God?

8. **What personal, life-orienting core commitments are consistent with this worldview?**[5]

A biblical worldview

How does a biblical worldview answer these questions? Here is a brief summary:

1. **What is prime reality – the really real?** There is one true and living God. He is eternal. He exists as three distinct, co-equal, and co-eternal persons: Father, Son and Holy Spirit. God is personal and knowable.

2. **What is the nature of external reality, that is, the world around us?** God created the universe – everything seen and unseen – out of nothing. He created it good, but humans fell into sin and the world is under a curse. God sent His Son to save lost sinners. One day He will restore creation to its sinless perfection.

3. **What is a human being?** God created human beings in His image – as personal beings with thoughts, emotions, and wills. He made us to enjoy intimate fellowship with Him. By faith in Jesus Christ, we are forgiven of our sins and brought into a proper relationship with God.

4. **What happens to a person at death?** At death, the soul and spirit continue to exist consciously. One day all people will be physically resurrected and stand before God in judgment. Those that have trusted in Christ will spend eternity with Him on a restored earth, while those who have rejected Jesus will spend eternity apart from God in hell.

5. **Why is it possible to know anything at all?** Since God made human beings in His image, He desires that we know Him and understand His purpose for our lives. God reveals Himself and His truths in creation, conscience, Christ, and the canon of Scripture.

6. **How do we know what is right and wrong?** God has revealed right and wrong to all people. One day every person will stand before God "without excuse" (Rom. 1:20).

7. **What is the meaning of human history?** God is working in and through human history to fulfill His purposes for mankind. Even the evil that people do will be called into account and

used for God's purposes. For example, the greatest evil ever done was the crucifixion of the sinless Son of God, yet in that evil God performed the ultimate good by paying our sin debt and providing us with everlasting life. One day Jesus will return, judge all people, set things right, and create new heavens and a new earth.

8. **What personal, life-orienting core commitments are consistent with this worldview?** We might offer a variety of responses here: To know God intimately; to seek His will in our lives; to seek first the kingdom of God; to walk in the path of good works He laid out for us in eternity past (Eph. 2:10).

C. Fred Smith, in *Developing a Biblical Worldview*, uses a simpler, four-question method for probing worldviews:

1. Who am I?

2. Where am I?

3. What's wrong?

4. What's the answer?[6]

Asking our friends these four questions can open up respectful discussions that help us understand how they see the world and their place it in. And, by listening respectfully, we may earn the right to ask one final question: "May I share with you what the Bible has to say about that?"

THINK *Questions for personal or group study*

How does the Bible answer the four simple worldview questions C. Fred Smith has raised: (1) Who am I? (2) Where am I? (3) What's wrong? (4) What's the answer?

How might an atheist answer these four questions?

How might someone who says she's "spiritual but not religious" answer them?

How do worldview questions prepare us to share our faith?

Can you name a friend or acquaintance – or even a celebrity – that embraces a naturalistic worldview? A Far Eastern worldview? An animistic worldview? How would you pray for them?

SHARE *Talking points for worldviews*

A worldview is how we view reality and make sense of life from a specific standpoint. It's like a pair of glasses – your belief glasses.

We can group worldviews into four general categories: naturalism, animism, Far Eastern thought, and theism.

Asking good questions helps us determine someone's worldview – questions such as, "What is a human being?" and "What happens to a person at death?"

DIVE *Go deeper in your study with these resources*

What's Your Worldview: An Interactive Approach to Life's Big Questions by James N. Anderson

Developing a Biblical Worldview: Seeing Things God's Way by C. Fred Smith

The Universe Next Door: A Basic Worldview Catalogue, 5th Edition by James W. Sire

Philosophical Foundations for a Christian Worldview by J.P. Moreland and William Lane Craig

MarketFaith Ministries (MarketFaith.org)

II.

THE EXISTENCE OF GOD

4
HOW DO I KNOW GOD EXISTS?

Scholars generally break down the arguments for God's existence into three broad categories: Scripture, nature, and philosophy. Unbelievers may reject arguments from Scripture as nothing more than myths and legends.

But the apostle Paul makes a good case from philosophy and nature in Romans 1. The argument is so clear that Paul states emphatically every person will stand before God one day without excuse. That's because God has revealed Himself to all people in at least two ways.

1. God has revealed Himself in conscience.

Rom. 1:19 reads: "... since what can be known about God is evident among them, because God has shown it to them."

"Them" refers to unbelievers who "by their unrighteousness suppress the truth." They do not allow the truth to work in their lives. Rather, they suppress it so they might continue to live their lives independently of God.

Later, Paul says they turn the truth into a lie, and become like brute beasts in their thinking, so that God gives them up to their way of living. This results in "godlessness" and "unrighteousness," which draw the "wrath" of God.

Willmington's Guide to the Bible explains it this way: "God does not reap wrath where he has not sown knowledge."[1]

A person will either acknowledge the truth and repent, or suppress the truth until the conscience is "seared" (1 Tim. 4:2).

God has placed within every human heart a knowledge of right and wrong, along with an understanding that these standards are objective – coming from outside ourselves.

Some people – even some cultures – suppress that knowledge, but that doesn't make it any less true. The fact that people around the world –

regardless of societal advancement or religious practice – know that stealing, murder, rape and other such actions are wrong is a testimony to the truth that there is a sovereign God who created us and to whom we must give an account.

2. God has revealed Himself in creation.

Rom. 1:20 reads: "From the creation of the world His invisible attributes, that is, His eternal power and divine nature, have been clearly seen, being understood through what He has made. As a result, people are without excuse."

Warren Wiersbe writes: "Human history is not the story of a beast that worshiped idols, and then evolved into a man worshiping one God. Human history is just the opposite: man began knowing God, but turned from the truth and rejected God. God revealed Himself to man through creation.... From the world around him, man knew that there was a God who had the wisdom to plan and the power to create."[2]

Psalm 19:1 says, "The heavens declare the glory of God, and the sky proclaims the work of His hands." The things that are invisible of God, namely, His eternal power and Godhead, are clearly seen in the things He made.

"What a paradox," writes Greek scholar Kenneth Wuest, "invisible things which are visible.... Man, reasoning upon the basis of the law of cause and effect, which law requires an adequate cause for every effect, is forced to the conclusion that such a tremendous effect as the universe, demands a Being of eternal power and of divine attributes. That Being must be the Deity who should be worshipped."

Wuest continues, "Thus, through the light of the created universe, unsaved man recognizes the fact that there is a supreme Being who created it, who has eternal power and divine attributes, a Being to whom worship and obedience are due. This is the truth which unsaved man is repressing."[3]

It's important to note that Paul is not saying the full gospel message of Christ's death, burial and resurrection is clear to all people from the testimony of conscience and creation alone, for that requires God's further revelation of His Son through the preaching of the Word and the convicting power of the Holy Spirit.

But Paul is saying that all people are rendered without defense for rejecting God because God has shown all people He exists and is to be the sole object of their worship.

So, how do we answer the person who asks, "Is God real?" A simple response is: "When I look at the universe – so big and complex – I am driven to the conclusion that someone started it all. And when I think that people everywhere somehow know in their hearts what's right and what's wrong, I feel certain someone put that conscience there. Because of these things – creation and conscience – I believe God is real. How about you?"

This response will not persuade skeptics, of course, but it may start a conversation with someone seeking the truth. In the end, the sovereign Creator of the universe gets to ask the questions. And as the apostle Paul makes clear, no one gets a pass for saying, "I didn't know there was a God."

THINK *Questions for personal or group study*

What are we to make of people who seem totally void of personal conscience?

What questions could we ask our friends who say they see no evidence of God's existence?

How would you respond to someone who says the natural world is chaotic, not orderly?

Why do you think some people are willing to accept the idea of a divine being but shy away from the concept of a personal God?

If creation and conscience are two ways God reveals Himself to all people, why do you think so many people believe in gods other than the God of Scripture?

SHARE *Talking points for the existence of God*

Scholars generally break down arguments for God's existence into three broad categories: Scripture, nature, and philosophy.

In Romans 1, the apostle Paul makes a biblical case by appealing to both nature and philosophy.

Paul writes that God has revealed Himself to all persons in conscience and creation so that they are without excuse for rejecting Him.

No one gets a pass for saying, "I didn't know there was a God."

DIVE *Go deeper in your study with these resources*

Reasonable Faith: Christian Truth and Apologetics by William Lane Craig

The Case for a Creator by Lee Strobel

God's Crime Scene: A Cold-case Detective Examines the Evidence for a Divinely Created Universe by J. Warner Wallace

Stealing from God: Why Atheists Need God to Make Their Case by Frank Turek

5
THE ARGUMENTS FOR GOD'S EXISTENCE

The Bible provides us with four strong evidences for the existence of God: creation, conscience, Christ, and the canon of Scripture. In addition, there are many non-biblically based arguments for God's existence. This chapter highlights a few of these arguments.

Cosmological arguments

Cosmological arguments offer reasons to believe that the cosmos – everything that exists; the universe and all its constituents – depends on someone or something outside itself. "The cosmological argument for the existence of God tries to show that because anything exists there must be a God who brought it into existence," according to Christian apologist Doug Powell.[1]

Norman Geisler adds, "There is a universe rather than none at all, which must have been caused by something beyond itself. The law of causality says that every finite thing is caused by something other than itself."[2]

Cosmological arguments take on various forms. The three basic kinds are Kalam, Thomist, and Leibnizian.

The Kalam cosmological argument was developed primarily by Muslim theologians in the Middle Ages. It is simple and elegant:

1. Whatever begins to exist has a cause.

2. The universe began to exist.

3. Therefore, the universe has a cause. (Theists argue that the cause of the universe is God.)

The Thomist cosmological argument was advanced by priest, philosopher, and theologian Thomas Aquinas in the 13th century. It may be summarized this way:

1. What we observe in this universe is contingent – in other words dependent or conditional.

2. A sequence of causally related contingent things cannot be infinite.

3. The sequence of causally dependent contingent things must be finite.

4. Therefore, there must be a first cause (God) in the sequence of contingent causes.

The Leibnizian cosmological argument was put forth by German philosopher G.W.F. von Leibniz. Instead of arguing from cause itself, as Aquinas did, Leibniz argued that there must be a sufficient reason for the existence of the universe. Leibniz wrote, "The first question which should rightly be asked is this: why is there something rather than nothing?"

His argument may be stated in this way:

1. Every existing thing has an explanation of its existence, either in the necessity of its nature or in an external cause.

2. If the universe has an explanation of its existence, that explanation is God.

3. The universe is an existing thing.

4. Therefore the explanation of the universe is God.

As Christian apologist Douglas Groothuis summarizes, "Does the cosmos stand alone and unsupported, or is its existence dependent on something outside of itself? This is the ultimate cosmological question. Cosmological arguments offer reasons to believe that the cosmos depends on something outside itself."[3]

The design argument

The design argument is formally called the teleological argument, taken from *telos*, a Greek word meaning purpose or ultimate end.

While this line of reasoning predates Christianity – Plato and Aristotle argued for the existence of God based on their observations of the stars – English philosopher William Paley published what is probably the most famous articulation of the design argument in his book *Natural Theology*.

In the book, Paley directs our attention to the watch to illustrate that its complexity, function, and usefulness point us to a human designer in the same way that the observable qualities of the universe point us to a divine designer.

In short, the design argument reasons from design to an intelligent designer:

1. All designs imply a designer.
2. There is great design in the universe.
3. Therefore, there must be a great designer of the universe.

There are many aspects of the design argument, including: the anthropic or "fine tuning" principle of the universe; the concept of information and order, for example in DNA, as proof of design; and the idea of "irreducible complexity," or the reality that some systems – like the human eye – would not function without all their parts and therefore could not have evolved incrementally over time.

In recent years the design argument has morphed into "intelligent design," championed by leading thinkers such as Michael Behe, Philip Johnson, William Dembski, and Hugh Ross, who use the latest scientific discoveries to cast the design argument in cutting-edge terms.

The moral argument

The moral argument also is known as the axiological argument, borrowing from the Greek word *axios*, meaning value or worth. In simplest terms, the moral argument tries to show that moral values must be objective and universal to make any sense. And if moral values are objective, the source must be a transcendent, personal being to whom people must give an account.

This argument finds biblical support in Romans 2:12-15, in which people have no excuse for rejecting God or sinning against Him because the law is "written on their hearts."

Though expressed in many ways, perhaps the most popular form comes from C.S. Lewis in *Mere Christianity* and follows this basic structure:

1. Moral laws imply a Moral Law Giver.
2. There is an objective moral law.
3. Therefore, there is a Moral Law Giver. [4]

The moral argument challenges the widely held view of relativism, which holds that people and/or societies decide what is right and wrong and that those values differ from person to person and from culture to culture.

As Doug Powell states, "Morals are not opinions. They are not personal, private decisions, and they are not descriptions of behavior and motive that have the force of a command. They contain a sense of obligation and oughtness that is universal, authoritative, and outweighs considerations of culture, time, and place."[5]

Moral laws are different from natural laws. Moral laws do not *describe* what is; they *prescribe* what ought to be. They cannot be known by observing *what* people do. They are what people *should* do, whether they do them or not.

But where does this "should" come from? Because morals deal with purpose and will, the source must have purpose and will. Because morals are universal and transcend people, societies, and time, the source must be transcendent. Since morals are authoritative, they must come from an authority that has the power to impose them. Thus, the argument goes, morals come from a transcendent lawgiver who has the authority to hold us accountable for our thoughts, words, and deeds. That lawgiver, Christians argue, is God.

The ontological argument

Anselm, a Benedictine monk and philosopher who served as the Archbishop of Canterbury in the late 11th and early 12th centuries, is the first to develop this argument, which basically argues from the *idea* of God as "the greatest conceivable being" to the *existence* of God.

In other words, once a person truly understands the notion of a greatest conceivable being, then he or she will see that such a being must exist. Ontology concerns the nature of being and is drawn form the Greek word *ontos*, which means being.

The ontological argument takes two primary forms. The first is the idea of a Perfect Being. The second is the idea of a Necessary Being. The Perfect Being form may be summarized in this manner:

1. God is by definition an absolutely perfect being.

2. But existence is a perfection.

3. Therefore, God must exist.

This form has been challenged on the grounds that existence is not perfection. Existence adds nothing to the concept of a thing; it merely gives a concrete instance of it.

The second form of Anselm's argument, however, is much stronger:

1. If God exists, we must conceive of him as a Necessary Being.
2. But by definition, a Necessary Being cannot not exist.
3. Therefore, if a Necessary Being can exist, then it must exist.

The ontological argument cannot prove the existence of God, although it can prove certain things about His nature. For example, God must necessarily exist, if He exists at all. He cannot cease to exist or exist contingently.

Why God's existence matters

Christian philosopher William Lane Craig offers three reasons why God's existence matters.

First, if God does not exist, life is ultimately meaningless. If your life is doomed to end in death, then it does not matter how you lived, or whether you existed at all. Your life might have relative significance insofar as you affected the lives of other people or impacted history, but even they are destined to pass away with the world. In contrast, the existence of God provides value and meaning to all life.

Second, if God does not exist, then we ultimately live without hope. If there is no God, then there is no hope of deliverance from the shortcomings of our finite existence. For example, there is no hope of deliverance from evil, aging, sickness, or death. However, the existence of God provides deliverance from sin and its consequences, including death and separation from our Creator.

Third, if God does exist, then there is meaning and hope, and the possibility of a personal relationship with Him. "Think of it!" he writes. "That the infinite God should love you and want to be your personal friend! This would be the highest status that a human being could enjoy! Clearly, if God exists, it makes not only a tremendous difference for mankind in general, but it could make a life-changing difference for you as well."

Craig then shares five reasons to believe in God:

1. God makes sense of the origin of the universe.
2. God makes sense of the fine-tuning of the universe for intelligent life.
3. God makes sense of objective moral values in the world.
4. God makes sense of the historical facts concerning the life, death, and resurrection of Jesus.
5. God can be immediately known and experienced.

He concludes: "I think that Christian theism is a plausible worldview which commends itself to the thoughtful consideration of every rational human being."[6]

THINK *Questions for personal or group study*

Of the various arguments for the existence of God, which one appeals most strongly to you? Why?

Put yourself in the shoes of an atheist friend and try forming an argument against the existence of God. What type of argument would you build?

If someone tells you her mind is made up and she is convinced God does not exist, what questions could you ask that challenge her certainty?

What reasons does the Bible give for a person concluding that there is no God?

How would you respond to a friend who says he believes in a supreme being but describes that being in an unbiblical way?

SHARE *Talking points for the existence of God*

The Bible provides us with four strong evidences for the existence of God: creation, conscience, Christ, and the canon of Scripture.

In addition, there are many non-biblically based arguments for God's existence.

Cosmological arguments try to show that because anything exists there must be a God who brought it into existence.

The design argument reasons from design to an intelligent designer.

The moral argument tries to show that moral values must be objective and universal to make any sense; and if moral values are objective, the source must be a transcendent, personal being to whom people must give an account.

The ontological argument argues from the *idea* of God as "the greatest conceivable being" to the *existence* of God.

God's existence matters. If He does exist, He offers meaning, hope, and the possibility of a personal relationship with our Creator.

DIVE *Go deeper in your study with these resources*

To Everyone an Answer: A Case for a Christian Worldview, edited by Francis J. Beckwith, William Lane Craig, and J.P. Moreland

The Existence of God, 2nd Edition by Richard Swinburne

Big Bang, Big God: A Universe Designed for Life? by Rodney D. Holder

Questions of Truth: Fifty-one Responses to Questions about God, Science, and Belief by John Polkinghorne and Nicholas Beale

The Creation Answer Book by Hank Hanegraaff

III.

THE BIBLE

6
HOW DO I KNOW THE BIBLE IS TRUE?

Christians may disagree about the interpretation of certain passages of Scripture, but generally we stand together in a firm conviction that the Bible is the inspired Word of God. In fact, we almost take it for granted that the Bible is God's complete written revelation to us – which is why we struggle to answer the question skeptics and seekers alike often ask: "How do you know the Bible is true?"

Some common replies include:

- "The Bible is true because I believe it." But believing something does not make it true.

- "The Bible is true because it's the best-selling book in the world." But popularity is not a reliable yardstick of truth.

- "The Bible is true because it changed my life." But people make the same claims about transcendental meditation, Scientology, Botox, or the latest diet fad.

- "The Bible is true because it has stood the test of time." But so have the Qur'an and the Hindu Vedas.

Here is a better response based on 2 Peter 1:16-21:

I believe the Bible is true because credible eyewitnesses accurately recorded the acts of God throughout human history, under divine direction, free of personal agendas, and in the presence of hostile witnesses who often made them pay for their testimonies with their lives.

Let's break this down.

Credible eyewitnesses

In 2 Peter 1, Peter builds a case for himself and the other apostles when he writes that "we did not follow cleverly contrived myths when we made known to you the power and coming of our Lord Jesus Christ; instead, we were eyewitnesses of his majesty" (v. 16). He recalls his experience with James and John on the Mount of Transfiguration, when they saw

Jesus in His glory and heard the Father speak from heaven: "For when He received honor and glory from God the Father, a voice came to Him from the Majestic Glory: This is My beloved Son. I take delight in Him. And we heard this voice when it came from heaven while we were with Him on the holy mountain. So we have the prophetic word strongly confirmed" (vv. 17-19a).

Consider that 40 different men record the Bible over a period of 1,500 years – credible eyewitnesses such as:

- Moses, who meets God in the burning bush; spends time with Him on Mt. Sinai; is empowered to perform miracles; leads the children of Israel through the Red Sea and during 40 years in the wilderness. He is called the most humble man who ever lived (Num. 12:3), and Ex. 33:11 says God spoke to him face to face as a man speaks to a friend. Moses is recognized as a trustworthy witness by the world's three great monotheistic religions – Christianity, Islam, and Judaism.

- David, a shepherd boy whom God uses to smite Goliath and become Israel's greatest king. He foreshadows the Messiah, is called a man after God's own heart (Acts 13:22), and is listed in the faith hall of fame in Hebrews 11. Christianity, Islam, and Judaism recognize him as a writer of Scripture.

- Daniel, a youngster taken to Babylon as a captive following the destruction of Jerusalem. He proves himself faithful through many trials. He firmly but diplomatically refuses to eat meat sacrificed to idols; interprets the king's dream; refuses to stop praying to the God of Israel despite declarations to the contrary, which gets him tossed into the lion's den; and observes visions God gives him of the future. The record of Daniel's life is one of faultless credibility.

- The apostle John, who emphasizes that he is an eyewitness of the life, death, burial and resurrection of Christ (1 John 1:1-4).

- Paul, who stresses his role as an eyewitness of the resurrected Christ (1 Cor. 9:1).

- Peter, who recalls his first-hand knowledge of the works of the Savior (2 Peter 1:16-21).

We could cite other examples, but the point is clear: The holy men of God who recorded His Word were credible eyewitnesses.

Accurately recorded the acts of God

The recorders of Scripture are **under divine direction**. The apostle Paul writes, "All Scripture is inspired by God and is profitable for teaching, for rebuking, for correcting, for training in righteousness, so that the man of God may be complete, equipped for every good work" (2 Tim. 3:16-17). Peter adds, "First of all, you should know this: no prophecy of Scripture comes from one's own interpretation, because no prophecy ever came by the will of man; instead, men spoke from God as they were moved by the Holy Spirit" (2 Peter 1:20-21).

Before His work on the cross, Jesus promises His followers that the Spirit would guide them into all truth and help them remember the things Jesus said and did (John 14:26; 16:13). God is quoted directly or is attributed with Scripture thousands of times throughout the Old and New Testaments. The Holy Spirit, we're told, is the divine Author of the Bible, working through men God selected, enabling them to use their own experiences and words, yet superintending their thoughts and written expressions in such a way that every word may be traced to a divine source.

Not only are the recorders of Scripture divinely inspired; they are **free of personal agendas**. Luke makes it clear to Theophilus that he has "carefully investigated everything from the very first, to write to you in an orderly sequence ... so that you may know the certainty of the things about which you have been instructed" (Luke 1:3-4). When Peter and John heal a lame man on the steps of the temple, Peter is careful not to take credit for the miracle. "Men of Israel," he proclaims, "why are you amazed at this? Or why do you stare at us, as though we had made him walk by our own power or godliness? The God of Abraham, Isaac, and Jacob, the God of our fathers, has glorified His Servant Jesus, whom you handed over and denied in the presence of Pilate ... By faith in His name, His name has made this man strong" (Acts 3:12-16).

Later, Peter and John rebuke Simon the sorcerer for offering them money in order to obtain the authority to confer the Holy Spirit on people; Paul refuses to be worshiped as a god; and the apostles carry the gospel throughout the world with no thought for their personal wealth, comfort, or stature. Their only agenda: to glorify Jesus and to make Him known.

Some may argue at this point that a defense of the recorders of Scripture is vain because we do not have their original writings, and the copies we have are filled with "errors." While other articles in this series address these objections in detail, a few brief remarks should be made.

First, it's true that we do not have the originals of the Bible, just as non-biblical originals from that era have not survived the ravages of time. But no other book from the ancient world has more, earlier, or better-copied manuscripts than the Bible. For example, there are between 25,000 and 30,000 handwritten New Testament manuscripts, nearly 5,800 in Greek – far more than the runner up, Homer's *Iliad*, with fewer than 1,800 copies (and no originals).

Further, the earliest New Testament manuscripts date back to about 40 years after the originals, while the earliest copy of Homer's classic work is found a full 400 years after the original. Finally, the variations in the manuscripts are almost universally minor – and none of the variants affects a single doctrine of Scripture. Truly, the Holy Spirit inspired the originals – and ensured the preservation of their message throughout time. By the way, even if no New Testament manuscripts existed, we could reconstruct nearly all of the 27 books because the early church fathers of the second and third centuries quoted the NT more than 36,000 times.[1]

In the presence of hostile witnesses

The New Testament writers recorded the words and deeds of Jesus at a time when others could have refuted their testimony – especially with respect to the resurrection. Yet there is a deafening silence in the historical record of ancient writers who attempted to disprove the testimony of the eyewitnesses. Disbelief, yes; but disproof, no.

Consider first that Jesus, Stephen, the apostles and others used the Old Testament to reason with the Jews about the prophesied person and work of the Messiah – fulfilled in Jesus of Nazareth. This does not prevent the Jewish leaders from refusing to acknowledge Jesus as Messiah, or from seeking His death, or from trying to stamp out Christianity after the resurrection and ascension of Jesus. But they are not successful in refuting the words and works of Jesus as Messiah.

As we read through the New Testament, we see there is widespread hostility toward Jesus and His followers. For example, Stephen becomes the first Christian martyr at the hands of the Jewish religious leaders because he boldly proclaims Jesus as Messiah and argues for belief in His resurrection (Acts 6-7). Idol makers are enraged with Paul (who had approved of the stoning of Stephen) because his preaching of the gospel is bad for business (Acts 19:23 ff.).

The Jewish religious leaders bribe the Roman soldiers who guarded Jesus' tomb to lie about the resurrection (Matt. 28:11-15). Some philosophers on Mars Hill ridicule Paul because He attests to Jesus' resurrection (Acts 17:32), and Festus cries out in a loud voice that Paul is mad from his religious studies (Acts 26:24), but no one is able to produce evidence that he is not telling the truth.

There is, however, evidence from non-Christians that Jesus exists, is called the Christ, is crucified, and rises from the dead. For example, Roman historian Tacitus reports on Nero's decision to blame Christians for the fire that destroys Rome in A.D. 64. He refers to "Christus, from whom the name (Christian) had its origin, suffered the extreme penalty (crucifixion) during the reign of Tiberius ..."[2]

Pliny the Younger, Roman governor of Bithynia in Asia Minor, writes to the emperor seeking advice about the appropriate way to conduct legal proceedings against those accused of being Christians. He relates that Christians meet on a certain fixed day, singing verses of a hymn to "Christ, as to a god ..." (A.D. 112).[3]

Twice in *Jewish Antiquities*, Josephus, a first century Jewish historian, mentions Jesus. He refers to James, "the brother of Jesus the so-called Christ."[4] In the other reference he writes: "About this time there lived Jesus, a wise man, if indeed one ought to call him a man. For he ... wrought surprising feats ... He was the Christ. When Pilate ... condemned him to be crucified, those who had ... come to love him did not give up their affection for him. On the third day he appeared ... restored to life ... And the tribe of Christians ... has ... not disappeared."[5] (It should be noted that some believe Josephus wrote the original, and that a Christian later edited it. In any case, this unbelieving historian acknowledges Jesus as a historical figure and does not dispute His resurrection.)

The Babylonian Talmud, a collection of Jewish rabbinical writings compiled between A.D. 75-100, records, "On the eve of the Passover Yeshu was hanged."[6] Yeshu, or Yeshua, is how Jesus' name is pronounced in Hebrew. Paul uses "hanged" in Galatians to refer to Jesus' crucifixion, and Luke records that the criminals crucified with Jesus are "hanged."

Finally, Lucian of Samosata is a second century Greek satirist who writes, "The Christians ... worship a man to this day – the distinguished personage who introduced their novel rites, and was crucified on that account ... they are all brothers, from the moment that they are converted, and deny the gods of Greece, and worship the crucified sage, and live after his laws."[7] While his writing is tongue-in-cheek, he confirms early Christian beliefs and practices.

At the cost of their lives

People have been known to die for something they truly believe in. But it's rare – and exceptionally foolhardy – to die for something one knows to be a lie. The faithfulness of the New Testament writers – many of whom suffered gruesome martyrs' deaths – is a testimony to the truth of their eyewitness accounts. Jesus prepares them for conflict when He assures them the world will hate them (John 15:18-19). He promises to be with His followers always – until the end of the age; to send them the Holy Spirit as another Comforter; to reward them in heaven for their faithfulness; to prepare a place for them and to return for them one day; but never does He guarantee they will not pay a price for sincere devotion to Him.

According to accounts from Scripture, church history and tradition, this is how, and in some cases where, eyewitnesses of Christ died (or may have died) in service to Him:

- Stephen is stoned to death as the first Christian martyr.
- Herod Agrippa kills James with the sword.
- Peter is crucified, reportedly upside-down, on an x-shaped cross in Rome.
- Matthew is beheaded in Ethiopia.
- Mark dies in Egypt after horses drag him through the streets of Alexandria.

- Luke is hanged in Greece as a result of his preaching.

- Andrew is crucified in Greece.

- Thomas is thrust through with pine spears, tormented with red-hot plates, and burned alive in India.

- Philip is tortured and then crucified in Phrygia.

- James the Great, son of Zebedee, is beheaded in Jerusalem.

- Nathanael (Bartholomew) is flayed with a whip and then crucified.

- James the Lesser, head of the Jerusalem church, is thrown down from the pinnacle of the temple; surviving, he is beaten to death.

- Simon the Zealot is crucified in Syria; another account says he was killed in Persia.

- Judas Thaddeus is beaten to death with sticks in Mesopotamia.

- Matthias, who replaces Judas Iscariot, is stoned while hanging on a cross; another account says he is burned to death in Syria.

- John is boiled in oil; when he miraculously survives, he is exiled to Patmos.

- Paul is beheaded in Rome.[8]

Time has not changed the price many Christians pay for standing with the apostles in their declaration that Jesus is the Christ. Today, Christians are the single most persecuted religious group in the world. This is confirmed in studies by sources as diverse as the Vatican, Open Doors, the Pew Research Center, *Commentary*, *Newsweek*, and the *Economist*. According to one estimate by the Catholic Bishops' Conferences of the European Community, 75 percent of acts of religious intolerance are directed against Christians.[9]

The Pew Forum on Religion and Public Life reports that Christians have suffered harassment by the state and / or society in 133 countries – two-thirds of the world's nation states – and suffer in more places than any other religious group.[10] Data from the late researcher David B. Barrett puts the number of Christians martyred since the time of Jesus at 70 million.[11]

Conclusion

There are many good reasons to trust the Scriptures. In our conversations with those who ask, "How do you know the Bible is true?" we may confidently respond, "I believe the Bible is true because credible eyewitnesses accurately recorded the acts of God throughout human history, under divine direction, free of personal agendas, and in the presence of hostile witnesses who often made them pay for their testimony with their lives."

THINK *Questions for personal or group study*

What questions raise the most doubt in your mind about the reliability of Scripture? Where could you go to find answers?

The Bible's "credible eyewitness" sometimes seem to disagree on particular details of commonly reported events, especially in the Gospels. So, why does "multiple attestation" strengthen rather than undermine the biblical record?

How would you explain that the Bible is both a divine and human document?

How does the gruesome death of so many biblical writers support the reliability of their testimony?

Why do you think there is an absence of first-century documentation refuting the life and times of Jesus?

SHARE *Talking points for the reliability of the Bible*

Christians believe the Bible is true because credible eyewitnesses accurately recorded the acts of God throughout human history, under divine direction, free of personal agendas, and in the presence of hostile witnesses who often made them pay for their testimonies with their lives.

Consider that 40 different men record the Bible over a period of 1,500 years – credible eyewitnesses such as Moses, David, Daniel, John, Paul, and Peter.

The recorders of Scripture operate under divine direction (2 Tim. 3:16-17; 2 Peter 1:20-21).

They also are free of personal agendas, seeking neither fame nor fortune.

The New Testament writers in particular pen their works in the presence of hostile witnesses; yet there is deafening silence when it comes to efforts to refute their testimonies.

People have been known to die for something they truly believe in. But it's rare – and exceptionally foolhardy – to die for something one knows to be a lie. The faithfulness of the New Testament writers – many of whom suffered gruesome martyrs' deaths – is a testimony to the truth of their eyewitness accounts.

DIVE *Go deeper in your study with these resources*

Has God Spoken? by Hank Hanegraaff

How We Got the Bible by Neil R. Lightfoot

Cold Case Christianity by J. Warner Wallace

Can We Still Believe the Bible? by Craig L. Blomberg

7
SEVEN REASONS TO TRUST THE SCRIPTURES

Here, in brief summary, are seven reasons anyone who seeks earnestly for the truth may have confidence that the Bible is God's Word.

Reason 1: The documents

While the autographs, or original manuscripts, of the Bible have not survived the ravages of time, no other book from the ancient world has more, earlier, or more accurately copied manuscripts than the Bible. (See "Comparing Ancient Works with the New Testament" at the end of the chapter.) For example, we have 25,000 – 30,000 handwritten manuscripts (copies consisting of fragments, portions of books, complete books, or collections of books) of the New Testament, nearly 5,800 of them in Greek. Even if no New Testament manuscripts existed, we could reconstruct nearly all of the 27 books because the early church fathers of the second and third centuries quoted the NT more than 36,000 times.[1] In addition, the existing Bible manuscripts are relatively older than other ancient documents, dating closer to the time of the originals, thus lending credence to their reliability. Finally, while these documents vary somewhat as they have been copied over the years, nearly all of the variants are minor, and none of them challenges a single doctrine of the Christian faith.

Reason 2: The scribes

The 40 men who penned the Scriptures over a period of 1,500 years insisted that their message came from God. Many were persecuted, or even martyred, for their faith. The authors of the Bible claimed to be under the direction of the Holy Spirit (2 Sam. 23:2; 2 Peter 1:20-21). The prophets ascribed their message to God. Phrases such as, "Thus saith the Lord," "God said," and "the Word of the Lord came to me," are found hundreds of times in the Bible. The apostle Paul declared, "All Scripture is inspired by God" (2 Tim. 3:16). Peter referred to the writings of Paul as "Scriptures" (2 Peter 3:16). Even non-Christian ancient writings attest to the truthfulness of the eyewitness accounts of Christ.

Reason 3: Fulfilled prophecy

Consider the Old Testament prophecies of the Messiah. There are nearly 300 such prophecies, the last of which dates more than four centuries before the birth of Jesus, who fulfills every Messianic prophecy except those pertaining to His glorious future return. (But remember His words recorded in John 14:3, "I will come back.") Many of these ancient prophecies are highly detailed, making it impossible – apart from divine intervention – for one man to fulfill them all. Yet Jesus did, confirming His identity as the Messiah (or Christ) and providing exceptional evidence for the reliability of Scripture. Among the Messianic prophecies fulfilled in Jesus are: His virgin birth (Isa. 7:14; Matt. 1:18-21); His birthplace in Bethlehem (Micah 5:2; Matt. 2:1; Luke 2:4-7); His miracle-working authority (Isa. 35:5-6; Matt. 9:35); His rejection by the Jews (Ps. 118:22; 1 Peter 2:7); His suffering and death (Psalm 22; Isaiah 53; Matt. 27:27ff); His resurrection (Ps. 16:10; Mark 16:6; Acts 2:31; 1 Cor. 15:3-8); His ascension into heaven (Ps. 68:18; Acts 1:9); and His place today at the Father's right hand (Ps. 110:1; Heb. 1:3).

Reason 4: Archaeology

The unearthing of ancient sites has confirmed the accuracy of the biblical record. Noted archaeologist Nelson Glueck states, "As a matter of fact … it may be stated categorically that no archaeological discovery has ever controverted a biblical reference. Scores of archaeological findings have been made which confirm in clear outline or exact detail historical statements in the Bible."[2] Examples of archaeological confirmations include the Tower of Babel (Genesis 11); Sodom and Gomorrah (Genesis 18-19); the fall of Jericho (Joshua 6); King David (2 Samuel); and the Assyrian Captivity (Isaiah 20). In the New Testament book of Acts alone there are hundreds of archaeological confirmations.

Reason 5: Jesus

Jesus claimed to be the Messiah (or Christ), the Son of God and the Son of Man (Matt. 16:16-18; 26:63-64; John 8:58). He was confirmed by acts of God (John 3:2; Acts 2:22) and declared that He had been given all authority in heaven and on earth to rule and to judge (Matt. 28:18; John 5:22). Therefore, His views on the Bible are extremely important. What did Jesus have to say? Norman Geisler writes, "Jesus declared that the Old Testament was *divinely authoritative* (Matt. 4:4,

7, 10); *imperishable* (Matt. 5:17-18); *infallible* (John 10:35); *inerrant* (Matt. 22:29; John 17:17); *historically reliable* (Matt. 12:40; 24:37-38); *scientifically accurate* (Matt. 19:4-5; John 3:12); and *ultimately supreme* (Matt. 15:3, 6)."[3] Jesus also personally affirmed many things that Bible critics deny, for example: 1) God created a literal Adam and Eve (Matt. 19:4); Jonah actually was swallowed by a great fish (Matt. 12:40); the whole world was destroyed by a flood in Noah's day (Matt. 24:36-39); and there was one prophet (not two or three) who wrote all of Isaiah (Mark 7:6-7; Luke 4:17-21).

Reason 6: The Holy Spirit

The same Holy Spirit who authored Scripture (2 Tim. 3:16-17) lives in believers' hearts and "testifies together with our spirit that we are God's children" (Rom. 8:16). This means the Holy Spirit confirms the truth of God's Word to us. Jesus taught that the Holy Spirit would convince the lost of their sin of unbelief, of the righteousness of Christ, and of the judgment they will share with Satan if they persist in their unbelief – all clear teachings of Scripture (John 16:7-11).

Reason 7: The redeemed

The Bible's life-changing power is widely known through the testimony of those who have come to know Christ. The apostle Paul, once known as a Christ-hating persecutor of the church, declared, "For I am not ashamed of the gospel, because it is God's power for salvation to everyone who believes, first to the Jew, and also to the Greek" (Rom. 1:16). Peter added, "… you have been born again – not of perishable seed but of imperishable – through the living and enduring word of God" (1 Peter 1:23). Millions of personal testimonies throughout the ages lend credence to the power of God's Word to convey truth, convict the spiritually dead of their sins, and bring new life through faith in Jesus Christ. As the writer of Hebrews declares, "For the word of God is living and effective and sharper than any two-edged sword, penetrating as far as to divide soul, spirit, joints, and marrow; it is a judge of the ideas and thoughts of the heart" (Heb. 4:12).

THINK *Questions for personal or group study*

Why is it significant that we have more, earlier, and better-copied manuscripts of the New Testament than of other contemporary ancient documents?

Why are the deity and personhood of the Holy Spirit important to the inspiration of Scripture?

How can Christians say the Bible is without error when sinful men are attributed with writing it down?

What did Jesus have to say about the reliability of the Old Testament?

Where in the Gospels does Jesus indicate that the future writings of the apostles will be faithful representations of the historical accounts of His life and words?

SHARE *Talking points for the trustworthiness of Scripture*

The reliability of the New Testament is based in part on the fact that we have more, earlier, and better-copied manuscripts of the NT than of other contemporary ancient documents.

Thousands of times in the Bible, God either is quoted directly or attributed with the words penned by human authors.

There is remarkable consistency in the Bible despite the fact that 40 different men contributed to the Scriptures over a period of 1,500 years.

The apostle Paul writes that all Scripture is inspired, or God-breathed (2 Tim. 3:16-17); and the apostle Peter reminds us that holy men of God spoke as they were moved by the Holy Spirit (2 Peter 1:20-21).

Jesus declared the Old Testament to be authoritative, imperishable, infallible, inerrant, historically reliable, scientifically accurate, and ultimately supreme.

DIVE *Go deeper in your study with these resources*

Systematic Theology, Vol. 1 by Norman Geisler

Christian Theology, Third Edition by Millard J. Erickson

Systematic Theology by Wayne Grudem

The Canon of Scripture by F.F. Bruce

In Defense of the Bible, edited by Steven B. Cowan and Terry L. Wilder

COMPARING ANCIENT WORKS WITH THE NEW TESTAMENT

Author	Title	Date Written	Earliest Manuscript	Time Gap (Years)	Number of Copies
Various	New Testament	AD 50-100	AD 130 or earlier	40	5,795 (Greek)
Homer	*Iliad*	BC 800	c. BC 400	400	1,757
Herodotus	*History*	BC 480-425	AD 900s	1,350	109
Sophocles	Plays	BC 496-406	BC 200s	100-200	193
Plato	Tetralogies	BC 400	AD 895	1,300	210
Caesar	*Gallic Wars*	BC 100-44	AD 800s	950	251
Livy	*History of Rome*	BC 59 – AD 17	AD early 400s	400	150
Tacitus	*Annals*	AD 100	AD 850 (first half) AD 1050 (2nd half)	750-950	33
Pliny, the Elder	*Natural History*	AD 49-79	AD 400s (fragment)	350-400	200
Thucydides	*History*	BC 460-400	BC 200s	200	96
Demosthenes	Speeches	BC 300	BC 1st Century (fragments)	200	340

Adapted from various sources including: "The Biographical Test Updated," *Christian Research Journal*, Vol. 35, No. 03 (2012); *The New Evidence that Demands a Verdict*, Josh McDowell; and *How We Got the Bible*, Neil R. Lightfoot.

"The number of manuscripts of the New Testament, or early translations from it, and of quotations from it in the oldest writers of the Church, is so large that it is practically certain that the true reading of every doubtful passage is preserved in some one or other of these ancient authorities.... This can be said of no other ancient book in the world" (Sir Frederick Kenyon, *Our Bible and the Ancient Manuscripts*, p. 55).

"If we compare the present state of the New Testament text with that of any other ancient writing, we must ... declare it to be marvelously correct. Such has been the care with which the New Testament has been copied – a care which has doubtless grown out of true reverence for its holy words.... The New Testament [is] unrivaled among ancient writings in the purity of its text as actually transmitted and kept in use" (Benjamin B. Warfield, *Introduction to Textual Criticism of the New Testament*, pp. 12-13).

8
ADDRESSING EIGHT COMMON OBJECTIONS

Here are eight objections critics commonly raise against the Bible, along with brief responses.

Objection 1

No one really knows what the Bible says because the original manuscripts are lost.

Response

True, the "autographs," or original documents, no longer exist, but a remarkable number of copies do. No other book from the ancient world has more, earlier, or better-copied manuscripts than the Bible. For example, nearly 5,800 Greek, 10,000 Latin, and 10,000-15,000 other early manuscripts of the New Testament are in existence, some dating to within a generation of the originals. Compare with fewer than 1,800 copies of Homer's *Iliad*, with the earliest copies dating 400 years *after* the original.

Objection 2

The Bible has been copied so many times, with so many variations, there's no way to know what was originally scripted.

Response

While it's true there are variations among the manuscripts – 150,000 by some counts – the vast majority have to do with changes in spelling, grammar, and style, or accidental omissions or duplications of words or phrases. Only about 400 variants in the New Testament manuscripts have any significant bearing on the meaning of the passage, and most of these are noted in the footnotes or margins of modern translations and editions of Scripture. The only textual variants that affect more than a sentence or two are John 7:53-8:11 and Mark 16:9-20.

Objection 3

Councils of men working in highly political processes decided which books belong in the Bible. As a result, they left out some very good books – perhaps some equally inspired writings.

Response

These oft-repeated charges are unfounded. They deny the supernatural inspiration and preservation of Scripture and instead emphasize the efforts of men who, it is argued, wanted only to maintain control over the early church. In truth, the Holy Spirit authored Scripture through the pens of human agents, managed its preservation, and decided which books belong in the canon (2 Tim. 3:16-17; 2 Peter 1:20-21). Councils of Christian leaders met in the fourth century and made important decisions about the New Testament based on evidence supporting the books' inspiration and authority, but in no way did they undermine God's revelation of Himself in Scripture. The God who hangs the stars in space and calls them by name (Isa. 40:26) has no problem guiding the means by which His very words are given to His most precious creation: mankind.

Objection 4

It's silly to assume that one book – the Bible – contains all of God's truth and that other great writings, from the *Vedas* to the *Book of Mormon*, do not come from God.

Response

We must begin with the claims of the documents themselves. The Bible specifically and repeatedly declares itself to be the written Word of God, while the *Vedas* do not. Even the *Book of Mormon* is called "another testament of Jesus Christ," dangerously ignoring a biblical mandate not to add to or take away from the Scriptures (Rev. 22:18-19). While many religious writings contain moral and ethical truths, some of which are consistent with Scripture, only the Bible claims to be God's written and complete revelation to mankind. The Bible's claim to be the Word of God is backed up by unparalleled textual, archaeological, and historical evidence. Most compelling, however, is the testimony of the Holy Spirit, who authored the Scriptures and who confirms in our human spirits the truth of God's Word.

Objection 5

The Bible is full of contradictions.

Response

The Bible *does* feature passages that are difficult to understand, or that report historical events from different perspectives. But that does not prove the charge of contradictions. Consider these guidelines for dealing with Bible difficulties: 1) logic and reason – examine the Bible like other documents; 2) translation – consider the nuances between various English versions; 3) time – some seemingly contradictory statements are separated by years and must be seen in their proper time frames; 4) context – study the chapters and books in which apparent contradictions occur; 5) sense – words and phrases may be used literally or figuratively; 6) quotations – many Old Testament passages are paraphrased or summarized in the New Testament; 7) perspective – when two or more writers provide separate accounts of the same events, differences in names, numbers, and conversations may be accounted for by each writer's perspective. One final thought: When a friend says the Bible is full of contradictions, ask her to name one; then, follow the guidelines listed above and explore the passage together.

Objection 6

The Bible can't be true because it depicts a different God in the Old and New Testaments.

Response

The Bible is God's progressive revelation of Himself and must be understood in context. When one reads both the Old and the New Testaments it becomes evident that God is the same yesterday, today, and forever (Mal. 3:6; Heb. 13:8). For example, both testaments tell us that God judges the unrepentant in time and eternity; He is compassionate and gracious; He desires a personal relationship with people; and He is actively engaged in human history. Concerning the Trinity, while the Bible emphatically declares that there is one true and living God (Deut. 6:4; James 2:19), the Old Testament hints at the triune Godhead and the New Testament more fully reveals one God in three persons (see Gen. 1:1-2, 26; 3:22; 11:7; Isa. 6:8; Matt. 3:16-17; John 1:1, 14; 10:30; Acts 5:3-4; Col. 1:16; 2:9; Heb. 1:8; 1 Peter 1:2).

Objection 7

There are so many English translations of the Bible, it's impossible to know which translation is the right one.

Response

There are many Bible translations available today, leading some to ask, "Which version is right?" and others to conclude that because there is so much variation between translations, none of them is correct. Keep in mind, however, that the *autographs,* or original documents, of Scripture are inerrant – not the subsequent copies and translations. Even though there are dozens of English translations that differ in varying degrees from one another, we have a high degree of confidence that the source documents from which these versions came are accurate representations of the autographs. For more information, see Chapter 10: Which Translation of the Bible Should I Use?

Objection 8

There are so many Christian denominations today, it's clear that Christians can't agree on what the Bible teaches.

Response

Christian denominations generally developed out of a desire for fellowship and joint ministry between individual churches – a biblical concept (Acts 11:27-30). There is a rich diversity among Christian denominations today, and the differences between them are not as wide as they appear. Many of the disagreements are over matters of conscience, such as which day of the week to worship, dietary restrictions, or which translation of the Bible to use (see Romans 14; 1 Cor.10:23-33), or they focus on lesser points of doctrine, such as the manner in which missions activities are organized and funded. It should be acknowledged that Christians often have engaged in petty squabbling, internal power struggles, political wrangling, and outright warfare – to the detriment of the gospel. The New Testament implores believers to be gracious toward and forgiving of one another (Eph. 4:32).

THINK *Questions for personal or group study*

Why do you think some people raise objections to the Bible? If you can, sort out reasons that are sincere versus reasons that simply are argumentative.

If further documentary evidence proved that the story of the woman caught in adultery (John 7:53-8:11) and the closing verses of the Gospel of Mark (Mark 16:9-20) were not part of the New Testament autographs (original documents), what difference would that make in your confidence in Scripture?

What are the challenges faced by having so many different Christian denominations? Do you see any strengths in the diversity of denominations?

How might you respond to a person who sincerely asks why there are so many contradictions in the Bible?

Do you think there's room for additional books in the canon of Scripture? In other words, is it possible God did not stop at 66 books?

SHARE *Talking points for addressing objections to the Bible*

While the original documents (autographs) of the Bible have not survived, we are confident of Scripture's reliability because we have more, earlier, and better-copied manuscripts of the Bible than we have of other contemporary ancient documents.

Variants in ancient manuscripts do not necessarily mean errors. Only about 400 variants in the New Testament manuscripts have any significant bearing on the meaning of the passage, and most of these are noted in the footnotes or margins of modern translations and editions of Scripture. No variant undermines a Christian doctrine.

The original documents of Scripture, not the subsequent copies and translations, are inerrant.

The Bible is God's progressive revelation of Himself and must be understood in context. When we read the Old and the New Testaments, it becomes evident that God is the same yesterday, today, and forever (Mal. 3:6; Heb. 13:8).

Even though there are dozens of English translations that differ in varying degrees from one another, we have a high degree of confidence that the source documents from which these versions came are accurate representations of the originals.

DIVE *Go deeper in your study with these resources*

Encyclopedia of Bible Difficulties by Gleason Archer

The Big Book of Bible Difficulties: Clear and Concise Answers from Genesis to Revelation by Norman L. Geisler and Thomas Howe

Is God a Moral Monster? Making Sense of the Old Testament by Paul Copan

Questioning the Bible: 11 Major Challenges to the Bible's Authority by Jonathan Morrow

One Bible, Many Versions: Are All Translations Created Equal? by Dave Brunn

9
IS THE NEW TESTAMENT CANON CLOSED?

Muslim and Mormon apologists have attempted to justify their collections of "divinely inspired" literature by casting doubt over the biblical canon – those 66 books that the church has long held to be the complete written revelation of God. They justify their views by claiming: (1) that surviving texts of the Old and New Testaments are corrupt and therefore unreliable (a typical Muslim claim), or (2) that early church leaders deliberately excluded certain books for personal or political reasons (a typical Mormon claim).

As Craig L. Blomberg responds in his book – *Can We Still Believe the Bible?* – "there is not a shred of historical evidence to support either of these claims; anyone choosing to believe them must do so by pure credulity, flying in the face of all the evidence that actually exists."[1]

Even so, modern-day critics and best-selling authors, from Bart Ehrman to Dan Brown, weave intricate arguments against the certainty of the "closed" canon of 27 New Testament books. Why are these books included? And why exclude other leading candidates like the *Apocalypse of Peter*, the *Epistle of Barnabas*, and the *Shepherd of Hermas*?

Let's carry the argument one step further, into the 21st century: What if we discovered an apostolic writing that has remained hidden for the last 2,000 years?

For example, in 1 Cor. 5:9, Paul alludes to an earlier letter to fellow believers in Corinth. We don't have that letter, nor are we aware of its specific contents. Let's say, however, that archaeologists unearth a clay pot containing a manuscript dating from the mid-first century and fitting the description of Paul's letter.

Should the church welcome 3 Corinthians as the 28th book of the New Testament? Not so fast.

The New Testament canon

We should begin by noting that the word "canon" is derived from the Hebrew word *qaneh*, which means "reed" or "measuring rod." In essence, the canon is the full expression of God's written revelation and therefore is a valid measurement of truth.

Judaism accepted the concept of a closed Hebrew canon (Old Testament) by the end of the first century at the latest. The books of Moses, also known as the Pentateuch, were the first Scriptures canonized, with the Prophets and the Writings coming later. After His resurrection, Jesus spoke of Himself as the fulfillment of the Law of Moses, the Prophets, and the Psalms (Luke 24:44).[2]

The New Testament offers hints of the process of canonization, but little more. As Jesus prepares His followers for His passion and return to heaven, He promises to send the Holy Spirit, who will enable the disciples to remember Jesus' teaching (John 14:26), testify further about Him (John 15:26), and proclaim truth (John 16:13).

In other words, the same Holy Spirit who authored the Old Testament will ensure that authentic testimonies about Jesus are written, preserved, and shared.

Some New Testament books received a great deal of scrutiny before their inclusion, most notably Hebrews, James, 2 Peter, 2-3 John, Jude, and Revelation. And some didn't make the cut for a variety of reasons; examples include the gnostic gospels of Judas, Barnabas, and Thomas.

So, what criteria did the early church use as a guide? Blomberg notes three main requirements: apostolicity, catholicity, and orthodoxy.[3]

Apostolicity. This does not mean every book is written by an apostle, but rather that each book is written during the apostolic age.

In addition, no book in the New Testament is more than one person removed from an apostle or another authoritative eyewitness of the life of Christ.

Mark, for example, is not an apostle, but he is a traveling companion of both Peter and Paul. Early church tradition attributes much of Mark's Gospel to the memoirs of Peter.

Luke, in a similar manner, travels with Paul and interviews eyewitnesses of Jesus.

Catholicity. This has nothing to do with the Roman Catholic Church. The word "catholic" simply means "universal." Catholicity means that believers throughout the world to which Christianity was spreading were in agreement on the value of these books – and used them widely.

No books that were found only among one sect of Christianity or in a single geographical location are included in the New Testament canon.

Orthodoxy. This refers to the faithfulness of the books to the teachings of Jesus and the apostles. Blomberg writes, "It is a criterion that could not have developed if people had not recognized that the heresies afflicting the church in its earliest centuries were parasitic on orthodoxy. That is to say, the heresies developed in response to apostolic doctrine – modifying it, challenging it, trying to refute it, supplementing it, or simply rejecting it."[4]

By the late second century, we see lists of 20 to 22 books accepted as authoritative, increasing to 23 early in the third century, and finally to 27 by no later than A.D. 367, when Athanasius, bishop of Alexandria, writes his Easter encyclical to the rest of the church and lists the books that most Christians still accept today.

So, back to our original question: What if Paul's earlier letter is discovered? While the letter would be instructive, and likely would pass the tests of apostolicity and orthodoxy, it would fail the test of catholicity. There is no evidence this letter was read widely in the early church.

The key is to remember that the Holy Spirit ultimately fixes the canon of Scripture. The New Testament tests of apostolicity, catholicity, and orthodoxy do not *determine* which books are inspired; they simply help us *discover* them.

THINK *Questions for personal or group study*

How would you respond to your Roman Catholic friends who say the Reformers removed inspired books from the Bible? (For a good start, see Craig Blomberg, *Can We Still Believe the Bible?* pp. 43-82.)

Why do you think God did not simply declare a book to be Scripture as soon as it was finished? Put another way, why rely on the counsel of men to affirm the inspired books?

What purpose do you think God had for giving us the Bible over a period of 1,500 years through 40 human authors? Why didn't He just hand it down all at once through a single person – or by divine fiat?

Why is the canon of Scripture closed? That is, why hasn't God given us any more "God-breathed" writings since the first century?

What reasons can you cite for believing the Bible to be the complete written revelation of God, as opposed to, say, the gnostic gospels, the Qur'an, or the *Book of Mormon*?

SHARE *Talking points for addressing the canon of Scripture*

Jesus affirmed the closed canon of the Old Testament, describing Himself as the fulfillment of the Law of Moses, the Prophets, and the Psalms.

In the Gospels, Jesus assures His followers that the same Holy Spirit who inspired the Old Testament will ensure that authentic testimonies about Him are written, preserved, and shared.

The early church used three main requirements for discovering the New Testament canon: apostolicity, catholicity, and orthodoxy.

The tests of apostolicity, catholicity, and orthodoxy do not *determine* which New Testament books are inspired; they simply help us *discover* them.

The Holy Spirit ultimately fixes the canon of Scripture.

DIVE *Go deeper in your study with these resources*

Can We Still Trust the Bible? by Craig Blomberg

The Canon of Scripture by F.F. Bruce

The Missing Gospels: Unearthing the Truth Behind Alternative Christianities by Darrell L. Bock, Ph.D.

10

WHICH TRANSLATION OF THE BIBLE SHOULD I USE?

There is an alphabet soup of Bible translations available today, from the KJV to the NIV, and the NASB to the HCSB. This has led some critics to conclude that because there is so much variation between translations, no one really knows what the Bible says.

This attack on inerrancy is misplaced. Keep in mind that the Bible's *autographs*, or original documents, are inerrant – not subsequent copies and translations. Even though there are dozens of English translations that differ in varying degrees, we are highly confident that the source documents from which these versions came – more than 25,000 New Testament manuscripts alone – are accurate representations of the autographs.

A more practical question for Christians today is, "Which translation of the Bible should I use?" To answer that question, let's look at four types of translations, then match our intended use with the translators' intended goals.

Four types of translations

While scholars and Bible publishers offer varying lists, we will pursue four general classifications of Bible translations:

Formal equivalence. Often called a "word-for-word" translation, formal equivalence "seeks to represent each word of the translated text with an exact equivalent word in the translation so that the reader can see word for word what the original human author wrote," according to The Apologetics Study Bible.[1]

Advantages include: (a) consistency with the conviction that the Holy Spirit inspired not just the thoughts but the very words of Scripture; (b) access to the structure of the text in the original language; and (c) accuracy to the degree that English has an exact equivalent for each word. Drawbacks include sometimes-awkward English or a misunderstanding of the author's intent.

Translations that tend to follow a formal equivalence philosophy include the King James Version (KJV), the New American Standard Bible (NASB), and the English Standard Version (ESV).

Dynamic or functional equivalence. Known as a "thought-for-thought" approach, dynamic equivalence attempts to distinguish the meaning of a text from its form and then translate the meaning so that it makes the same impact on modern readers that the ancient text made on its original readers.

Strengths include readability and an acknowledgement that accurate and effective translation requires interpretation. Drawbacks include: (a) the meaning of a text cannot always be neatly separated from its form; (b) the author may have intended multiple meanings; and (c) difficulty in verifying accuracy, which may affect the usefulness of the translation for in-depth study.

Translations that tend to employ dynamic equivalence include the New International Version (NIV), the Contemporary English Version (CEV), and the Good News Translation (GNT).

Optimal equivalence. This translation philosophy seeks to combine as much clarity as the original text and the translation language permit. The theory is to use formal equivalence where possible and dynamic equivalence where needed to clarify the text.

The main advantage is the combination of accuracy and readability. One drawback is that some people prefer either a more formal equivalence or dynamic equivalence translation. Translations that employ optimal equivalence include the Holman Christian Standard Bible (HCSB); the NET Bible; and God's Word.

Paraphrase. Paraphrased versions are loose translations that are highly readable and contemporary but lack the accuracy of word-for-word translations and at times add meaning beyond what a thought-for-thought translation would allow.

Examples of paraphrased translations include The Living Bible (TLB) and The Message (TM).

Rule of thumb

To find a good translation for your needs, ask two questions: What am I using the translation for? And what is the translators' intent?

For example, if you're engaged in scholarly study, you may prefer accuracy over readability, so a formal equivalence translation like the NASB or ESV might make the most sense.

If you're leading corporate worship or teaching a class, you may want a good balance between accuracy and readability such as the HCSB (optimal equivalence) or NIV (dynamic equivalence).

If you're interested in a highly readable translation for devotional purposes, you might enjoy a paraphrase like The Message or The Living Bible.

For a well-rounded understanding of Bible passages, some students use several translations side-by-side – for example the NASB (accuracy), NIV (readability), and The Message (contemporary language). They also may consult a variety of classic and contemporary Bible commentaries, or popular Bible computer programs such as Logos Bible Software.[2]

THINK *Questions for personal or group study*

Why is it wrong to argue that a certain translation of Scripture is inerrant?

Do you think the many different English translations of the Bible available today are helping or hurting serious Bible study?

Under what circumstances might it be best to use a word-for-word translation? A thought-for-thought translation? A paraphrase?

In your opinion, should church leaders instruct their congregations to use a certain translation in corporate worship and church-led Bible studies? What are the potential advantages of this? The potential disadvantages?

Why should some translations be avoided altogether, such as the New World Translation (Jehovah's Witness Bible) and the Joseph Smith Translation (also known as the "Inspired Version" of Mormonism)?

SHARE *Talking points for addressing various translations of Scripture*

Keep in mind that the Bible's autographs, or original documents, are inerrant; subsequent copies and translations are not.

There are four basic types of Bible translations: (1) formal equivalence (word-for-word); (2) dynamic equivalence (thought-for-thought); (3) optimal equivalence (a combination of formal and dynamic); and (4) paraphrase.

Formal equivalence translations focus on accuracy; dynamic equivalence translations emphasize readability; optimal equivalence translations seek a balance between accuracy and readability.

Paraphrased versions of the Bible are rich with imagery and contemporary language, but should not be used in isolation for in-depth Bible study.

In selecting a translation, it's helpful to ask yourself two questions: (1) What am I using the translation for? and (2) What is the translators' intent?

DIVE *Go deeper in your study with these resources*

One Bible, Many Versions: Are All Translations Created Equal? by Dave Brunn

The King James Only Controversy: Can You Trust Modern Translations? by James R. White

COMPARING ENGLISH BIBLE TRANSLATIONS[3]

Translation	Translation Type	Year Released	Reading Level (grade)
Amplified Bible (AMP)	Formal Equivalence; amplification of word meanings	1965; updated 1987	11
Contemporary English Version (CEV)	Dynamic Equivalence	1995	5-6
English Standard Version (ESV) – based on Revised Standard Version (RSV) 1951	Formal Equivalence	2001	7-8
Good News Translation (GNT)	Dynamic Equivalence	1976	5-6
Holman Christian Standard Bible (HCSB)	Optimal Equivalence*	2004	7-8
King James Version (KJV)	Formal Equivalence	1611	11-12
New King James Version (NKJV)	Formal Equivalence	1982	7-8
The Living Bible (LB)	Paraphrase	1971	8
The Message (MSG)	Paraphrase	2002	5-6
New American Standard Bible (NASB)	Formal Equivalence	1971	11
New Century Version (NCV)	Dynamic Equivalence	1988	5-6
New International Version (NIV)	Dynamic Equivalence **	1978	7-8
New Living Translation (NLT)	Dynamic Equivalence	1996	6-7
New Revised Standard Version (NRSV)	Formal Equivalence	1989	10-11

* Also known as a "hybrid" – formal equivalence with dynamic balance
** Some consider this translation a "hybrid"

JOHN 3:16-17 IN FOUR TRANSLATIONS

Translation	Translation Type	John 3:16-17	Reading Level (grade)
King James Version (KJV)	Formal Equivalence	For God so loved the world, that he gave his only begotten Son, that whosoever believeth in him should not perish, but have everlasting life. For God sent not his Son into the world to condemn the world; but that the world through him might be saved.	11-12
New International Version (NIV)	Dynamic Equivalence	For God so loved the world that he gave his one and only Son, that whoever believes in him shall not perish but have eternal life. For God did not send his Son into the world to condemn the world, but to save the world through him.	7-8
Holman Christian Standard Bible (HCSB)	Optimal Equivalence	For God loved the world in this way: He gave His One and only Son, so that everyone who believes in Him will not perish but have eternal life. For God did not send His Son into the world that He might condemn the world, but that the world might be saved through Him.	7-8
The Message (MSG)	Paraphrase	This is how much God loved the world: He gave his Son, his one and only Son. And this is why: so that no one need be destroyed; by believing in him, anyone can have a whole and lasting life. God didn't go to all the trouble of sending his Son merely to point an accusing finger, telling the world how bad it was. He came to help, to put the world right again.	5-6

IV.

JESUS CHRIST

11
WHO IS THE REAL JESUS?

Jesus of Nazareth is among the world's most famous and admired persons. Amazon.com offers more than 295,000 book titles about Him. Google lists about 169 million references to Jesus Christ. The world's major religions hold a high view of Jesus, although they do not agree on who He is or what He accomplished. For example:

Islam teaches that Jesus was a great prophet who performed miracles and lived a sinless life; but He is not the Son of God, nor did he die on the cross.

Hinduism teaches that Jesus was an avatar, or incarnation of God, a great spiritual teacher, a guru, or even a major god in the Hindu pantheon of 330 million gods; but He is not unique as the Son of God or Savior.

Buddhism tells us Jesus was a teacher who may have possessed Buddhahood or enlightenment; but He is not unique and is not mankind's Savior.

Judaism teaches that Jesus was a humble and insignificant prophet, a reformer who performed good deeds; but He is not the Messiah and certainly is not divine.

Christianity, of course, professes that Jesus is the Son of God, Messiah, and Savior, whose death and resurrection paid our sin debt and provided forgiveness of sins and eternal life. Even so, not all who profess Christianity agree about Jesus' life and work. Mormons, for example, say Jesus attained godhood in pre-human existence; and Jehovah's Witnesses insist that Jesus was Jehovah's first creation and therefore is not divine.

The debate over Jesus is nothing new. It raged 2,000 years ago in Israel and involved everyone from John the Baptist to Jesus' own family members, many of whom initially did not believe He was the promised Messiah. Jesus was fully aware that His life and ministry produced tension, and He challenged His followers to examine the evidence and decide for themselves.

In Matt. 16:13-17, Jesus asks His disciples two questions. First, "Who do people say that the Son of Man is?" A loaded question to be sure, since by calling Himself "Son of Man" Jesus is claiming to be both divine and the Messiah (see Dan. 7:13-14). Second, Jesus asks a more pointed question, "Who do *you* say that I am?"

Notice several keys in these verses:

- There are many opinions about Jesus – all of them good. Some say He is John the Baptist, Elijah, Jeremiah, or one of the prophets. Today, members of nearly every major world religion agree that Jesus is someone to be admired, even followed. But it's not enough to have a high view of Jesus; one must have the *correct* view of Jesus.

- Peter offers a different answer – and the correct one: "You are the Messiah, the Son of the living God!"

- Jesus acknowledges Peter's answer as the proper one and states that it was not revealed by human wisdom but "by My Father in heaven." Flesh-and-blood opinions about Jesus are subject to error because people are sinful and fallen and prone to mistakes. God the Father, however, is not. He sent Jesus to earth and reveals the person and work of Christ to human hearts. In fact, Jesus made it clear that no one can be saved unless the Father draws him or her to the Son (John 6:44).

Today, we have God's complete written revelation to us, the Bible, which features convincing evidence that Jesus is who He claimed to be: Messiah, Son of God, Son of Man, Savior, King of kings and Lord of lords. So let's go to the evidence in Scripture. We will use the Bible because it records the words of Jesus and features the accounts of eyewitnesses.

Some may raise objections to using the Bible instead of other sources, but keep in mind:

- The New Testament is the most accurate set of ancient documents available to us concerning the life of Jesus.

- The eyewitnesses wrote their accounts in the presence of hostile witnesses, who could have refuted them if they were wrong, but didn't.

- The apostles willingly suffered – and most died – for their testimony.

- More recent "new" gospels challenging the historical view of Jesus were penned much later (mostly in the 2nd – 4th centuries) and were recognized as false teachings or even forgeries.

So, let's turn our attention to seven keys that depict the real Jesus. Each key centers on three important questions:

1. What does Jesus say about Himself?

2. What do the eyewitnesses say about Jesus?

3. What do you say? (Specifically: What other Scriptures address this doctrine? Do you agree with the view of Jesus and the eyewitnesses? Why or why not?)

THINK *Questions for personal or group study*

Why do you think the story of Jesus is woven into so many major world religions?

What are the non-negotiable truths about Jesus that are core to the Christian faith? For example, we may not agree on the exact date of Jesus' birth, but can we afford to "agree to disagree" about His place of birth? His virgin birth? Deity? Sinless humanity? Death on a cross? Physical resurrection?

What are some of the most important truths Jesus reveals about Himself in the Gospels?

How much about Jesus does a person need to know to be saved?

What are some good questions we could ask our friends to determine their beliefs about Jesus?

SHARE *Talking points for addressing the real Jesus*

The world's major religions hold a high view of Jesus, although they do not agree on who He is or what He accomplished.

Jesus was fully aware that His life and ministry produced tension, and He challenged His followers to examine the evidence and decide for themselves.

The most important question in all of Scripture – the question on which our eternal destiny hangs – is the question Jesus asks in Matthew 16, "Who do you say that I am?"

It's not good enough to have a high view of Jesus; we must have the correct view of Jesus.

God has given us the Bible, which offers convincing eyewitness testimony that Jesus is who He claimed to be: Messiah, Son of God, Son of Man, Savior, King of kings and Lord of lords.

DIVE *Go deeper in your study with these resources*

The Case for Christ and *The Case for the Real Jesus* by Lee Strobel

The Jesus I Never Knew by Philip Yancey

The Missing Gospels: Unearthing the Truth Behind Alternative Christianities by Darrell L. Bock

12

SEVEN KEYS TO UNLOCKING THE REAL JESUS

In this chapter, we address seven keys that depict the real Jesus. Each key opens the door to three important questions:

1. What does Jesus say about Himself?

2. What do the eyewitnesses say about Jesus?

3. What do you say? Specifically: What other Scriptures address this doctrine? Do you agree with the view of Jesus and the eyewitnesses? Why or why not?

1. His origin

What Jesus says about Himself: He is eternal and uncreated.

- John 8:58 – "I assure you: Before Abraham was, I am" (I AM is the name God gives Himself at the burning bush [Ex. 3:13-14]).

- John 17:5 – "Now, Father, glorify Me in Your presence with that glory I had with You before the world existed."

- Rev. 1:17-18 – "Don't be afraid! I am the First and the Last, and the Living One. I was dead, but look — I am alive forever and ever, and I hold the keys of death and Hades."

What the eyewitnesses say about Jesus: He has always existed and is the uncreated Creator.

- John 1:1-3 – In the beginning was the Word, and the Word was with God, and the Word was God. He was with God in the beginning. All things were created through Him, and apart from Him not one thing was created that has been created.

- Col. 1:15-17 – He is the image of the invisible God, the firstborn over all creation; because by Him everything was created, in heaven and on earth, the visible and the invisible, whether thrones or dominions or rulers or authorities – all things have been created through Him and for Him.

What do you say about Jesus' origin?

- What other Scriptures address Jesus' origins?

- Do you agree Jesus is eternal and uncreated – the uncreated Creator of all?

- Why or why not? What's the strongest case you can make for or against the eternal nature of Jesus?

2. His deity

What Jesus says about Himself: He is co-equal and co-eternal with the Father and the Holy Spirit.

- Mark 14:61b-62 – Again the high priest questioned Him, "Are You the Messiah, the Son of the Blessed One?" "I am," said Jesus, "and all of you will see the Son of Man seated at the right hand of the Power and coming with the clouds of heaven."

- John 8:24 – "Therefore I told you that you will die in your sins. For if you do not believe that I am [He], you will die in your sins." (I AM is the name God gives Himself at the burning bush [Ex. 3:13-14]).

- John 10:30 – "The Father and I are one."

What the eyewitnesses say about Jesus: He is God, co-equal and co-eternal with the Father and the Holy Spirit; the fullness of deity in the flesh.

- John 1:1 – In the beginning was the Word, and the Word was with God, and the Word was God.

- John 5:18 – This is why the Jews began trying all the more to kill Him: not only was He breaking the Sabbath, but He was even calling God His own Father, making Himself equal with God.

- Col. 2:9 – For in Him the entire fullness of God's nature dwells bodily …

- Heb. 1:3 – He is the radiance of His glory, the exact expression of His nature, and He sustains all things by His powerful word. After making purification for sins, He sat down at the right hand of the Majesty on high.

What do you say about Jesus' deity?

- What other Scriptures address Jesus' deity?

- Do you agree Jesus is co-equal and co-eternal with the Father and the Holy Spirit; the fullness of deity in the flesh?

- Why or why not? What's the strongest case you can make for or against Jesus' deity?

3. His humanity

What Jesus says, does, or experiences: He is fully human, sharing the full range of mankind's experiences from thirst to temptation.

- Matt. 4:1-11 – Jesus is hungry and tempted by Satan.

- Luke 19:41; John 11:35 – Jesus weeps over Jerusalem and at the tomb of Lazarus, expressing human emotions.

- John 11:33, 38 – Jesus is "angry in His spirit."

- John 19:28, 30 – "I'm thirsty," he says, and then He dies.

What the eyewitnesses say about Jesus: He is virgin born, adding sinless humanity to His deity; His humanity enables Him to serve as our great high priest.

- Matt. 1:18-25 – The birth of Jesus Christ came about this way: After His mother Mary had been engaged to Joseph, it was discovered before they came together that she was pregnant by the Holy Spirit.... Now all this took place to fulfill what was spoken by the Lord through the prophet: See, the virgin will become pregnant and give birth to a son, and they will name Him Immanuel, which is translated "God is with us."

- John 1:14 – The Word became flesh and took up residence among us. We observed His glory, the glory as the One and Only Son from the Father, full of grace and truth.

- Phil. 2:5-8 – Make your own attitude that of Christ Jesus, who, existing in the form of God, did not consider equality with God as something to be used for His own advantage. Instead He emptied Himself by assuming the form of a slave, taking on the likeness of men. And when He had come as a man in His external form, He humbled Himself by becoming obedient to the point of death — even to death on a cross.

- Heb. 2:17-18 – Therefore He had to be like His brothers in every way, so that He could become a merciful and faithful high priest in service to God, to make propitiation for the sins of the people. For since He Himself was tested and has suffered, He is able to help those who are tested.

What do you say about Jesus' humanity?

- What other Scriptures address Jesus' humanity?

- Do you agree Jesus is fully human, sharing the full range of mankind's experiences; the virgin-born God-Man who serves today as our great High Priest?

- Why or why not? What's the strongest case you can make for or against Jesus' humanity?

4. His purpose

What Jesus says about Himself: He came to bring God's kingdom; to seek and save the lost; to pay mankind's sin debt; to defeat Satan and his works; and to offer us eternal life.

- Matt. 12:28 – "If I drive out demons by the Spirit of God, then the kingdom of God has come to you."

- Luke 19:10 – "For the Son of Man has come to seek and to save the lost."

- John 10:10-11 – "A thief comes only to steal and to kill and to destroy. I have come that they may have life and have it in abundance. I am the good shepherd. The good shepherd lays down his life for the sheep."

- John 12:32-33 – "As for Me, if I am lifted up from the earth I will draw all [people] to Myself." He said this to signify what kind of death He was about to die.

What the eyewitnesses say about Jesus: He came to die and rise from the dead in fulfillment of Scripture; to save sinners and reconcile them to God; to destroy the works of Satan.

- Rom. 5:6-11 – For while we were still helpless, at the appointed moment, Christ died for the ungodly. For rarely will someone die for a just person – though for a good person perhaps someone might even dare to die. But God proves His own love for us in that while we were still sinners Christ died for us! Much more then, since we have now been declared righteous by His blood, we will be saved through Him from wrath. For if, while we were enemies, we were reconciled to God through the death of His Son, [then how] much more, having been reconciled, will we be saved by His life! And not only that, but we also rejoice in God through our Lord Jesus Christ, through whom we have now received reconciliation.

- 1 Cor. 15:3-4 – For I passed on to you as most important what I also received: that Christ died for our sins according to the Scriptures, that He was buried, that He was raised on the third day according to the Scriptures ...

- 2 Cor. 5:21 – He made the One who did not know sin to be sin for us, so that we might become the righteousness of God in Him.

- 1 Tim. 1:15 – This saying is trustworthy and deserving of full acceptance: "Christ Jesus came into the world to save sinners" – and I am the worst of them.

- Heb. 2:9 – But we do see Jesus – made lower than the angels for a short time so that by God's grace He might taste death for everyone – crowned with glory and honor because of the suffering of death.

- 1 John 3:8b – The Son of God was revealed for this purpose: to destroy the Devil's works.

What do you say about Jesus' purpose?

- What other Scriptures address Jesus' purpose?

- Do you agree Jesus came to bring God's kingdom; to seek and save the lost; to die and rise from the dead in fulfillment of Scripture; to defeat Satan and his works; to save us and reconcile us to God?

- Why or why not? What's your strongest case for or against Christ's purpose in coming to earth?

5. His proof

What Jesus says about Himself: He fulfills Messianic prophecies, most notably by rising physically from the dead.

- Matt. 12:39-40; 26:31-32 – "An evil and adulterous generation demands a sign, but no sign will be given to it except the sign of the prophet Jonah. For as Jonah was in the belly of the great fish three days and three nights, so the Son of Man will be in the heart of the earth three days and three nights.... Tonight all of you will run away because of Me, for it is written: I will strike the shepherd, and the sheep of the flock will be scattered. But after I have been resurrected, I will go ahead of you to Galilee."

- Luke 18:31-33; 24:38-39 – "Listen! We are going up to Jerusalem. Everything that is written through the prophets about the Son of Man will be accomplished.... they will kill Him, and He will rise on the third day.... Why are you troubled ... And why do doubts arise in your hearts? Look at My hands and My feet, that it is I Myself! Touch Me and see, because a ghost does not have flesh and bones as you can see I have."

- John 2:18-22 – So the Jews replied to Him, "What sign [of authority] will You show us for doing these things?" Jesus answered, "Destroy this sanctuary, and I will raise it up in three days." Therefore the Jews said, "This sanctuary took 46 years to build, and will You raise it up in three days?" But He was speaking about the sanctuary of His body. So when He was raised from the dead, His disciples remembered that He had said this. And they believed the Scripture and the statement Jesus had made.

What the eyewitnesses say about Jesus: He fulfills Messianic prophecies, most notably by dying on the cross for mankind's sins and rising physically from the dead.

- Mark 15:25-28 – Now it was nine in the morning when they crucified Him. The inscription of the charge written against Him was THE KING OF THE JEWS. They crucified two criminals with Him, one on His right and one on His left.

[So the Scripture was fulfilled that says: And He was counted among outlaws.]

- John 19:33-37 – When they came to Jesus, they did not break His legs since they saw that He was already dead. But one of the soldiers pierced His side with a spear, and at once blood and water came out.... For these things happened so that the Scripture would be fulfilled: Not one of His bones will be broken. Also, another Scripture says: They will look at the One they pierced.

- Acts 2:22-27 – "Men of Israel, listen to these words: This Jesus the Nazarene was a man pointed out to you by God with miracles, wonders, and signs that God did among you through Him, just as you yourselves know. Though He was delivered up according to God's determined plan and foreknowledge, you used lawless people to nail Him to a cross and kill Him. God raised Him up, ending the pains of death, because it was not possible for Him to be held by it. For David says of Him: I saw the Lord ever before me; because He is at my right hand, I will not be shaken. Therefore my heart was glad, and my tongue rejoiced. Moreover my flesh will rest in hope, because You will not leave my soul in Hades, or allow Your Holy One to see decay."

- 1 Cor. 15:3-4 – For I passed on to you as most important what I also received: that Christ died for our sins according to the Scriptures, that He was buried, that He was raised on the third day according to the Scriptures.

What do you say about Jesus' proof?

- What other Scriptures show that Jesus fulfilled Messianic prophecies?

- Do you agree Jesus fulfills Messianic prophecies, most notably by dying on the cross and rising physically from the dead?

- Why or why not? What's your strongest case for or against His physical resurrection from the dead?

6. His uniqueness

What Jesus says about Himself: He is the Messiah/Christ; the Son of God; the Alpha and the Omega; the only means of salvation; and the One who will return to set things right.

- Matt. 25:31 – "When the Son of Man comes in His glory, and all the angels with Him, then He will sit on the throne of His glory."

- Matt. 26:63-64; 27:11 – Then the high priest said to Him, "By the living God I place You under oath: tell us if You are the Messiah, the Son of God!" "You have said it," Jesus told him. "But I tell you, in the future you will see the Son of Man seated at the right hand of the Power and coming on the clouds of heaven" … Now Jesus stood before the governor. "Are You the King of the Jews?" the governor asked Him. Jesus answered, "You have said it."

- John 14:1-3 – "Your heart must not be troubled. Believe in God; believe also in Me. In My Father's house are many dwelling places; if not, I would have told you. I am going away to prepare a place for you. If I go away and prepare a place for you, I will come back and receive you to Myself, so that where I am you may be also."

- John 14:6 – "I am the way, the truth, and the life. No one comes to the Father except through Me."

- Rev. 1:17-18 – "Don't be afraid! I am the First and the Last, and the Living One. I was dead, but look – I am alive forever and ever, and I hold the keys of death and Hades."

- Rev. 22:13 – "I am the Alpha and the Omega, the First and the Last, the Beginning and the End."

What the eyewitnesses say about Jesus: He is the unique Son of God; divine; the Creator; the only means of salvation; and the One who will return to set things right.

- John 1:1, 14, 18 – In the beginning was the Word, and the Word was with God, and the Word was God…. The Word became flesh and took up residence among us. We observed His glory, the glory as the One and Only Son from the Father, full of grace and truth.... No one has ever seen God. The One and Only Son – the One who is at the Father's side – He has revealed Him.

- Acts 4:11-12 – This [Jesus] is The stone despised by you builders, who has become the cornerstone. There is salvation in no one else, for there is no other name under heaven given to people by which we must be saved.

- Col. 1:16; 2:9 – [B]ecause by Him everything was created, in heaven and on earth, the visible and the invisible, whether thrones or dominions or rulers or authorities – all things have been created through Him and for Him.... For in Him the entire fullness of God's nature dwells bodily.

- 2 Thess. 2:8 – The Lord Jesus will destroy him [the lawless one] with the breath of His mouth and will bring him to nothing with the brightness of His coming.

- Heb. 1:3 – He is the radiance of His glory, the exact expression of His nature, and He sustains all things by His powerful word. After making purification for sins, He sat down at the right hand of the Majesty on high.

What do you say about Jesus' uniqueness?
- What other Scriptures support Jesus' claims to be one of a kind?

- Do you agree Jesus is the Messiah/Christ; the Son of God; the Alpha and the Omega; and the only means of salvation?

- Why or why not? What's your strongest case for or against Jesus as one of a kind?

7. His call to us

What Jesus says about Himself: He calls sinners to trust in Him for eternal life; He invites the weary to rest in Him; He beckons the spiritually thirsty to be satisfied in Him; He warns of the danger of rejecting Him.
- Matt. 11:28 – "Come to Me, all of you who are weary and burdened, and I will give you rest."

- John 3:16-18 – "For God loved the world in this way: He gave His One and Only Son, so that everyone who believes in Him will not perish but have eternal life. For God did not send His Son into the world that He might condemn the world, but that the world might be saved through Him. Anyone who believes in Him is not condemned, but anyone who does not believe is already condemned, because he has not believed in the name of the One and Only Son of God."

- John 5:24 – "I assure you: Anyone who hears My word and believes Him who sent Me has eternal life and will not come under judgment but has passed from death to life."

- John 7:37b-38 – "If anyone is thirsty, he should come to Me and drink! The one who believes in Me, as the Scripture has said, will have streams of living water flow from deep within him."

- John 8:24 – "Therefore I told you that you will die in your sins. For if you do not believe that I am [He], you will die in your sins."

What the eyewitnesses say about Jesus: He calls sinners to receive forgiveness of sins and everlasting life by believing in Him; He grants salvation by grace through faith; He calls us to salvation and to service.

- Acts 2:39 – For the promise is for you and for your children, and for all who are far off, as many as the Lord our God will call.

- Rom. 4:4-5 – Now to the one who works, pay is not considered as a gift, but as something owed. But to the one who does not work, but believes on Him who declares righteous the ungodly, his faith is credited for righteousness.

- Eph. 1:18 – [I pray] that the eyes of your heart may be enlightened so you may know what is the hope of His calling, what are the glorious riches of His inheritance among the saints ...

- Eph. 2:8-10 – For by grace you are saved through faith, and this is not from yourselves; it is God's gift – not from works, so that no one can boast. For we are His creation – created in Christ Jesus for good works, which God prepared ahead of time so that we should walk in them.

- Eph. 4:1 – I, therefore, the prisoner in the Lord, urge you to walk worthy of the calling you have received ...

- 1 Thess. 2:12 – [W]e encouraged, comforted, and implored each one of you to walk worthy of God, who calls you into His own kingdom and glory.

- 2 Tim. 1:9 – [God] has saved us and called us with a holy calling, not according to our works, but according to His own purpose and grace, which was given to us in Christ Jesus before time began.

- Titus 3:5 – He saved us – not by works of righteousness that we had done, but according to His mercy, through the washing of regeneration and renewal by the Holy Spirit.

What do you say about Jesus' call to you?

- What other Scriptures support Jesus' personal interest in you – and plan for you?

- Do you agree Jesus calls you to trust Him for forgiveness of sins and eternal life; to receive salvation and satisfaction in Him by grace alone through faith alone; and to serve Him with the resources and spiritual gifts He has entrusted to you? Why or why not?

- What's your strongest case for or against God's call to salvation and service?

THINK *Questions for personal or group study*

Do you think it's contradictory for the Bible to record that God created all things, and then to say that Jesus created all things, too? Why or why not?

What are some things Jesus says and does that support His claims of deity?

Isn't it possible that any number of men could fulfill the Messianic prophecies Jesus fulfilled? Why or why not?

Why does Jesus say that people who refuse to believe in Him will die in their sins?

No one disagrees that Jesus was a good man, or even a great prophet. Why isn't that good enough? Why do Christians insist on His virgin birth, sinless life, deity, death on the cross, and physical resurrection from the dead?

SHARE *Talking points for unlocking the real Jesus*

Jesus is the eternal, uncreated Creator of all things.

Jesus is the second person of the triune Godhead and is co-equal and co-eternal with the Father and the Holy Spirit.

Through the miracle of the virgin birth, Jesus added sinless humanity to His deity and became the unique God-Man, Savior of the world, and our great High Priest.

Jesus' sinless life, death on the cross, and physical resurrection from the dead conquered Satan, sin, and death for us. As a result, people may be forgiven of their sins, restored to a right relationship with God, and granted everlasting life by trusting in Jesus.

Jesus fulfilled all Old Testament prophecies of the Messiah except those relating to the physical establishment of His kingdom of earth – but He promised, "I will come again."

DIVE *Go deeper in your study with these resources*

The Case for Jesus the Messiah by John Ankerberg, John Weldon, and Walter Kaiser, Jr.

The Case for the Resurrection of Jesus by Gary R. Habermas and Michael R. Licona

Jesus Among Other Gods: The Absolute Claims of the Christian Message by Ravi Zacharias

The Life and Times of Jesus the Messiah by Alfred Edersheim

13
DID JESUS EVER CLAIM TO BE GOD?

Muslims, Jehovah's Witnesses, and atheists often argue, "Jesus never claimed to be God." They assert that Christians have corrupted or misinterpreted the New Testament, or they reject the Bible outright.

But for those willing to consider the eyewitness testimony of the New Testament writers, and the convincing evidence that their words are accurately preserved, we may point our unbelieving friends to seven ways that Jesus does, in fact, claim deity.

First, Jesus calls Himself God. In John 8:58 He tells the religious leaders, "I assure you: Before Abraham was, I am." These words hark back to Exodus 3 where God reveals Himself to Moses in the burning bush as I AM, or YHWH. The Jewish leaders clearly understand Jesus' declaration of deity.

Second, Jesus claims equality with God. In John 10:30 He states, "The Father and I are one." His frequent reference to God as Father – especially by the intimate Aramaic term *Abba*, or Father dearest – rankles the religious leaders. John writes, "This is why the Jews began trying all the more to kill Him ... He was even calling God His own Father, making Himself equal with God" (John 5:18).

In His high priestly prayer, Jesus anticipates once again sharing the glory He had with the Father before the world existed (John 17:5). This is a telling claim, for the Old Testament makes it clear that God does not share His glory with anyone (Isa. 42:8; 48:11).

Also note that more than four dozen times Jesus calls Himself the Son of Man – a term that illuminates the Messiah's deity (Dan. 7:13-14).

Third, Jesus receives worship. After Jesus' resurrection, Thomas examines Jesus' hands and side and declares, "My Lord and my God" (John 20:28). Jesus commits blasphemy if He receives Thomas' worship unless He really is God. Similarly, when Peter declares Jesus to be the Messiah, the Son of the living God, Jesus' reaction is not to correct Him but to affirm the truth of Peter's statement (Matt. 16:13-17).

Fourth, Jesus forgives sins. When He tells a paralytic man, "Son, your sins are forgiven," the scribes immediately think, "Why does He speak like this? He's blaspheming! Who can forgive sins but God alone?" Jesus exposes their private thoughts and demonstrates His authority to forgive sins by healing the paralyzed man (see Mark 2:1-12).

Fifth, Jesus teaches with divine authority. In John 8 the Pharisees say to Him, "You are testifying about Yourself. Your testimony is not valid." Jesus responds, "My judgment is true because I am not alone, but I and the Father who sent Me judge together. Even in your law it is written that the witness of two men is valid. I am the One who testifies about Myself, and the Father who sent Me testifies about Me" (see John 8:13-20).

Sixth, Jesus affirms the apostles' statements of His deity. He promises the apostles that the Holy Spirit will guide them into all truth and bring to their minds the things He says and does. In effect, He confirms what they write later. For example, John calls Jesus God and says He is the Creator who took on human flesh (John 1:1-3, 14). Paul tells us that in Jesus the fullness of deity dwells bodily (Col. 2:9); that He added to His deity sinless humanity (Phil. 2:5-11); and that He is the Creator (Col. 1:15-16). The writer of Hebrews records the deity of Jesus (Heb. 1:1-4).

Seventh, Jesus fulfills the attributes unique to God. In John 16:30 His disciples exclaim, "Now we know that you know everything" (omniscience). In Matt. 28:20 Jesus assures His followers He is with them always (omnipresence). And in Matt. 28:18 He claims all authority (omnipotence). In addition, He is eternal (John 1:1), immutable (Heb. 13:8), and the judge of all people (John 5:22). Even the Father calls Jesus God (Heb. 1:8).

Finally, the names used to portray God in the Old Testament – Alpha and Omega, Lord, Savior, King, Judge, Light, Rock, Redeemer, Shepherd, Creator – are applied to Jesus in the New Testament.

THINK *Questions for personal or group study*

Why do you think Muslims and Jehovah's Witnesses, who have a high regard for Jesus, are not willing to accept His deity?

If Jesus really is God, how could He get tired, hungry, and thirsty, and how could He die?

What Old Testament passages describe the deity of the Messiah?

How would you respond to the Jehovah's Witness claim that Jesus never said He was God?

Jesus could read people's thoughts and He predicted many future events, including His own death and resurrection. So, if He's really God, why doesn't He know certain things, like the day and hour of His return to earth?

IV. Jesus Christ

Jesus reveals His deity through His words and deeds.

Jesus calls Himself "I am," a clear tie to YHWH in the burning bush of Exodus, and the "Son of Man," a term that illuminates the Messiah's deity in the Book of Daniel.

Jesus did certain things only God can do, such as receive worship and forgive sins.

The New Testament writers affirm the deity of Jesus, calling Him the Creator, the Word who became flesh, and the exact image of God. Even the Father calls His Son "God."

Jesus fulfills attributes unique to God, such as omniscience, omnipotence, and omnipresence. He is eternal, immutable, and the judge of all people.

Jesus is the "God Man," eternally existing God who adds sinless humanity to His deity via the miracle of the virgin birth. Thus, Jesus in His incarnation is fully divine and fully human.

DIVE *Go deeper in your study with these resources*

Putting Jesus in His Place: The Case for the Deity of Christ by Robert M. Bowman Jr. and J. Ed Komoszewski

Christ the Eternal Son: A Beautiful Portrait of Deity from the Gospel of John by A.W. Tozer

The Man Christ Jesus: Theological Reflections on the Humanity of Christ by Bruce A. Ware

14
WHAT HAVE WE DONE WITH THE CHRISTMAS STORY?

Christians love to hear and tell the traditional Christmas story. The birth of Jesus includes Mary and Joseph seeking shelter on a winter night, no room in the inn, a baby born in a stable, and angels visiting lowly shepherds nearby.

But our modern telling of the account in Luke 2:1-20 embraces critical flaws, according to Kenneth E. Bailey, who spent 40 years teaching the New Testament in the Middle East and who authored *Jesus Through Middle Eastern Eyes: Cultural Studies in the Gospels.*

According to Bailey, a careful reading of the text, along with an understanding of Jewish culture, illuminate five biblical truths that challenge our Westernized version of the Christmas story:

1. Joseph is returning to the village of his origin. Simply entering Bethlehem and telling people, "I am Joseph, son of Heli, son of Matthat, the son of Levi" instantly would have opened most homes to him.

2. Joseph is a "royal." That is, he is from the family of King David. He would have been welcome anywhere in the city of David (Luke 2:4).

3. Villagers would have paid special attention to a pregnant woman. To turn away Mary would have brought unspeakable shame on Bethlehem.

4. Mary has relatives nearby. Elizabeth and her husband Zechariah live in the hill country of Judea. Even if Bethlehem rejected Mary and Joseph, Elizabeth – who knew Mary was bearing the Son of God – would have welcomed them.

5. Joseph has adequate time to make living arrangements. Luke 2:4 says that Joseph and Mary "went up from the town of Nazareth in Galilee, to Judea," and verse 6 states, "While they were there, the time came for her to give birth."

Bailey comments, "This late-night-arrival-imminent-birth myth is so deeply engrained in the popular Christian mind that it is important to inquire of its origin."[1]

The source of this embellishment is an expanded account of Jesus' birth by an anonymous novelist 200 years after the fact. Called *The Protevangelium of James*, it adds many fanciful details and exposes the author as a non-Jew who did not understand Judean geography or Jewish tradition.

Jerome, the Latin scholar, attacks the novel. Still, some of its heart-rending details stick and become imbedded in modern Christmas tales.

Two key questions

Still, two key questions arise: What is the "inn?" And where is the manger?

Bailey says the answers to both questions are found in the authentic account of Luke, who understands the geography and history of the Holy Land.

The "inn" in Luke 2:7 uses a Greek word that means "place to stay." It is the same word Jesus uses in Luke 22:10-12 to describe the guest room where He and the disciples celebrate the Passover.

A simple village home has but two rooms; one is exclusively for guests. That room could be attached to the end of the house or be a "prophet's chamber" on the roof. The main room is a family room where the entire family cooks, eats, and sleeps.

One end of the family room is either a few feet lower than the rest of the house or blocked off with heavy timbers. There, the family cow, donkey and a few sheep are brought in for the night. A "manger" is dug out of the lower end of the family room, and from it the animals help themselves to food.

Taken together, it becomes clear that when Joseph and Mary arrive in Bethlehem, a hospitable family welcomes them but cannot offer them the "inn" because other guests are staying there. As a result, Mary and Joseph likely share the family room with their hosts, and when Jesus is born, He is laid in clean, fresh straw in the manger.

So, what are we to do with our nativity scenes?

Luke's account does not minimize the discomfort Mary experiences, the efforts of Joseph to secure a place for his pregnant fiancée, or the awe-stricken response of the shepherds and wise men to the news of the Incarnation.

But we should be careful not to take liberties with the wondrous story Luke tells, knowing the Holy Spirit entrusts the story to a faithful human author who understands the culture and geography of Judea in the days that "the Word became flesh and took up residence among us" (John 1:14).

THINK *Questions for personal or group study*

Which parts of the traditional Christmas story are at odds with the account of Luke, who understands the geography and history of the Holy Land?

Why should we be as historically accurate as possible when telling Bible stories? Put another way, what's the harm in a little exaggeration for dramatic effect?

What are the five biblical truths that challenge a Westernized version of the Christmas story, according to Kenneth E. Bailey?

What do you believe are the essential elements of the story of Jesus' birth? Why are they important?

If Mary were not a virgin, as some liberal scholars argue, what difference would that make to the Christmas story?

Our modern telling of the Christmas story embraces critical flaws, such as the idea that Mary and Joseph are forced to spend the night in a stable.

The source of these embellishments is an expanded account of Jesus' birth, *The Protevangelium of James*, written by an anonymous novelist 200 years after the fact.

We should be careful not to take liberties with the Christmas story, but to stay true to the biblical account.

Among the facts are: Joseph is returning to his village of origin and is a "royal," being of the house of King David; he and Mary would be welcome in any home in Bethlehem.

The "inn" likely refers to a guest room in a house in Bethlehem; being occupied, it means Mary and Joseph probably share the family room with their hosts, placing the newborn Jesus in a fresh bed of straw in a part of the room normally reserved for animals.

DIVE *Go deeper in your study with these resources*

Jesus Through Middle Eastern Eyes: Cultural Studies in the Gospels by Kenneth E. Bailey

Misreading Scripture with Western Eyes: Removing Cultural Blinders to Better Understand the Bible by E. Randolph Richards and Brandon J. O'Brien

V.

FALSE RELIGIONS, CULTS, AND CHRISTIAN SECTS

Roman Catholicism

The Word of Faith Movement

Snake-handling Pentecostals

15
WHAT DO FALSE PROPHETS HAVE IN COMMON?

But I fear that, as the serpent deceived Eve by his cunning, your minds may be corrupted from a complete and pure devotion to Christ. For if a person comes and preaches another Jesus, whom we did not preach, or you receive a different spirit, which you had not received, or a different gospel, which you had not accepted, you put up with it splendidly!

- 2 Cor. 11:3-4

The words of the apostle Paul are clear: Those who are not grounded in the Word of God are subject to deceptive teachings about "another Jesus … a different spirit … a different gospel" – three distinctive markers that help us identify false prophets.

Whether they are Muslim prophets like Muhammad, or self-proclaimed messiahs like the Rev. Sun Myung Moon, these false prophets invariably promote an unbiblical view of Jesus, the Holy Spirit, and the gospel. In the chapters ahead (chapters 16-34) we use these three markers, along with comparative charts, to examine the teachings of Islam, Mormonism, and the Jehovah's Witnesses in light of what God's Word proclaims.

The Bible cautions us to beware of false messiahs, false prophets, and false teachers who "disguise themselves as servants of righteousness" and promote "doctrines of demons" (see Matt. 24:24; 2 Cor. 11:13-15; 1 Tim. 4:1; 2 Tim. 4:3-4).

Defining our terms

Before we go deeper, let's define some key terms.

False religion. From a New Testament perspective, a false religion is any system of belief that opposes the central teachings of the Christian faith. While all cults of Christianity (such as Mormonism and the Jehovah's Witnesses) are false religions, not all false religions are cults, because not all religions claim to be Christian. Islam, for example, is a false religion but not a cult, because Islam does not claim to be Christian.

Cult. A cult is a religious organization whose members claim to be Christians, and who use the Bible and Christian terms, yet who deny the central beliefs of historical Christianity. Simply put, a cult is a counterfeit form of Christianity.

Heresy. This may be defined as a teaching strongly opposed to the doctrines of historical Christianity, for example the denial of Christ's deity, virgin birth, or bodily resurrection.

Sect. A sect is an otherwise orthodox group having established its own identity and teachings distinct from the group to which it belongs. In Jesus' day, for example, the Pharisees, Sadducees, and Essenes were sects of Judaism.

False prophet. A false prophet is one who preaches, teaches, or foretells events contrary to the Word of God. Some false prophets claim to speak for the God of the Bible, such as Muhammad and Joseph Smith, yet their teachings conflict with Scripture. Others make no claims to speaking for Yahweh, yet they are false prophets in that what they teach clearly is unbiblical; L. Ron Hubbard, the founder of Scientology, is a modern-day example.

Three key questions

In his classic book, *The Kingdom of the Cults*, the late Walter Martin tells about a training program the American Banking Association offers. Each year the ABA sends hundreds of bank tellers to Washington to teach them to detect counterfeit money.

Martin writes: "It is most interesting that during the entire two-week training program, no teller touches counterfeit money. Only the original passes through his hands. The reason for this is that the American Banking Association is convinced that if a man is thoroughly familiar with the original, he will not be deceived by the counterfeit bill, no matter how much like the original it appears. It is the contention of this writer that if the average Christian would become familiar once again with the great foundations of his faith, he would be able to detect those counterfeit elements so apparent in the cult systems, which set them apart from Biblical Christianity."[1]

This is a great lesson. Even though it's good for us to know at least something about other belief systems, our focus should be on the Word of God. Then it won't matter what the counterfeit doctrines are; we will be able to identify them and lovingly steer their proponents toward the truth.

In light of the clear teaching of Scripture, every Christian can identify false belief systems by asking three important questions: 1) Who is Jesus? 2) Who is the Holy Spirit? 3) How am I saved? As we go to the text and comparative charts on the following pages and place the teachings of God's Word against the teachings of Islam, Mormonism, and the Jehovah's Witnesses, let's remind ourselves of some key biblical truths that address these crucial questions.

Key truths about the real Jesus

Jesus is:

- The eternal Son of God, without beginning or end
- God / deity
- Creator of all things
- Co-equal and co-eternal with the Father and the Holy Spirit
- Virgin born
- The God-Man / fully divine and fully human
- Sinless in His humanity
- Our substitute through His sacrificial death on the cross
- Alive, having been raised physically from the dead
- The only way of salvation
- Seated today in heaven as our Mediator and Intercessor
- Coming visibly and physically one day in power and great glory
- The one who will judge all people and to whom, one day, all creatures will bow

Key truths about the real Holy Spirit

The Holy Spirit is:

- The eternal Spirit, without beginning or end
- God / deity
- Creator of all things
- Co-equal and co-eternal with the Father and the Son
- Personal (not an impersonal force)
- The author of scripture
- The one who convicts the lost of their need for Christ
- The one who regenerates sinners, causing them to be made spiritually alive
- The one who indwells, seals, and sanctifies believers, and who places them into the Body of Christ
- The giver of spiritual gifts
- God's down payment/guarantee of our home in heaven

Key truths about the real gospel

We must understand that:

- All people are sinners
- Sin separates us from holy God, resulting in spiritual and physical death and, ultimately, hell
- People are incapable of saving themselves
- Christ died on the cross for our sins and, as our substitute, paid our sin debt in full
- Christ was buried and rose physically from the dead
- His finished work at Calvary conquered Satan, sin, and death for us
- As a result, salvation is by God's grace alone through faith alone – not by works
- Salvation is God's gift – an everlasting, unbreakable, covenant relationship with Him

THINK *Questions for personal or group study*

Read 2 Corinthians 11. What are some terms Paul uses to describe false prophets? Whose servants are they?

In 2 Corinthians 10-12, why is it so important for Paul to defend his apostleship?

Why do you think so many religious groups honor Jesus as a great spiritual leader yet fail to embrace all the Bible teaches about Him?

What practical difference does it make if the Holy Spirit is personal or impersonal?

When our Catholic friends (who are not cultists) tell us a person is saved by grace, but not by grace alone (meaning meritorious works are required to achieve "progressive" justification), how might we respond?

SHARE *Talking points for discussing false prophets*

According to the apostle Paul, false prophets promote an unbiblical view of Jesus, the Holy Spirit, and the gospel.

A false prophet is one who preaches, teaches, or foretells events contrary to the Word of God.

From a New Testament perspective, a false religion is any system of belief that opposes the central teachings of the Christian faith.

A cult is a religious organization whose members claim to be Christians, and who use the Bible and Christian terms, yet who deny the central beliefs of historical Christianity. Simply put, a cult is a counterfeit form of Christianity.

Every Christian can identify false belief systems by asking three important questions: 1) Who is Jesus? 2) Who is the Holy Spirit? 3) How am I saved?

DIVE *Go deeper in your study with these resources*

Scripture Twisting: 20 Ways the Cults Misread the Bible by James W. Sire

The Kingdom of the Cults by Walter Martin

God is Not One: The Eight Rival Religions That Run the World – and Why Their Differences Matter by Stephen Prothero (Note: While not written from an evangelical perspective, this book provides a good overview of major world religions.)

When Cultists Ask: A Popular Handbook on Cultic Misinterpretations by Norman L. Geisler and Ron Rhodes

They Can't All be Right: Do All Spiritual Paths Lead to God? by Steve Russo

ISLAM

16
ISLAM: AN OVERVIEW

Islam is the youngest major world religion, and one of the fastest growing. Arabian visionary Muhammad (570-632 A.D.), who was born in the city of Mecca in Arabia, founded Islam as a restoration of true monotheism. Muhammad claimed he received supernatural revelations from Allah through the angel Gabriel. These revelations were written down by others and compiled into a book called the Qur'an.

Islam today is comprised of two main schools: the majority Sunni school and the minority Shi'ite school. In addition, there are millions of Muslim mystics called Sufis. Islam is the second-largest religion in the world (behind Christianity) with about 1.6 billion followers. Interestingly, the four nations with the largest number of Muslims today are all outside the Middle East – Indonesia, Pakistan, Bangladesh, and India. If current trends continue, India will have the largest Muslim population of any country in the world, surpassing Indonesia by 2050.[1]

Purpose

The ultimate goal of Islam is to subjugate the world and then rule it according to Islamic law. Islam claims to be the restoration of true monotheism and thus supersedes both Judaism and Christianity. Islamic law teaches that conversion may be achieved through persuasion or subjugation, but some hold that if these fail, unbelievers (or "infidels") may be eliminated if necessary. As such, hostility toward non-Muslims is accepted and even encouraged in some Islamic cultures, based on passages from the Qur'an such as, "Fight those who believe not in Allah, nor in the Last Day, nor forbid that which Allah and His Messenger have forbidden, nor follow the Religion of Truth, out of those who have been given the Book, until they pay the tax in acknowledgement of superiority and they are in a state of subjection."[2]

Islam's beginnings

Islam began with supernatural visions and revelations that Muhammad claimed he received from Allah through the angel Gabriel. He committed these revelations to memory and ordered his followers to write them

V. False Religions, Cults, and Christian Sects

down. These writings became Islam's holy book, the Qur'an. Muhammad at first feared his revelations came from a *jinn*, or evil spirit, but later he accepted their source as divine and taught that he alone was the true recipient of Allah's truth.

Muhammad was born in the Arabian city of Mecca in 570 A.D. Mecca was an important economic center, serving as a resting place for trading caravans. But it also was an important religious city because the *Ka'bah* was located there. The *Ka'bah* is a cubic structure that in the days of Muhammad housed 360 deities. Each Arabian tribe selected its own deity and came to Mecca each year to pay homage to its god.

Muhammad's monotheistic preaching threatened the economic and religious livelihood of Mecca and set him against his own tribe. He and about 100 Muslim families were forced to flee to Medina, a city 200 miles north of Mecca. Muslims look to the year of Muhammad's flight, 622 A.D., as the beginning of the Muslim calendar. In 630 A.D., Muhammad and his army returned and took control of Mecca. He personally destroyed the idols in the *Ka'bah* and within a year succeeded in unifying the tribes of the Arabian Peninsula under Islam. Muhammad died in 632 A.D. without appointing a successor.

The sects of Islam

The two major sects of Islam, Sunni and Shi'ite, were established after Muhammad's death in a dispute over who should serve as his successor, or *caliph*. Sunni Muslims insisted that Muhammad's successor be elected, while Shi'ite Muslims felt he should be of Muhammad's bloodline, which would have meant that Ali, Muhammad's cousin and son-in-law, would have become *caliph*. The Sunnis prevailed and today account for more than 80 percent of the Muslim population. Sunnis and Shi'ites differ in other ways as well.

Authority. Sunnis emphasize the authority of the written traditions, which include the Qur'an and the Sunna ("custom"), from which they derive their name. They also receive guidance from a consensus of elders (*ulama*), who base their decisions on Islam's writings. Shi'ites look more to human authority. Initially, they believed Allah spoke through the *Imam*, roughly the equivalent of the Catholic pope. In the ninth century, however, the twelfth *Imam*, known as the *Mahdi*, became hidden; Shi'ites today await his return, much as Christians await the return of Christ.

Civil and religious power. Sunnis believe there should be a separation between civil and religious authorities, while Shi'ites believe the religious authorities should exercise both political and religious power. Iran's Ayatollah Khomeini, for example, was a Shi'ite leader.

Other sects of Islam include Sufism, which is mystical in nature; Wahhabism (primarily in Saudi Arabia); Druze (mostly in Lebanon, Syria and northern Israel); Alawi (mainly in Syria); and Ahmadiyya (primarily in Pakistan). Beyond this, Islam has been influential in the founding of two other religions: Sikhism and Baha'i.

Source of authority

Muslims believe Allah has revealed many written works, including the Old and New Testaments. But these revelations ended with the Qur'an ("recitations"), which supersedes all others. For all practical purposes, Muslims accept only the Qur'an as the Word of God. They believe Christians and Jews have corrupted Allah's earlier revelations in the Bible and therefore the Bible is not trustworthy, except as interpreted by the Qur'an. Sunni Muslims, as mentioned above, also place strong emphasis on the Sunna, which includes the Hadith, in which the sayings and conduct of Muhammad and his companions are recorded.

Basic beliefs

Muslims hold to six articles of faith:

Faith in Allah. The central doctrine of Islam is that God is one and that no one may be associated with his deity. To associate someone like Jesus with Allah by calling him God's Son is to commit the unpardonable sin of *shirk* (see Surah 4:48).

Belief in angels like Gabriel, whom they claim transmitted the Qur'an to Muhammad. Each person has two angels assigned to him or her – one to record the person's good deeds and the other to record the person's evil deeds. Muslims also believe in evil spirits called *jinn*, from which we get the word "genie."

Acceptance of the Qur'an. Four high-ranking prophets were given books by divine revelation. Moses was given the *Tawrat* (Torah); David, the *Zabur* (his Psalms); Jesus, the *Injil* (Gospel); and Muhammad, the Qur'an. Muslims teach that only the Qur'an has been preserved in perfection; Jews and Christians have corrupted the Bible.

Acceptance of Islam's prophets, with Muhammad as the greatest. The Qur'an says Allah has sent prophets to every nation, proclaiming the truth of the one true God. In all, 124,000 prophets have been sent. Most are unknown, but many include biblical characters such as Adam, Noah, Abraham, Moses, David, Solomon, Jonah, John the Baptist, and Jesus. Muhammad is the only prophet who is for all time; he is called the "Seal of the Prophets."

Belief in predestination – that is, everything that happens, good and evil, is predestined by Allah's will.

Preparation for the Day of Judgment, in which each person's good and evil works will be measured, resulting in heaven or hell. Only Allah knows – and has predetermined – who will go to heaven and who will go to hell. Hell is not an eternal place of torment, but a place where evil is purged from its inhabitants.

Religious duties

Every Muslim must practice at least five fundamental religious duties. These are known as the Pillars of Religion and they are:

The confession of faith or *Shahada*: "There is no god but Allah; Muhammad the Messenger of Allah." Sincerity in voicing the confession is essential. If a Muslim repudiates the *Shahada* it nullifies his or her hope of salvation.

Prayer (*Salat*). Muslims must recite 17 cycles of prayer each day. These cycles usually are spread over five times while the supplicant faces Mecca – dawn, noon, midafternoon, dusk, and two hours after sunset. The noon service on Friday is the only time Muslims are expected to gather together at the mosque. Muslims wash themselves ceremonially before praying; this is called ablution or *wudu*.

Observing *Ramadan*, a month of fasting throughout the daylight hours to commemorate the first revelation of the Qur'an to Muhammad. During the day, Muslims must refrain from food, drink, smoke, and sexual relations. After sundown, all of these pleasures may be enjoyed until sunrise the next day.

Almsgiving or *Zakat*. Muslims are required to give 2.5 percent of their currency, plus other forms of wealth, as determined by a complicated system that purifies their remaining wealth.

Pilgrimage, or *Hajj*, to Mecca, Muhammad's place of birth. Every Muslim who is physically and financially able must make this trek at least once is his or her lifetime. Pilgrims must wear white garments to eliminate all class distinctions. The process of visiting several sacred sites usually takes more than a week.

A sixth religious duty is sometimes associated with these: *Jihad*, or Muslim holy war. When the situation warrants it, this duty requires Muslims to go to war to defend Islam against "infidels." Anyone who dies in a holy war is guaranteed everlasting life in heaven and is considered a martyr for Islam.

Are Yahweh and Allah the same?

While many people assume that Muslims and Christians worship the same God, differing only in the name upon which they call, this simply is not true. The god of the Qur'an and the God of the Bible share some similarities, but the differences are profound. Following are some similarities and differences highlighted in *The Illustrated Guide to World Religions*:

Similarities

- Both are one.

- Both are transcendent creators of the universe.

- Both are sovereign.

- Both are omnipotent.

- Both have spoken to humanity through messengers or prophets, through angels, and through the written word.

- Both know in intimate detail the thoughts and deeds of men.

- Both will judge the wicked.

Differences

- Allah is a singular unity, while God is a compound unity who is one in essence and three in persons (Matt. 28:19; John 10:30; Acts 5:3-4).

- Allah is not a father and has begotten no sons (Surahs 19:88-92; 112:3), but God exists in an eternal relationship as Father, Son, and Holy Spirit (Matt. 28:19; Luke 3:21-22; John 5:18).

- Through the Qur'an, Allah broke into history through a word that is written, but the God of the Bible broke into history through the Word who is a person (John 1:1, 14; Col. 1:15-20; Heb. 1:2-3; 1 John 1:1-3; 4:9-10).

- Allah "loves not the prodigals" (Surahs 6:141; 7:31), but Jesus tells the story of a father, a metaphor for God the Father, who longs for the return of his prodigal son (Luke 15:11-24).

- "Allah loves not those that do wrong" (Surah 3:140), and neither does he love "him who is treacherous, sinful" (Surah 4:107), but the God of the Bible "proves his own love for us in that while we were still sinners Christ died for us" (Rom. 5:8).

- The standard of judgment for Allah is the Qur'anic teaching that our good deeds must outweigh our bad deeds (Surahs 7:8-9; 21:47), but the standard of the God of the Bible is complete perfection as measured by the holy character of God Himself (Matt. 5:48; Rom. 3:23).

- Allah provided a messenger, Muhammad, who warned of Allah's impending judgment (Surahs 2:119; 5:19; 7:184, 188; 15:89-90) and who declared that "No bearer of a burden can bear the burden of another" (Surahs 17:15; 35:18). But God provided a sinless Savior who took our sins upon Himself and bore God's wrath in our place (Matt. 20:28; 26:28; Luke 22:37; John 3:16; 10:9-11; 2 Cor. 5:21; Gal. 3:13; 1 Thess. 5:9-10).[3]

For more on this topic, see Chapter 18: Do Christians and Muslims Worship the Same God?

THINK *Questions for personal or group study*

Why do you think Islam is such a widely embraced and fast-growing religion?

What are the similarities and differences between the *Shahad*a, or Muslim confession of faith, and the Christian's public profession of faith in Jesus?

How would you respond to the person who says Christians and Muslims worship the same God, differing only by the name we call Him and a few other minor details?

When Muslims say the Qur'an supersedes all previous revelations of God, particularly the Old and New Testaments, what are they actually saying about the Bible?

How does the Muslim doctrine of predestination compare with the Christian doctrine of election? Is it fair to say the Muslim view of Allah's will is fatalistic?

SHARE *Talking points for discussing Islam*

Islam is the youngest major religion in the world, and one of the fastest growing.

Islam claims to be the restoration of true monotheism and thus supersedes both Judaism and Christianity.

Islam began with supernatural visions and revelations that Muhammad claimed he received from Allah through the angel Gabriel.

The ultimate goal of Islam is to subjugate the world and then rule it according to Islamic law. Islamic law teaches that conversion may be achieved through persuasion or subjugation, but some hold that if these fail, unbelievers (or "infidels") may be eliminated if necessary.

The two major sects of Islam, Sunni and Shi'ite, were established after Muhammad's death in a dispute over who should serve as his successor, or *caliph*.

While there are some similarities between Allah (the god of the Qur'an) and Yahweh (the God of the Bible), there are profound differences, leading us to conclude that Christians and Muslims do not worship the same God.

DIVE *Go deeper in your study with these resources*

Encountering the World of Islam, edited by Keith E. Swartley

The 10 Things You Need to Know about Islam by Ron Rhodes

The Islamic Invasion: Confronting the World's Fastest Growing Religion by Robert Morey

What Every Christian Should Know about Islam by Rob Phillips

17

COMPARING CHRISTIANITY AND ISLAM

The following table compares key Christian doctrines with those of Islam. The source of authority for Christians is the Bible. Muslim doctrines come from the Qur'an, the Hadith (sayings and teachings of Muhammad), and the Sira (the biography of Muhammad).

What the Bible says about God:	What Islam says about God:
There is one true and living God, who exists as three distinct, co-equal, co-eternal persons: Father, Son, and Holy Spirit. While the Bible is clear that there is one God (Deut. 6:4), the Scriptures also call the Father, Son, and Holy Spirit God (e.g., John 20:28; Acts 5:3-4), and in some places the three persons of the Godhead are depicted together (Matt. 3:16-17; 2 Cor. 13:13; Eph. 1:3-14; 1 Peter 1:2). God is personal, knowable, approachable, and loves all people.	The one true god is Allah. He is a distant god, unknowable and unapproachable. He does not love all people, only those who do well. He is the author of evil as well as good since he predestines all things. He is not triune but singular, and no partner is to be associated with him. To associate a person with Allah – such as by calling Jesus the Son of God – is to commit the unpardonable sin known as *shirk*.
What the Bible says about Jesus:	**What Islam says about Jesus:**
He is the virgin-born Son of God, conceived by the Holy Spirit (Isa. 7:14; Matt. 1:18-25; Luke 1:35). He is the eternal God, the Creator, co-equal and co-eternal with the Father and Holy Spirit (John 1:1-14; Col. 1:15-20; Phil. 2:5-11; Heb. 1:1-13). Jesus died for our sins (1 Cor. 15:3), rose physically from the dead (Matt. 12:38-40; Rom. 1:4; 1 Cor. 15:4-8; 1 Peter 1:18-21), and is coming back physically and visibly one day (Matt. 24:29-31; John 14:3; Titus 2:13; Rev. 19:11-16).	He was one of Allah's prophets or messengers, but inferior to Muhammad, who brought Allah's final revelations to man. The Qur'an denies that Jesus is the Son of God, and any Muslim who believes in the deity of Jesus has committed *shirk* – an unforgiveable sin that sends a person to hell. Muslims do believe Jesus is the Messiah, was born of a virgin, lived a sinless life, and is coming back one day – to establish Islam throughout the earth. They do not believe He died on the cross, but was rescued by Allah.

What the Bible says about the Bible:	What Islam says about the Bible:
The Bible is the inerrant, infallible, inspired Word of God, and is His sole written authority for all people (2 Tim. 3:16-17; 2 Peter 1:20-21).	The Bible is corrupted and untrustworthy. Islam claims the Qur'an is the eternally existing, literal Word of God, received supernaturally by Muhammad from the angel Gabriel. It supersedes the Bible, which also was given by Allah. The Qur'an does assert, however, that the teachings of the Qur'an are in harmony with those of the Bible: "We have revealed to thee the Book [the Qur'an] with the truth, verifying that which is before it [the Bible]" (5:48). Yet the Qur'an and the Bible clearly contradict in countless ways. For example, the Qur'an teaches a monolithic God; the Bible, a Trinitarian God. The Qur'an says Jesus was just a man; the Bible, that He is God incarnate. The Qur'an stresses salvation by works; the Bible, salvation by grace alone through faith alone in Christ.
What the Bible says about salvation:	**What Islam says about salvation:**
Christ's death at Calvary completely paid our sin debt so that salvation comes by grace alone through faith alone in Jesus (John 3:16; 5:24; Rom. 4:4-5; 1 Cor. 15:1-4; Eph. 2:8-9; Titus 3:5).	The Qur'an teaches, "Surely the (true) religion with Allah is Islam" (3:19). This means salvation is achieved only through submission to the teachings of Islam. Forgiveness is based on good works and Allah's choice of mercy. The Muslim's chances for heaven are good if he or she: 1) accepts Allah and his apostle Muhammad; 2) does good works; and 3) is predestined to Allah's favor. Islam teaches that Christ was neither crucified for our sins nor resurrected; therefore salvation cannot possibly be attained through faith in Jesus.

What the Bible says about sin:	What Islam says about sin:
Sin is the violation of God's perfect and holy standards. All people are sinners (Rom. 3:10, 23) and are under the curse of sin – spiritual and physical death (Gen. 2:17; 3:17-19; Rom. 6:23). Only faith in Christ and His work on our behalf frees us from sin and its consequences (John 3:16; 5:24; Eph. 2:8-9).	Sin is lack of obedience to Allah. Man is sinful by act only, not by nature. Original sin is viewed as a "lapse" by Adam. Man is not really "fallen" in his sin nature; he is merely weak and forgetful. The most serious sin is *shirk*; for example, considering God as triune. Sin is thought of in terms of rejecting right guidance. It can be forgiven through repentance. No atonement is necessary.
What the Bible says about heaven and hell:	What Islam says about heaven and hell:
Hell is a place of everlasting conscious existence, where the unbeliever is forever separated from God (Matt. 25:46; Rev. 14:9-11; 20:10, 15). As for heaven, all believers have God's promise of a home in heaven, will go there instantly upon physical death, and will return with Christ from heaven to earth one day (John 14:1-3; 2 Cor. 5:8; Rev. 19:11-16).	Muslims believe in heaven and hell. Allah predetermines the eternal destiny of each person, and the hope of salvation for the Muslim is based on works, although no Muslim has the assurance of heaven (unless he or she dies a martyr). Islam teaches its followers to prepare for the Day of Judgment, in which each person's good and evil works are measured, resulting in heaven or hell.

THINK *Questions for personal or group study*

What are the key differences between the God of the Bible and the god of Islam?

What beliefs about Jesus do Christians and Muslims hold in common? Where do our beliefs about Jesus differ?

In what ways do Christians and Muslims view salvation differently?

Why do you think the Christian and Muslim views of original sin are so important to their doctrines of salvation?

How are the Christian and Muslim views of final judgment different?

SHARE *Talking points for discussing Islam*

While there are some similarities between the god of Islam and the God of the Bible, there are profound differences, leading to the conclusion that Christians and Muslims do not worship the same God.

Muslims affirm the virgin birth, sinless life, and miracle-working power of Jesus but deny His deity, death on the cross, and resurrection.

Muslims teach that Jews and Christians have corrupted the Bible. They believe the Qur'an supersedes the Old and New Testaments. Christians may rightly ask our Muslim friends to produce evidence of the Bible's "corruption."

The Bible teaches that man's problem is sin, which separates him from God – a reality that led Jesus to the cross, where He paid our sin debt. In contrast, the Qur'an teaches that people are not fallen in their nature; they are merely weak and forgetful. Forgiveness may be sought through works, but no atonement is necessary.

Christians believe salvation is God's gift to sinful people. Muslims believe works (and Allah's predestination) determine the difference between heaven and hell.

DIVE *Go deeper in your study with these resources*

Secrets of the Koran: Revealing Insights into Islam's Holy Book by Don Richardson

What Every Christian Needs to Know about the Qur'an by James R. White

Breaking the Islam Code: Understanding the Soul Questions of Every Muslim by J.D. Greear

Inside Islam: Exposing and Reaching the World of Islam by Reza F. Safa (a former radical Shi'ite Muslim)

V. False Religions, Cults, and Christian Sects

18
DO CHRISTIANS AND MUSLIMS WORSHIP THE SAME GOD?

Several years ago, El Arabiya TV asked President George W. Bush whether he was anti-Islam. He responded, "I believe in an almighty God, and I believe that all the world, whether they be Muslim, Christian, or any other religion, prays to the same God." In the same interview he added, "I believe there is a universal God. I believe the God that the Muslim prays to is the same God that I pray to. After all, we all came from Abraham. I believe in that universality."[1]

While the president's comments may have soothed the minds of some viewers, they had just the opposite effect on me. The god of Islam (Allah) and the God of the Bible (Yahweh) clearly are different. We can see this by asking three personal questions:

1. Does God know me?

Allah. The Qur'an teaches that Allah is the transcendent creator. He knows who you are; in fact, he has fatalistically determined your thoughts, words, and deeds – and even your eternal destiny, which is why Muslims so often say, "If Allah wills it." So, Allah does indeed know you.

But Allah is neither knowable nor approachable. The Qur'an depicts him as a singular being with no "partners." To call Jesus the Son of God is to commit *shirk*, the unpardonable sin. Of the 99 names for God in the Qur'an, none is intimate. Allah reveals his will, not himself.

Yahweh also is depicted as the transcendent Creator. He knows us; but more than that, He is knowable and approachable. He created us in His image – with personality, thought, and will – for the purpose of enjoying an everlasting, intimate relationship with Him. He exists as a Trinity in eternal relationship as Father, Son, and Holy Spirit.

In fact, God is so knowable, He came in the flesh as Jesus of Nazareth. As the apostle John writes, "The Word became flesh and took up residence among us. We observed His glory, the glory as the One and Only Son from the Father, full of grace and truth" (John 1:14). The Message, a biblical paraphrase, puts it this way: "The Word became flesh and blood, and moved into the neighborhood ..."

Does God know me? Allah and Yahweh are depicted as supreme beings that know everything and everyone. But … only the God of the Bible is truly personal and knowable.

2. Does God love me?

Allah. The Qur'an teaches that Allah loves those he chooses to love and hates those he chooses to hate. "Allah loves not the wrongdoers," says the Qur'an (3:140), neither does he love "him who is treacherous, sinful" (4:107). "Those who disbelieve and act unjustly – Allah will not forgive them, nor guide them to a path, Except the path to hell, to abide in it for a long time. And that is easy to Allah" (4:168-169). Other types of people Allah hates include the proud and boastful (4:36; 16:23; 31:18; 57:23); those given to excess (5:87); and the ungrateful (22:38).

Yahweh, on the other hand, loves all people (John 3:16). He demonstrated His love for us in that while we were still sinners, Christ died for us (Rom. 5:8). John writes, "Herein is love, not that we loved God, but that He loved us and sent His Son to be the propitiation for our sin" (1 John 4:10 KJV). Even though God hates sin, He loves sinners and takes no pleasure in punishing them (Eze. 18:23).

Does God love me? Only the God of the Bible loves all people unconditionally.

3. Did God die for me?

Allah. The Qur'an teaches that Allah did not and would not die for you, nor would he send anyone to die for you. In fact, Islam claims that Jesus did not die on the cross but was taken up into heaven, and Judas, or someone who looked like Judas, was crucified in His place.

Further, the Qur'an states that there is no need for Allah to provide a sacrifice for sin because ignorance of Islam, not sin, is man's problem. The possible exceptions are apostasy from Islam and refusal to convert to Islam. Staying away from major sins (whatever those are) will automatically result in one's "small" sins being overlooked by Allah (4:31).

Yahweh, on the other hand, loves us so much He sent His Son to die for us. This was determined in eternity past; Jesus is declared to be the Lamb of God slain from the foundation of the world (Rev. 13:8). Jesus, who knew no sin, became sin for us (2 Cor. 5:21). Christ not only died for us; He rose from the dead, conquering sin and death. And He offers us forgiveness of sins and eternal life by grace through faith in Him.

Did God die for me? Only the God of the Bible sent His Son to die for us, securing eternal life for those who trust in Him.

So, are Allah and Yahweh just two different names for the same God? You decide:

- Allah is distant and unknowable. The God of the Bible is close and personal.

- Allah does not love every person. Yahweh does.

- Allah did not and would not die for you, nor would he send anyone to do so; rather, he sends you to die for him. But the God of the Bible loves you so much He sent His one and only Son to die for you. And He stands ready to grant you everlasting life if you will receive Him by faith.

THINK *Questions for personal or group study*

Why is it important that Yahweh (the God of the Bible) is both personal and knowable?

Why do you think Muslims are so opposed to the deity of Jesus that they claim calling Jesus the Son of God is the unpardonable sin?

If God's love for us is conditional, as Muslims claim, do you think it's ever possible to know for certain that God loves you?

If Jesus is divine and died on the cross, as the Bible teaches, then didn't God die? How can that be? If God is dead, how can God bring Himself back to life?

Is there really that much difference between Allah and Yahweh? How important are the differences?

V. False Religions, Cults, and Christian Sects

SHARE *Talking points for discussing Allah and Yahweh*

We can see that Allah and Yahweh are different deities by asking three personal questions: (1) Does God know me? (2) Does God love me? (3) Did God die for me?

Of the 99 names for God in the Qur'an, none is intimate. Allah reveals his will, not himself.

The God of the Bible is personal and knowable – in stark contrast to Allah, who is neither.

Allah's love for people is conditional, while the God of the Bible loves all people unconditionally.

Allah sends people to kill for him; Yahweh sent His Son to die for us.

DIVE *Go deeper in your study with these resources*

Who Is This Allah? by G.J.O. Moshay

Seeking Allah, Finding Jesus: A Devout Muslim Encounters Christianity by Nabeel Qureshi

A God Who Hates by Wafa Sultan

Unveiling Islam by Ergun Mehmet Caner and Emir Fethi Caner

19
THE REAL TRAGEDY OF JIHAD

The 2012 terrorist attack on the U.S. embassy in Libya, resulting in the deaths of four Americans, brought the Muslim doctrine of *jihad* back into our living rooms as we watched in horror the murderous rage of people acting in the name of Allah.

The rise of the Islamic State in 2014, and the televised beheadings of Western journalists, Middle Eastern and African Christians, and Kurdish-speaking Yazidis, amplified the message that "holy war" is meant to establish Islam as the dominant faith on the planet by whatever means necessary.

But what, exactly, is *jihad*?

The Arabic term means to endeavor, strive, struggle, or fight. It is sometimes translated "holy war."

Generally speaking, there are two ways Muslims embrace *jihad*.

First, the "greater *jihad*" is the internal struggle against evil inclinations. It might be compared to the Christian's battle against the flesh. Surah 9:20 reads, "Those who believed and fled (their homes), and strove hard in Allah's way … are much higher in rank with Allah."

Second, the "lesser *jihad*" is warfare in the cause of Allah. Surah 9:29 says, "Fight those who believe not in Allah, nor in the Last Day, nor forbid that which Allah and His Messenger have forbidden, nor follow the Religion of Truth, out of those who have been given the Book, until they pay the tax [*jizyah*, a non-believer's tax] in acknowledgment of superiority and they are in a state of subjection."

Circumstances seem to have dictated whether Muhammad employed "greater" or "lesser" *jihad*, according to Bill Warner, director of the Center for the Study of Political Islam: "In Mecca, Mohammed demonstrated the initial practice of *jihad* when Islam was weak: persuasion and conversion. When he moved to Medina, he demonstrated how *jihad* worked when Islam was strong: using immigration against inhabitants, creating political power by struggling against the host, dominating other religions, using violence, and establishing a government."[1]

V. False Religions, Cults, and Christian Sects

The purpose of *jihad*

Muslims contend that the main purpose of *jihad* is to protect and preserve the *haqq* (truth), according to scholar N.S.R.K. Ravi of the North American Mission Board's Evangelism Response Center. Some believe the way to deal with those who pose obstacles to the spread of Islam is to declare *jihad* against them. This can take on peaceful forms: *jihad* with the tongue (speaking the truth), *jihad* with the heart (feelings and intentions), and *jihad* with the hand (good works).

However, the Qur'an also encourages *jihad* with the sword to defend Islam from attack, or to forcefully establish Islam in foreign lands where Islam is not granted free expression. In this sense, *jihad* may be waged against oppressors, disbelievers, idolaters, and even Christians and Jews.

"Those who participate in *jihad* are told they will receive rewards from Allah, ranging from the spoils of war if they survive, to entrance into paradise if they're killed in battle," says Ravi.[2]

There is little doubt that the 9/11 terrorists, the Islamist Army major who gunned down U.S. soldiers at Ft. Hood in 2009, and the men who stormed the U.S. embassy in Benghazi in 2012 believed they were serving Allah, advancing Islam, and securing their place in paradise.

But a finer point needs to be made here. Whether a Muslim engages in "greater *jihad*" or "lesser *jihad*," ultimately he is striving for Allah's acceptance, for salvation in Islam is achieved through external acts, specifically the five pillars of Islam (with *jihad* a possible sixth pillar).

Missing the point

At its core, Islam misses the point because Muhammad's followers teach a flawed view of man's problem, which is sin. They insist that ignorance of Islam, not sin, is man's problem. We do not need a Messiah to die for us, they argue. In fact, Allah would never permit a great prophet like Jesus to die a shameful death on a Roman cross; therefore, they teach, Allah swept Jesus alive off the cross and into heaven.

Embrace the five pillars, Islam teaches, and hope that Allah, who predestines good and evil, is kindly predisposed toward you. The Bible, however, takes a much different view. Sin *is* our problem. We are by nature creatures who desire to live independently of God. Our sin creates a chasm between us and our Creator that no amount of "struggling" could ever bridge.

That's why Jesus came. He left the glory of heaven, was born of a virgin, lived a sinless life and offered it up on the cross, where the Father "made the One who did not know sin to be sin for us, so that we might become the righteousness of God in Him" (2 Cor. 5:21).

Through His finished work, Jesus conquered sin and death for us. He has taken up our struggle and paid our sin debt in full. The fight is over. By faith we are accepted by God, brought into His kingdom, and made His adopted children.

Unlike our Muslim friends, we do not strive to be accepted by a distant deity. Rather, we enjoy intimate fellowship with a personal God who loves us, makes peace with us, and assures us of a place in His kingdom.

Scholars will continue to debate the legitimacy and extent of *jihad*. Meanwhile, we can help our Muslim friends understand that one of the most brutal acts in history, the crucifixion of Jesus, accomplished what *jihad* will never attain – peace with God, eternal life, and an intimate, everlasting relationship with the sovereign Creator of the universe.

THINK *Questions for personal or group study*

The authoritative Islamic writings – the Qur'an, Hadith, and Sira – speak mostly of violent forms of *jihad*. So why do you think Muslims refer to peaceful expressions of holy war as the "greater *jihad?*"

How does the Muslim view of *jihad* as a primary means of protecting the *haqq* (truth) compare with Jesus' instructions for spreading the gospel?

What are some different ways Muslims engage in *jihad?*

What does it say about Allah that he only guarantees paradise to martyrs who die in *jihad?*

What did the crucifixion of Jesus accomplish that *jihad* will never attain?

SHARE *Talking points for discussing jihad*

The Arabic word *jihad* means to endeavor, strive, struggle, or fight. It is sometimes translated "holy war."

Generally speaking, there are two ways Muslims embrace *jihad*: the "greater *jihad*," or internal struggle against evil inclinations; and the "lesser *jihad*," or warfare in the cause of Allah.

Muslims contend that the main purpose of *jihad* is to protect and preserve the *haqq* (truth).

Whether a Muslim engages in "greater *jihad*" or "lesser *jihad*," ultimately he is striving for God's acceptance, for salvation in Islam is achieved through external acts, specifically the five pillars of Islam (with *jihad* a possible sixth pillar).

We can help our Muslim friends understand that one of the most brutal acts in history, the crucifixion of Jesus, accomplished what *jihad* will never attain – peace with God, eternal life, and an intimate, everlasting relationship with the sovereign Creator of the universe.

DIVE *Go deeper in your study with these resources*

The Cross in the Shadow of the Crescent: An Informed Response to Islam's War with Christianity by Erwin W. Lutzer with Steve Miller

Islam and Terrorism: What the Qur'an Really Teaches about Christianity, Violence and the Goals of the Islamic Jihad by Mark A. Gabriel

Spring Fever: The Illusion of Islamic Democracy by Andrew C. McCarthy

V. False Religions, Cults, and Christian Sects

20

THE ULTIMATE ROLE MODEL: JESUS OR MUHAMMAD?

Muslims have a high regard for Jesus. They believe He was born of a virgin, lived a sinless life, performed miracles, and spoke prophetic truth. He is in heaven today and is poised to return triumphantly to earth.

Yet it is Muhammad to whom Muslims pin their hopes. While they confess Jesus as a prophet, they say Muhammad is the greatest of Allah's messengers and the one through whom Allah chose to reveal supreme truth in the Qur'an. Indeed, the Qur'an refers to Muhammad as the *al-Insan al-Kamil* – the "perfect model" or "excellent exemplar" (33:21). Therefore, Muhammad, not Jesus, is the ultimate role model.

Okay. So let's look at the record. We'll focus on three areas.

1. Lifestyle. Jesus lived the most exemplary life in human history. He was tempted in every way we are tempted, yet without sin (Heb. 4:15). He successfully rebuffed intense temptation in the desert as Satan sought to entice the physically weakened Messiah to swap His earthly mission for personal comfort and human adoration.

Denying Himself, He never turned away the poor, sick, outcast, or spiritually barren, noting, "For even the Son of Man did not come to be served, but to serve, and to give His life – a ransom for many" (Mark 10:45).

Muhammad, in sharp contrast, did not profess to be sinless. Even so, the Qur'an establishes him as the highest model of virtue for the faithful in all circumstances (33:21). Indeed, he often was kind, generous, and brave, yet his life was deeply flawed.

Despite the Qur'an's prohibition against marrying more than four wives, Muhammad had at least nine wives at one time – justified by a special revelation giving him, and him alone, the right to exceed the legal limit (33:50).

One of his wives was only nine years old when the marriage was consummated. Another was taken from an adopted son, who divorced his wife so Muhammad could have her. Further, the prophet allowed his followers to possess an unlimited number of concubines, and to practice a form of prostitution called *muta*.

More could be written about the prophet's brutal treatment of critics and apostates, but this should suffice to help you decide whether Jesus or Muhammad lived a more consummate lifestyle.

2. Source of authority. Jesus is co-equal and co-eternal with the Father and the Holy Spirit; thus, He is the divine second person of the triune Godhead. The Father sent Jesus to be the Savior of the world (1 John 4:14) and entrusted all judgment to Him (John 5:22). Before ascending into heaven, Jesus told His disciples that all authority in heaven and on earth had been given to Him (Matt. 28:18).

Jesus demonstrated His authority through teaching, miracles, forgiveness of sins, and resurrection from the dead. He claimed equality with the Father and never refused to be worshiped.

According to the Qur'an, Muhammad's only miracle was the Qur'an itself (29:48-51). Yet when he first began receiving revelations in a cave on Mount Hira, Muhammad thought he had been possessed by a poetry demon. He later became suicidal and tried to throw himself off a cliff.

His first wife Khadijah and her cousin convinced him he was not possessed; rather, he was a prophet of God. At one point late in life, Muhammad claimed he was the victim of a magic spell, which witnesses said made him delusional.

When Muhammad recited the 53rd chapter of the Qur'an to his followers, it featured verses allowing Muslims to pray to three pagan goddesses: al-Lat, al-Uzza, and Manat (53:19-20). He later ordered the scribes to strike these so-called "Satanic Verses," which he said came from Satan and not from God.

These examples should cast considerable doubt on Muhammad's claim to speak authoritatively for God.

3. Historical record. Christian beliefs about Jesus are based entirely on sources written within the lifetimes of eyewitnesses. As David Wood, host of the talk show "Jesus or Muhammad," notes, "Having multiple, independent, early sources allows us to form a reliable picture of the historical Jesus."[1]

Further, we have thousands of manuscript copies of the Gospels and other New Testament books – some of them dating back to the early second century. These documents, plus thousands of New Testament quotes from the early church fathers, confirm the veracity of the texts. In addition, several ancient non-Christian writings refer to Jesus.

In contrast, the Qur'an tells us very little about Muhammad. Our earliest detailed biographical source, Ibn Ishaq's *Life of Muhammad*, was written more than a century after Muhammad's death. Modern Muslims cast doubt on this book, however, and turn to works written more than two centuries after Muhammad's life – plenty of time to embellish or fabricate stories.

But perhaps the most telling historical contrast comes in the record of each leader's dying words. On the cross, bloodied and beaten beyond recognition, Jesus asks the Father to forgive His tormentors. Six centuries later, as Muhammad lay dying from the effects of poison given to him by a Jewish woman whose family his followers had slaughtered, the prophet of Islam gasps, "May Allah curse the Jews and Christians, for they built the places of worship at the graves of their Prophets."[2]

Which is the ultimate role model: Jesus or Muhammad? You make the call.

THINK *Questions for personal or group study*

Given the clear contrast between the sinless life of Jesus and the flawed life of Muhammad, why do you think Muslims honor the "Messenger of Allah" above Jesus?

What events in the life of Muhammad cast doubt on his authority to speak for God?

How do Christians become more like Jesus? How do Muslims become more like Muhammad?

Why is it so important that the Gospels were written within the lifetimes of the eyewitnesses?

What do the dying words of Jesus and Muhammad reveal about their characters?

SHARE *Talking points for discussing Jesus and Muhammad*

Muslims have a high regard for Jesus, but they look to Muhammad as their ultimate role model.

Jesus lived the most exemplary life in human history, being sinless. While Muhammad often was kind, generous, and brave, he was deeply flawed; the Qur'an acknowledges him as a sinner.

Muhammad had at least nine wives at one time. He consummated one marriage when his bride was only nine years of age, and he took another bride from an adopted son, who divorced his wife so Muhammad could have her.

Jesus demonstrated His authority through teaching, miracles, forgiveness of sins, and resurrection from the dead. He claimed equality with the Father and never refused to be worshiped. As for Muhammad, incidents such as the "Satanic Verses" debacle cast doubt on his authority to speak for God.

Christian beliefs about Jesus are based entirely on sources written within the lifetimes of eyewitnesses. In contrast, the earliest biography of Muhammad was written more than a century after his death, leaving a gap for embellishment.

DIVE *Go deeper in your study with these resources*

Christ, Muhammad and I by Mohammad Al Ghazoli

The Truth about Muhammad: Founder of the World's Most Intolerant Religion by Robert Spencer

Did Muhammad Exist? An Inquiry into Islam's Obscure Origins by Robert Spencer

Paul Meets Muhammad: A Christian – Muslim Debate on the Resurrection by Michael R. Licona

21
SEVEN WORDS THAT REVEAL ISLAM'S WORLDVIEW

Sharing our faith with Muslims requires Christians to know at least something about the religion Muhammad established 14 centuries ago.

Particularly enlightening are seven words that reveal Islam's view of the non-Muslim world and help us understand why Muhammad and his followers have consistently treated Christians with disdain.

Kafir

A *kafir* is "one who covers or conceals the known truth; an unbeliever." In other words, a *kafir* is any non-Muslim.

Since *kafirs* reside outside the "world of Islam" and thus are in the "world of war," they may be deceived, lied to, plotted against, enslaved, subjugated, mocked, tortured, driven from their homes, or killed.

Nearly two-thirds of the Qur'an is devoted to the *kafir*, according to Bill Warner, founder of the Center for the Study of Political Islam. Thirteen verses in the Qur'an instruct Muslims not to befriend *kafirs*. Further, 81 percent of the Sira (the life of Muhammad) deals with the prophet's struggle with *kafirs*. And the Hadith (traditions) devotes one-third of the text to *kafirs*. Overall, the trilogy devotes 60 percent of its content to the *kafir*.[1]

It's clear that Muhammad directed a great deal of animosity toward those who rejected his teachings.

Dhimmi

A *dhimmi* is a second-class citizen in a Muslim-dominated society. By signing a *dhimma* treaty, Jews and Christians (because they are "People of the Book") are offered protection from physical harm or religious targeting. Other *kafirs* must choose between conversion and death. But even for *dhimmis* there's a catch.

Christians under the treaty, for example, may not renovate churches or monasteries, display crosses in public, or conduct religious ceremonies outside the church.

In addition, they must pay the Islamic tax (*jizyah*) equal to 50 percent of their income, shaving their heads and kneeling before Muslim authorities as they render the tax, according to Warner.[2]

Jews and Christians who want to avoid becoming *dhimmis* may either convert to Islam or "face the sword."

Taqiyya

This doctrine of deception empowers Muslims to deny their faith or commit otherwise illegal or blasphemous acts while they are at risk of persecution. It was developed to protect Shi'ite Muslims, who usually were in the minority and under pressure from rival Sunnis.

For all practical purposes, however, the doctrine has been expanded to encourage any deceit that advances Islam.

Qur'anic scholar Al-Tabari explains, "If you [Muslims] are under their [infidels'] authority, fearing for yourselves, behave loyally to them, with your tongue, while harboring animosity for them.... Allah has forbidden believers from being friendly or on intimate terms with the infidels in place of believers – except when infidels are above them [in authority]."[3]

Dawa

Also known as "stealth jihad," *dawa* is the spread of sharia law by subtle, non-violent means, including resistance to assimilation; intimidation of critics; exploitation of democratic legal systems; and the portrayal of any scrutiny of Islamic doctrine as "Islamophobia."

Abrogation

This doctrine states that when two passages in the Qur'an contradict, the more recent passage "abrogates," or overrides, the earlier one.

The Qur'an was written in two places at two different times. The Meccan passages are earlier, mostly religious, poetic, and peaceful. The Medinan passages are later, more historical and political, and quite violent.

For example, one earlier passage reads that Muslims should tolerate and forgive People of the Book (Jews and Christians – 2:219). But a later passage (9:29) commands Muslims to attack People of the Book until they pay the *jizyah*, submit to sharia law, and are humbled.

Which one is true? Using dualistic logic, Muslims argue that both are true – but the later passage takes precedence over the earlier one. Thus, hatred and violence are more obedient ways to treat Christians than peaceful coexistence.

Shirk

This is the unpardonable sin of practicing idolatry or polytheism. For example, the Christian belief that Jesus is the Son of God is blasphemous to Muslims, resulting in hell.

Muslims have a high regard for Jesus, believing Him to be one of Islam's greatest prophets, and also to be virgin-born, sinless, and a miracle worker.

But they deny that Jesus died on the cross or rose from the dead, and they flatly reject His deity.

Jihad

The Arabic word means to strive or struggle. Muslims explain that there are two kinds of *jihad* – the "greater *jihad*," an internal struggle to resist temptation and obey Allah; and the "lesser *jihad*," or taking up the sword.

Interestingly, there is very little in Islam's authoritative writings about the "greater *jihad*." The life and teachings of Muhammad are almost exclusively devoted to actual fighting in order to defend Islam or to propagate the religion.

In that respect, *jihad* is Islam's Great Commission, and it has resulted in the deaths of 270 million non-Muslims over the last 14 centuries.

THINK *Questions for personal or group study*

Why do you think Muhammad expressed such animosity toward those who rejected his message? How does that contrast with Jesus' reaction to those who rejected Him as Messiah?

Only Jews and Christians are given the option of becoming *dhimmis* if they refuse to convert to Islam. What are the two options for all other *kafirs*?

How should Christians treat Muslims, understanding that their kind words and gestures of friendship toward us may in fact be intended to deceive?

What are some ways Muslims wage *dawa*, or "stealth *jihad*," in the political, economic, educational, and cultural arenas of the West?

Why do you think there is so little in Islam's authoritative writings about peaceful "greater *jihad*," and so much about violent "lesser *jihad*?"

SHARE *Talking points for discussing key terms in Islam*

Kafirs, or non-Muslims, may be deceived, lied to, plotted against, enslaved, subjugated, mocked, tortured, driven from their homes, or killed.

Jews and Christians who want to avoid becoming *dhimmis*, or second-class citizens in Muslim-dominated societies, may either convert to Islam or "face the sword."

Taqiyya is a doctrine encouraging any deceit that advances Islam.

The doctrine of abrogation states that when two passages in the Qur'an contradict, the more recent passage "abrogates," or overrides, the earlier one.

Christians are accused of committing the unpardonable sin, known as *shirk*, for proclaiming that Jesus is the Son of God.

DIVE *Go deeper in your study with these resources*

Questioning Islam: Tough Questions & Honest Answers About the Muslim Religion by Peter Townsend

Anatomy of the Qur'an by G.J.O. Moshay

The Islamic Doctrine of Christians and Jews by Bill Warner

Understanding Dhimmitude by Bat Ye'or

22
CHRISTIANITY COMES TO QATAR

Saudi Arabia, by fiat, has snuffed out religious liberty. All churches are banned there, as are all public displays of non-Muslim faiths.

The hardline Wahhabi version of Islam has been the official religion of the Saudi state since 1932. All Saudis are required to be Muslim. The law of the land is sharia. The Qur'an is the constitution. In fact, life is so tough for "infidels" there that the state outlaws freedom of thought because "[f]reedom of thinking requires permitting the denial of faith," according to the Center for Religious Freedom.[1]

The Saudi stance is severe but common in Muslim majority countries, where Christians in particular are persecuted. In fact, Christians are the most ill treated religious group in the world today, according to studies by the Vatican, Pew Research Center, the *Economist,* and others. Christians are the victims of three-quarters of the world's recorded acts of religious intolerance.[2]

But why? *Persecuted: The Global Assault on Christians,* offers three reasons. "First is the hunger for total political control, exhibited by the communist and post-communist regimes," according to authors Paul Marshall, Lela Gilbert, and Nina Shea. "The second is the desire by some to preserve Hindu or Buddhist privilege, as is evident in South Asia. The third is radical Islam's urge for religious dominance, which at present is generating an expanding global crisis."[3]

The stories are chilling, and the case against Islamist states is deeply disturbing. Still, there's hope. A case in point: Saudi Arabia's tiny neighbor, Qatar.

A diplomat's coup

Qatar (pronounced "Cutter") shares the Saudis' Wahhabi brand of Islam and banned Christianity for 1400 years. That changed in 1988, when the government for the first time allowed a public Christian service. Thanks for this monumental shift in policy goes to a U.S. diplomat.

Joseph Ghougassian was born in Egypt. Fluent in Arabic and well versed in Islam, he reached out to the head of Qatar's Sharia Court. Over a period of months, the U.S. envoy to Qatar engaged him on the points of religion and history.

"His extraordinary experience deserves examination," according to the authors of *Persecuted*. Ghougassian "challenged the principal rationale Saudi Arabia offers today for why it bans churches – that all the country is sacred ground that 'infidels' like Christians and Jews must not defile with their prayers. The ambassador pointed out this applied only to Mecca and Medina, which are only a small part of the country, a country whose national borders did not exist at the time of Islam's prophet Muhammad."[4]

Equally compelling, Ghougassian said to the Sheikh of Qatar's Sharia Court: "Well, Allah forbid, if you were to die tomorrow, and you appeared in front of Allah, do you think Allah would be pleased with you? Do you think that Allah might complain by telling you, 'My son, what have you done to those hundreds of thousands of Christian souls who lived and worked in Qatar when you were the head of the Sharia Court? Look in the Gehennam [hell]. There they are. Because you prohibited them from openly professing their faith and performing their religious duties toward me, they forgot me, stopped worshipping me, and went astray on the wrong path.'"[5]

The Sheikh accepted the ambassador's request for a public gathering of Christians to pray to "Allah" (the Arabic term for God that Arab Christians used long before the rise of Islam). And on Friday, Sept. 3, 1988, for the first time since the 7th century, the nation's first Catholic Holy Mass and Christian service was publicly celebrated. It was followed by at least one every week thereafter. Today even Hindus and Buddhists are permitted to hold worship services in Qatar.

It's an extraordinary story of one man's conviction that every person should be free to worship according to the dictates of his or her own conscience. And it's a reminder that the glorious gospel of Christ still penetrates the darkest places on earth.

May God place daring diplomats like Joseph Ghougassian in Saudi Arabia, Iran, and other Islamist states.

THINK *Questions for personal or group study*

Consider the reasons the authors of *Persecuted* gave for the widespread mistreatment of Christians in nations where communist, Hindu, Buddhist, and Muslim ideologies dominate. Are there ways in which Western nations restrict Christians or other religious adherents from exercising their religious freedoms?

What does the story of Joseph Ghougassian tell us about the hope for greater religious tolerance in Muslim-dominated societies?

What are some ways we can help persecuted Christians around the world?

How do you think God is working in the persecuted church?

Do you think Muslims should have any restrictions on the practice of their religion in the United States? Why or why not?

SHARE *Talking points for discussing Christianity in Muslim-dominated societies*

Saudi Arabia is a leading example of Muslim-dominated nations that restrict, or ban, religious liberty.

In fact, life is so tough for "infidels" in Saudi Arabia that the state outlaws freedom of thought because "[f]reedom of thinking requires permitting the denial of faith."

U.S. envoy Joseph Ghougassian engaged Qatar's Sharia Court on the points of religion and history, and through persistence won the right of Christians to worship publicly there.

Today in Qatar, even Hindus and Buddhists are permitted to hold religious services.

Ghougassian was convinced that people should be free to worship according to the dictates of their conscience. And he reminds us that the glorious gospel of Christ still penetrates the darkest places on earth.

DIVE *Go deeper in your study with these resources*

Chrislam: How Missionaries are Promoting an Islamized Gospel, edited by Joshua Lingel, Jeff Morton & Bill Nikides

Reasoning from the Scriptures with Muslims by Ron Rhodes

Why I Am Not a Muslim by Ibn Warraq

MORMONISM

23
MORMONISM: AN OVERVIEW

As the official version of the story goes, in 1820, 14-year-old Joseph Smith, Jr. had a vision in which God the Father and Jesus Christ appeared to him. Caught up in the Protestant revivalism of his day, Smith inquired as to which of the Christian denominations he should join. None of them, he was told, because they were all "wrong" and their creeds "were an abomination" in God's sight. Rather, God would use Smith to reinstate the true church, which had been in apostasy since the death of the apostles.[1]

Thus began the saga of the Church of Jesus Christ of Latter-day Saints, or Mormons, which today is the largest form of counterfeit Christianity in the world, increasing at an average rate of 300,000 converts a year – as many as 75 percent of whom may be former Protestants.[2]

Today the LDS Church, headquartered in Salt Lake City, Utah, boasts roughly 13 million members in more than 160 countries; about 6 million members reside in the United States. In addition, the church has more than 50,000 missionaries who spread the Mormon message around the world. Its current leader is Thomas S. Monson, who, like founder Joseph Smith and subsequent presidents, is considered the church's "prophet, seer, and revelator."

The LDS Church initially stood in defiance of historical Christianity, claiming that after the death of the apostles the Christian church fell into "the great apostasy." Joseph Smith taught that he alone was called to restore the true church, and that the revelations God gave him – particularly as recorded in the *Book of Mormon, Doctrine and Covenants,* and *Pearl of Great Price* – would guide the church back to its historic foundation.

In recent years, however, the LDS Church has minimized, refuted, or re-interpreted many earlier teachings of its leaders – such as polygamy, the multiple marriages of Jesus, and the curse of African Americans – and has launched a concerted effort to promote Mormonism as mainstream Christianity. This leads some to ask legitimately whether the LDS Church can have it both ways. Either Mormonism is true and all other forms of Christianity are false, or the LDS Church is not really needed, since historic Christianity is true after all, despite Joseph Smith's claims to the contrary.

Mormon leaders are exceptionally vague in their official statements about what the LDS Church really believes. A visit to the church's official websites (lds.org and mormon.org) will frustrate any sincere inquirer who wants to know what Mormons really believe about the nature and character of God, the Trinity, the atonement, and man's potential for godhood. Of course, web surfers can always click on the link for a free *Book of Mormon* and have Mormon missionaries deliver a copy personally to their door, although the answers these missionaries give likely will be as vague as the answers their leaders provide.

A brief history

After Joseph Smith's initial visit from Heavenly Father and Jesus Christ in 1820, he allegedly saw the angel Moroni appear at his bedside in 1823 to tell him of golden plates on which was inscribed a record of the ancient American people.

During his earthly life, Moroni had been a great warrior who lived among the Nephite people, descendants of Jews who fled Israel for North America around 600 B.C. Moroni's father, Mormon, commander in chief of the Nephites, had given the golden plates to his son, who added a few words of his own before hiding the plates in Hill Cumorah near Palmyra, New York.

These plates featured "the fullness of the everlasting gospel." In 1827, after further visits from Moroni, Smith dug up the plates and began translating the "Reformed Egyptian" with the assistance of two special stones called "Urim" and "Thummim." The result was the *Book of Mormon*. By 1830 the book was published and Smith founded the "Church of Christ" (not affiliated with the Church of Christ denomination) with five of his followers.

From 1831 to 1844, Smith gained converts and established strongholds in Ohio, Missouri, and Illinois. Wherever they went, Mormons attracted curiosity and even hostility, either because non-Mormons did not trust Smith or were suspicious of Mormon beliefs and practices. During this time, Smith said he continued to receive revelations.

In 1835 he released *Doctrine and Covenants*, which would become "inspired Scripture" along with the *Book of Mormon*. By 1838 the Mormons had been driven from Missouri to Illinois, where they converted a swampy area on the banks of the Mississippi River into a thriving community called Nauvoo. It was here that Smith claimed to receive revelations concerning the Godhead, the origin and destiny of the human race, eternal progression, baptism for the dead, polygamy, and other unique doctrines.

The fourth "standard work" of Mormonism (after the King James Version of the Bible, the *Book of Mormon*, and *Doctrine and Covenants*), *Pearl of Great Price* was first compiled and published in 1851 and brought into the LDS canon in 1880.

Tensions in Nauvoo arose between Mormons and non-Mormons and came to a head when the local paper, the *Expositor*, published stories exposing the LDS practice of polygamy. Smith, who had risen to power as mayor of Nauvoo and "lieutenant general" of the 4,000-man Nauvoo legion, ordered the paper destroyed. For this he was arrested and jailed in Carthage, Illinois. While awaiting trial, a mob of 200 attacked the jail and a gunfight ensued. Smith, using a six-shooter that had been smuggled into the jail, killed at least two attackers before he succumbed to gunshot wounds.

Following Smith's death, Brigham Young emerged as successor and led a large number of Mormons west, where they settled in the Valley of the Great Salt Lake in 1847. Today, Salt Lake City is home to the LDS Church. But all LDS members did not follow Young west. Smith's widow, Emma, stayed behind in Illinois. Those who affirmed her son, Joseph Smith III, as the true successor helped found the "Reorganized Church," now called the Community of Christ and headquartered in Independence, Missouri.

Four standard works

Mormons recognize four written volumes as inspired and authoritative:

The King James Version of the Bible – "as far as it is translated correctly." This caveat enables Mormons to question the Bible's veracity and authority. Joseph Smith made more than 600 "corrections" to its text. According to the *Book of Mormon*, the Bible is missing "plain and most precious" parts (1 Nephi 13:26), which the other three standard volumes complete.

The Book of Mormon, also called "Another Testament of Jesus Christ." According to one of the church's official websites (mormon.org), "By the power of God, Joseph Smith translated this book from an ancient record written on gold plates. The Book of Mormon is 'a record of God's dealings with the ancient inhabitants of the Americas and contains, as does the Bible, the fullness of the everlasting gospel.'"

Doctrine and Covenants. This volume features 138 revelations given to Mormon prophets, along with two "declarations." Here, much of Mormon doctrine may be found, including teachings on the priesthood, baptism for the dead, exaltation (or godhood), and polygamy.

Pearl of Great Price, which contains Smith's religious history, the Articles of Faith, the Book of Abraham, and the Book of Moses.

Basic Mormon beliefs

"The first difference to grasp between the Mormon Church and biblical Christianity is one of semantics," writes Fritz Ridenour in *So What's the Difference?* "The Mormons use but have redefined many key terms employed by evangelical Christians – a definitive sign of a cult. Analysis of Mormon views, past and present, reveals that they dismiss, twist, change, or add to all biblical doctrines, particularly revelation, the Trinity, and salvation by grace alone through faith alone."[3]

Here is a glimpse of several key doctrines of the Mormon Church:

One true church. Joseph Smith declared that all Christian denominations were false and apostate. Mormons teach that after the death of the apostles, all churches became heretical and no true saints existed until the LDS Church was established. Full salvation and "exaltation" (godhood) is found only in the LDS Church.

LDS president as living prophet, seer, and revelator. Joseph Smith and his successors are considered the sole spokesmen and revelators of God through whom God's will is made known to the church. These revelations are considered authoritative, although some early revelations have been superseded by more recent ones; others are minimized by the church today; and still others, such as Smith's prophecy that the temple would be built in Independence, Missouri, in his lifetime, have not been fulfilled.

Mormon scripture. Mormons accept "four standard works" – The King James Version of the Bible ("as far as it is translated correctly"); the *Book of Mormon; Doctrine and Covenants*; and *Pearl of Great Price*. In addition, LDS presidents may receive new revelations from God, and these may become scripture.

God as an exalted man. Elohim, or Heavenly Father, is the god of this world. He was a man in prior existence, but by keeping the requirements of Mormonism, he was exalted to godhood and inherited his own universe. There are an infinite number of gods with their own worlds; these gods, too, once were men. The Father, Son, and Holy Ghost are three separate and distinct gods. The Father and Son have bodies of flesh and bone; the Holy Ghost is a "personage of spirit."

Jesus is God's "Son." Jesus (also called Jehovah) was Elohim's firstborn spirit child in heaven. (Lucifer also was a spirit child, but his plan of redemption was rejected in favor of Jesus' superior plan.) Jesus was begotten by God through Mary in a "literal, full and complete sense."[4] Principally in the Garden of Gethsemane (and not on the cross), Jesus atoned for Adam's sin and guaranteed all people resurrection and immortality (salvation). Jesus visited the Israelites (ancestors of Native Americans) after his resurrection and established the true church among them. We are the spiritual younger brothers and sisters of Christ. Jesus was married at Cana in Galilee (John 2); in fact, He had numerous wives and fathered many children Himself.

Humans are gods in embryo. Every person has the potential to become a god by keeping the requirements of Mormonism. A key phrase in Mormonism, coined by fifth LDS President Lorenzo Snow, is, "As man is, God once was; as God is, man may become." From a prior spirit existence in heaven, people are born on earth in order to exercise freedom to choose good or evil and to have a body for the resurrection. By obeying Mormon teachings and performing required duties, worthy Mormon males may pass the celestial guards, bring their wives with them, and achieve a status similar to Elohim. In the resurrection, faithful Mormons receive exaltation (godhood) and have authority over their own worlds.

Salvation by works. When Mormons say people are "saved" by grace through faith, they mean "resurrection." In this sense, virtually all people will be saved. To achieve the highest tier of the highest level of heaven, Mormons must exercise faith in the god of Mormonism, in Christ, and in the Church of Jesus Christ of Latter-day Saints; exercise repentance; and be baptized in the LDS Church. Additionally, they must keep the "Word of Wisdom" by abstaining from alcohol, tobacco, and caffeine; tithe to the church; attend weekly meetings; support the Mormon prophet; do temple works; and be active in their support of the church. "Full salvation" or "exaltation" (godhood) is only available through the LDS Church.

Eternal progression. All people, as well as all gods, have existed eternally. There are four stages in "eternal progression" through which people may pass: 1) eternally existing intelligence; 2) pre-mortal spirit; 3) mortal probation; 4) resurrection and eternal life in one of several places: outer darkness; the telestial kingdom (lowest level of heaven); the terrestrial kingdom (next-highest level of heaven); or the celestial kingdom, consisting of three levels, the highest of which leads to exaltation/godhood.

THINK *Questions for personal or group study*

Why do you think Mormonism appeals to so many people?

What are some biblical terms Mormons distort? How are the LDS definitions in conflict with the historic Christian understanding of these terms?

What must Mormons do to attain "full salvation" or "exaltation?"

Why is Mormonism a counterfeit form of Christianity? Specifically, which doctrines set the LDS Church apart as a cult?

In terms of receiving revelation from God, how is the LDS president similar to the Roman Catholic pope?

SHARE *Talking points for discussing Mormonism*

LDS Founder Joseph Smith claimed God chose him to reinstate the true church, which fell into complete apostasy after the death of the apostles.

In recent years, however, the LDS Church has launched a concerted effort to promote Mormonism as mainstream Christianity.

Mormons draw their doctrines from four "standard works:" The King James Version of the Bible ("as far as it is translated correctly"); the *Book of Mormon; Doctrine and Covenants*; and *Pearl of Great Price*. In addition, the LDS president may receive direct revelations from God.

Mormonism may be summarized with this phrase: "As man is, God once was; as God is, man may become."

While most people enter some level of heaven beyond the grave, faithful Mormons hope for a place in the highest level of the celestial kingdom, where "exaltation" or godhood is possible.

DIVE *Go deeper in your study with these resources*

Mormonism 101: Examining the Religion of the Latter-day Saints by Bill McKeever and Eric Johnson

Where Mormonism Meets Biblical Christianity Face to Face by Shawn Aaron McCraney

Doctrine and Covenants (This LDS "standard work" reveals a number of the church's key doctrines but should be read with discernment.)

24
COMPARING CHRISTIANITY AND MORMONISM

The following table compares key Christian doctrines with those of the LDS Church. The source of authority for Christians is the Bible. Mormon doctrines come from the "four standard works:" The King James Version of the Bible ("as far as it is translated correctly"); the *Book of Mormon; Doctrine and Covenants;* and *Pearl of Great Price.* Additional writings by LDS leaders help explain Mormon beliefs. All sources are cited in the table rather than in the end notes.

What the Bible says about Jesus:	What Mormonism says about Jesus:
1. He is the virgin-born Son of God, conceived by the Holy Spirit (Isa. 7:14; Matt. 1:18-23; Luke 1:34-5).	"Jesus was not the son of Joseph, nor was He begotten by the Holy Ghost. He is the Son of the Eternal Father" (Ezra Taft Benson, *Teachings of Ezra Taft Benson,* 7, quoted in the *Ensign,* April 1997, 15). "God the Father became the literal father of Jesus Christ. Jesus is the only person on earth to be born of a mortal mother and an immortal father" (*Gospel Principles,* 64). "Jesus is the only person who had our Heavenly Father as the father of his body" (Joseph F. Smith, *Family Home Evening Manual,* 125-26). "Jesus Christ is the Son of Elohim both as spiritual and bodily offspring; that is to say, Elohim is literally the Father of the spirit of Jesus Christ and also of the body in which Jesus Christ performed His mission in the flesh" (James E. Talmage, *The Articles of Faith,* 466-67). "Let it not be forgotten, that He is essentially greater than any and all others, by reason (1) of His seniority as the oldest or first born; (2) of His unique status in the flesh as the offspring of a mortal mother and of an immortal, or resurrected and glorified, Father …" (James E. Talmage, *The Articles of Faith,* 426).

[Satan is a created – and fallen – angel].	"Long before you were born a program was developed by your creators…. The principal personalities in this great drama were a Father Elohim, perfect in wisdom, judgment, and person, and two sons, Lucifer and Jehovah" (Spencer W. Kimball, *Teachings of Spencer W. Kimball*, 32-33).
	"The appointment of Jesus to be the Savior of the world was contested by one of the other sons of God. He was called Lucifer … this spirit-brother of Jesus desperately tried to become the Savior of mankind" (Milton R. Hunter, *The Gospel through the Ages*, 15).
	"Both the scriptures and the prophets affirm that Jesus Christ and Lucifer are indeed offspring of our Heavenly Father and, therefore, spirit brothers…. Both Jesus and Lucifer were strong leaders with great knowledge and influence. But as the First-born of the Father, Jesus was Lucifer's older brother" (Jess L. Christensen, *A Sure Foundation: Answers to Difficult Gospel Questions*, 223-24; this teaching also appears in other Mormon publications).
2. Jesus did not marry.	"Jesus was the bridegroom at the marriage of Cana – We say it was Jesus Christ who was married, to be brought into relation whereby he could see his seed" (Orson Hyde, apostle, *Journal of Discourses*, Vol. 2, 82).
	"From the passage in the forty-fifth Psalm, it will be seen that the great Messiah who was the founder of the Christian religion, was a Polygamist…. the Messiah chose to take upon himself his seed; and by marrying many honorable wives himself, show to all future generations that he approbated the plurality of Wives under the Christian dispensation, as well as under the dispensations in which His Polygamist ancestors lived" (Orson Pratt, *The Seer*, 172).
3. Jesus is the foundation of the true church (Matt. 16:18; Acts 4:11-12; Col. 1:18).	Joseph Smith: "I have more to boast of than ever any man had. I am the only man that has ever been able to keep a whole church together since the days of Adam. A large majority of the whole have stood by me. Neither Paul, John, Peter, nor Jesus ever did it. The followers of Jesus ran away from Him, but the Latter-day Saints never ran away from me yet" (*History of the Church*, Vol. 6, 408-9).

4. Jesus is the judge of all (John 5:22).	"No man or woman in this dispensation will ever enter into the celestial kingdom of God without the consent of Joseph Smith ... Every man and woman must have the certificate of Joseph Smith, Junior, as a passport to their entrance into the mansion where God and Christ are" (Brigham Young, *Journal of Discourses*, vol. 7, 289).
5. Jesus is the one who resurrects all (John 5:28-29).	Joseph Smith will receive the keys of the resurrection. "If we ask who will stand at the head of the resurrection in this last dispensation, the answer is – Joseph Smith, Junior, the Prophet of God. He is the man who will be resurrected and receive the keys of the resurrection, and he will seal this authority upon others, and they will hunt up their friends and resurrect them" (Brigham Young, *Discourses of Brigham Young*, 116).
6. Jesus is the eternal God, the Creator, co-equal and co-eternal with the Father and Holy Spirit (John 1:1-14; Col. 1:15-20; Phil 2:5-11; Heb. 1:1-13).	A "council of the Gods" created the world. "In the beginning, the head of the Gods called a council of the Gods; and they came together and concocted a plan to create the world and people it ... In all congregations when I have preached on the subject of the Deity, it has been the plurality of Gods" (Joseph Smith, *History of the Church*, Vol. 6, 308, 474). "He [Jesus] is the Firstborn of the Father. By obedience and devotion to the truth he attained that pinnacle of intelligence which ranked him as a God, as the Lord Omnipotent, while yet in his pre-existent state.... Inasmuch, however, as Christ attained Godhood while yet in pre-existence, he too stood as a God to the other spirits" (Bruce McConkie, *Mormon Doctrine*, 129, 323).

What the Bible says about the Holy Spirit:	What Mormonism says about the Holy Spirit:
1. The Holy Spirit is the third person of the triune Godhead (Matt. 3:16-17; 28:19-20).	Joseph Smith taught that the Father, Son, and Holy Spirit "constitute three distinct personages and three Gods" (*Teachings of the Prophet Joseph Smith*, 370).
2. The Holy Spirit is co-equal and co-eternal with the Father and the Son (Acts 5:3-4).	The Father has a body of flesh and bones. So does the Son. But the Holy Ghost is "a personage of spirit" (*Doctrine and Covenants* 130:22).
3. The Holy Spirit and the Holy Ghost are two biblical names for the same person.	"The Holy Ghost ... is a personage distinct from the Holy Spirit. As a personage, the Holy Ghost cannot any more than the Father and the Son be everywhere present in person" (John A. Widtsoe, *Evidences and Reconciliations*, 76).
4. The Holy Spirit/Holy Ghost is God (Acts 5:3-4).	"The Holy Ghost is yet a spiritual body and waiting to take to himself a body as the Saviour did or as the gods before them took bodies" (Joseph Smith, April 6, 1843; see *Discourses on the Holy Ghost* compiled by N.B. Lundwall, 73).

What the Bible says about the gospel of Jesus Christ:	What Mormonism says about the gospel of Jesus Christ:
1. Christ's death at Calvary completely paid our sin debt so that salvation comes by grace through faith in Jesus (John 3:16; 5:24; Rom. 4:4-5; 1 Cor. 15:1-4; Eph. 2:8-9; Titus 3:5-7).	Jesus' death, burial, and resurrection made it possible for mankind to be resurrected, but "men will be punished for their own sins." (*Article of Faith #2* by Joseph Smith). Through the atonement of Christ "all mankind may be saved, by obedience to the laws and ordinances of the gospel" (*Article of Faith #3* by Joseph Smith). "There is *no salvation* outside The Church of Jesus Christ of Latter-day Saints" (Bruce McConkie, *Mormon Doctrine*, 670). "Baptism ... is for the remission of sins ... (and) is the gate to the celestial kingdom of heaven" (Bruce McConkie, *Mormon Doctrine*, 70). There is "no salvation without accepting Joseph Smith ... No man can eject that testimony without accepting most dreadful consequences, for he cannot enter the kingdom of God" (Joseph Fielding Smith, *Doctrines of Salvation*, Vol. 1, 188). A summary of Mormon teaching on grace and works: • The grace of God provides for resurrection from the dead • Works are necessary for a person to achieve exaltation, or godhood • Salvation by grace alone is a pernicious doctrine • Perfection is an achievable goal (Bill McKeever and Eric Johnson, *Mormonism 101*, 169)

2. The Bible teaches that at death, man's eternal destiny is fixed in one of two places: heaven or hell (Luke 16:19-31; John 5:28-29; 2 Cor. 5:6-8; Heb. 9:27; Rev. 20:11-15).	Virtually all men are saved in "General Salvation … meaning resurrection" (*Contributions of Joseph Smith* by Stephen L. Richards, 5). Then, based on works, all men will spend eternity in one of three levels of heaven – telestial, terrestrial, or celestial. A few "sons of perdition" will not be saved/resurrected. More specifically, Mormonism teaches that a person is destined for one of several places after death: • **Outer darkness** – reserved for Satan and his demons and the extremely wicked, including apostate Mormons • **Telestial kingdom** – the lowest of the three heavens; the wicked spend eternity here • **Terrestrial kingdom** – the second of the three heavens; honorable people and "lukewarm" Mormons live here • **Celestial kingdom** – the highest of the three heavens consisting of three separate levels; the top level is where Mormons hope to be exalted
3. All men are sinners by nature and by volition (Rom. 3:23; 5:12; 1 Cor. 15:21-22).	There is no such thing as original sin. All men are gods in embryo. "God and man are of the same race, differing only in their degrees of advancement" (Apostle John Widtsoe, *Rational Theology*, 61).
4. There is no second chance for salvation after death (Heb. 9:27).	Mormons may be baptized on behalf of the dead for their salvation. "If a man cannot enter the kingdom of God without baptism, then the dead must be baptized" (Joseph Fielding Smith, *Doctrines of Salvation*, Vol. II, 141).

5. A justified person is eternally secure, based on the finished work of Christ at Calvary and the faithfulness of God (John 5:24;10:27-30; Rom. 4:21; 8:28-39; Heb. 7:25; 10:14; 1 Peter 1:1-5).	Believers must do works to earn a level of heaven and risk losing their position in that heaven if they are not faithful in service. For example, failure to marry in an LDS temple will "damn" persons so that their eternal progression will be stopped short of godhood (see *Doctrine and Covenants* 132:16-20).
6. Each individual is a uniquely created person whose beginning came at the moment of conception; after death, that person retains his or her personhood and spends eternity in heaven or hell.	Each individual has four stages of life (eternal progression): (1) Eternally existing intelligence; (2) pre-mortal spirit born by procreation of God and one of his wives; (3) mortal probation (present life on earth); and (4) post-mortal status that depends on works done in this life. Eternity is spent in one of three heavens: telestial (almost everyone makes it at least this far); terrestrial (good and religious folk make it here); and celestial (only Mormons who have fulfilled the proper requirements make it into one of this heaven's three levels).

THINK *Questions for personal or group study*

What are the key differences between the Jesus of the Bible and the Jesus of Mormonism?

How would you respond to a Mormon who says there is additional revelation beyond the Bible that gives us a more complete understanding of Jesus, including His being born into the spirit world and achieving deity in pre-mortal existence?

What are the possible destinies for people after death, according to LDS teachings?

How does the LDS Church distinguish between "general salvation" and "individual salvation?"

Why do you think it's impossible for a Mormon to know for certain where he or she will spend eternity?

SHARE *Talking points for discussing Mormon beliefs*

Mormonism draws from extra-biblical sources to promote false teachings about Jesus, such as the false teaching that He and Lucifer are spirit brothers; that Jesus is the physical offspring of Elohim and Mary; and that He was the bridegroom at the wedding in Cana.

According to LDS teachings, God the Father has a body of flesh and bones. So does the Son. But the Holy Ghost is "a personage of spirit."

Mormonism teaches that all men are gods in embryo. As fifth LDS President Lorenzo Snow proclaimed, "As man is, God once was; as God is, man may become."

Mormons may be baptized on behalf of the dead for their salvation.

In Mormon theology, each person experiences four stages of eternal progression: (1) eternally existing intelligence; (2) pre-mortal spirit born by procreation of God and one of his wives; (3) mortal probation (present life on earth); and (4) post-mortal status that depends on works done in this life.

DIVE *Go deeper in your study with these resources*

Mormonism Unmasked by R. Philip Roberts

The God Makers: A Shocking Expose of What the Mormon Church Really Believes by Ed Decker and Dave Hunt

25
DOES THE BIBLE PROVE PREEXISTENCE?

Our Mormon friends teach the doctrine of eternal progression. Among other things, it means that all people were born into the spirit world – through sexual relations between God and one of his wives – prior to taking on earthly bodies.

As Mormon.org puts it: "Your life didn't begin at birth and it won't end at death. Before you came to earth, your spirit lived with Heavenly Father who created you. You knew Him, and He knew and loved you. It was a happy time during which you were taught God's plan of happiness and the path to true joy. But just as most of us leave our home and parents when we grow up, God knew you needed to do the same. He knew you couldn't progress unless you left for a while. So he allowed you to come to earth to experience the joy – as well as pain – of a physical body."[1]

While this is a troubling doctrine that departs from orthodox Christianity, it is even more disturbing to learn that Mormons claim the Bible supports this belief.

Before I formed you ...

Specifically, Mormons cite two passages of Scripture.

The first is Jeremiah 1:5, where the Lord declares, "Before I formed you in the womb I knew you, and before you were born I consecrated you; I appointed you a prophet to the nations."

Mormons believe this verse supports the doctrine of pre-mortal existence since God says He "knew" Jeremiah prior to the prophet's conception.

But as Ron Rhodes points out in *The 10 Most Important Things You Can Say to a Mormon*, "This verse does not imply Jeremiah's preexistence; rather, it affirms Jeremiah's preordination to a special ministry."[2]

Taken in context, the verse speaks of God's omniscience and sovereignty. Because neither space nor time can bind God, He sees the future with the same clarity He views the past. The Lord knew His plans for Jeremiah and set him apart as a prophet before knitting Jeremiah in his mother's womb.

It's also good to keep in mind Genesis 2:7, which says "the Lord God formed the man out of the dust from the ground and breathed the breath of life into his nostrils, and the man became a living being." Adam *became* a living being at creation, not in pre-mortal existence.

The glory I had with you ...

The second passage Mormons quote is John 17:5 – "Now, Father, glorify Me in Your presence with that glory I had with You before the world existed."

Mormons say this verse proves spirit existence prior to mortal existence. They further believe everyone – not just Jesus – preexisted as spirit offspring of the Father. In this respect, Jesus is our "elder brother."

The Bible, however, teaches that God alone is eternal. Jesus' prayer to the Father is grounded both in His deity and eternality. Jesus set aside His heavenly position – but not His deity – to come to earth to die on the cross, after which He returned to heaven and sat at the Father's right hand. His prayer in John 17 anticipates the ascension.

John the Baptist said that even though Jesus was born six months after him, the Son of God preceded John (John 1:30). Isaiah 9:6 refers to the coming Messiah as the Eternal Father. And Jesus affirms to a Jewish audience, "Before Abraham was, I am" (John 8:58).

Jesus is both divine and eternal, and humans are neither. We are everlasting, not eternal; that is, we came into existence at conception, and our lives continue into eternity future either in heaven or in hell.

The danger of the doctrine of preexistence is three-fold. First, it is not taught in Scripture. Second, it equates all humans with Jesus, who is eternal and divine, while we are not. And third, it introduces the possibility that mere humans may become gods.

The Bible, in contrast, teaches that Jesus is the uncreated, eternal Son of God, the Creator and sovereign Lord of the universe. Human beings are not eternal; we are everlasting creatures made in the image of God and invited to join Him in an unbreakable relationship.

The clearer we are with our Mormon friends about this doctrine, the more we can help them see their need to acknowledge their mortality, sinfulness, and need of a Savior.

THINK *Questions for personal or group study*

How does the Mormon doctrine of eternal progression depart from biblical truths about God, human beings, and salvation?

While Mormons distort Jeremiah 1:5 and John 17:5 to support the notion of pre-mortal existence, what are some passages of Scripture that refute that teaching?

If humans beings truly existed in the spirit world prior to their physical birth, how would that change the orthodox teaching that life begins at conception?

How do you think the doctrine of pre-mortal existence influences the prolife stance of the LDS Church?

In what ways is the uniqueness of Christ undermined by the LDS teaching of pre-mortal existence and eternal progression?

V. False Religions, Cults, and Christian Sects

SHARE *Talking points for discussing the Mormon doctrine of preexistence*

The LDS Church teaches that all people, including Jesus, were born into the spirit world – through sexual relations between God and one of his wives – prior to taking on earthly bodies.

Mormons distort Jeremiah 1:5 and John 17:5 to support their belief in preexistence.

Jeremiah 1:5 does not imply the prophet's preexistence; rather, it affirms his preordination to a special ministry.

Jesus' prayer in John 17:5 is grounded both in His deity and eternality – neither of which human beings may claim. His prayer in John 17 anticipates the ascension.

The danger of the doctrine of preexistence is three-fold. First, it is not taught in Scripture. Second, it equates all humans with Jesus, who is eternal and divine, while we are not. And third, it introduces the possibility that mere humans may become gods.

DIVE *Go deeper in your study with these resources*

The 10 Most Important Things to Say to a Mormon by Ron Rhodes

Inside Today's Mormonism by Richard Abanes

26
IS MORMONISM NECESSARY?

As the official version of the story goes, in 1820, 14-year-old Joseph Smith went into the woods near his home in rural New York to pray. There, God the Father and Jesus Christ appeared to him.

Caught up in the Protestant revivalism of his day, Smith inquired as to which of the Christian denominations he should join. None of them, he was told, because they were all wrong. "[T]he Personage who addressed me said that all their creeds were an abomination in his sight; that those professors were all corrupt; that: 'they draw near to me with their lips, but their hearts are far from me, they teach for doctrines the commandments of men, having a form of godliness, but they deny the power thereof,'" Smith later recalled.[1]

Smith was urged to take heart. God would use him to reinstate the true church, which had fallen into complete apostasy after the death of the apostles.

The Church of Jesus Christ of Latter-day Saints professes to be the restored true church. Its leaders claim that Joseph Smith faithfully rediscovered proper church organization – that is, the Aaronic and Melchizedek priesthoods – and the true gospel, which was lost due to "ignorant translators, careless transcribers, or designing and corrupt priests."[2]

In short, the LDS Church declares itself the one true church, while all other forms of Christianity remain apostate.

Total apostasy?

Our Mormon friends say the great apostasy is prophesied in Scripture. For example, Acts 20:30-31 says, "And men will rise up from your own number with deviant doctrines to lure the disciples into following them. Therefore be on the alert ..."

So it's fair to ask: Does the Bible really predict total apostasy? And if so, is the Mormon Church the only form of Christianity to be trusted?

To the first question, the answer is an emphatic no. Paul's plea to the Ephesian elders in Acts 20 is to be on guard against false teachers, whom he calls "savage wolves" (v. 29), but the apostle does not predict a total apostasy of that local church, or of the universal body of Christ.

In Gal. 1:6-8, another passage Mormons cite, Paul simply warns against believing a different gospel. There is no hint of total apostasy in Galatia or throughout the world.

And in 2 Thess. 2:3, another favorite Mormon passage, Paul is not referring to a general global apostasy beginning in the first century but rather to a specific apostasy that is yet to come.

As to the second question – Is the LDS Church the only form of Christianity to be trusted? – the answer again is no. The Bible does not feature a restored church because the true church will never be extinguished.

In Matt. 28:20 Jesus promises to be with His followers to the end of the age. His sustaining power is with us, uninterrupted, until He returns.

In Eph. 3:21 Paul writes, "[T]o Him be glory in the church and in Christ Jesus to all generations, forever and ever." How could God be glorified in the church throughout all generations if the entire church fell into apostasy?

Further, the Mormon claim of restoring the Melchizedek priesthood cannot be true because that priesthood belongs only to Christ. Psalm 110 is a messianic psalm pointing to the person and work of Christ, not a role in the church. In Heb. 7:23-24 Christ's priesthood is eternal because He is an eternal being.

In a similar manner, the Aaronic priesthood was done way with and replaced with something better – the priesthood of Jesus Christ, our eternal priest. And we should note that Mormons are not physical descendants of Aaron, a key requirement for the Aaronic priesthood (see Num. 3:6-10).

Just another denomination?

Today the LDS Church downplays its founder's claim to be the only true church. On its website and in its publications, the church seems to promote itself as just another Christian denomination.

Which begs the question for our Mormon friends: Is the LDS Church restored Christianity and therefore the only true church?

If they answer no, then we should ask why Joseph Smith claimed the church he founded is the only true church.

If they answer yes, then we may ask, "Is it possible for a non-Mormon to be a Christian?"

Our Mormon friends cannot have it both ways: Either the LDS Church is the only true church, a claim that Mormons should state clearly and unapologetically, or the LDS Church is not the only true church, in which case it is reasonable to conclude that Mormonism is not necessary.

THINK *Questions for personal or group study*

If Mormons truly believe the LDS Church is the only true church, why do you think the church positions itself publicly as one of many evangelical denominations?

How would you explain to a Mormon friend the biblical definition of the one true church?

Why isn't it possible for the true church – the body of Christ – to fall into complete apostasy?

Why do you think Joseph Smith argued for the LDS Church as the restored true church? Rather than take on historic Christianity, couldn't he have positioned Mormonism as a Christian sect, or as a completely new religion altogether?

Do you think it's possible for a Mormon to be a born-again Christian? Why or why not?

SHARE *Talking points for discussing the LDS claim to be the one true church*

According to LDS founder Joseph Smith, God appointed him to restore the one true church, which had fallen into complete apostasy after the death of the apostles.

Today, the LDS Church declares itself the one true church, while all other forms of Christianity remain apostate.

While the apostle Paul and other New Testament writers warn against falling away from the core doctrines of the Christian faith, nowhere do they – or Jesus – predict a fully apostate church.

The Bible does not feature a restored church because the true church will never be extinguished.

Jesus promises to be with His followers to the end of the age. His sustaining power is with us, uninterrupted, until He returns.

Our Mormon friends cannot have it both ways: Either the LDS Church is the only true church, or it is not, in which case it is reasonable to conclude that Mormonism is not necessary.

DIVE *Go deeper in your study with these resources*

Reasoning from the Scriptures with the Mormons by Ron Rhodes & Marian Bodine

27

JOSEPH SMITH AND POLYGAMY: A TEACHABLE MOMENT

Does it make any difference that Joseph Smith, founder of the Church of Jesus Christ of Latter-day Saints, married as many as 40 women, some of whom already were married?

Smith's marital history has been the subject of much debate, but until a 2014 essay by the Mormon Church acknowledging the founding prophet's multiple wives, the church has maintained that Smith was happily married to one woman.

The essay explains that Smith was a reluctant polygamist, agreeing to multiple marriages only after an angel threatened him with a sword. Further, the essay notes that Smith was restoring the "ancient principles" of biblical prophets like Abraham, who took secondary wives.[1]

In appealing to Scripture to address the inconvenient truth of Smith's polygamy, the LDS Church offers evangelical Christians a unique opportunity to urge our Mormon friends to revisit the Bible, which takes a back seat to the *Book of Mormon* and other church documents in LDS theology and practice.

Consider three biblical perspectives: (1) God's creative intent; (2) His divine accommodation; and (3) His warning against polygamy.

One flesh

Let's begin with God's design for men and women created in His image. In Gen. 2:18, the Lord says, "It is not good for the man to be alone. I will make a helper as his complement." Adam acknowledges Eve as a perfect fit for him – "bone of my bone, and flesh of my flesh." Scripture then says, "This is why a man leaves his father and mother and bonds with his wife, and they become one flesh" (Gen. 2:24).

When the Pharisees press Jesus about the legitimacy of divorce on any grounds, He takes them back to this passage to emphasize God's creative intent: "So they are no longer two, but one flesh. Therefore what God has joined together, man must not separate" (Matt. 19:6).

When they ask why Moses allowed divorce, Jesus explains that it is due to the hardness of people's hearts, but "it was not like that from the beginning" (Matt. 19:8).

It is clear that God's ideal is a monogamous, lifelong marriage between a man and a woman.

Divine accommodation

The Mosaic Law deals with such realities as divorce (which God hates) and polygamy (which He warns against). The Law is a great improvement over the pagan practices of Israel's neighbors while making allowances for the fallen state of God's people. It's what some scholars call "divine accommodation."

In his book *Is God a Moral Monster?* Paul Copan writes that the Law of Moses is "a gracious gift temporarily given to national Israel that bridged God's ideals and the realities of ancient Near Eastern life and human hard-heartedness.... Much in the Old Testament visibly reminds us of God's abundant grace despite human sin and fall-damaged social structures."[2]

While Scripture nowhere instructs God's people to engage in polygamy, the Law provides protection for women involved in polygamous relationships.

Warning against polygamy

In addition to God's clear intention for monogamous marriage, and His divine accommodation to protect the victims of sinful behavior like divorce and polygamy, several passages of Scripture warn us of the danger of taking multiple wives. Here's a brief sampling:

From Lamech, the first recorded polygamist in Scripture (Gen. 4:19, 23-24), to Abraham, Esau, Jacob, David, and Solomon, wherever we see God's ideal of monogamy ignored, the result is bickering, strife, and often idolatry.

Lev. 18:18 is a strong teaching against polygamy: "You are not to marry a woman as a rival to her sister and have sexual intercourse with her during her sister's lifetime."

In Deut. 17:17, God prohibits Israel's king from acquiring many wives "so that his heart won't go astray." Solomon, of course, takes 700 wives and 300 concubines (1 Kings 11:3), often from foreign nations for political reasons. The result: They turn his heart away from God.

It also should be noted that just because Old Testament characters like David and Solomon took multiple wives does not mean God endorses the practice. We need to draw a distinction between what the Bible *records* and what it *commands*.

Those who point to the Bible to endorse their polygamous practices, or to ridicule Scripture's "outdated" and "archaic" teachings, need to study the passages in context and against the historical backdrop of the times in which they are given.

God's creative intent remains the same: one man and one woman, becoming one flesh through marriage, until death. This is a teachable moment for all of us, including our Mormon friends.

THINK *Questions for personal or group study*

If the U.S. Supreme Court, which affirmed same-sex marriage in 2015, were to make polygamy legal, would you support it? Why or why not?

Why do you think King David, a man after God's own heart (Acts 13:22), and King Solomon, one of the wisest men ever to live (1 Kings 4:30), took multiple wives if they knew it displeased God?

Read about Jesus' encounter with the Pharisees in Matt. 19:1-13. While Jesus does not directly address polygamy in this exchange, how do His words apply?

How would you respond to the Mormon who defends Joseph Smith's polygamy by saying God spoke to him and commanded him to take multiple wives, even though he was reluctant to do so?

What do you think about "divine accommodation" – that is, God making allowances for the fallen state of His people, such as permitting divorce under certain circumstances?

SHARE *Talking points for discussing Joseph Smith's polygamy*

The LDS Church acknowledges that Joseph Smith, founder of the Church of Jesus Christ of Latter-day Saints, married as many as 40 women, ranging from age 15 to 56.

God's ideal, clearly expressed in Scripture, is a monogamous, lifelong marriage between a man and a woman.

While Scripture nowhere instructs God's people to engage in polygamy, the Mosaic Law provides protection for women involved in polygamous relationships.

In Scripture, wherever we see God's ideal of monogamy ignored, the result is bickering, strife, and often idolatry.

Just because Old Testament characters like David and Solomon took multiple wives does not mean God endorses the practice. We need to draw a distinction between what the Bible *records* and what it *commands*.

DIVE *Go deeper in your study with these resources*

Answering Mormons' Questions: Ready Responses for Inquiring Latter-day Saints by Bill McKeever and Eric Johnson

Wife No. 19: The Story of a Life in Bondage, Being a Complete Expose of Mormonism, and Revealing the Sorrows, Sacrifices and Sufferings of Women in Polygamy by Ann Eliza Young

28
WHEN THE BIBLE SPEAKS TO MORMONS

Lynn Wilder and her husband were quintessential Mormons.

Lynn had served for 8 years as a professor at Brigham Young University, the flagship school of the Church of Jesus Christ of Latter-day Saints.

Michael was a high priest, temple worker, seminary teacher, and Sunday school president.

Their eldest sons had completed two-year missions assignments, and their daughter was demonstrating a strong faith in the LDS Church's founder, Joseph Smith.

Then, as Lynn explains it, their world came crashing down. In 2006 their third son, Micah, was only three weeks from completing his two-year mission when he called to report that he was being sent home early in disgrace.

His sin: He read the New Testament and confessed to a roomful of missionaries that the Bible offered a different Jesus than the LDS Church — a Jesus of grace, not works. He professed belief in Jesus and confessed he had found a deep and genuine faith.

Church leaders told his parents that Micah had the spirit of the Devil in him and sent him home to face the LDS high council. To prevent excommunication, the Wilders put their son on a plane out of Utah.

Before entering the jetway, Micah pleaded, "Mom and Dad, please read the New Testament."[1]

A call to Scripture

They did. And as Lynn tells it in her book, *Unveiling Grace: The Story of How We Found Our Way Out of the Mormon Church*, "I heeded Micah's advice.... As I read [the Bible], I became increasingly consumed by reading about the God of grace. I barely ate or slept. It's all I wanted to do."[2]

Several months later, after watching the film *Luther* with her family, her heart pounded as she faced a similar struggle: "Did I believe the Mormon system of obedience to laws and ordinances would secure my forgiveness? Or did I believe what the Bible taught, that Jesus alone was the Way, the Truth, and the Life?"

That night she lay face-down on the carpet, arms extended, and cried out to Jesus, "I am yours. Save me."

From that point on God became personal, she reports. "I discovered this Jesus could not be confined by the laws and ordinances of a religion. Jesus is real. This palpable relationship transformed me."[3]

Her husband and daughter followed in faith. They left the Mormon Church and God provided another job for Lynn. "This is the Jesus my family and I know now. He loves me personally. I devour His word and find him there. He knows me and teaches me. I do not need the laws and ordinances of the Mormon Church to be saved. Only my beloved Jesus."[4]

Being held captive

Wilder's story reveals several truths about those held captive in counterfeit forms of Christianity.

First, they "accept" the Bible. Mormons consider the Bible to be "the word of God as far as it is translated correctly."[5] The King James Version is one of the four standard works of the LDS Church. But for all practical purposes, the Bible takes a back seat to the alleged revelations God gave LDS founder Joseph Smith.

In a similar manner, Jehovah's Witnesses say they believe the Bible is God's Word. Yet the official New World Translation has stripped away the deity of Christ so that Witnesses cannot find the truth in their own organization's Bible.

Second, Scripture remains a most powerful evangelistic tool. The Wilders' son simply requested that they read the Bible, and the Word of God proved itself "living and effective and sharper than any two-edged sword" (Heb. 4:12).

Third, God redeems people out of darkness and uses their experiences to magnify His work in their lives. The apostle Paul was a killer of

Christians, but after his conversion he never failed to share his testimony of how the risen Jesus changed his life.

Think of how God is using the Wilders to reach Mormons in ways that non-Mormons never could.

Lynn Wilder's breath-taking testimony reminds us of the power of God's written word. We don't always have to explain it or even understand its more difficult texts. Mostly, we just need to urge our friends to read the Bible and then allow its author to draw them to faith in Jesus.

THINK *Questions for personal or group study*

If Mormons believe the Bible is the Word of God, why do you think reading the New Testament had such a profound effect on turning the Wilders' hearts away from the LDS Church?

Think back on what you've learned about Mormonism. What are the key differences between the Jesus of the LDS Church and the Jesus of the Bible?

What are some passages of Scripture that describe unbelievers as captives, blind, and in spiritual darkness? How do these verses help us explain the sincerely held, but false, beliefs of our Mormon friends?

In what ways do you think the Wilders are more effective witnesses to Mormons than Christians who have never been in the LDS Church?

How does the New Testament describe the work of the Holy Spirit in drawing unbelievers to faith in Christ? Cite specific passages.

SHARE *Talking points for discussing the Bible and Mormonism*

In contrast to the Mormon system of obedience to laws and ordinances to secure forgiveness, the Bible teaches that Jesus alone is the Way, the Truth, and the Life.

Many counterfeit forms of Christianity "accept" the Bible but then make it secondary to other forms of "revelation."

Some translations of the Bible – like the Jehovah's Witnesses' New World Translation, and the LDS Church's Joseph Smith Translation – remove, distort, or add to the plain reading of Scripture.

Scripture is a most powerful evangelistic tool.

God redeems people out of darkness and uses their experiences to magnify His work in their lives.

DIVE *Go deeper in your study with these resources*

Unveiling Grace: The Story of How We Found Our Way Out of the Mormon Church by Lynn Wilder

The 10 Most Important Things You Can Say to a Mormon by Ron Rhodes

JEHOVAH'S WITNESSES

29
JEHOVAH'S WITNESSES: AN OVERVIEW

Some 50 years after Joseph Smith claimed God the Father and Jesus Christ visited him – an event that launched the Mormon Church – another teenage boy began an inconspicuous Bible study in Allegheny, Pennsylvania, in 1870. The result: a second major worldwide cult in the 19th century, known today as the Jehovah's Witnesses.

Known over the years by several names – including The Watch Tower Bible and Tract Society of Pennsylvania, and the International Bible Students Association – the Jehovah's Witnesses today boast more than 8.2 million active participants (known as "publishers") in more than 230 countries, with more than 115,000 Kingdom Halls, one of the largest publishing operations in the world, and an aggressive door-to-door "preaching" ministry.[1]

A brief history

It all began with Charles Taze Russell (1852-1916). As a teenager he rejected many of the views taught in his Congregational church, particularly the doctrines of hell and the Trinity, which he found unreasonable. Influenced by Adventists, who assured him there is no eternal punishment and who focused on the return of Christ, he formed his own Bible study and began to develop his unique theology.

In 1879, Russell began publishing his own magazine, eventually known as *The Watchtower*, predicting that the battle of Armageddon would take place in 1914, at which time Jehovah would destroy all earthly governments, end the "Gentile times," and establish His kingdom on earth. Russell believed and taught that Jesus had returned to earth invisibly in 1874.

By 1896 Russell had founded the Watch Tower Bible and Tract Society. In 1908 he moved his headquarters from Pennsylvania to Brooklyn, New York, where it remains today, along with a massive printing operation, an apartment building, offices, and a Bible school. When the First World War began in 1914, Russell claimed his prophecy of Armageddon was on the verge of being fulfilled, but he died a failed prophet two years later.

Joseph F. Rutherford, legal advisor to Russell's organization, became its new president in 1917. He set a new date of 1925 for Armageddon, but when it didn't happen, the charismatic and domineering Rutherford backed away from his prediction, claiming that his followers misunderstood him.

Undaunted, he changed the name of the society to the Jehovah's Witnesses, taken from Isaiah 43:10, in part to distance his followers from splinter groups forged by former, disillusioned members. He also escalated the aggressive door-to-door "preaching" that distinguishes Jehovah's Witnesses today. In fact, Jehovah's Witnesses logged more than 1.9 billion hours of "preaching" door-to-door in 2014.[2]

In an effort to rapidly increase membership, Rutherford proclaimed that only 144,000 people would make it to heaven. When Watch Tower ranks swelled beyond this number, Rutherford announced that everyone who had become a Witness before 1935 would go to heaven (the "little flock"), while everyone who joined after 1935 would be among the "great crowd" that would not go to heaven but could live in an earthly paradise after Armageddon and the Millennium.

Rutherford died in 1942. His successor, Nathan Knorr, was less flamboyant than Rutherford and changed Watch Tower policy so that all publications from that point forward were released anonymously. Under his direction, the society issued a new Armageddon dating system, teaching that Jesus had not returned invisibly in 1874, as Russell had taught, but in 1914. Further, the generation that had been alive in 1914 would not "pass away" (see Matt. 24:34) before Armageddon would occur – an "absolutely final" date of 1975. Knorr died in 1977 with the final battle yet to be waged.

Frederick Franz became the next president. While he would not permit the society to set any more dates for Armageddon, he insisted that persons alive in 1914 would witness this cataclysmic event. He died in 1992 at age 99. Successor Milton G. Henschel discarded the entire end-times scenario in favor of "new light" that made the "generation" of Matt. 24:34 apply to any generation that sees the signs of Christ's return. Don Adams heads the organization today – a society that remains prolific in its publications and aggressive in its evangelism.

The Watchtower, a semimonthly magazine that instructs the society's members in faith and practice, is published in 190 languages. *Awake!* is designed for non-members and is published in 80 languages. Each issue of these magazines has a print run of more than 42 million.[3] The society's official website may be found at jw.org.

Basic Jehovah's Witness beliefs

Jehovah's Witnesses acknowledge that Charles Taze Russell was the prime mover of the group but seek to distance themselves from claims that he founded the organization.[4] Unfortunately, Jehovah's Witnesses today still cling to Russell's main false teachings: a denial of the Trinity; a denial of the deity of Christ and His bodily resurrection; a denial of the Holy Spirit's deity and personality; a denial of hell as a place of everlasting punishment; and more.

Here is a glimpse of several key Jehovah's Witnesses doctrines:

God's name is Jehovah; He is not triune. No other names must be used to depict the one true and living God. Jehovah is a "spirit being," invisible and eternal, but He has a spiritual body and is not omnipresent.[5] Neither Jesus nor the Holy Spirit is God; the Trinity is strenuously denied.

Jesus is Jehovah's first created being. Jesus had three periods of existence. In his pre-human existence he was called "God's only begotten Son" because Jehovah created him. Jesus then created all other things. He also had the personal name Michael the Archangel. The second stage of Jesus' life was on earth as Jehovah transferred Jesus' life from heaven to the womb of Mary. Jehovah's Witnesses are adamant that this was not an incarnation. Jesus became Messiah at his baptism, was executed on a torture stake, and his humanity was annihilated. He then began the third stage of his life, being raised an immortal spirit who returned to heaven once again as Michael the Archangel. He returned invisibly to earth, but now rules from heaven, and "very soon now, he will manifest his rulership over our troubled earth."[6]

Jesus is not God. Jehovah's Witnesses teach a type of polytheism with a doctrine of "two gods." They say Jehovah is Almighty God who created Jesus, and Jesus is mighty god who created everything else. This is simply a modern version of an ancient heresy. Arius, a pastor's assistant in Alexandria, Egypt, taught that Christ was a created being. He captured a strong following, which necessitated the Council of Nicea in A.D. 325.

Jesus rose spiritually, not physically, from the dead. Jehovah's Witnesses claim that Christ was raised from the dead as a spirit who only appeared to have a body. What the disciples saw three days after Christ's death was Jesus' "re-created body." Because in Watchtower reasoning the body and soul of an individual become extinct at death, God must re-create the "life pattern" of a person, and He does so by retrieving the life pattern from His memory.

The "holy spirit" is not God. Jehovah's Witnesses teach that the spirit is an "invisible act or force" that Jehovah uses to inspire His servants to accomplish His will. Put simply, the "holy spirit" is like electricity, according to Watch Tower reasoning.

Christ's death did not provide full atonement. Jehovah's Witnesses teach that Jesus was a "ransom to God for Adam's sin." By this, they mean that Jesus (Michael the Archangel in human form) was a fair exchange for Adam's sin. As such, he made it possible for all people to be saved by obedience to Jehovah. Christ died on a torture stake, not a cross. After lying in death for parts of three days, Jesus was re-created by Jehovah as a mighty spirit person.

Salvation is by faith and obedience. Requirements for salvation are "exercising faith in Jesus' ransom sacrifice," baptism by immersion, active association with the Watch Tower society, righteous conduct, and absolute loyalty to Jehovah. There is no assurance of salvation, only hope for a resurrection.

There are two classes of saved people. Only 144,000, known as the "Anointed Class," go to heaven at death to rule with Jesus. Most Jehovah's Witnesses hope to be among the "other sheep" or "great crowd" that do not go to heaven but live forever in paradise on earth after Armageddon and the Millennium.

Hell is mankind's common grave. The body and soul sleep at death, say Jehovah's Witnesses. When Jehovah raises them from the dead one day, righteous Witnesses populate paradise on earth (the 144,000 "Anointed Class" are the only people in heaven). Apparently, the wicked have a second chance for life, but if they don't measure up, they are annihilated, ceasing to exist forever. Jehovah's Witnesses deny the biblical teaching that hell is a place of conscious, everlasting separation from God.

THINK *Questions for personal or group study*

What are the primary differences between the beliefs of Jehovah's Witnesses and the doctrines of historical Christianity?

Why do you think someone like Charles Taze Russell, who studied the Bible, abandoned so many of the Scripture's core doctrines?

How does the Jesus of the Watch Tower differ from the Jesus of the Bible?

In what ways is the JW belief in soul sleep contrary to the teachings of both the Old and New Testaments? What did Jesus teach about life after death?

Visit the Jehovah's Witnesses official website (jw.org) and search for articles about the "cross" and the "torture stake." Why do JWs deny that Jesus died on a cross? How would you respond?

SHARE *Talking points for discussing the Watch Tower*

Charles Taze Russell denied many key biblical doctrines, including the Trinity, the deity of Christ, His death on the cross, and His physical resurrection. While distancing themselves from Russell, Jehovah's Witnesses today embrace most of his teachings.

Jehovah's Witnesses teach a type of polytheism with a doctrine of "two gods." They say Jehovah is Almighty God who created Jesus, and Jesus is mighty god who created everything else.

The Watch Tower teaches that Christ died on a torture stake, not a cross, and was raised from the dead as a spirit who only appeared to have a body.

Salvation in JW theology is a combination of faith and works, and there is no assurance of everlasting life.

Jehovah's Witnesses teach that the souls of departed humans sleep in the grave ("soul sleep") until the resurrection. After final judgment, non-JWs are cast into hell and annihilated.

DIVE *Go deeper in your study with these resources*

Jehovah's Witnesses Answered Verse by Verse by David A. Reed

Apocalypse Delayed: The Story of Jehovah's Witnesses, Third Edition by M. James Penton

30
COMPARING CHRISTIANITY AND THE JEHOVAH'S WITNESSES

The following table compares key Christian doctrines with those of the Watch Tower Bible and Tract Society. The source of authority for Christians is the Bible. Jehovah's Witness doctrines come from a Watch Tower version of the Bible called the New World Translation of the Holy Scriptures, as well as from various JW publications, cited below rather than in the end notes.

What the Bible says about the Bible:	What Jehovah's Witnesses say about the Bible:
The Bible is the inerrant, infallible, inspired Word of God, and is His sole written authority for all people (2 Tim. 3:16-17; 2 Peter 1:20-21).	The New World Translation of the Holy Scriptures is the official version for Jehovah's Witnesses. It essentially strips out key doctrines such as the deity of Christ. The Bible is authoritative only when interpreted by the Watch Tower Bible and Tract Society, because only the Watch Tower Society receives divine illumination as to its true meaning. During the era of founder Charles Taze Russell, it was stated that his *Studies in the Scriptures* were necessary to understand the Bible accurately: "They are not mere comments on the Bible, but they are practically the Bible itself ... if anyone lays the 'Scripture Studies' aside ... and ignores them and goes to the Bible alone, though he has understood his Bible for ten years, our experience shows that within two years he goes into darkness" (*The Watchtower*, Sept. 15, 1920).

What the Bible says about God:	What Jehovah's Witnesses say about God:
There is one true and living God, who exists as three distinct, co-equal, co-eternal persons: Father, Son, and Holy Spirit (Deut. 6:4; John 10:30; Acts 5:3-4; 2 Cor. 13:13; 1 Peter 1:2). The Father, Son, and Holy Spirit are described as deity using similar terms: Omniscient (Matt. 9:4; Rom. 11:33; 1 Cor. 2:10); God (John 10:30; Acts 5:3-4; 1 Peter 1:2); Lord (Luke 2:11; Rom. 10:12; 2 Cor. 3:17); almighty (Gen. 17:1; Rom. 15:19; Rev. 1:8); truth (John 7:28; 1 John 5:6; Rev. 3:7); eternal (Ps. 90:2; Micah 5:2; Heb. 9:14); and powerful (Jer. 32:17; Matt. 28:18; Luke 1:35; Rom. 15:19; Heb. 1:3; 1 Peter 1:5).	The Christian God is, in fact, the devil, according to Charles Taze Russell: "The clergy's God is plainly not Jehovah but the ancient deity, hoary with the iniquity of the ages – Baal, the Devil Himself" (*Studies in the Scriptures*, Vol. 7, 410). "Jehovah" is the only name by which God rightly may be called. "… the Bible plainly states that in his prehuman existence, Jesus was a created spirit being, just as angels were spirit beings created by God…. The fact is that Jesus is not God and never claimed to be" (*Should You Believe in the Trinity?* 14, 20). "… it is logical to conclude that the holy spirit is the active force of God. It is not a person but is a powerful force that God causes to emanate from himself to accomplish his holy will" (*Reasoning from the Scriptures*, 381). "Satan is the originator of the trinity doctrine" (*Let God Be True*, 101).

What the Bible says about Jesus:	What Jehovah's Witnesses say about Jesus:
He is the virgin-born Son of God, conceived by the Holy Spirit (Isa. 7:14; Matt. 1:18-23; Luke 1:35). He is eternal God, the Creator, co-equal and co-eternal with the Father and Holy Spirit (John 1:1-3, 10, 14; 10:30; Col. 1:15-20; Phil. 2:5-11; Heb. 1:1-3).	Jesus is the first creation of Jehovah; Jesus then made all "other" things (see Col. 1:16 in the New World Translation). "In other words, he was the first and direct creation of Jehovah God" (*The Truth Shall Make You Free*, 47). "... Jesus was conceived by a sinless, perfect Father, Jehovah God ... Jehovah took the perfect life of his only-begotten Son and transferred it from heaven to ... the womb of the unmarried girl Mary ... Thus God's Son was conceived or given a start as a human creature ... Jesus' birth on earth was not an incarnation" (*From Paradise Lost to Paradise Regained*, 126-27; *What Has Religion Done for Mankind?* 231). "... the true Scriptures speak of God's Son, the Word, as 'a god.' He is a 'mighty god,' but not the Almighty God, who is Jehovah" (*The Truth Shall Make You Free*, 47).
Jesus rose physically from the dead (Matt. 12:38-40; 28:5-10; Rom. 1:4; 1 Cor. 15:4-8; 1 Peter 1:18-21).	"This firstborn from the dead was raised from the grave, not a human creature, but a spirit" (*Let God Be True*, 276).
Jesus is coming back physically and visibly one day (Matt. 24:29-31; John 14:3; Titus 2:13; Rev. 19:11-14).	"Christ Jesus returns, not again as a human, but as a glorious spirit person" (*Let God Be True*, 196). "Some wrongfully expect a literal fulfillment of the symbolic statements of the Bible. Such hope to see the glorified Jesus coming seated on a white cloud where every human eye will see him ... Since no earthly men have ever seen the Father ... neither will they see the glorified Son" (*Let God Be True*, 186). "Jesus returned to earth in 1914, has expelled Satan from Heaven and is proceeding to overthrow Satan's organization, establish the Theocratic Millennial Kingdom, and vindicate the name of Jehovah God. He did not return in a physical form and is invisible as the Logos" (Walter Martin, summarizing the beliefs of Jehovah's Witnesses in *Kingdom of the Cults*, 52).

What the Bible says about the Holy Spirit:	What Jehovah's Witnesses say about the Holy Spirit:
The Holy Spirit is the third person of the triune Godhead (Matt. 3:16-17; 28:19-20).	"…The holy spirit is the invisible active force of Almighty God that moves his servants to do his will" (*Let God Be True*, 108). "The Scriptures themselves unite to show that God's holy spirit is not a person but is God's active force by which he accomplishes his purpose and executes his will" (*Aid to Bible Understanding*, 1543).
The Holy Spirit is co-equal and co-eternal with the Father and the Son (Acts 5:1-11).	"As for the 'Holy Spirit,' the so-called 'third Person of the Trinity,' we have already seen that it is not a person, but God's active force" (*The Truth That Leads to Eternal Life*, 24).
What the Bible says about the gospel of Jesus Christ:	**What Jehovah's Witnesses say about the gospel of Jesus Christ:**
Christ's death at Calvary paid our sin debt and purchased our salvation so that everlasting life is received by grace through faith in the person and work of Jesus (John 3:16; 5:24; Rom. 4:4-5; 1 Cor. 15:1-4; Eph. 2:8-9; Titus 3:5-7).	"The atonement is a ransom paid to Jehovah God by Christ Jesus and is applicable to all who accept it in righteousness. In brief, the death of Jesus removed the effects of Adam's sin on his offspring and laid the foundation of the New World of righteousness including the Millennium of Christ's reign" (Walter Martin, *Kingdom of the Cults*, 52). "Those people of good will today who avail themselves of the provision and who steadfastly abide in this confidence will find Christ Jesus to be their 'everlasting Father'" (*Let God Be True*, 121).
Believers are eternally secure based on the finished work of Christ at Calvary and the faithfulness of God (John 5:24; 10:27-30; Rom. 8:28-39; Heb. 7:25; 10:14; 1 Peter 1:1-5).	"We have learned that a person could fall away and be judged unfavorably either now or at Armageddon, or during the thousand years of Christ's reign, or at the end of the final test … into everlasting destruction" (*From Paradise Lost to Paradise Regained*, 241).

All who receive Christ by faith enter immediately and everlastingly into Christ's kingdom (John 1:12; 3:16; 5:24; Rom. 10:9-10, 13).	"Who and how many are able to enter in (the Kingdom)? The Revelation limits to 144,000 the number that become a part of the Kingdom and stand on heavenly Mount Zion" (*Let God Be True*, 136).
What the Bible says about life after death:	**What Jehovah's Witnesses say about life after death:**
At death, man's eternal destiny is fixed in one of two places: heaven or hell (Luke 16:19-31; John 5:28-29; 2 Cor. 5:6-8; Heb. 9:27; Rev. 20:11-15).	"… the claim of religionists that man has an immortal soul and therefore differs from the beast is not Scriptural" (*Let God Be True*, 68).
Hell is a place of everlasting conscious existence, where the unbeliever is forever separated from God (Matt. 25:46; Rev. 14:9-11; 20:10).	"Who is responsible for this God-defaming doctrine of a hell of torment? The promulgator of it is Satan himself. His purpose in introducing it has been to frighten the people away from studying the Bible and to make them hate God" (*Let God Be True*, 98). "Hell is mankind's common grave" (Jehovah's Witnesses official website). "The doctrine of a burning hell where the wicked are tortured eternally after death cannot be true, mainly for four reasons: (1) Because it is wholly unscriptural; (2) it is unreasonable; (3) it is contrary to God's love; and (4) it is repugnant to justice" (*Let God Be True*, 99). "Would a loving God really torment people forever? … The wicked, of course, are not literally tormented because, as we have seen, when a person is dead he is completely out of existence…. And it is also a lie, which the Devil spread, that the souls of the wicked are tormented …" (*You Can Live Forever in Paradise on Earth*, 81, 88-89).

All believers have God's promise of a home in heaven, will go there instantly upon physical death, and will return with Christ to earth one day (John 14:1-3; 2 Cor. 5:8; Rev. 19:11-16).	Only 144,000 Jehovah's Witnesses, chosen by Jehovah, will be in heaven. The remaining faithful Witnesses, after an indefinite length of time in a state of soul sleep, are raised to populate Paradise Earth. "So this 'congregation of God' is made up of all Christians on earth who have the hope of heavenly life. In all, only 144,000 persons finally make up the 'congregation of God.' Today, only a few of these, a remnant, are still on the earth. Christians who hope to live forever on earth look for spiritual guidance from members of this 'congregation of the living God'" (*You Can Live Forever in Paradise on Earth*, 125-26).
There is no opportunity for salvation beyond the grave (Luke 16:19-31; Heb. 9:27).	"Many millions that have lived in centuries past and who were not Jehovah's Witnesses will come back in a resurrection and have an opportunity for life. Many now living may yet take a stand for truth and righteousness before the 'great tribulation,' and they will gain salvation" (Jehovah's Witnesses official website).

THINK *Questions for personal or group study*

Why do you think Jehovah's Witnesses have their own version of the Bible, the New World Translation of the Holy Scriptures? Why is there so little information available about the translators of this version?

What other religious organizations deny the deity of Christ? The Trinity? The deity and personhood of the Holy Spirit?

In what three ways does 2 Cor. 11:4 help us identify Charles Taze Russell as a false prophet?

What's the rationale behind the JW teaching that only 144,000 make up the "congregation of God?"

How do JWs explain their conviction that unbelievers are annihilated rather separated eternally from God in hell?

SHARE *Talking points for discussing Christianity and the Jehovah's Witnesses*

The New World Translation of the Holy Scriptures is the official version of the Bible for Jehovah's Witnesses. It essentially strips out key Christian doctrines such as the deity of Christ.

Christians embrace a triune God while Jehovah's Witnesses argue against the deity of Jesus, as well as the personhood and deity of the Holy Spirit. JWs' rejection of Christ's deity is a modern version of the ancient Arian heresy.

The Bible assures Christians of their everlasting security in Jesus, while the Watch Tower warns that Jehovah's Witnesses may fall away and be lost to "everlasting destruction."

Christianity teaches that a person's eternal destiny is fixed at death, while Jehovah's Witnesses contend that millions of people are given a second chance after the resurrection.

The Bible speaks of hell as a place of everlasting conscious existence apart from Jesus. The Watch Tower, in contrast, argues that people cast into hell (*gehenna*) cease to exist.

DIVE *Go deeper in your study with these resources*

The 10 Most Important Things You Can Say to a Jehovah's Witness by Ron Rhodes

Reasoning from the Scriptures with the Jehovah's Witnesses by Ron Rhodes

31
DID JESUS DIE ON A TORTURE STAKE?

Jehovah's Witnesses deny the deity of Christ and His bodily resurrection. These unbiblical views are nothing new; the apostles wrestled with them in the days following the ascension of Jesus, and the church invested much of the fourth century in the Arian controversy, which challenged the Trinitarian view of God.

But one of the more curious doctrines of the Watch Tower is the view that Jesus died, not on a cross, but on a "torture stake."

According to Watch Tower publications, "no biblical evidence even intimates that Jesus died on a cross.... Jesus most likely was executed on an upright stake without any crossbeam."[1]

Jehovah's Witnesses (JWs) argue that the Greek word for cross – *stauros* – in classical Greek means an upright stake. Further, they teach that the cross is a pagan religious symbol adopted in the early centuries of the church after Satan took control of "Christendom."

Therefore, JWs insist that their members reject the notion of Jesus' death on a cross. They should not wear crosses as jewelry or display the symbols in their homes or places of worship.

Say what?

In response, let's begin with the word *stauros*. Robert Bowman, in *Understanding Jehovah's Witnesses,* notes that *stauros* as a wooden structure represents shapes "similar to the Greek letter tau (T) and the plus sign (+), occasionally using two diagonal beams (X), as well as (infrequently) a simple upright stake with no crosspiece. To argue that only the last-named form was used ... is contradictory to the actual historical facts and is based on a naïve restriction of the term to its simplest meaning."[2]

We should invite our JW friends to consult their own New World Translation and read John 20:25, in which Thomas says, "Unless I see in his hands the print of the <u>nails</u> and stick my finger into the print of the <u>nails</u> and stick my hand into his side, I will certainly not believe."

V. False Religions, Cults, and Christian Sects

If Jesus is crucified on a stake, then a single nail is driven through both hands. But twice Thomas insists that more than one nail is used for his hands, lending support to a cross as the means of Jesus' crucifixion.

Later, when Jesus speaks of Peter's future crucifixion, he indicates that Peter's arms will be outstretched, not above his head, foretelling Peter's death on a cross (John 21:18-19).

Our younger JW friends might not be aware that until the late 1920s Watch Tower publications commonly referred to Jesus' death on the cross and featured artwork depicting it that way. That changed in the 1930s when JWs sought to distance themselves primarily from Roman Catholics, so the argument was put forth that the cross is a pagan symbol.

We also could point to the crucifixion accounts in all four Gospels, which show that Jesus is forced to follow the well-known Roman practice of carrying a heavy crosspiece to the place of execution, where it is then affixed to an upright post. But a more effective approach is to ask our JW friends why they find the cross so offensive.

The real issue

Perhaps the real reason JWs despise the cross has less to do with historical integrity and more to do with doctrinal distortion. For orthodox Christians, the cross symbolizes the finished work of Jesus, who died and rose physically from the dead to conquer sin and death for us.

JWs don't see it that way. They believe Jesus died as a "ransom sacrifice" to buy back what Adam lost: the right to perfect life on earth. Therefore, they argue, salvation is not the gift of God; it is a works-based quest for future life on earth – apart from Jesus, who reigns in heaven with the 144,000.

The apostle Paul puts it well: "For to those who are perishing the message of the cross is foolishness, but to us who are being saved it is God's power" (1 Cor. 1:18).

To lay it on the line: The cross symbolizes salvation by grace; the torture stake depicts salvation by works.

THINK *Questions for personal or group study*

What reasons do Jehovah's Witnesses offer for believing Jesus died, not on a cross, but on a torture stake? How might you respond?

How does the JW belief in a torture stake reflect the Watch Tower view of salvation?

When Jehovah's Witnesses say there is no biblical evidence that Jesus died on a cross, what passages of Scripture could you use to support the historical Christian view?

Besides the manner of Jesus' death, what other unbiblical views of Christ do Jehovah's Witnesses hold?

What questions could you ask Jehovah's Witnesses to challenge their unbiblical view of Jesus' death and resurrection?

SHARE *Talking points for discussing the Jehovah's Witness view of Jesus' death*

Jehovah's Witnesses contend that Jesus died, not on a cross, but on a "torture stake." They say the cross is a pagan symbol introduced later in church history.

However, the Bible is clear that Jesus was crucified on a *stauros*, or cross, a common form of Roman execution in His day.

Younger Jehovah's Witnesses may not know that until the late 1920s Watch Tower publications commonly referred to Jesus' death on the cross and featured artwork depicting it that way.

Perhaps the real reason JWs despise the cross is because of its true meaning. The cross symbolizes the finished work of Jesus, who died and rose physically from the dead to conquer sin and death for us.

To lay it on the line: The cross symbolizes salvation by grace; the torture stake depicts salvation by works.

DIVE *Go deeper in your study with these resources*

Understanding Jehovah's Witnesses by Robert M. Bowman, Jr.

Jehovah's Witnesses, Jesus Christ, and the Gospel of John by Robert M. Bowman, Jr.

32
IS THE HOLY SPIRIT LIKE ELECTRICITY?

A 2015 survey by LifeWay Research, as reported in *Facts & Trends* magazine, revealed that 59 percent of American evangelicals believe the Holy Spirit is a force, not a personal being.[1]

This lack of understanding of the divine and personal nature of the Spirit is more at home in counterfeit forms of Christianity like the Watch Tower Bible and Tract Society, whose adherents are known as Jehovah's Witnesses.

Our JW friends promote a "holy spirit" that is neither personal nor divine. A teaching guide called *Aid to Bible Understanding* explains, "The Scriptures themselves unite to show that God's holy spirit is not a person but is God's active force by which he accomplishes his purpose and executes his will."[2]

Some Jehovah's Witnesses liken the "holy spirit" to electricity – a powerful, unseen force under the sovereign control of Jehovah.

But is that truly the Holy Spirit of the Scriptures? Or does the Bible present a Holy Spirit who is personal, divine, co-equal, and co-eternal with the Father and the Son?

Let's explore two simple truths from Scripture.

The Spirit is divine

First, the Bible clearly establishes the deity of the Holy Spirit as the third person of the triune Godhead.

The Bible uses the words "Holy Spirit" and "God" interchangeably. We find a classic example in Acts 5, where Ananias and Sapphira sell a piece of property and bring a portion of the proceeds to the church while claiming to have contributed the full amount.

Peter rebukes Ananias for lying to the Holy Spirit (Acts 5:3) and then, in the next verse, tells Ananias he has not lied to men, but to God.

The apostle Paul uses "Holy Spirit" and "God" interchangeably as well. In

1 Cor. 3:16 he calls Christians "God's sanctuary," and then in 1 Cor. 6:19 he says our bodies are "a sanctuary of the Holy Spirit."

It is the divine Holy Spirit who inhabits the temple of believers' bodies.

In addition, the Bible ascribes the same divine attributes to the Spirit as it does to the Father and the Son. To cite just a few examples, the Holy Spirit is omnipotent (Luke 1:35); omniscient (1 Cor. 2:10-11); omnipresent (Ps. 139:7); eternal (Heb. 9:14); and sovereign (John 3:8; 1 Cor. 12:11).

The Spirit is the fullness of the Godhead acting upon humans, convicting the lost of sin, righteousness, and judgment (John 16:7-11), and guiding believers into all truth (John 16:13). He is the author of the Bible (2 Peter 1:21). The Father sent Him into the world in the Son's name (John 14:26). He dwells within believers (John 14:17), fills them (Acts 4:31), and confirms that we belong to God (Rom. 8:16).

We also might note that the Spirit demonstrates His deity by doing what only God can do. For example, He creates (Gen. 1:2; Ps. 104:30) and imparts new life (Joel 2:28; John 3:5-8; Acts 2:17).

Finally, the New Testament witnesses that the Father, Son, and Holy Spirit are equal agents in baptism (Matt. 28:19-20), salvation (Eph. 1:3-14; 2:18), the distribution of spiritual gifts (1 Cor. 12:4-6), and even a benediction (2 Cor. 13:13).

The Spirit is a person

The second scriptural truth is that the Holy Spirit is a person.

In Greek, "spirit" is a neuter noun, meaning you would expect a neuter pronoun to go with it. However, Jesus and the New Testament writers consistently call the Spirit "He" or "Him" by using a masculine pronoun.

Jesus, who never refers to the Spirit as an "it," calls the Spirit "another Counselor," with the Greek word *allos* meaning "another of the same kind." As Jesus is a divine person who comforts His followers, so is the Spirit (John 14:16).

Further, the Spirit is described in personal terms. He testifies (John 15:26); guides (John 16:13); glorifies Jesus (John 16:14); decides (Acts 15:28); prevents (Acts 16:6-7); appoints (Acts 20:28); intercedes (Rom.

8:26); speaks (John 16:13; Rev. 2:7); and is self-aware (Acts 10:19-20).

He can be blasphemed (Matt. 12:31-32); lied to (Acts 5:3-4); grieved (Eph. 4:30); and insulted (Heb. 10:29).

In short, the Holy Spirit has the same divine and personal attributes as the Father and the Son. As such, we owe Him the same honor and worship as the other members of the Trinity.

Our Jehovah's Witness friends may contend that the Bible never calls Him "God the Spirit," but that is an argument from silence, refuted convincingly by the Holy Spirit's self-revelation in the book He authored.

THINK *Questions for personal or group study*

Why do you think Jehovah's Witnesses deny the personhood and deity of the Holy Spirit?

What passages of Scripture could you share with Jehovah's Witnesses to demonstrate the personal attributes of the Spirit?

How do Jesus' teachings reveal the Spirit's divine and personal nature?

Think about the roles the Holy Spirit plays in salvation (regeneration, indwelling, sealing, gifting, etc.). How do these activities illustrate both the deity and personality of the Spirit?

What questions could you ask Jehovah's Witnesses that might get them to consider a biblical view of the Holy Spirit?

SHARE *Talking points for discussing the Jehovah's Witness view of the Holy Spirit*

Jehovah's Witnesses promote a "holy spirit" that is neither personal nor divine.

Some Jehovah's Witnesses liken the "holy spirit" to electricity – a powerful, unseen force under the sovereign control of Jehovah.

However, the Bible presents a Holy Spirit who is personal, divine, co-equal, and co-eternal with the Father and the Son.

The Bible clearly establishes the deity of the Holy Spirit as the third person of the triune Godhead.

The Holy Spirit has the same divine and personal attributes as the Father and the Son. As such, we owe Him the same honor and worship as the other members of the Trinity.

DIVE *Go deeper in your study with these resources*

Jehovah's Witnesses: What You Need to Know – Quick Reference Guide by Ron Rhodes

10 Questions & Answers on Jehovah's Witnesses by Rose Publishing

Reasoning from the Scriptures by the Watch Tower Bible and Tract Society (read this JW publication with discernment; it offers insight into how JWs defend their doctrines)

33
WHAT IS THE NEW WORLD TRANSLATION?

Jehovah's Witnesses regard the New World Translation of the Holy Scriptures (NWT) as "an accurate, easy-to-read translation of the Bible" that has been published in more than 120 languages.[1] What many don't realize is that four of the five men on the translation committee producing the complete 1961 edition had no Hebrew or Greek training whatsoever. The fifth, who claimed to know both languages, failed a simple Hebrew test while under oath in a Scottish court.

What all this means is that the Watch Tower's official version of the Bible is "an incredibly biased translation," writes Ron Rhodes in *Reasoning from the Scriptures with Jehovah's Witnesses*.[2]

British scholar H.H. Rowley calls it "a shining example of how the Bible should not be translated," classifying the text as "an insult to the Word of God."[3] Revisions in 1984 and 2013 have not improved the translation.

What's so wrong with it? In a phrase, the translation committee plainly sought to conform the text to Watch Tower theology, particularly with respect to the person and work of Christ.

A few examples should make this clear.

John 1:1
This verse in the NWT 2013 reads: "In the beginning was the Word, and the Word was with **God**, and the Word was *a god*." The Watch Tower goes to great lengths to explain why this is an accurate rendering of the Greek, citing grammatical rules and misquoting Greek scholars to support their belief that the Word is "godlike, divine, a god," but not co-equal and co-eternal with the Father.

In truth, as the late professor and dean Charles L. Feinberg noted, "I can assure you that the rendering which the Jehovah's Witnesses give John 1:1 is not held by any reputable Greek scholar."[4]

Compare the King James Version (KJV): "In the beginning was the Word, and the Word was with God, and the Word was God." The New

American Standard (NASB) and Holman Christian Standard (HCSB) versions read exactly the same.

John 8:58

The New World Translation 2013 renders this: "Jesus said to them: 'Most truly I say to you, **Before Abraham came into existence, I have been.**'" Because Jehovah's witnesses deny the deity and eternality of Jesus, their translators had to change the biblical text to match their errant doctrines.

Compare the KJV: "Jesus said to them, Verily, verily, I say unto you, Before Abraham was, I am."

Or consider the NASB: "Truly, truly, I say to you, before Abraham was born, I am." And the HCSB renders it, "I assure you: Before Abraham was, I am."

Here, Jesus harks back to Exodus 3 where God reveals Himself to Moses in the burning bush as I AM, or YHWH, a unique name Jesus applies to Himself as He speaks to the religious leaders of His day.

Acts 20:28

The NWT 2013 reads: "Pay attention to yourselves and to all the flock, among which the holy spirit has appointed you overseers, to shepherd the congregation of God, which he purchased with *the blood of his own Son.*"

Since Jehovah's Witnesses deny the deity of Christ, they cannot allow God to shed His blood to pay our sin debt.

Consider the plainer language of the KJV: "… feed the church of God, which he hath purchased with his own blood."

The NASB and HCSB both render it "His own blood."

Colossians 1:17

The NWT 2013 reads: "Also, he is before all other things and *by means of him all other things were made to exist.*"

Jehovah's Witnesses argue that Jesus is the first of Jehovah's created beings, who then created all "other" things. Again, the biblical text is bent to match JW doctrine.

The KJV reads: "And he is before all things, and by him all things consist."

The NASB reads: "He is before all things, and in Him all things hold together."

And the HCSB reads: "He is before all things, and by Him all things hold together."

No English translation distorts the true meaning of this verse like the NWT.

Hebrews 1:8

The NWT 2013 reads: "But about the Son, he says: '**God is your throne** forever and ever ...'"

So, according to Watch Tower thinking, God is the eternal throne upon which Jesus relies, not the eternal Son of God who is co-equal with the Father.

But what does God actually say? Consider the KJV: "But unto the Son he saith, Thy throne, O God, is for ever and ever ..."

The NASB and HCSB render it, "... Your throne, O God, is forever and ever ..."

We could cite many other examples – Col. 2:9 and Titus 2:13 to name two – but the point is that Scripture must dictate doctrine, not the other way around. And that is the fatal flaw of the five "scholars" who gave us what the late Bruce Metzger of Princeton Theological Seminary called "a frightful mistranslation," "erroneous," "pernicious," and "reprehensible."[5]

As Tal Davis of MarketFaith Ministries points out: "[T]he 2013 New World Translation of the Holy Scriptures, as was also seen in previous editions, is still one of the most biased, distorted, and deceptive Bible versions ever published. The NWT is an unreliable and unscholarly corruption of God's Word. It should be avoided, condemned, and exposed by all Bible loving and believing Christians."[6]

THINK *Questions for personal or group study*

Why do you think Jehovah's Witnesses have their own translation of the Bible?

Considering the key verses listed in this chapter, do you believe it's possible to build a biblically sound case against the deity of Christ using the King James Version or any widely accepted modern translation?

Look in the introductory pages of modern Bible translations and you'll find a list of translators, plus information on their translation method and purpose. What does it say about the Watch Tower organization when it declines to name the NWT "translators?"

Compare the verses listed in this chapter from the 2013 Revised NWT with the 1961 and 1984 editions. Do you think the latest revisions are an improvement? Why or why not?

Why do you suppose Jehovah's Witnesses are so determined in their version of the Bible to deny the Trinity, the deity of Christ, and the deity and personhood of the Holy Spirit?

SHARE *Talking points for discussing the New World Translation*

Jehovah's Witnesses regard the New World Translation of the Holy Scriptures as "an accurate, easy-to-read translation of the Bible."

However, four of the five men on the 1961 translation committee had no Hebrew or Greek training, and the fifth, who claimed to know both languages, failed a simple Hebrew test.

At least one scholar calls the NWT "a shining example of how the Bible should not be translated."

The NWT translation committee plainly sought to conform the text to Watch Tower theology, particularly with respect to the person and work of Christ.

The Watch Tower issued a revised translation in 2013 but it fares no better than the 1961 original or the 1984 revision.

DIVE *Go deeper in your study with these resources*

The Facts on Jehovah's Witnesses by John Ankerberg and John Weldon

Conversations with Jehovah's Witnesses by Ron Rhodes

34

SHARING YOUR FAITH WITH MORMONS AND JEHOVAH'S WITNESSES

Every Christian can successfully engage a Mormon or Jehovah's Witness at the door by following three biblical imperatives: be ready, be gracious, and be clear.

It's Saturday morning. You have a full day planned as you fix breakfast for the family. Suddenly, the doorbell rings. "I'll get it," you volunteer. As you open the door, two young men in white shirts and ties greet you. They smile, say good morning, and ask if they can talk to you about something very important.

What should you do?

- Invite them in for pancakes.
- Slam the door in their face.
- Pretend you don't speak English.
- Quote 2 John 10-11 to them.
- Step outside and engage them in a brief conversation.

The young men at your door are Mormons. They are from the Church of Jesus Christ of Latter-day Saints. Mormons, as well as Jehovah's Witnesses, often visit door to door. They are members of what may be called "cults" or counterfeit forms of Christianity, claiming to be orthodox in their faith but denying important biblical truths, especially about Jesus, the Holy Spirit, and the gospel (see 2 Cor. 11:3-4).

Three simple rules

So what should you do about your uninvited guests?

1. Be ready.

- The apostle Peter urges us to "set apart the Messiah as Lord in your hearts, and always be ready to give a defense to anyone who asks you for a reason for the hope that is in you" (1 Peter 3:15).

- Be ready with your personal testimony, a simple narrative highlighting your life before Christ, how you came to know Him, and your life since receiving Christ.

- Be ready with a basic understanding of key Christian doctrines, particularly those regarding Jesus, the Holy Spirit, and the gospel.

- Be ready with a basic understanding of the teachings of Mormons and Jehovah's Witnesses and how they differ from those of historical Christianity.

2. Be gracious.

- Consider the example of Jesus: "They were all speaking well of Him (Jesus) and were amazed by the gracious words that came from His mouth ..." (Luke 4:22).

- Consider Paul's exhortation: "Your speech should always be gracious, seasoned with salt, so that you may know how you should answer each person" (Col. 4:6).

- Be nice. Smile and say good morning. Your kindness could surprise your uninvited guests, many of whom have been the victims of verbal assaults.

- Respect their sincerity. Your guests really believe they have the truth, and they want you to have it, too.

- Thank them for coming, for sharing their views, and for listening to yours.

3. Be clear.

- Have a clear head: "Keep a clear head about everything ..." (2 Tim. 4:5).

- Have a clear conscience: "Pray for us; for we are convinced that we have a clear conscience, wanting to conduct ourselves honorably in everything" (Heb. 13:18; see also Acts 24:16; 1 Tim. 3:9; 2 Tim. 1:3; 1 Peter 3:16).

- Have a clear resolve: "Now it is clear that no one is justified before God by the law, because the righteous will live by faith" (Gal. 3:11).

- Step outside. This puts you in control of how long the conversation lasts. Make it clear you will grant your guests limited time.

- Take control. Your visitors have a well-rehearsed "sales pitch." Don't let them lead you through a series of questions you may not be prepared to answer. Instead, you might say, "I'd like to ask you a few questions."

- Define your terms. Mormons and Jehovah's Witnesses may use Christian terms like faith, salvation, Scripture, and eternal life but mean something totally different.

- Stay focused. Your questions could include: Who is Jesus, in your opinion? What did His death accomplish for you? What is mankind's biggest problem, and what's the solution? How does a person receive eternal life? Do you know for certain where you'll spend eternity? Your questions should revolve around the person and work of Christ – and you should know the biblical answers.

- Get personal. Tell your guests how you came to realize you were a sinner. Share your belief that Jesus died on the cross to pay your sin debt and rose physically from the dead. Emphasize your gratefulness to God that through Christ's finished work on the cross you have eternal life – not by your works but by His grace.

- Do not agree to let them start a "Bible study" in your home (although some well-grounded evangelicals do this as an outreach to Mormons and JWs). Instead, offer to trade a Christian booklet or New Testament for some of their literature.

Mormons and Jehovah's Witnesses are working for their salvation. A smile, a kind word, and a testimony about your personal relationship with Jesus may just surprise them and plant a seed of God's love in their minds as they leave your doorstep.

Christian apologist Gregory Koukl shares these words of encouragement, "Our job is to communicate the gospel as clearly, graciously, and persuasively as possible. God's job is to take it from there. We may plant the seeds or water the saplings, but God causes whatever increase comes from our efforts.... Sharing the gospel is our task, but it's God's problem."[1]

THINK *Questions for personal or group study*

Why do you think Mormons and Jehovah's Witnesses go door to door to share their faith? What's their objective in a first visit? Their ultimate objective?

What advantages does a Mormon or Jehovah's Witness have by coming to your home uninvited?

How can you be prepared for an unexpected encounter at your front door?

Why do you think treating Mormons and Jehovah's Witnesses with respect is important, even when they knock on your door at the worst times and may even frustrate you with their approach?

How can you take control of a visit at your front door? Why is this important?

SHARE *Talking points for discussing encounters with Mormons and Jehovah's Witnesses*

Every Christian can successfully engage a Mormon or Jehovah's Witness at the door by following three biblical imperatives: be ready, be gracious, and be clear.

In any witnessing encounter, it's vital to have a basic understanding of key Christian doctrines, particularly those regarding Jesus, the Holy Spirit, and the gospel (see 2 Cor. 11:3-4).

We should respect the sincerity of Mormons and Jehovah's Witnesses. They are seeking the truth, believe they have found it, and want us to have it, too.

It's important to take control of a conversation at your door. Stepping outside and asking good questions of your Mormon or Jehovah's Witness guests are good ways to interrupt the "sales pitch" of well-rehearsed questions and answers on their agenda.

We may not win our guests to Christ in our first encounter with them at the door, but we can share our personal testimony and leave them with some biblical truths to ponder – what Gregory Koukl refers to as putting a stone in their shoes.

DIVE *Go deeper in your study with these resources*

Tactics: A Game Plan for Discussing Your Christian Convictions by Gregory Koukl

Answering Mormons' Questions by Bill McKeever and Eric Johnson

Reasoning from the Scriptures with Mormons by Ron Rhodes

Answering Jehovah's Witnesses Subject by Subject by David A. Reed

Conversations with Jehovah's Witnesses by Ron Rhodes

V. False Religions, Cults, and Christian Sects

ROMAN CATHOLICISM

35
ROMAN CATHOLICISM: AN OVERVIEW

The Roman Catholic Church traces its beginning to the apostle Peter, claiming he is the rock upon whom Jesus built His church (Matt. 16:18). As the first pope, Peter is followed by an unbroken line of successors stretching to Pope Francis today. Non-Catholics establish the beginning of the Roman Catholic Church at A.D. 590 with Gregory I, who consolidated the power of the bishopric in Rome.

In any case, the Catholic Church is the world's largest Christian denomination, with 1.2 billion members, according to Vatican figures. The Catholic hierarchy includes cardinals and bishops and is led by the bishop of Rome, also known as the pope.

The Catholic Church teaches that it is the one true church divinely founded by Jesus Christ. In addition, it teaches that its bishops are the successors of Jesus' apostles, and that the pope, as the successor to the head of the apostles (Peter), has supreme authority over the church.

Categories of Catholics

While the Catholic Church claims to be the one true church, Catholics worldwide hold to a diversity of beliefs. Researcher Kenneth R. Samples has concluded that there are six primary categories of Roman Catholics:

Ultratraditional Catholics defend historical Catholicism and are critical of recent changes such as those coming out of Vatican II in the 1960s.

Traditional Catholics resist liberalism and modernism within the church, yet they generally accept the reforms of Vatican II.

Liberal Catholics celebrate human reason over the authority of the church; they also question the infallibility of the pope, church councils, and the Bible.

Charismatic/Evangelical Catholics emphasize the gifts of the Holy Spirit, the importance of being baptized in the Holy Spirit, and the Spirit-filled life.

Cultural Catholics are "womb-to-tomb" Catholics – born, baptized, married, and buried in the church. However, they essentially go through the motions of their faith without much regard for its meaning.

Popular folk Catholics predominate Central and South America. They combine elements of animistic or nature-culture religion with traditional medieval Catholicism.[1]

Common ground

Roman Catholics and evangelical Christians agree on a number of Christian doctrines. For example, Catholics generally defend:

- The doctrine of the Trinity – one true and living God who exists as three distinct, co-equal, co-eternal persons: Father, Son, and Holy Spirit

- The full theistic attributes of God, from His holiness and love to His jealousy and wrath

- God as creator and sustainer of the universe

- The deity of Christ

- Jesus' virgin birth and incarnation

- Jesus' sinless life, death on the cross, burial, and physical resurrection

- Jesus' ascension into heaven and His imminent return

- The doctrine of the Holy Spirit, including His deity, personality, and involvement in redemption

- Other key tenets of the Christian faith

Historically, the church has emphasized that union with the Catholic Church is essential to salvation. The Council of Trent in the 16th century affirmed a long-held belief that anyone holding to the doctrine of salvation by grace alone through faith alone is anathema. However, the Second Vatican Council in the 1960s declared that non-Catholics are "separated brethren," even though the church continues to hold to the findings of its historical councils. In other words, the church insists that Rome is the narrow way to eternal life.

It's important to caution evangelical Christians not to paint Roman Catholics as unbelievers. The Lord judges the heart, and some practicing Catholics today clearly hold to an evangelical understanding of Scripture while remaining active participants in Catholicism.

However, differences between Catholic doctrine and evangelical beliefs are profound, leading Ron Rhodes, author of *Reasoning from the Scriptures with Catholics,* to write, "If the 'gospel' of Rome is a different gospel than that of Scripture, if Mary is *not* the exalted personage Roman Catholics make her out to be, if the pope is *not* the visible representative of Christ on earth who makes 'infallible' statements on matters of faith and practice, if the doctrine of the Mass has *no biblical support whatsoever*, then those who place faith in such doctrines have a false hope for the future. They may believe they have been made right with God when they are not right at all."[2]

Divergent doctrines

Protestant theologian Harold Brown once warned that while Catholicism holds to key fundamental articles of the faith, the church "so overlays them with extraneous and sometimes false doctrines that the foundations are no longer accessible to the majority of Catholic believers."[3]

Here are some key Roman Catholic doctrines that evangelical Christians reject as inconsistent with Scripture:

The Apocrypha. While evangelicals hold to the "canon" of 66 books in the Bible, Catholics argue that the apocryphal books – seven books and four parts of other books – belong in the canon. They call them deuterocanonical – literally, "second canon." The Council of Trent (A.D. 1545-1563) canonized these books. Among other things, these books support such Catholic teachings as prayers for the dead and justification by faith plus works.

Tradition. Evangelicals believe that Scripture alone (*sola scriptura*) speaks with God's voice and is authoritative in matters of faith and practice. Roman Catholics, however, believe that both Scripture and tradition constitute the Word of God.

Papal authority and infallibility. Evangelicals believe Christ is the head of the church and that every believer is a priest. This means we may go directly to God in prayer and confess our sins without the need for a human mediator because Jesus is our mediator (1 Tim. 2:5). In addition, God has given us the Bible as His written authority.

In the Roman Catholic Church, the seat of power is the pope, "the Supreme Pontiff." As the "Vicar of Christ," he acts for and in the place of Jesus. He exercises authority over the cardinals, archbishops, and bishops. The *Catechism of the Catholic Church* tells us that the pope has "full, supreme, and universal power over the whole Church, a power which he can always exercise unhindered."[4]

In addition, Catholics believe that when the pope speaks *ex cathedra* ("from the chair" in Latin) on issues pertaining to faith and morals, he is infallible. The bishops also are infallible when they speak "with one voice" – that is, when all the bishops agree on a doctrine, so long as they are in union with the pope and their teaching is subject to his authority.

Meritorious justification. Evangelicals believe the Bible teaches salvation by grace alone through faith alone. Catholics generally deny that their church teaches a works-based salvation, but, in fact, a life of meritorious works is required to gain eternal life in Catholic theology. In other words, grace alone is not sufficient without works to yield final and full justification. Further, the Catholic Church teaches that justification may be lost through serious sins; therefore, no Catholic is certain of everlasting life.

Sacramentalism. The Bible reveals that salvation is a gift of God received by faith in Jesus Christ. The Christian partakes of baptism and the Lord's Supper as acts of obedience. Baptism by immersion publicly proclaims the believer's identification with the crucified, buried, and risen Savior. The Lord's Supper is a communal meal in which believers honor the sacrifice of Jesus and anticipate His return. These acts of obedience – often called ordinances, although some evangelicals call them sacraments or "means of grace" – have no saving value.

Roman Catholics, however, teach seven sacraments that are essential to an individual's eternal destiny: baptism, penance, the Eucharist, confirmation, matrimony, holy orders, and the anointing of the sick.

Sacraments in Roman Catholic theology do not merely symbolize grace; they are said to be containers of grace, which the participant receives as he or she partakes of the sacraments. The Council of Trent declared that a sacrament has the power "not only of signifying, but also of efficiently conveying grace."[5] The *Catechism of the Catholic Church* states plainly: "The Church affirms that for believers the sacraments of the New Covenant are necessary for salvation."[6]

The sacraments convey two kinds of grace: sanctifying grace and actual grace. Through participation in the sacraments, the Roman Catholic is infused with sanctifying grace, which makes him or her holy and acceptable to God. Actual grace is God's way of enlightening the mind and strengthening the will to do good and avoid evil; this grace becomes depleted and therefore must be replenished through the sacraments.

Understanding the Catholic view of the sacraments helps us see why the church historically has viewed salvation outside the church as impossible, although Vatican II softened this stance to some degree.

A brief summary of the sacraments:

Baptism. This is said to confer initial justification and new birth upon the participant, purifying the person from sin, making him or her a new creature, and placing sanctifying grace in his or her soul.

Penance. If someone commits a mortal sin following baptism, that person must participate in penance or else be assured of going to hell at death. The sinner must confess his or her sins to the priest, be sorry for the sins, and then carry out acts of penance as prescribed by the priest to ensure that saving grace is restored.

The Eucharist (Mass). This is the single most important Catholic sacrament because it involves the re-presenting or renewing of the sacrifice of Jesus. During Mass, the bread and wine actually become the body and blood of Jesus (transubstantiation), whose continual sacrifice is said to appease God's wrath and cover people's sins. Catholics claim that the Mass does not diminish the work of Christ on the cross but rather is the primary means of applying the benefits of His death to the faithful. The Eucharist is the primary and most sacred channel of grace to Catholics. That is why refusing to attend Mass is a mortal sin.

Confirmation. This is the second of three Sacraments of Initiation (the first being baptism and the third being communion). It is regarded as the perfection of baptism because, as the Introduction to the Rite of Confirmation states, "by the sacrament of Confirmation, [the baptized] are more perfectly bound to the Church and are enriched with a special strength of the Holy Spirit."[7] The bishop administers confirmation by laying hands on the head of the parishioner, resulting in the receiving of the Holy Spirit.

Matrimony. Through marriage, two people of different sexes receive grace to fulfill their special duties. There is a triple good attached to this sacrament: first, the begetting of children and their education to worship God; second, the faithfulness each party owes to the other; and third, the permanence of marriage, which represents the unbreakable union between Christ and His Church.

Holy orders. This involves ordination to the offices of bishop, priest, or deacon, conferring on a man the spiritual power and grace to sanctify others.

The anointing of the sick. This sacrament is intended for those who are sick or near the point of death. It is said to remove the infirmity left by sin, and it is carried out for the purpose of commending to the Lord "the faithful" who are "dangerously sick" so He can relieve them and save them.

As important as the sacraments are to Roman Catholics, it should be noted that the sevenfold sacramental system was not initiated until the 12th century and was not a permanent part of Catholicism until the Council of Florence in A.D. 1439.

Purgatory and indulgences. The Bible teaches that Christ paid our sin debt in full on the cross. There is nothing a sinner can do to be forgiven of sins except to believe on the Lord Jesus Christ, at which time that person's sins – past, present, and future – are forgiven. He or she is declared in right standing with God (justified) and granted everlasting life. Believers' sins after justification affect their fellowship with Christ and should be confessed, but justification is never revoked. Evangelicals believe that immediately upon death, the souls/spirits of Christians enter directly into the presence of God in heaven, where they await resurrection, final judgment, and glorification.

Catholic theology, in contrast, teaches that not all Christians enter heaven immediately upon death. The doctrine of purgatory became official Catholic dogma in A.D. 1438. Simply put, purgatory is a temporary place of suffering where the dead who are bound for heaven are purified from unpaid sins. The *Catechism of the Catholic Church* states that all "who die in God's grace and friendship, but still imperfectly purified, are indeed assured of their eternal salvation; but after death they undergo purification, so as to achieve the holiness necessary to enter the joy of heaven."[8]

In other words, purgatory is an intermediate state in which departed souls, bound for heaven, are purged of the stain of venial sins before receiving their final reward.

Catholics believe that the living can shorten the stay of a departed friend or relative in purgatory. Ron Rhodes writes, "You can say prayers, give alms, and perform a variety of good works. All of these are viewed as meritorious and can aid a soul in purgatory. But if you really want to help your loved one, ask the priest to say a Mass on his or her behalf. That yields big results."[9]

Catholics are taught that they may earn "indulgences" for themselves or departed loved ones to shorten the time spent in purgatory. By doing the sign of the cross, reciting the rosary in a family group, visiting a Catholic shrine, or performing other duties, a person may draw from the "treasury of the Church" – an inexhaustible fount of merit provided by Jesus, Mary, and the saints.

Incidentally, some Catholic theologians argue that unbaptized infants who die go to an eternal state known as limbo. They do not enjoy the glories of heaven because they are not baptized, but neither do they suffer the torments of hell.

The exaltation of Mary. Evangelicals hold Mary in high regard as the virgin mother of Jesus. Catholics, however, ascribe to Mary a much higher degree of admiration. She is said to have been immaculately conceived, or preserved from the stain of original sin, and therefore beyond sin altogether. She also is said to have been perpetually a virgin, meaning she never engaged in sexual relations although married to Joseph.

Other Catholic claims: Because she was sinless, Mary was taken to heaven bodily at the end of her earthly life. She has allegedly appeared to many people throughout history, including at Guadalupe, Mexico (1531); Lourdes, France (1858); and Medjugorje, Bosnia-Herzegovina (1980s). She bears numerous titles of honor that exalt her above mere humanity, including "Mother of God," "Mother of the Church," "Co-redeemer of Mankind," and "Queen of Heaven and Earth."

Evangelicals contend that the Bible offers no support for the veneration of Mary. She is a faithful servant of the Lord who humbly and obediently answers the call of God to be the vessel of His incarnation. At the same time, she acknowledges her need for a Savior (meaning she is a sinner, although Catholics assert her salvation is from original sin; see Luke 1:47); bears sons and daughters with Joseph (meaning she is not a perpetual virgin); and is nowhere in the New Testament found receiving worship, proclaiming herself a co-Redeemer, or claiming any exalted position in heaven. Mary deserves our respect and appreciation, not our worship.

THINK *Questions for personal or group study*

Why is it important to understand that all Catholics do not believe and practice exactly the same things? How do the six general types of Catholics, as depicted by Kenneth R. Samples in this chapter, vary from one another?

What Christian doctrines do evangelicals and Catholics hold in common?

If someone asked you whether you believed Roman Catholicism was a cult, how would you respond? What are the grounds for your position?

If someone is truly born again and a practicing Catholic, what are the greatest doctrinal challenges with which he or she must contend?

In your view, which Catholic doctrines are most difficult to defend biblically? Why?

SHARE *Talking points for discussing Roman Catholicism*

The Roman Catholic Church traces its beginning to the apostle Peter, claiming he is the rock upon whom Jesus built His church (Matt. 16:18).

The Catholic Church teaches that it is the one true church divinely founded by Jesus Christ. In addition, it teaches that its bishops are the successors of Jesus' apostles, and that the pope, as the successor to the head of the apostles (Peter), has supreme authority over the church.

Roman Catholics and evangelical Christians agree on a number of Christian doctrines, such as the Trinity, the full theistic attributes of God, and the virgin birth and deity of Christ.

But Catholics and evangelicals part company on many issues as well. Among these issues are: The Apocrypha, papal authority and infallibility, sacramentalism, purgatory and indulgences, and the veneration of Mary.

Another key difference deals with justification. Evangelicals believe a person is justified – declared righteous – by grace alone through faith alone in Christ, while Catholics teach a meritorious path to full justification.

DIVE *Go deeper in your study with these resources*

Catechism of the Catholic Church

Reasoning from the Scriptures with Catholics by Ron Rhodes

Talking with Catholics about the Gospel: A Guide for Evangelicals by Chris Castaldo

36
WAS SAINT PETER THE FIRST POPE?

After Simon Peter makes his famous declaration that Jesus is "the Messiah, the Son of the living God," Jesus tells the apostle, "you are Peter, and on this rock I will build My church, and the forces of Hades will not overpower it" (Matt. 16:16, 18).

Jesus further states, "I will give you the keys of the kingdom of heaven, and whatever you bind on earth is already bound in heaven, and whatever you loose on earth is already loosed in heaven" (v. 19).

Is Jesus declaring Peter the first pope and thus establishing apostolic succession? The Roman Catholic Church says yes, as the *Catechism of the Catholic Church* makes clear:

"The Lord made Simon alone, whom he named Peter, the 'rock' of His Church. He gave him the keys of his Church and instituted him the shepherd of the whole flock.... This pastoral office of Peter and the other apostles belongs to the Church's very foundation and is continued by the bishops under the primacy of the Pope.... For the Roman Pontiff, by reason of his office as Vicar of Christ, and as pastor of the entire Church has full, supreme, and universal power over the whole Church, a power which he can always exercise unhindered."[1]

Of course, not everyone agrees. Other interpreters say Jesus meant that He will build His church:

1. On Himself (He is "the rock")
2. On Peter's profession of faith, or
3. On the life and teachings of Jesus as revealed in the apostolic record

The third view has much to be commended. Christ's life and teachings are the foundation of the church. Ephesians 2:20 tells us Jesus is the cornerstone of the church, and the prophets and apostles are the foundation as the bearers of God's revealed truth preserved in the Scriptures.

As Michael F. Ross writes in *Christian Research Journal*, "Peter became 'the rock' not as an individual with an office, but as the leader of the apostolic band of men who received and recorded New Testament revelation."

Ross continues: "That he is the first among equals seems indisputable; that his is an office transferred to others is indefensible. In fact, in Matthew 18:1-6, the apostles argue over preeminence, something moot had Peter been made the first 'Pope' by Jesus. The New Testament knows no Head but Jesus Christ."[2]

We should acknowledge that Jesus, in referring to "Peter" (*petros*) and to "this rock" (*petra*), likely is speaking of the apostle in both instances, as the Catholic Church argues. However, we may appreciate Jesus' play on words as He foretells the impact of Peter's life and confession on the kingdom of God. We should not take the Lord's words beyond their intended meaning and exalt a mere man to the head of the church.

Consider also:

1. The New Testament nowhere mentions a line of apostolic succession.

2. Peter never claims to be head of the church, or even the chief among apostles. He even receives a public rebuke from the apostle Paul in Antioch (Gal. 2:11-14).

3. When Jesus gives Peter and the apostles the keys of the kingdom of heaven, He is talking symbolically about their authoritative preaching of the gospel, not of any power to forgive sins or condemn to hell. Peter understands clearly that only Jesus has authority to grant forgiveness based on His finished work on the cross (1 Peter 2:24-25).

4. "Binding and loosing" are rabbinical terms for approval or disapproval concerning the Law and the regulations of conduct, not the vested power to forgive sins.

5. Jesus tells the apostles "*whatever* you bind on earth," not "*whoever* you bind on earth" – a distinction that removes any doubt about their lack of authority to grant salvation or inflict damnation.

6. Peter shares his authority with the other apostles (John 20:23) and with the church in general (Matt. 18:18). The church, too, can bind or loose conduct and confession as it shares the gospel and engages in church discipline.

7. Peter is a married man (Matt. 8:14; 1 Cor. 9:5).

Christ is the head of the church, and the apostles and prophets are its foundation. We are to build upon that foundation, not move it perpetually into the rafters.

THINK *Questions for personal or group study*

In what ways is the Catholic understanding of Matt. 16:13-19 at odds with the life and teachings of Jesus?

What is a better understanding of "the rock" upon which Jesus builds His church than the Catholic explanation of Peter as the church's first pope?

What New Testament evidence argues against the office of pope?

How does Eph. 2:19-22 explain the relationship between Jesus, the prophets, and the apostles with respect to the church?

What potential dangers does the office of pope pose for the body of Christ?

SHARE *Talking points for discussing the role of Peter in the church*

The Catholic Church contends that Jesus declared Peter the first pope and thus established apostolic succession (see Matt. 16:13-19).

But a more biblically faithful response is that "the rock" upon which Jesus builds His church is the life of Jesus as revealed in the apostolic record.

Jesus is the cornerstone of the church, and the prophets and apostles are the foundation as the bearers of God's revealed truth preserved in the Scriptures (see Eph. 2:20).

The New Testament nowhere mentions a line of apostolic succession.

Christ is the head of the church, and the apostles and prophets are its foundation. We are to build upon that foundation, not move it perpetually into the rafters.

DIVE *Go deeper in your study with these resources*

Roman Catholics and Evangelicals: Agreements and Differences by Norman L. Geisler and Ralph E. MacKenzie

Answers to Catholic Claims: A Discussion of Biblical Authority by James R. White

The Great Gulf Between Catholicism and Christianity by Casey Smith

THE WORD OF FAITH MOVEMENT

37
THE WORD OF FAITH MOVEMENT: AN OVERVIEW

Does God want me to be rich? Can my words, spoken in faith, create reality? Are human beings little gods? Do our words and actions result in blessings or curses for future generations?

Almost without exception, leaders of today's Word of Faith movement answer these questions with a resounding, "Yes!"

While elements of the Word of Faith movement are as old as first-century false teachings, the so-called Prosperity Gospel has borrowed from more recent "mind sciences" and radical Pentecostalism to become a leading form of wayward Christianity today.

Using satellite broadcasts, the Internet, best-selling books, social media, and stadium-size venues, today's "health and wealth" preachers are convincing millions of people that material wealth and physical well-being are available through the creative power of our words.

But is the Word of Faith movement truly orthodox in its doctrine? What exactly is the Word of Faith movement? Where did it come from? Who are its leaders? What do they teach? What, if anything, is wrong with this global movement? And what should be our attitude toward money and health?

The following pages seek to answer these questions.

What is the Word of Faith movement?

Also known as the Health & Wealth Gospel and the Prosperity Gospel, the Word of Faith movement is an errant stream of Christianity that places strong emphasis on the power of our words to claim wealth and healing. Essentially, its leaders teach that God wills our prosperity and health; therefore, to be a Christian in poverty or ill health is to be outside God's will.

Prosperity preachers say that if we confess – or say out loud – that we believe, we will enjoy health and wealth. In other words, our own words have creative power. The idea of confessing that we have these blessings in spite of appearances is known as "positive confession." In a similar manner, it is because of the idea of speaking words of faith that the teaching is known as the "Word of Faith" or "Word-Faith" doctrine.

Where did the movement come from?

Some critics of Word of Faith say the movement arose out of 19th century New Thought metaphysics and mind-science cults, such as Christian Science, or even from the occult. Others argue that its roots are in Pentecostalism.

Many point to E.W. Kenyon as the father of the Word of Faith movement. Kenyon, a one-time Methodist minister who pioneered religious broadcasting through his radio program, *Kenyon's Church of the Air*, evidently drew some teachings from New Thought and the mind-science cults. He also was part of the evangelical faith-cure movement of the 19th century.

However, most consider Kenneth Hagin (1917-2003) the true father of the Word of Faith movement. Known as "Dad Hagin," he claimed visitations to heaven and hell as well as being resurrected on three separate occasions.

Hagin drew much of his theology from Kenyon. Following Hagin, or contemporary with him, are a number of 20th and 21st century Word of Faith leaders who represent diversity within the movement and who hold teachings that range from orthodox to heretical.

Who are its leaders?

Following is an abbreviated listing of popular Word of Faith leaders (some are deceased). Much of this information comes from *Christianity in Crisis 21st Century* by Hank Hanegraaff, who writes that these Word of Faith preachers hold several methods in common: (1) They work their subjects into altered states of consciousness; (2) they use peer pressure to conform followers to predictable patterns; (3) they elevate the expectations of followers with fanciful stories, undocumented reports of miracles, and occasional urban legends; and (4) they employ the power of suggestion.[1]

E.W. Kenyon

Kenyon is considered by many to be the father, or at least the grandfather, of the Word of Faith movement. Saved in a Methodist church, he later served as pastor of a Freewill Baptist congregation. A pioneer of religious broadcasting, he launched a radio program in 1931 called *Kenyon's Church of the Air.*

Among his teachings:

- "The believer is as much an incarnation as was Jesus of Nazareth."[2]
- "If Jesus' physical death could pay the penalty of sin as some contend, then why is it necessary that a Christian die? ... But we hold that the physical death of Jesus did not touch the sin issue at all."[3]

Kenneth Hagin

Also known as "Dad Hagin," he is widely recognized as the father of the modern-day Faith movement. He claims his teaching authority came from personal contacts with Jesus and alleged visits to heaven and hell as well as numerous out-of-body experiences. He claims to have died and been resurrected on three separate occasions.

Among his key teachings:

- "Man was created on terms of equality with God, and he could stand in God's presence without any consciousness of inferiority."[4]

Kenneth Copeland

A devoted student of Hagin, Copeland and his wife Gloria use television to share their false teachings with audiences around the world, teachings that include:

- "Adam, in the Garden of Eden, was God manifested in the flesh."[5]
- "God cannot do anything for you apart or separate from faith" because "faith is God's source of power."[6]
- "Satan conquered Jesus on the cross."[7]
- Jesus went to hell as an "emaciated, poured out, little wormy spirit."[8]

V. False Religions, Cults, and Christian Sects

- The apostle Paul did not receive the healing he asked for in 2 Cor. 12:8 because he asked God to heal him when in reality he could have done it himself (Gloria).[9]

Benny Hinn

Hinn claims that God instructed him to begin monthly crusades in 1990, and he has used these events, as well as books and television, to reach a worldwide audience.

Among his teachings:

- The Father, Son, and Holy Spirit each consist of body, soul, and spirit. "There's nine of them!" he proclaims.[10] (Hinn later said he regretted making the statement.)

- "That's why you never ever, ever, ever ought to say, 'I'm sick.' How can you be sick if you're the new creation? Say, 'I'm healed!' Don't say, 'I'm a sinner.' The new creature is no sinner. I'm the righteousness of God in Christ."[11]

- Hinn says he frequents the gravesites of Kathryn Kuhlman and Aimee Semple McPherson to get the "anointing" from their bones.[12]

- He has offered numerous false prophecies, including that Fidel Castro would die in the 1990s and that God would destroy the gay community in the U.S. before the year 2000.[13]

Joel Osteen

Osteen is arguably the most popular prosperity preacher on earth today. He pastors Lakewood Church in Houston, with weekly attendance reaching three times the facility's capacity of 16,800. His books, personal appearances and impressions on social media prove that his message is sought after around the globe.

Among his teachings:

- "It's not enough to simply see it by faith or in your imagination. You have to begin speaking words of faith over your life. Your words have enormous creative power. The moment you speak something out, you give birth to it. This is a spiritual principle, and it works whether what you are saying is good or bad, positive or negative."[14]

- Jesus did not finish the work of redemption on the cross. He triumphed over the demonic hordes in hell.[15]
- Generational curses and generational blessings are handed down via "the bloodline being formed in your DNA."[16]

Joyce Meyer

Best-selling author and star of radio and TV programs, Meyer enjoys a worldwide following. Among her teachings:

- "You cannot go to heaven unless you believe with all your heart that Jesus took your place in hell."[17]
- "Words are containers for power. They carry creative or destructive power.... What you say today you'll probably end up having tomorrow."[18]
- "I didn't stop sinning until I finally got it through my thick head I wasn't a sinner anymore.... I am not poor, I am not miserable, and I am not a sinner. That is a lie from the pit of hell. That is what I were and if I still was, then Jesus died in vain."[19]

Creflo Dollar

Dollar is founder and senior pastor of World Changers Church International. He denies the deity of Christ and rebukes pastors that proclaim Christ is fully God, calling them "fantasy preachers."

Among his teachings:

- "Because you came from God you are gods – you're not just human."[20]
- "Around 2003-2005, Jesus will break through the sky, and those of us who remain shall be changed and caught up to meet Him in the air."[21] [Clearly, he was wrong.]

T.D. Jakes

Bishop Jakes leads the Potter's House megachurch in Texas. His books and appearances on broadcasts influence people around the world.

Among his teachings:

- He serves in a Oneness Pentecostal network of churches, which reduces the Trinity to three "manifestations" of God and insists that a person must be baptized in the name of Jesus only.

- God "manifests himself in many different ways.... He just kept turning into stuff.... He became quail and started flying through the air.... He became water, came gushing out of a rock.... He became a tree and turned the bitter water sweet. I mean, He just kept turning into stuff! One God manifesting in a multiplicity of ways!"[22]

- "You gotta be careful what you speak to, because the power of life and death is in your tongue."[23]

Rod Parsley

Televangelist, best-selling author and founder of World Harvest Church in Ohio, Parsley teaches that God cannot do anything on earth apart from the word of man.

Specifically, he states, "Why does God say, 'Ask of me?' [Psalm 2:8]. Why does He say that? Because He can't do it on His own! He can't get what He wants on His own because He placed you in authority on this earth."[24]

Among Parsley's other teachings:

- The size of your miracle corresponds directly to the size of your donation to his ministry.[25]

- Demons, not people, are responsible for all sorts of personal problems, from headaches to financial difficulties to addiction to pornography.[26]

Frederick K.C. Price

Price leads the Crenshaw Christian Center in Los Angeles and calls himself the "chief exponent of Name It and Claim It," adding, "That's the reason why I drive a Rolls Royce – I'm following Jesus' steps."[27]

Among his teachings:

- Jesus took on the nature of Satan sometime between the Garden of Gethsemane and the cross, thus experiencing spiritual death.[28]

- Jesus "must have had a whole lot of money" since Judas Iscariot stole out of the apostles' moneybag for three years and "nobody knew."[29]

Charles Capps

Kenneth Copeland ordained Capps as a minister in the International Convention of Faith Churches and Ministers.

Among Capps' teachings:

- "This is the key to understanding the virgin birth. God's Word is full of faith and Spirit power. God spoke it. God transmitted that image to Mary. She received the image inside of her ... The embryo that was in Mary's womb was nothing more than the Word of God."[30]

- The tongue is a creative force, meaning what you speak out in faith creates reality for you; even Jesus was the product of His positive confession.[31]

Morris Cerullo

Cerullo is a Pentecostal televangelist whose ministry is based in southern California. Among other false doctrines, he teaches:

- God is about six feet tall and twice as broad as a human being.[32]

- He (Cerullo) was transported to heaven and had a face-to-face meeting with God. He also gazed into hell.[33]

- God's purpose is to "reproduce Himself." He adds, "And when we stand up here, brother, you're not looking at Morris Cerullo, you're looking at God. You're looking at Jesus."[34]

Paula White

A senior pastor in Florida, an internationally known evangelist, speaker and author, White claims a divine visitation in which God gave her a vision of millions of people to whom she would impart truth.

Among her teachings:

- "God does not want us to live in poverty or lack for he wants you to be prosperous. God wants you to have it all."[35]

- "Your words create your world.... If God can create something out of nothing, and we are created in his image, then if we can image it, or imagine it, then, so it can be for us."[36]

What does the Word of Faith movement teach?

The central teaching of the Word of Faith movement is that God wills your prosperity and health; therefore, to be a Christian in poverty or ill health is to be outside the will of God.

There is great diversity within the Word of Faith movement, but here are some of the core doctrines that most prosperity teachers embrace. The following are drawn largely, but not exclusively, from Robert M. Bowman Jr. in *The Word-Faith Controversy: Understanding the Health and Wealth Gospel.*[37]

Human beings are little gods.

Human nature consists of body, soul, and spirit, but the spirit is the real person made in God's image; therefore, human beings are exact duplicates of God, or little gods. Our problem is that we allow our bodies and souls to control our lives.

This is fundamental for Word of Faith teachers. From their perspective, we should not trust our senses when they tell us we are sick or poor, neither should we rely on reason when it tells us the Word of Faith teaching makes no sense.

In addition, prosperity preachers urge Christians to see themselves just as much "incarnations of God" as was Jesus because we have the Holy Spirit dwelling in us.

God is like us.

He is a God that possesses faith. He created the world by faith and accomplishes His will by believing things in His heart and speaking words of faith, thereby bringing things into existence. We may do the same. Incidentally, God, like us, is spirit, soul, and body.

Jesus came to restore our godhood.

When Adam fell, he forfeited his status as the god of this world by obeying Satan, who in turn gained legal dominion over this world and passed Satan's nature of death, along with sickness and poverty, down to the rest of humanity. Jesus came to create a new race of humans who, like Jesus, would be God incarnate.

Some Word of Faith teachers, like Kenneth Copeland and Charles Capps, teach that the Word that became incarnate was not the eternal Son of God but God's Word of promise that He would redeem humanity, and that this Word was "positively confessed" into personal existence through the Virgin Mary.

Jesus went to hell.

Jesus died both physically and spiritually on the cross. In dying spiritually he took on Satan's nature and went to hell, where he was "born again," rising from the dead with God's nature. In hell, not on the cross, Jesus secured our salvation. This paved the way for us to be born again and exhibit God's nature in our lives.

Faith is believing we have whatever we say.

God has faith, and we should, too. Faith is not only believing what God says but believing that we have whatever we say. Prayer is not just speaking to, or with, God. It is speaking to things and circumstances – like check books and illnesses – and commanding them to do as we say. This is the basis of positive and negative confession, the idea that what we believe and say, whether good or bad, comes to pass.

Our divine birthright is financial prosperity and good health.

Since we are divine spirits created and redeemed to rule our circumstances by speaking words of faith, we are to obtain health and wealth. Since Christ died to free us from the curse of the law, Christians need no longer accept sickness or poverty in their lives. Christians ought to live in divine health and wealth as a testimony to the power of God and as evidence that they are children of God.

What's wrong with the Word of Faith movement?

The Health & Wealth Gospel is wayward Christianity and is leading millions of people to embrace false teachings about the nature of God, the deity of Christ, and God's purpose for human beings.

Consider the following errors in the Word of Faith movement.

The Word of Faith movement abuses the Bible.

While prosperity preachers proclaim the Bible as God's Word and the source of their teaching, they consistently fail to correctly teach the word of truth (2 Tim. 2:15).

Specifically, they commit three common errors of biblical interpretation:

1. They ignore the context. A single verse, such as 3 John 2, must be read as part of the full narrative, and the full narrative must be considered in light of the intended audience and in comparison with the rest of Scripture.

We must bear in mind that the Bible originally was written to certain people at specific times. As Hank Hanegraaff often notes in his *Bible Answer Man* radio broadcasts, "The Bible was not written *to* us; it was written *for* us."

That doesn't mean the Bible is less authoritative or less relevant today. It simply means we cannot disregard the historical setting of each book. The primary audience was never intended to be 21st century Americans.

2. They rely on extra-biblical experiences to establish their interpretations of Scripture. It is not uncommon to hear leaders like Kenneth Copeland say that God spoke to them in an audible voice or appeared to them in a vision.

This is not to deny that the Lord uses dreams and visions to speak to people today. For example, many former Muslims report appearances by Jesus to them in visions, leading them to consider the Christ of the Bible rather than the "Isa" of the Qur'an. But this is not the norm.

Further, we must lay all experiences against the yardstick of Scripture. The canon is closed, and we must take pains not to add to or take away from God's Word.

As a caution, Mormonism is based largely on the alleged visions of Joseph Smith. These visions led to false doctrines concerning the nature of God, the finished work of Jesus on the cross, and the ultimate destiny of human beings.

3. They begin with doctrine rather than with the Bible. Based on "dreams," "visions," "prophecies," and other subjective experiences, they formulate new teachings that tickle the ear rather than lead to godliness (2 Tim. 4:3).

Many counterfeit forms of Christianity begin this way. Charles Taze Russell, who established a Bible study that morphed into the Watch Tower Bible and Tract Society (the Jehovah's Witnesses), rejected the

Trinity, the deity of Christ, and the doctrine of an eternal hell because he found them unreasonable. The end result is a worldwide organization that follows the teachings of the Watch Tower rather than the truth of God's Word.

The Word of Faith movement is man-centered rather than God-centered.

Some leaders go so far as to describe God as having a body similar to that of man, and conversely describe humans as "little gods."

We are exact duplicates of God, say several prosperity preachers. This deifies people and demotes God to a subservient role in which He waits for us to grant Him permission to work in the world.

The Word of Faith movement promotes a false theology of giving.

God's gifts to us – for example, His creation, grace, mercy, and eternal life – are unmerited; they cannot be bought or paid for. The Word of Faith movement, however, seeks to pursue a *quid pro quo* approach to giving; in other words, if Christians say and do certain things, God is honor-bound to grant their wishes.

The Word of Faith movement oppresses the poor and the sick.

Since prosperity preachers insist that our words of faith create wealth and healing, a lack of these blessings is due to an absence of faith. People in poverty, for example, are not where God intends them to be; their poverty is their own fault. Similarly, people who are disabled, ill, or riddled with cancer are failing to appropriate the faith that would make them well.

The Word of Faith movement denies the cost of discipleship.

The claim of some prosperity preachers that Jesus and the apostles are wealthy and never suffer illness or hardship requires them to ignore the plain teaching of Scripture. Jesus, in fact, is an itinerant teacher who places little value on an earthly home, warning those who seek to follow Him that "the Son of Man has no place to lay His head" (Matt. 8:20b).

He further tells His followers that those who cling to possessions fail to be kingdom-minded. "I assure you," He says, "it will be hard for a rich person to enter the kingdom of heaven! Again I tell you, it is easier for a camel to go through the eye of a needle than for a rich person to enter the kingdom of God" (Matt. 19:23-24).

The disciples react in amazement, and Peter responds to Jesus, "Look, we have left everything and followed you. So what will there be for us?" (Matt. 19:27) Jesus assures the apostles that when the Son of Man sits on His glorious throne, they also will sit on 12 thrones. He further promises that "everyone who has left houses, brothers or sisters, father or mother, children, or fields because of My name will receive 100 times more and will inherit eternal life" (Matt. 19:28-29).

Our Lord makes no promises of prosperity and comfort in this life. Those who claim that "100 times more" means a hundred-fold increase of material blessings on earth are guilty of taking the Savior's words out of context and twisting them to enlarge their own tents.

If the Health & Wealth Gospel is true, the apostles are miserable failures. According to biblical accounts, tradition, and church history, all of the apostles suffer martyrs' deaths with the exception of John, who is boiled in oil and, after surviving the ordeal, exiled to Patmos. This is hardly a rousing endorsement of the Prosperity Gospel.

Finally, the Bible tells us that all true followers of Jesus are to expect hardship – not wealth, health, and leisure – as a result of their faith. Writing about his "persecutions and sufferings" at Antioch, Iconium, and Lystra, Paul warns, "In fact, all those who want to live a godly life in Christ Jesus will be persecuted" (2 Tim. 3:12).

Paul writes to the Philippians that his goal is "to know Him and the power of His resurrection and *the fellowship of His sufferings*, being conformed to His death" (Phil. 3:10, emphasis added).

After being stoned, dragged outside the city of Lystra, and left for dead, Paul returns to the city, strengthening the hearts of the disciples and "encouraging them to continue in the faith, and by telling them, 'It is necessary to pass through many troubles on our way into the kingdom of God'" (Acts 14:22).

Writing to believers in the provinces of Pontus, Galatia, Cappadocia, Asia, and Bithynia, Peter reminds his readers to expect suffering for the sake of Christ. "Dear friends," he says, "when the fiery ordeal arises among you to test you, don't be surprised by it, as if something unusual were happening to you. Instead, as you share in the sufferings of the Messiah rejoice, so that you may also rejoice with great joy at the revelation of His glory. If you are ridiculed for the name of Christ, you are blessed, because the Spirit of glory and of God rests on you. None of you, however, should suffer as a murderer, a thief, an evildoer, or as a meddler. But if anyone suffers as a Christian, he should not be ashamed, but should glorify God with that name" (1 Peter 4:12-16).

Other passages of Scripture could be cited, but the point is this: Even a casual reader of the New Testament finds that suffering, persecution, and poverty are far more prevalent among believers than riches and comfort.

This is not to say wealth is evil; it is, in fact, morally neutral. However, the desire for riches is a snare that leads many believers down a path of destruction, as Paul notes: "For the love of money is a root of all kinds of evil, and by craving it, some have wandered away from the faith and pierced themselves with many pains" (1 Tim. 6:10).

What scriptural texts do Word of Faith leaders use?

Following are a few examples of Scriptures prosperity preachers use to promote their health-and-wealth gospel:

Gen. 1:26-27 – *Then God said, "Let us make man in Our image, according to Our likeness" .... So God created man in His own image; He created him in the image of God; He created them male and female.*

Some Word of Faith leaders suggest that the Hebrew word for "likeness" (*demuth*) literally means "an exact duplication in kind." In other words, God created us as "little gods."

But as Hebrew scholars R. Laird Harris, Gleason L. Archer Jr., and Bruce K. Waltke point out in the *Theological Wordbook of the Old Testament*, the word *demuth* defines and limits the other word translated as "image" (Hebrew *tselem*) to avoid the implication that man is a precise, albeit miniature, copy of God.[38]

Prov. 6:2 – *You have been trapped by the words of your lips – ensnared by the words of your mouth.*

Word of Faith leaders quote this verse to illustrate that our words have power. If we speak positively, we get positive results. But if we speak "negative confessions," we get negative results.

V. False Religions, Cults, and Christian Sects

In truth, this proverb teaches nothing of the kind. Solomon simply points out that whenever you enter into an agreement with someone, you are honor-bound to fulfill it.

In a similar manner, prosperity preachers quote Prov. 18:21 to support the notion that words create reality: *Life and death are in the power of the tongue, and those who love it will eat its fruit.*

But as Matthew Henry points out, "A man may do a great deal of good, or a great deal of hurt, both to others and to himself, according to the use he makes of his tongue."[39]

Matt. 9:29 – *Then He touched their eyes, saying, "Let it be done according to your faith!"*

Joyce Meyer, referring to this passage, remarks, "The Bible says it will be unto us as we believe. That principle works in the negative as well as the positive. We can receive by fear as well as by faith."[40]

She and other Faith teachers add that the Old Testament figure Job got what he deserved because he spoke words of fear.

But a simple reading of Matt. 9:27-31 shows that the two blind men express their faith in Jesus – not faith in their faith or faith in their healing. Jesus asks them point blank: "Do you believe that I can do this?" They reply, "Yes, Lord."

As for Job, the first two chapters of the book make it clear that Job is blameless and upright, one who fears God and shuns evil. To accuse him of suffering the loss of his family, health, and property because he spoke out "negative confessions" is to twist the Scriptures in a most horrible fashion.

Mark 11:22-23 – *Jesus replied to them, "Have faith in God. I assure you: If anyone says to this mountain, 'Be lifted up and thrown into the sea,' and does not doubt in his heart, but believes that what he says will happen, it will be done for him."*

Several Word of Faith leaders insist that a more proper translation of verse 22 is, "Have the God kind of faith," or, "Have the faith of God." They twist this verse to support their view that God has faith; further, God used "faith substance" to create the universe. "Cut God open," says Creflo Dollar, "and you'd see nothing but faith."[41]

Ultimately, this flawed view of God is intended to bring Him down to our level. If God conceives of something, like the universe, and has sufficient faith, then when He speaks, it comes to pass. The same is true of human beings, who are, the prosperity preachers tell us, "little gods."

But Greek scholars like A.T. Robertson assure us that the Faith preachers' interpretation is faulty. "It is *not* the faith that God *has*," he writes, "but the faith of which *God is the object*."[42]

A being who exercises faith is limited in knowledge and power. If God must have faith, as some prosperity preachers claim, He is therefore necessarily dependent upon something or someone outside of Himself for knowledge or power. Such a divine being is not the God of Scripture.

Rom. 4:17 – *As it is written: I have made you the father of many nations. He believed in God, who gives life to the dead and calls things into existence that do not exist.*

Joel Osteen uses this verse to support the notion that our words have creative power. Scripture tells us we are to "call the things that are not as if they already were," he says.[43] We must conceive them in our minds, believe them, and speak them out. "You've got to give life to your faith by speaking it out."[44]

Is that really what the apostle Paul means in this verse? Of course not. Abraham does not believe in himself, in his faith, or in his own power to create reality. Abraham believes in God. And it is God who gives life to the dead and calls things into existence that do not exist.

Only the sovereign Lord of the universe has the power to create reality.

Heb. 11:1, 3 (KJV) – *Now faith is the substance of things hoped for, the evidence of things not seen.... Through faith, we understand that the worlds were framed by the word of God, so that things which are seen were not made of things which do appear.*

Prosperity preachers prefer to quote these verses from the King James Version because faith is called a "substance." As Kenneth Copeland says, "Faith was the raw material substance that the Spirit of God used to form the universe."[45]

By extension, say the Faith teachers, faith is the "stuff" we can use to create reality.

V. False Religions, Cults, and Christian Sects

Not so. The Greek word translated "substance" in the KJV is more accurately rendered "assurance." The Greek word is *hupostasis* and in the context of Heb. 11:1 means "[t]he ground of confidence, assurance, guarantee or proof."[46]

It's also important to note that the writer of Hebrews emphasizes *God* as the object of our faith. Faith is not the stuff God uses to create; it is the trust we place in the Creator, who called everything into existence by His word.

"Through faith, we understand that the worlds were framed by the word of God" (v. 3).

"By faith Abel offered ..." (v. 4).

"By faith Enoch was translated [taken away] ..." (v. 5).

"By faith Noah ... prepared an ark ..." (v. 7).

"By faith Abraham ... obeyed ..." (v. 8).

The entire eleventh chapter of Hebrews is an encouragement to trust in God, who is sovereign over our circumstances. Some believers witness great works of God – the crossing of the Red Sea, the destruction of Jericho, the resurrection of the dead, and so on. Others, however, experience torture, mocking, scourging, and all manner of suffering.

"All these," says the writer of Hebrews, "were approved through their faith" (v. 39). It is not their positive or negative confessions that created their circumstances; rather, it is their unwavering faith in God that carried them through their circumstances and led the Holy Spirit to include them in the faith hall of fame.

2 Peter 1:4 – *By these [God's divine power, knowledge of Him, glory and goodness] He has given us very great and precious promises, so that through them you may share in the divine nature ...*

Kenneth Copeland explains, "Now, Peter said by exceeding great and precious promises you become partakers of the divine nature. All right, are we gods? We are a class of gods!"[47]

But this is not at all what Peter means, as the context makes clear. Verses 5-11 describe a moral transformation that Jesus produces in Christians, so that they overcome evil desires with goodness, knowledge, self-control, endurance, godliness, brotherly affection, and love.

Prosperity preachers also cite passages such as Ex. 4:16 (Moses serves as "God" to pharaoh); Exodus 21-22 (the Israelite judges are called *elohim*, or gods); John 10:31-39 (Jesus quotes Ps. 82:6, in which the judges are called gods); and 2 Cor. 4:4 (Satan is the god of this age) to bolster their claim that humans, and perhaps angelic beings, are little gods.

None of these passages ascribes deity to human beings or to Satan. Rather, they describe people or angelic beings granted limited authority for a period of time under the sovereign hand of God. Believers are "sons" of the Most High, not by nature but by adoption (Gal. 4:5-8).

3 John 2 – *Dear friend, I pray that you may prosper in every way and be in good health, just as your soul prospers.*

Word of Faith leaders say this passage proves God's desire for us to prosper financially and live out our days in complete health.

But the word "prosper" in the Greek simply means "to go well with someone," not to strike it rich. Further, John is sharing with his friend Gaius a standard form of greeting in a personal letter in antiquity.

The prosperity preachers take this verse out of context.

What should be our attitude toward wealth and health?

We should be content with what we have.

Paul experiences many hardships in his ministry – beatings, being left for dead, shipwreck, hunger, cold, imprisonment, and much more. Yet he writes that he has "learned" to be content (see Phil. 4:11-12). Further, he reminds Timothy that "godliness with contentment is great gain" (1 Tim. 6:6).

In "What is the Secret to Contentment?" John MacArthur outlines six steps to a contented life, based on the life and teaching of Paul:

1. Learn to give thanks in all things (Eph. 5:18-20; 1 Thess. 5:18).

2. Learn to rest in God's providence (Rom. 8:28; see also 1 Peter 4:12-13).

V. False Religions, Cults, and Christian Sects

3. Learn to be satisfied with little (1 Tim. 6:6-8).

4. Learn to live above life's circumstances (2 Cor. 12:9-10).

5. Learn to rely on God's power and provision (Eph. 3:16; Heb. 13:5; Phil. 4:13, 19).

6. Become preoccupied with the well-being of others (Phil. 2:3-4).[48]

We should be indifferent toward wealth.

Prosperity is neither good nor evil. But our attitude toward it reveals a great deal about us (see 1 Tim. 6:6-10, 17-19).

Agur's request of the Lord in Prov. 30:8b-9 expresses a proper attitude toward worldly gain: "Give me neither poverty nor wealth; feed me with the food I need. Otherwise, I might have too much and deny You, saying, 'Who is the Lord?' or I might have nothing and steal, profaning the name of my God."

Jesus specifically warns us against laying up treasures on earth (Matt. 6:19-21) and reminds us that we cannot be slaves to both God and money (Matt. 6:24).

We should see poverty and sickness in light of the Fall.

Sin and its consequences affect all people. Our mortal bodies are subject to the ravages of the curse. We get sick, contract diseases, suffer injuries, grow old, and ultimately die. Poverty may afflict us if we are slothful, disadvantaged, or oppressed. Jesus' story of Lazarus and the rich man tells us that the wicked sometimes prosper and the righteous sometimes suffer, but in the end God, who sees the heart, sets everything right (Luke 16:19-31).

It is important to note that God entrusts every human being with an ability to make choices for which we experience consequences. Oftentimes, these choices reflect an eternal perspective (see, for example, Matt. 19:16-22; Luke 12:16-21).

We also should remember that God sometimes uses sickness and death as acts of divine discipline (see Acts 5:1-11; 1 Cor. 11:27-32).

Signs, wonders, and miracles accompany Paul's ministry (Rom. 15:19; 2 Cor. 12:12). Yet neither he nor his associates experience health at all times. "And *never* is their sickness attributed to lack of faith, nor their recovery to great faith," writes Gordon D. Fee in *The Disease of the Health and Wealth Gospels.*[49]

For example, Epaphroditus falls ill and nearly dies, yet "God had mercy on him" (Phil. 2:27). Paul leaves Trophimus sick in Miletus (2 Tim. 4:20). When Timothy suffers frequent stomach disorders, Paul does not tell the young pastor to claim healing but to "use a little wine" (1 Tim. 5:23).

We should look ahead.

For Christians, a day is coming when God wipes every tear from our eyes. Death exists no longer. Grief, crying, and pain are gone "because the previous things have passed away" (Rev. 21:4).

A day of health and prosperity is coming for all who call upon the Lord. As adopted children of God and joint-heirs with Jesus, we are to dwell in the heavenly city that knows nothing of darkness or doom. The Father and the Lamb light the New Jerusalem with their presence, and nothing profane ever enters it.

While faithful saints on this side of heaven may endure torture, mocking, scourging, bonds, imprisonment, stoning, death by the saw and sword, destitution, affliction, mistreatment, sheepskins for clothing, living in caves and holes in the ground, they are "approved through their faith" and in heaven one day they walk the streets of gold (see Heb. 11:35-40; Rev. 21-22).

We should understand that God deals harshly with false teachers.

Prosperity preachers will give an account before God one day for the degree to which they fleeced the flock.

Jesus tells His disciples, "Much will be required of everyone who has been given much. And even more will be expected of the one who has been entrusted with more" (Luke 12:48). No doubt the Word of Faith leaders are gifted communicators with worldwide platforms to proclaim the gospel. Unfortunately, they misuse their gifts and abuse the Word of God, keeping many from the kingdom and driving believers away in despair because they lack the "faith" to see their dreams come true.

Jesus calls the scribes and Pharisees "hypocrites" and tells them, "You lock up the kingdom of heaven from people. For you don't go in, and you don't allow those entering to go in.... Snakes! Brood of vipers! How can you escape being condemned to hell?" (Matt. 23:13, 33). In a similar manner, today's prosperity preachers prevent their followers from entering the kingdom by proclaiming "another Jesus ... a different spirit ... a different gospel" (2 Cor. 11:4).

In the Sermon on the Mount, Jesus warns of false prophets who come in sheep's clothing but inwardly are ravaging wolves. "You'll recognize them by their fruit," He says; that is, their unbiblical doctrine exposes their true nature. Jesus describes their day of reckoning: "On that day many will say to Me, 'Lord, Lord, didn't we prophesy in Your name, drive out demons in Your name, and do many miracles in Your name?' Then I will announce to them, 'I never knew you! Depart from Me, you lawbreakers'" (Matt. 7:15-22).

The apostle Peter writes, "But there were also false prophets among the people, just as there will be false teachers among you. They will secretly bring in destructive heresies, even denying the Master who bought them, and will bring swift destruction on themselves. Many will follow their unrestrained way, and because of them the way of truth will be blasphemed. In their greed they will exploit you with deceptive words. Their condemnation, pronounced long ago, is not idle, and their destruction does not sleep" (2 Peter 2:1-3).

It's not too late for false prophets to repent. Meanwhile, faithful teachers are urged to remain true to the Lord. Peter exhorts elders of the Dispersion to "shepherd God's flock among you, not overseeing out of compulsion but freely, according to God's will; not for the money but eagerly; not lording it over those entrusted to you, but being examples to the flock. And when the chief Shepherd appears, you will receive the unfading crown of glory" (1 Peter 5:2-4).

Conversation starters for people caught in the Word of Faith trap

Respectfully challenge your friends in the Word of Faith movement with the following questions:

Little gods? Are you aware that many Word of Faith teachers proclaim that we are "little gods?" Do you believe the Bible teaches this? If so, in what way are you a little god? Are you equal with Jesus in divinity? Do you realize that Satan tempted Eve with the promise of becoming like God?

How much is enough? How much wealth are you entitled to as a child of God? How much is enough, and when will you know you are there? What do you think God wants you to do with your financial blessings?

Why did Jesus die? Did Jesus die because He made "negative confessions" about going to the cross? Why couldn't He defeat Satan through "positive confessions" rather than through His suffering and death? Are you aware that many Word of Faith leaders say Jesus suffered in hell for three days at the hands of Satan and his demons? How is this possible when Jesus said hell was created for Satan and demons as a place for *their* punishment, not His (Matt. 25:41)? And are you aware that Satan is not in hell yet? He will be sent there at the return of Jesus (Rev. 20:10). Today, Satan is roaming the earth, according to the apostle Peter (1 Peter 5:8).

Can God discipline us? Do you believe God has a right to discipline us for sin? If so, might that discipline include illness, or even death (see Acts 5:1-11; 1 Cor. 11:27-32)?

Does God have faith? Are you aware that prosperity preachers claim God has faith, which He uses to create reality? If God has faith, how can He be all-knowing and all-powerful, since faith implies an absence of knowledge and power?

Who creates wealth? Where do prosperity preachers get their wealth? Do they follow the same rules they impose on you? For example, has a prosperity preacher ever given away all of his or her earthly wealth in order to claim a "hundred-fold increase" from God? Then why do some of them ask you to give your last dollar to their ministry?

Whose fault is poverty and sickness? If you get sick or become poor, is it due to your lack of faith? Are you aware that many Word of Faith leaders suffer illness and disease, and all of them eventually die? Could the actions of other people make you sick or poor, even though you positively confess health and prosperity? Whose lack of faith leads to the suffering and death of children, and to the abortion of unborn babies?

Does God have a body? Did you know that many Word of Faith leaders teach that God has a physical body? Are you aware that Mormons and Jehovah's Witnesses teach the same doctrine, but the Bible does not?

What is your motive? Do you love God for who He is, or for what He can do for you? Is it possible that you embrace the Word of Faith movement because you like the idea of being healthy and prosperous, not because it's true?

What does the Bible say? How carefully have you tested the prosperity preachers' doctrine against the Bible? When they claim out-of-body experiences or personal encounters with Jesus, do you test their alleged experiences by the Word of God? If their "revelations" are contrary to the Bible, which will you believe?

THINK *Questions for personal or group study*

Why do you think the Prosperity Gospel is so popular among poor populations when it's clear that the movement's doctrines are unbiblical and its techniques don't work?

What are some common methods prosperity preachers employ to gain followers (and financial supporters)?

How do Word of Faith leaders twist the Scriptures?

Why can't God have faith?

What does the Bible teach about a proper attitude toward wealth and health?

How will God deal with those who fleece the flock rather than feed it?

What divine purposes can poverty or suffering play in the life of a Christian?

V. False Religions, Cults, and Christian Sects

The Word of Faith movement is an errant stream of Christianity that places strong emphasis on the power of our words to claim wealth and healing.

Prosperity preachers say that if we confess – or say out loud – that we believe, we will enjoy health and wealth. In other words, our own words have creative power.

Word of Faith preachers work their devotees into altered states of consciousness; use peer pressure to manipulate the masses; elevate the expectations of followers with fanciful stories; and employ the power of suggestion.

The Word of Faith movement abuses the Bible; is man-centered rather than God-centered; promotes a false theology of giving; oppresses the poor and sick; and denies the cost of discipleship.

Prosperity preachers will give an account before God one day for the degree to which they fleeced the flock.

DIVE *Go deeper in your study with these resources*

Christianity in Crisis 21st Century by Hank Hanegraaff

The Word-Faith Controversy by Robert M. Bowman Jr.

The Disease of the Health and Wealth Gospels by Gordon D. Fee

The OSTEENification of American Christianity by Hank Hanegraaff

38
DOES GOD HAVE A BODY?

Mormons teach that God the Father has a body of flesh and bones. And Jehovah's Witnesses say Jehovah has a "spiritual body" that prevents Him from being omnipresent.

While these unbiblical views from our LDS and JW friends are not surprising, it may come as a shock to hear that some leaders of the Christian Word of Faith movement hold a similar view – and quote the Bible to support it.

A case in point: Kenneth Copeland and Isaiah 40:12.

Copeland, perhaps more than any other prosperity preacher, has gone into great detail about God's alleged bodily existence.

In a letter responding to an inquiry on the subject, Copeland lists a number of God's bodily attributes, including back parts, a heart, hands, a finger, nostrils, a mouth with lips and a tongue, feet, eyes and eyelids, a voice, breath, ears, hair, head, face, arms, and loins.

Further, says Copeland, he wears clothes, eats, sits on His throne, and walks. Copeland has made the outrageous claim that God lives on a planet, of which the earth is an exact, albeit smaller, copy. Says the televangelist: Earth is "a copy of the Mother Planet."[1]

Unpacking Isaiah

From Isaiah 40:12, Copeland concludes that God is six feet two or three inches tall and weighs a little more than 200 pounds. All of this comes from the word "span" in the passage.

For context, let's quote the entire verse: "Who has measured the waters in the hollow of his hand or marked off the heavens with the span of his hand? Who has gathered the dust of the earth in a measure or weighed the mountains in a balance and the hills in scales?"

The word translated "span" is a standard of measurement based on the distance from the tip of the thumb to the tip of the little finger when the hand is stretched out, or about nine inches. Therefore, argues Copeland, since Isaiah says God has a hand-span, He must be a little over six feet tall. That's absurd.

For starters, Isaiah says God measures the waters in the hollow of His hand, or the middle of His palm. If this imagery were pressed literally, God would not be six feet tall, but gargantuan – able to hold the seas in His cupped hands.

Next, marking off the heavens by a "span" would require a God who is not slightly taller than six feet, but larger than we could comprehend.

Does Copeland really expect us to take passages literally that describe God in anthropomorphic terms? Does God literally blow smoke out of His nostrils (Ps. 18:8)? Does He have eyelids (Ps. 11:4)? Does He literally rest because He gets tired (Gen. 2:2-3)?

"A more striking set of problem passages for the view that God has a body are those that say heaven is God's 'throne' and the earth his 'footstool,'" writes Robert M. Bowman in *The Word-Faith Controversy*. "Obviously, if the earth is God's literal footstool, God is enormous! Not even the nine-hundred-feet-tall 'Jesus' that Oral Roberts claims to have seen could use the earth as a literal footstool."[2]

God's omnipresence

The claim that God has a body is incompatible with the omnipresence of God. The Bible says God is present everywhere (Ps. 139:1-10; Acts 17:28), that the universe cannot contain Him (1 Kings 8:27; Isa. 66:1; Acts 7:48-49), and that His presence fills all things (Jer. 23:23-24).

It's true that Jesus has a body, which He took on in the Incarnation. As John writes, "The Word *became* flesh" (John 1:14). Through the miracle of the virgin birth, Jesus added to His deity sinless humanity, and He demonstrated His victory over sin and death through His physical resurrection, corroborated by hundreds of eyewitnesses. But nowhere does Scripture teach that the Father or the Holy Spirit has a body.

Finally, the expression "spirit body" is a contradiction in terms. A spirit does not occupy three-dimensional space whereas a body does. A careful examination of the biblical occurrence of the word "body" will show that it is applied only to physical beings, never to spirits.

God does not have a body. Those in the Word of Faith movement – as well as in Mormonism and the Jehovah's Witnesses – who insist that He does are trying to make God more like us. Then, it's no great leap of faith to say we are in turn "little gods."

Not every teaching of the Word of Faith movement is heretical, but the idea of making God in man's image is a very bad start.

THINK *Questions for personal or group study*

If God the Father had a physical body, how would that change our understanding of the nature and attributes of God?

What are some anthropomorphic terms the biblical writers use to describe God? (Anthropomorphism is attributing human characteristics to non-human beings.) Why do you think the authors of Scripture use these terms to depict God?

Do you think Word of Faith preachers like Kenneth Copeland are deceived? Or are they knowingly deceiving others? If the latter, what seems to be the goal of their false teaching?

Jesus is the only member of the Trinity to have a physical body. How would you explain to someone when, how, and why this occurred?

What do Word of Faith preachers mean when they say human beings are "little gods?"

SHARE *Talking points for discussing the false teaching that God has a body*

Word of Faith leaders like Kenneth Copeland twist the Bible in order to teach that God has a physical body.

The biblical writers often use anthropomorphic terms to describe God, allowing us to better comprehend His divine attributes. These terms are not to be taken literally. Anthropomorphism is attributing human characteristics to non-human beings.

God is spirit and cannot be confined to a physical space; He is omnipresent, meaning always present everywhere.

Jesus is the only member of the Trinity to have a physical body. The apostle John records, "The Word became flesh," meaning that through the miracle of the virgin birth, the eternal Son of God added to His deity sinless humanity, and in so doing, secured our salvation through His finished work on the cross.

If one believes that God has a physical body, then it's no great leap to falsely conclude that people are "little gods."

DIVE *Go deeper in your study with these resources*

Strange Fire by John MacArthur

Charismatic Chaos by John MacArthur

Blessed: A History of the American Prosperity Gospel by Kate Bowler

39
WAS THAT A MIRACLE?

An elderly woman tosses aside her walker and sprints around a crowded auditorium amidst thunderous applause. Hundreds of congregants gasp as a faith healer lengthens a man's shortened leg in the name of Jesus. Throngs of worshipers fall backward, seemingly lifeless, as an evangelist breathes the Holy Spirit on them.

These are common sights on Christian television, meant to convince us that God continues to perform signs, wonders, and miracles through His anointed servants.

But are these truly miracles? Is God really at work, or is some charlatan playing on our emotions so we'll pull out our checkbooks and "release" our faith with a generous donation?

It's not always easy to tell. Thankfully, Christian apologists Norman Geisler and Frank Turek offer some good advice in their book, *I Don't Have Enough Faith to Be an Atheist.*[1] The authors remind us that miracles are possible today – God still deals in the supernatural – but it's important to separate the miraculous from a host of counterfeits.

Six categories of the unusual

Geisler and Turek say there are at least six categories of "unusual events," only one of which is a miracle. A brief summary follows.

Miracle. A miracle is an unmistakable sign from God that meets certain criteria. It must be unique, easily recognizable, and something only God can do. God alone has infinite power, supreme design and purpose, and complete moral purity.

In other words, to be miraculous, the act or event cannot be explained naturally. In addition, the act may not be performed for entertainment purposes or personal gain, but to exalt God. Further, there may be no error or immorality or it is not from God.

Examples of miracles are raising the dead, calming the stormy seas, and restoring sight to the blind. These acts are instantaneous, complete, purposeful, and moral.

Providence. God indirectly causes providential events. That is, He uses natural laws to accomplish them. These may be quite remarkable and may stimulate faith, but they are not provable as supernatural.

Examples include answered prayers for healing, deliverance from danger, and protection from natural disasters. Geisler and Turek cite the fog at Normandy in June of 1944, which shielded the Allied forces from detection by Nazi defenders.[2]

Satanic signs. "Satan can perform tricks better than the best magicians – and there are many examples of these in the Bible – but those tricks fail to meet the characteristics of a true miracle," write Geisler and Turek.[3] True miracles cause one to think more highly of God, tell the truth, and promote moral behavior. Counterfeit signs do not do this.

Paul writes that Satan masquerades as an angel of light, so we should not be surprised when his minions counterfeit the things of God (2 Cor. 11:13-14).

Psychosomatic. These are psychological cures. To be sure, mental stress often leads to physical ailments, while positive attitudes, faith, and happiness have a healing effect (see Prov. 17:22). The power of suggestion is mighty indeed, and it proves that the mind can have a limited but significant impact on the body.

Magic. We're talking slight-of-hand tricks or misleading the mind. A good magician can make you think he has sliced a person in half, and a good illusionist can cause you to believe a jumbo airliner has vanished into thin air.

In a similar fashion, some faith healers seemingly cure crooked backs and wobbly knees, but it's all for show.

Anomalies. These are unexplained freaks of nature, like the bumblebee. For years, scientists could not explain how the bumblebee flies. Its wings are too small for its body. But they later discovered that bees have a "power pack" that makes up for their small wings.

A quick review

So, what about the elderly lady who chucks her walker? Chalk that up to magic or perhaps a psychosomatic cure. Fully documented cures at faith-healing services are as rare as televangelists on food stamps.

The leg-lengthening incident? Pure slight of hand – an old faith healer's trick with willing participants.

Those slain in the Spirit? The power of suggestion – the religious equivalent of the "wave" at a football game. If you watch closely, you'll see people fall down only when those around them do the same.

True slaying in the Spirit may be found in Acts 5, when Ananias and Sapphira lie to the Holy Spirit – with fatal consequences. Today's faith healers would do well to keep that divine discipline in mind when they demean the third person of the Godhead.

THINK *Questions for personal or group study*

How can you tell whether a televangelist has truly healed a lame person? What makes "faith healings" difficult to verify?

In what ways does a genuine miracle differ from a counterfeit miracle?

Why are acts of divine providence difficult to prove as coming from God?

How does the power of suggestion play into faith healing?

Why do you think Satan is interested in the miraculous?

How can Christians maintain a high level of trust in God's ability to perform miracles while at the same time guard against charlatans?

SHARE *Talking points for discussing the miraculous*

Miracles are possible today – God still deals in the supernatural – but it's important to separate the miraculous from a host of counterfeits.

A miracle is an unmistakable sign from God. It must be unique, easily recognizable, and something only God can do. God alone has infinite power, supreme design and purpose, and complete moral purity.

God indirectly causes providential events, using natural laws to accomplish them. These may be quite remarkable and may stimulate faith, but they are not provable as supernatural.

Satan masquerades as an angel of light, so we should not be surprised when his minions counterfeit the things of God (2 Cor. 11:13-14).

Some faith healers use age-old tricks to seemingly cure crooked backs and wobbly knees, but these are not miracles.

True slaying in the Spirit is not knocking people down with your breath. It may be found in Acts 5, when Ananias and Sapphira lie to the Holy Spirit – with fatal consequences.

DIVE *Go deeper in your study with these resources*

I Don't Have Enough Faith to Be an Atheist by Norman L. Geisler and Frank Turek

Strange Fire: The Danger of Offending the Holy Spirit with Counterfeit Worship by John MacArthur

Christianity in Crisis 21st Century by Hank Hanegraaff

Miracles: What they are, why they happen, and how they can change your life by Eric Metaxas

SNAKE-HANDLING
PENTECOSTALS

40
THERE'S DEATH IN THAT BOX

When the Rev. Jamie Coots died in 2014, it made national news.

The co-star of National Geographic Channel's reality TV show, "Snake Salvation," was bitten on the hand by a rattlesnake as he led services at the Full Gospel Tabernacle in Jesus' Name in Middlesboro, Ky. He died less than two hours later after refusing medical treatment.

Coots and his followers represent a sect of Christianity that incorporates snake handling into worship, relying heavily on Mark 16:17-18 for support. The beloved pastor, having survived numerous snakebites in the past, is not the first to die in this manner since George Went Hensley introduced snake handling to Appalachian churches in 1910. Coots died the way he lived, faithful to his beliefs.

Some people classify snake handlers like Coots as cultists, but that is neither fair nor gracious. In defending the Christian faith we need to draw a distinction between *cults* and *sects*.

A cult is a religious organization whose members claim to be Christians, and who use the Bible and Christian terms, yet who deny the central beliefs of historic Christianity. More to the point, a cult is *counterfeit Christianity*.

Our Jehovah's Witness and Mormon friends, for example, belong to counterfeit Christian movements, which deny biblical doctrines that define orthodox Christianity.

Jehovah's Witnesses deny the Trinity, the deity of Christ, His atonement on the cross, His physical resurrection, and salvation by grace alone through faith alone – all non-negotiable Christian doctrines.

Mormons, too, have unbiblical views of God, teach that Jesus and Lucifer were brothers born into the spirit world through sexual relations between Elohim and a goddess wife, and argue that "as man is, God once was; as God is, man may become."[1]

Clearly, these views distinguish the Watch Tower and the LDS Church as counterfeit forms of Christianity.

V. False Religions, Cults, and Christian Sects

They will pick up snakes

Our snake-handling Pentecostal friends, however, also reject these false teachings and embrace the core doctrines of the Christian faith. Therefore, they are not members of a cult, but of a sect, which may be defined as an otherwise orthodox group having established its own identity and teachings distinct from the group to which it belongs.

Coots truly believed that Mark 16:17-18 is a command: "And these signs will accompany those who believe: In My name they will drive out demons; they will speak in new languages; they will pick up snakes; if they should drink anything deadly, it will never harm them; they will lay hands on the sick, and they will get well."

As Andrew Hamblin, 21, pastor of Tabernacle Church of God in LaFollette, Tenn., told *The Tennessean*, "To me it's a mandate. You don't have to do it to go to heaven, but you do have to believe it is the word of God to take up serpents." Hamblin begins each service with a warning: "There's death in that box," pointing to snakes in stacked wood-and-glass containers.[2]

There are sound reasons to reject the interpretation of Mark 16 that Hamblin and others embrace. First, manuscript evidence indicates that this Gospel probably did not originally include any of verses 9-20. As the HCSB Study Bible explains, "These verses do not appear in the oldest and best manuscripts of Mark's Gospel."[3] Either Mark ended his Gospel after verse 8, never wrote an intended ending, or his original ending has been lost.

A second reason to reject snake handling as normative for the church is that we see no commands for it elsewhere in Scripture, either in the Gospels or the epistles. Nor do we see it practiced in the early church.

Third, we must distinguish between what the writers of Scripture *record* and what they *command*. If this passage truly is canonical, it likely describes God's miraculous preservation of His people under extraordinary circumstances. For example, Paul is bitten by a viper, yet survives (Acts 28:3-6).

Finally, God does not instruct us to entertain death in a box. We should never tempt God or test His sovereign will. The "spiritual high" described in these worship services may be more of an adrenaline rush than "the closest thing to heaven," as Hamblin describes it.[4]

God may allow us to live to a ripe old age or take us home prematurely in divine discipline (see 1 Cor. 11:27-32). We do not need to test His sovereignty by claiming snake salvation.

Even so, we should remember that snake-handling Pentecostals are our brothers and sisters in Christ. We should love them and speak well of their passion for God, even if we do not agree with their interpretation of a disputed passage of Scripture.

THINK *Questions for personal or group study*

What do snake-handling Pentecostals say is the reason they incorporate serpents into their worship services?

Why are snake handlers on shaky biblical ground when they cite Mark 16:17-18 for support?

Are there sound biblical reasons for *not* taking up serpents? If so, what are they?

What is the difference between a "cult" and a "sect?" Why are snake-handling Pentecostals more accurately depicted as members of a sect?

How do Pentecostals explain the death of a snake-handling preacher?

SHARE *Talking points for discussing snake-handling Pentecostals*

Snake-handling Pentecostals rely heavily on Mark 16:17-18 to support their incorporation of poisonous serpents into worship services.

Those who take up serpents in worship services are better classified as members of a Christian *sect* rather than a *cult*. Unlike a cult, which is counterfeit Christianity, a sect like snake-handling Pentecostalism is an otherwise orthodox group that has established its own identity and teachings distinct from the group to which it belongs.

There are sound reasons to reject the snake handlers' interpretation of Mark 16:17-18, not least of which is the likelihood that the final 12 verses of Mark 16 are not part of the Gospel writer's original work.

We should never tempt God or test His sovereign will. The "spiritual high" described in these worship services may be more of an adrenaline rush than "the closest thing to heaven," as one preacher describes it.

We should love our snake-handling Pentecostal friends and speak well of their passion for God, even if we do not agree with their interpretation of a disputed passage of Scripture.

DIVE *Go deeper in your study with these resources*

Taking Up Serpents: Snake Handlers of Eastern Kentucky by David L. Kimbrough

VI.

OTHER APOLOGETICS TOPICS

Evangelism and the Exclusivity of Christianity

The Unseen Realm, the Afterlife, and the End of the World

Tough Questions About God

Science and Religion

Relativism and Unbelief

Homosexuality

Stewardship

EVANGELISM AND
THE EXCLUSIVITY OF
CHRISTIANITY

41

WHAT ABOUT THOSE WHO HAVEN'T HEARD?

The story is told of a Christian missionary who traveled deep into the heart of a distant land, bringing the gospel message to its inhabitants for the first time. The missionary labored for years learning the language and adapting to the culture.

At long last, he was able to clearly communicate the story of Jesus. Many of the once animistic people eagerly became Christians.

But not their chief. He listened intently and weighed the missionary's every word. Finally, he asked, "Would I go to this place called hell if I never heard about Jesus?"

"Well, no," the missionary replied.

The chief said, "Then why did you come?"

The story illustrates an issue that has perplexed us for centuries. If faith comes by hearing, as the apostle Paul makes clear (Rom. 10:17), then what about those who have never heard of Jesus?

Are they going to hell? Getting a second chance in the afterlife? Will everyone be saved in the end, anyway? Or is this an unanswerable question – perhaps even a foolish one akin to asking whether God could create a stone too heavy for Him to lift?

No doubt, some people ask the question in an effort to justify their unbelief. And for them, we may simply respond, "Well, you *have* heard of Jesus. What will you do with Him?"

Still, the question is a haunting one. And the Scriptures seem to lack a single, clear proof text that satisfies those who like their answers in 20-second sound bites or 140-character tweets. Take heart, though. There are a number of biblical truths to ponder as we share our faith with others and trust the Holy Spirit to draw them to Christ.

10 simple truths

Consider these 10 simple truths:

1. Jesus Christ is the only Savior. Jesus declares this when He says, "I am the way, the truth, and the life. No one comes to the Father except through Me" (John 14:6). Peter affirms it in Acts 4:12: "There is salvation in no one else, for there is no other name under heaven given to people by which we must be saved."

2. God loves all people and desires their salvation (John 3:16; 1 Tim. 2:4; 2 Peter 3:9).

3. God is just and will judge all people justly (Job. 34:10-12; Ps. 9:8; 98:9; Jer. 11:20; Acts 17:31; Rom. 2:5-11).

4. All people are aware of God's existence (Rom. 1:18-23). They have failed to act responsibly on what God has revealed to them, whether through the light of creation (Romans 1), the light of conscience (Romans 2), or the light of Christ (Romans 3).

5. All people are sinners and know it. God has written His law in their hearts and all people are aware that they have violated the law of God (Rom. 2:1-16). No one will be able to stand before God in judgment and claim that he or she never willfully did wrong.

6. Men and women are not sentenced to hell based upon whether they heard of Jesus. Rather, they are justly and fittingly condemned based upon the fact that they are sinners (Rom. 3:10, 23; 6:23).

7. It appears that if people respond to the light they are given, God sends them the brighter light of the gospel. Consider the Ethiopian eunuch, for example, in Acts 8:26ff, and Cornelius in Acts 10:17ff.

8. Evidently, God will judge people based on their response to the light He has given them as expressed in their deeds (Rom. 2:6-11), words (Matt. 12:36-37), and thoughts (Heb. 4:12). This does not mean good works save people, or that salvation is found in other religions; rather it means that people's response to God in faith, or lack thereof, is evident in their thoughts, words, and actions.

9. It appears there is stricter judgment for those who reject the gospel than for those who have never heard it (John 3:36; 12:48). Jesus told the Jewish leaders – who had greater degrees of knowledge of the Scriptures – they would receive "greater damnation," and He pronounced many "woes" on them (Matthew 23).

10. Christian evangelism is essential for at least three reasons: (1) God commands us to go and make disciples (Matt. 28:19-20); (2) the preaching of the gospel is the means by which people hear and are saved (Rom. 10:13-17); and (3) all people may share in the blessings of eternal life, not only beyond the grave, but now (John 10:10).

THINK *Questions for personal or group study*

In what ways has God revealed Himself to all people so that they are without excuse for rejecting Him? (See Rom. 1:18-25.)

Why do you think God has chosen not to speak more plainly in Scripture on the status of those who haven't heard of Jesus?

Who is subject to greater damnation: a person who has never heard of Jesus but rejects God's revelation in creation and conscience, or a person who has heard and understood the gospel but has chosen to reject it? Can you cite passages of Scripture to support your position?

If God loves all people and desires their salvation, why doesn't He get what He wants?

Why doesn't God just accept people who do their best according to the light they've been given?

SHARE *Talking points for discussing the destiny of those who haven't heard of Jesus*

There are a number of biblical truths to ponder as we consider the destiny of those who have never heard of Jesus.

The exclusivity of Christ is a key Christian doctrine – and a stumbling block to many. Jesus declares, "I am the way, the truth, and the life. No one comes to the Father except through Me" (John 14:6).

In the end, we know that God is just and will judge all people justly.

People aren't sentenced to hell based upon whether they heard of Jesus. Rather, they are justly and fittingly condemned based upon the fact that they are sinners (Rom. 3:10, 23; 6:23).

It appears there is stricter judgment for those who reject the gospel than for those who have never heard it (John 3:36; 12:48).

DIVE *Go deeper in your study with these resources*

What About Those Who Have Never Heard? Three Views on the Destiny of the Unevangelized edited by Gabriel Fackre, Ronald H. Nash, and John Sanders

Jesus: The Only Way to God: Must You Hear the Gospel to be Saved? by John Piper

What About Those Who Have Never Heard the Gospel? (The Christian Apologetics Program), Audio CD by Gregory P. Koukl

42

WHEN WORDS LOSE THEIR MEANING

A panda walks into a café and orders a sandwich. He eats it, then draws a gun and shoots the other patrons.

A surviving waiter, quivering as he looks up from the carnage, asks, "Why?"

Before walking out the door, the panda tosses the waiter a poorly punctuated wildlife manual and replies, "Look it up."

The waiter searches for the relevant entry and reads aloud: "Panda. Large, black-and-white bear-like mammal, native to China. Eats, shoots and leaves."

This joke serves as the namesake for Lynne Truss's best-selling book, *Eats, Shoots & Leaves: The Zero Tolerance Approach to Punctuation.*[1]

It also reminds us how easily our language may be mangled – or manipulated – so that two people using the same words can intend totally different meanings.

Consider this

This is an important truth in apologetics, where our defense of the Christian faith often focuses on the correct – that is, biblical – meaning of words.

Take, for example, the word "salvation." For historic Christianity, the term describes a personal relationship with Jesus Christ provided through His death, burial, and resurrection and received by God's grace through faith, resulting in forgiveness of sins and everlasting life.

Our Mormon friends, however, describe two types of salvation. First, there is general salvation, which essentially means resurrection and is given to nearly all people. Second, there is individual salvation, which is a level of life beyond the grave earned through works, the ultimate goal of which is godhood.

Or consider the name "Jesus." The Bible teaches that He is the eternal Son of God, co-equal and co-eternal with the Father and the Spirit; the virgin-born God-man who lived a sinless life, died on the cross for our sins, rose physically from the dead, is seated today at the Father's right hand as our Mediator and Intercessor, and is coming back one day physically and visibly in power and great glory to set things right. Because He loved us first, we love Jesus.

Well, our Muslim friends love Jesus, too. They say the Qur'an teaches that Jesus is a great prophet, a miracle worker, and a sinless messenger of Allah. But He is not the Son of God, is not divine, does not die on the cross and therefore does not rise from the dead.

Our Hindu friends love Jesus, and many accept Him as one of their gods, or even as the primary god they worship. But He is not the exclusive Son of God.

Our Mormon friends also love Jesus but believe He is the spirit brother of Lucifer and acquired deity in His pre-earthly life. His death did not pay our sin debt, for each person must pay for his or her own sins.

And our Jehovah's Witness friends love Jesus but deny His deity, death on the cross, and physical resurrection.

A stone in the shoe

The bottom line is that words have meaning. It's important for us to understand what other people mean by their words so that we may earn the right to be understood ourselves. There are three reasons to ask for definitions.

First, it shows respect. It shows we value the people with whom we are speaking, and we sincerely want to know what views they hold.

Second, asking for definitions provides clarity. If I love a Jesus who is divine and my Jehovah's Witness friend loves a Jesus who is not, then obviously we don't love the same Jesus.

Third, seeking definitions gives us an opportunity to share our faith. Once we have earned the right to be heard, we can say something like this: "May I share with you what I believe the Bible teaches about ...?"

You may not come to an agreement with your friends, but you have listened to them, clarified similarities and differences, and had an opportunity to leave a lasting impression.

In *Tactics: A Game Plan for Discussing Your Christian Convictions*, Christian apologetics instructor Gregory Koukl, writes: "All I want to do is put a stone in someone's shoe. I want to give him something worth thinking about, something he can't ignore because it continues to poke at him in a good way."[2]

A simple biblical truth – Christ's sacrificial and substitutionary death, the certainty of future resurrection and judgment, the reality of heaven and hell – may be just that tiny stone that leads unbelieving persons to deal with the uncomfortable reality of their need for Christ.

The end result may be that your friend becomes a brother or sister in Christ.

THINK *Questions for personal or group study*

Why do you think there is so much disagreement between evangelical Christians and members of other religious groups about the meaning of key words such as salvation, Jesus, and Scripture?

Why is it important in witnessing to ask our friends to define their terms?

How can we know if our understanding of biblical terms is truly faithful to Scripture? Wouldn't our Mormon and Jehovah's Witness friends make the same claim?

Which biblical words and phrases would you say are absolutely essential to a discussion with a Mormon? A Jehovah's Witness? A Muslim?

How can focusing on defining biblical terms put a "stone" in the shoe of our lost friends?

SHARE *Talking points for discussing the importance of defining our terms*

Our defense of the Christian faith requires us to pay particular attention to the biblical meaning of words.

Words have meaning, so it's important to understand what other people mean by such terms as salvation, Jesus, and Scripture.

Our Mormon, Jehovah's Witness, and Muslim friends all profess faith in Jesus but describe Him and His work on the cross in unbiblical ways.

Asking our friends to define their terms shows we value them and sincerely want to know their views. It also may earn us the right to share our beliefs.

When discussing the meaning of biblical terms, we may not end in agreement, but we have listened to our friends, clarified similarities and differences, and perhaps left a lasting impression.

DIVE *Go deeper in your study with these resources*

Tactics: A Game Plan for Discussing Your Christian Convictions by Gregory Koukl

Holman Illustrated Bible Dictionary edited by Charles W. Draper, Chad Brand, and Archie England

Expository Dictionary of Bible Words edited by Stephen D. Renn

43

WHEN A QUESTION IS BETTER THAN AN ANSWER

Has anyone asked you:

"Why are all Christians homophobes?"

"Why should I worship a God who allows children to starve?"

"If Jesus is so great, why are so many of His followers jerks?"

Tough questions, to be sure. And making matters worse is the questioner's tone, implying that he or she is not really looking for an answer.

So how should we reply?

Questioning evangelism

That's a topic Randy Newman addresses in his book, *Questioning Evangelism: Engaging People's Hearts the Way Jesus Did.*

Newman, who has served in ministry on college campuses, at the Pentagon, in churches, and in various academic settings, writes that a diverse audience requires diverse approaches. "If Jesus teaches us anything about evangelism, it's that He used a variety of methods with a variety of people," he notes.[1]

Newman says any evangelistic approach requires three skills: (1) declaring the gospel; (2) defending the gospel (Christian apologetics); and (3) dialoguing the gospel. That third skill is the focus of his book.

"Often neglected, difficult to master, but absolutely essential, this skill of giving and taking – asking questions and bouncing ideas back and forth – might be just what our postmodern audience needs," he writes. "We need all three skills if we're to be Christ's ambassadors in the twenty-first century."[2]

Reading the Gospels, we see that Jesus often responds to questions with a question of His own. His goal is to get beneath the question to the heart of the matter – whether strict legalism, as in the case of the Jewish religious leaders who chide Jesus for healing on the Sabbath, or a faulty view of Christ's divinity, as in the case of the rich young ruler.

Fight or flight

So, how might we respond to someone looking for a debate rather than a sincere answer?

One option is to walk away. "When a person's choice of words or tone of voice tells you that he or she isn't looking for an answer, it's best not to give one," says Newman.[3] At times, Jesus cuts His encounters short with hardened unbelievers. Most of the time, though, He finds a way to engage them.

Newman challenges us to ask probing questions that neither launch a red-faced debate nor confirm the questioner's suspicion that all Christians are simpletons with pat answers.

Here are a few questions we might consider asking:

Really? When someone makes a self-refuting statement such as, "All religions are true," a good response is to challenge the statement. We may follow up with questions like, "Do you think a religion that leads people to commit mass suicide is true?" The purpose of the "really" question is to help our friends discover that their statements make no sense.

Isn't it possible? If someone charges that the Bible cannot be trusted because the originals are lost, we might respond, "Isn't it possible that the copies we have are faithful to the originals?"

As Newman notes, "'Isn't is possible' may be one of the most important ways to begin a question. It helps people consider that something *might* be true so that they ultimately can accept that it *is* true."[4]

What do you think? We might ask this of a person who wonders how a loving God can send people to hell, followed by questions about what the person thinks of God, of good and evil, of justice, and of life beyond the grave.

How do you know that? A person who claims, for example, that miracles are impossible may rightfully be challenged to defend her position.

Would you like it if …? This question helps explore motives and expose agendas. For example, we might ask: "Would you like it if there were a God who knows everything about you?" Or, "Would you like it if Jesus really did perform miracles?"

Other good questions include: "What convinces you of that?" "Where have you heard that?" And, "What is the strongest case for that?"

Well-placed questions put the burden of proof on those who challenge biblical truth and, if asked respectfully, may open the door to a gospel presentation.

THINK *Questions for personal or group study*

Why do you think some unbelievers ask Christians questions they know are difficult to answer?

What made Jesus' use of questions so effective in His encounters with people?

If someone said to you in an angry tone, "All Christians are homophobes!" how might you respond?

Why is a well-placed question sometimes better than an answer?

What questions are you most afraid someone will ask about your Christian faith? What questions could you employ in your response?

SHARE *Talking points for discussing when a question is better than an answer*

Any evangelistic approach requires three skills: (1) declaring the gospel; (2) defending the gospel (Christian apologetics); and (3) dialoguing the gospel. We need all three skills if we're to be Christ's ambassadors in the 21st century.

Jesus' goal in asking questions is to get to the heart of the matter – whether strict legalism, as in the case of the Jewish religious leaders who chide Him for healing on the Sabbath, or a faulty view of Christ's divinity, as in the case of the rich young ruler.

If someone is looking for an argument rather than a sincere discussion, it's probably best to walk away.

Sincerely asking, "What do you think?" may open the door to honest discussion – and perhaps a gospel presentation.

Well-placed questions put the burden of proof on those who challenge biblical truth. If asked respectfully, these questions may open the door to a gospel presentation.

DIVE *Go deeper in your study with these resources*

Questioning Evangelism: Engaging People's Hearts the Way Jesus Did by Randy Newman

Good Leaders Ask Great Questions: Your Foundation for Successful Leadership by John C. Maxwell

The Questions Christians Hope No One Will Ask by Mark Mittelberg and Lee Strobel

What Would Jesus Ask? by Paul Welter

44
WHY MANY NON-WESTERNERS REJECT THE GOSPEL

Missionaries to Muslims often report resistance to the gospel message – not because Muslims reject Jesus as a great prophet, but because the Qur'an denies the doctrines of original sin and the atonement.

The idea of natural-born sinners runs counter to the Islamic belief that man is basically good but ignorant of Allah's will. This may be overcome by repeating the *shahada* – "There is no god but Allah; Muhammad is the Messenger of Allah" – and by embracing the five pillars of Islam.

In addition, Muslims deny Jesus' substitutionary death because they cannot believe Allah would allow his second greatest prophet to suffer shame on a Roman cross.

In other words, many Muslims reject the gospel because it does not align with their cultural perspective that stresses shame and honor rather than guilt and innocence.

So, how can Christians, who embrace the doctrines of original sin and the substitutionary death of Jesus, present the gospel cross-culturally? Is it even possible?

Shame and honor

Ronald Muller answers with a resounding yes! Muller has devoted his life to understanding and communicating the gospel to Muslims in the Middle East.

In his book, *Honor & Shame: Unlocking the Door*, Muller writes about the importance of communicating through culture. He argues that the gospel answers the questions posed by the three main types of cultures in the world.

First, there is the guilt-innocence culture primarily embraced by the West. Second is the shame-honor culture that dominates the Middle East, Northern Africa, and Asia – the so-called 10/40 window. Third comes the fear-power culture that is seen mostly in the animistic religions of Southern Africa, Latin America, and some islands in the Far East.

Because these cultures are so different, the gospel must be communicated in a way that makes sense to the lost persons who embrace them. Fortunately, the gospel applies to all three types of cultures.

Three effects of the Fall

Muller points out that the Fall affected Adam and Eve in three ways. They experienced guilt, shame, and fear – the negative side of the three cultural types that dominate the world's population today.

"Down through history and across the world, these three emotional reactions to sin became the three basic building blocks that exist in all cultures today," writes Muller. "Some cultures have more of one than another, but all three are present in all cultures today."[1]

When sharing the gospel with Westerners, the emphasis on guilt, and the promise of justification by faith in Christ, is a strong message that resonates with people immersed in a guilt-innocence culture. But the message loses impact with Muslims who hold a shame-honor worldview, or with animists who thrive in a fear-power culture.

More effective with Middle Eastern Muslims is a message about the shame that Adam and Eve experienced when they rebelled against God ("they suddenly felt shame at their nakedness," Gen. 3:7 NLT). The good news is that Jesus, through His sinless life and sacrificial death, bore Adam's shame – and ours – and restores our honor.

Animists live in fear of the unseen spiritual realm that interacts with the physical world. There is constant fear that gods, demons, ghosts, or ancestors may be displeased and cause the offender sickness, poverty, or other forms of suffering.

The message of the fear Adam and Eve felt after they rebelled strikes a chord ("So they hid from the Lord God among the trees," Gen. 3:8 NLT). However, Jesus conquered Satan, sin, and death for us. He is all-powerful over the forces in the spiritual realm and thus calms our fears.

One gospel message

So, do we need to come up with three different gospel messages, one for each type of culture? No, says Muller. There is one gospel – the good news of Jesus Christ to lost people everywhere.

At the same time, we need to communicate the gospel in a way that addresses the full spectrum of sin's consequences – guilt, shame, and fear – and explains how Jesus restores innocence, honor, and peace to the believing sinner.

Where we begin to tell the story depends on the culture in which we share it.

Christ bore, not only our sin on the cross, but also our shame and our fear. That is truly good news for lost people everywhere.

THINK *Questions for personal or group study*

Why do you think culture plays such an important role in the way a person hears the gospel?

What is a more effective way of sharing Christ with a Middle Eastern Muslim than focusing on sin and guilt?

In witnessing to friends in animistic cultures, how would you explain that Christ has overcome the fear of the unseen realm?

How does Jesus reverse three main consequences of the Fall – guilt, shame, and fear?

Why do you think we only need one gospel message for people of all cultures?

SHARE *Talking points for discussing cultural influences and the gospel*

Many Muslims reject the gospel because it does not align with their cultural perspective that stresses shame and honor rather than guilt and innocence.

There are three main types of cultures: guilt-innocence, shame-honor, and fear-power.

The Fall affected Adam and Eve in three ways. They experienced guilt, shame, and fear – the negative side of the three cultural types that dominate the world's population today.

But we don't need three different gospel messages. There is one gospel – the good news of Jesus Christ to lost people everywhere.

We should communicate the gospel in a way that addresses the full spectrum of sin's consequences – guilt, shame, and fear – and explains how Jesus restores innocence, honor, and peace to the believing sinner.

DIVE *Go deeper in your study with these resources*

Honor & Shame: Unlocking the Door by Ronald Muller

Jesus Through Middle Eastern Eyes: Cultural Studies in the Gospels by Kenneth E. Bailey

Misreading Scripture with Western Eyes: Removing Cultural Blinders to Better Understand the Bible by E. Randolph Richards and Brandon J. O'Brien

45
HOW CAN 5 BILLION PEOPLE BE WRONG?

The world's population stands at more than 7.1 billion people. According to Adherents.com, this number includes 1.5 billion Muslims, 1.1 billion nonreligious people, 900 million Hindus, nearly 400 million Buddhists, and millions of followers of other faiths.

The website also reports there are 2.1 billion "Christians," a broad category that includes Catholics and Protestants, Mormons and Jehovah's Witnesses, and so-called "nominal" Christians. If the exclusive claims of Jesus are true, and even if everyone who claims to be a Christian really is, then roughly 5 billion people still stand outside the kingdom of heaven.[1]

By all appearances, these people are sincere. They want to know the truth and believe they have found it. So, how can 5 billion people be wrong? One way to approach the question is to understand the biblical descriptions of the lost.

Eight characteristics

What, specifically, does the Bible teach about the state of those who don't know Christ? Let's look at eight ways the Word of God describes unbelievers, regardless of their religions views.

1. Natural. The apostle Paul writes that "the natural man does not welcome what comes from God's Spirit, because it is foolishness to him; he is not able to know it since it is evaluated spiritually" (1 Cor. 2:14).

Unlike the "spiritual person" who has "the mind of Christ" (v. 16), unbelievers see God's revealed truth through the lens of their fallen natures and thus declare it foolishness.

2. Blind. Paul tells the Corinthians the gospel is "veiled to those who are perishing" because "the god of this age has blinded the minds of unbelievers so they cannot see the light of the gospel of the glory of Christ" (2 Cor. 4:4).

Satan often blinds the lost with half-truths. For example, many counterfeit forms of Christianity emphasize salvation through a combination of faith and works rather than by faith alone in Christ alone.

3. Bound. Timothy, a young pastor, is urged to instruct his opponents with gentleness, trusting God to grant them repentance to know the truth. "Then they may come to their senses and escape the Devil's trap, having been captured by him to do his will" (2 Tim. 2:25-26).

4. Alienated. Unbelievers, who walk "in the futility of their thoughts" and are "darkened in their understanding," are therefore "excluded from the life of God" (Eph. 4:17-18).

Paul goes on to say that unbelievers become callous as they give themselves over to ungodly practices, a state he calls "the old man ... corrupted by deceitful desires" (v. 22).

5. Enemies. Christians should remember that we once were helpless "enemies" of God – a situation God remedied through the death of His Son (Rom. 5:6-11).

Though once "alienated and hostile in mind," believers have been reconciled to God by Christ's body through His death (Col. 1:21).

6. Condemned. God sent His Son so that the world might be saved through Him. "Anyone who believes in Him is not condemned," says Jesus, "but anyone who does not believe is already condemned, because he has not believed in the name of the One and Only Son of God" (John 3:18).

7. In darkness. Jesus sends Paul to the Gentiles "to open their eyes, that they may turn from darkness to light" (Acts 26:18).

Believers once were "darkness, but now [they are] light in the Lord" (Eph. 5:8). Christ came to rescue us from "the domain of darkness" (Col. 1:13), and He calls us "out of darkness into His marvelous light" (1 Peter 2:9).

8. Spiritually dead. Paul reminds the Ephesian believers they once were "dead in trespasses and sins" (Eph. 2:1). That is, while alive in body and soul, unbelievers are dead in their spirits – their innermost beings God created for His habitation via the indwelling Holy Spirit.

If these eight characteristics truly describe the lost, what hope exists for these 5 billion people?

First, remember that God has revealed Himself to all people in creation and conscience, meaning they have no defense on judgment day for rejecting Him (see Romans 1). What's more, God has given us His written word, the Bible – and the Word who became flesh, Jesus Christ (John 1:14).

Along with the Father and Son, the Holy Spirit does the necessary work of convincing unbelievers of their need for Christ (see John 16:7-11).

If that's the work of the triune God, what's our part? As Peter and John tell the Sanhedrin, "We are unable to stop speaking about what we have seen and heard" (Acts 4:20).

THINK *Questions for personal or group study*

Statistically, the vast majority of people in the world today believe in some deity. What right do we as Christians have to say they are wrong if they don't accept the God of the Bible?

If the world's first inhabitants worshiped God exclusively, as the Bible records, how do you think we developed such a diversity of religious beliefs?

If non-Christians truly are blinded, bound, in darkness, and spiritually dead, as the Bible teaches, what hope exists for them?

Read 2 Cor. 11:4. What are three common threads that run through many false belief systems?

Read John 16:7-11. In what three ways does the Holy Spirit convict unbelievers of their need for Christ?

SHARE *Talking points for discussing the state of the lost*

According to current statistical records, as many as 5 billion people in the world today are outside the kingdom of heaven – that is, they do not profess a personal relationship with Christ.

The Bible describes unbelievers in many ways, among them: blind, bound, condemned, and in spiritual darkness.

Those who reject Christ see God's revealed truth through the lens of their fallen natures and thus declare it foolishness.

Remember that God has revealed Himself to all people in creation and conscience, meaning they have no defense on judgment day for rejecting Him (see Romans 1).

What's more, God has given us His written word, the Bible – and the Word who became flesh, Jesus Christ (John 1:14).

DIVE *Go deeper in your study with these resources*

Eternity in Their Hearts: Startling Evidence of Belief in the One True God in Hundreds of Cultures Throughout the World by Don Richardson

Evangelism and the Sovereignty of God by J.I. Packer and Mark Dever

The Master Plan of Evangelism by Robert E. Coleman

They Can't All be Right: Do All Spiritual Paths Lead to God? by Steve Russo

THE UNSEEN REALM, THE AFTERLIFE, AND THE END OF THE WORLD

46
SHOULD YOU BELIEVE IN GHOSTS?

Ghosts are everywhere. They star in major motion pictures from *The Shining* to *Scary Movie 2*. Some ghosts are friendly (Casper) and some arc frightening (Bloody Mary).

Popular television shows like *Ghost Adventures* use the latest technologies to "prove" that spirits of the dead are all around us – and want to make their presence known.

But is this true? The short answer is no. As Christians, we must gauge all truth claims by the Bible, the ultimate and unchanging measure of reality.

Ghost stories in the Gospels

Some people argue that the apostles believed in ghosts and even thought Jesus was one when He walked toward their boat on the Sea of Galilee (Matt. 14:22-33).

Later, after Christ's resurrection, the apostles once again mistook Jesus for a ghost. He assured them that "a ghost does not have flesh and bones as you can see I have" (Luke 24:39).

Don't the beliefs of the apostles and the words of Jesus prove that ghosts are all around us?

Let's be clear on two points. First, Scripture teaches that all humans possess both physical and non-physical properties – the body and the soul/spirit, the second of which survives physical death.

Second, nowhere does the Bible support the notion that spirits of the dead (*phantasma* or *pneuma* in the Greek) are free to return to the physical realm prior to their future resurrection.

In other words, the departed are just that – departed.

Heaven or Hades

The souls of the dead either are in the presence of God in heaven or separated from Him in torment in *Hades*.

In Jesus' story of Lazarus and the rich man, the righteous beggar at death is carried by the angels to Abraham's side and is comforted there, while the unrighteous aristocrat finds himself in torment beyond the grave.

The rich man petitions Abraham to send Lazarus to warn his brothers, but Abraham makes it clear that is not permitted. "They have Moses and the prophets; they should listen to them," Abraham explains (Luke 16:29).

The apostle Paul reminds us that when Christians die, their souls/spirits go directly into the presence of God (2 Cor. 5:8).

The appearances of the righteous dead on earth are brief and rare exceptions to the rule. For example, Moses and Elijah appear briefly on the Mount of Transfiguration with Jesus and His inner circle of apostles (Matt. 17:1-9).

In the Old Testament, we read the story of Samuel, who appears on earth after his death. King Saul has gone to the witch of Endor, seeking to engage her in necromancy – communicating with the dead, a practice denounced in Scripture and banished by fiat from the land of Israel in Saul's day.

The appearance of Samuel shocks the witch as much as it surprises Saul. As Hank Hanegraaff describes it, "When the departed Samuel appeared to the living Saul, the witch of Endor immediately recognized the occasion as a non-normative act of God – a divine display of judgment rather than a haunting."[1]

In other words, God called the witch's bluff. She dabbled in deception and demonic activity to ply her trade but had no real power to bring back the spirits of the dead.

Ghost adventures

So, what are we to make of reports of modern-day hauntings?

First, understand that ghosts – the spirits of the departed – do not roam unseen among us; they are with the Lord in heaven or apart from him in *Hades*.

Second, avoid fascination with modern-day "ghost adventures." At best, they rob you of your time; at worst, they draw you into demonic deception.

While Satan has no power to raise the dead or create human flesh, he and his demons play on the field of superstition.

Third, stay armed. Paul exhorts us to put on the full armor of God so we can evade Satan's fiery darts (Eph. 6:11ff).

Finally, measure all experiences by the Scriptures, "which are able to make you wise for salvation through faith in Jesus Christ" (2 Tim. 3:15).

Who you gonna call? The Word of God is the ultimate Ghostbuster.

THINK *Questions for personal or group study*

What are the dangers for a Christian pursuing paranormal experience?

Suppose your friend tells you her deceased mother visited her in the night. What biblically faithful explanations might you offer?

Why do you think the Bible prohibits us from seeking communication with the deceased?

Why doesn't God permit Satan to resurrect the dead? The Lord seems to give the Devil considerable latitude in other areas, doesn't He (see 1 Peter 5:8)?

Read 2 Cor. 11:14-15. How does this passage provide an explanation for some of today's ghost stories?

SHARE *Talking points for discussing ghosts and the unseen realm*

Despite alleged "proof" that spirits of the dead are all around us and want to make their presence known, Christians must gauge all truth claims by the Bible, the ultimate and unchanging measure of reality.

Scripture teaches that all humans possess both physical and non-physical properties – the body and the soul/spirit, the second of which survives physical death.

Nowhere does the Bible support the notion that spirits of the dead (*phantasma* or *pneuma* in the Greek) are free to return to the physical realm prior to their future resurrection.

The souls of the dead either are in the presence of God in heaven or separated from Him in torment in *Hades*.

In Scripture, appearances of the righteous dead on earth (for example, Samuel, Moses, and Elijah) are brief and rare exceptions to the rule.

We should avoid fascination with modern-day "ghost adventures." At best, they rob us of our time; at worst, they draw us into demonic deception. While Satan has no power to raise the dead or create human flesh, he and his demons play on the field of superstition.

DIVE *Go deeper in your study with these resources*

Afterlife: What You Need to Know about Heaven, the Hereafter & Near-death Experiences by Hank Hanegraaff

The Truth Behind Ghosts, Mediums, and Psychic Phenomena by Ron Rhodes

47
TEN BIBLICAL TRUTHS ABOUT THE AFTERLIFE

Three-year-old Colton Burpo had a near-death experience (NDE) while on the operating table. When it was over, he described his "three minutes in heaven" in vivid detail, including encounters with Samson, John the Baptist, and Jesus, who had sea-blue eyes and owned a rainbow-colored horse.

Colton's father, a Wesleyan pastor, believes the lad's experience was real because he shared it with "the simple conviction of an eyewitness."[1]

You may read Colton's story in *Heaven is for Real: A Little Boy's Astounding Story of His Trip to Heaven and Back*,[2] which ruled the best-seller list for 44 weeks. Millions of people have devoured the book, watched the youngster's appearances on TV shows, and viewed the major motion picture based on his story.

Less popular but equally intriguing are books about NDEs in which people "die" for brief periods and experience the horrors of hell. *To Hell and Back* by cardiologist Maurice Rollins, for example, tells us that hellish NDEs have to be recorded and verified immediately after the person "returns" or the horrifying memories are repressed.[3]

In any case, stories like Colton's appeal to our desire to know more about the afterlife.

Sincerely wrong

I have never met Colton or his father. And I have no reason to doubt that Colton had an experience of some kind, or that his father is sincere in sharing what his son observed. What concerns me is something Christian apologist Hank Hanegraaff articulated when he wrote that "our culture has forgotten one very simple fact: you can be sincere and still be wrong."[4]

It is important for Christians to realize that any reports of the afterlife must be measured against Scripture. God has chosen not to answer every question about life after death in His Word, but He gives us enough information to know at least 10 biblical truths:

1. Death is not the end of life. In perhaps the earliest biblical reference to resurrection, Job expresses confidence that in his flesh he will see God (Job 19:26). Samuel appears to Saul after his death (1 Samuel 28), and Moses and Elijah appear with Jesus on the Mount of Transfiguration (Matt. 17:1-4). Jesus tells the story of Lazarus and the rich man to describe life beyond the grave (Luke 16:19-31). And the apostles Paul and John are given glimpses into heaven (2 Cor. 12:1-4; Revelation 1-22).

2. There is conscious existence beyond the grave. Jesus' story of Lazarus and the rich man offers graphic details of the afterlife, showing us that people continue to think, remember, experience pain, communicate, and understand where they are – and why (Luke 16:19-31).

3. We maintain our identities. King Saul recognizes Samuel after the witch of Endor (or more properly, the Lord) summons him from the dead (1 Samuel 28). Peter, James, and John identify Moses and Elijah on the Mount of Transfiguration even though they have never met (Matt. 17:1-4). The rich man in Jesus' parable sees both Lazarus and Abraham across the great divide in *Hades* (Luke 16:19-31).

4. We have memories of life on earth. The rich man remembers that he has five brothers, and he asks Abraham to send Lazarus back to earth to warn them of Torment (apparently realizing he is not permitted to be set free).

5. We await future resurrection. Jesus tells us all who are in the graves will hear His voice one day and "come forth" (John 5:29). Paul writes that Christians will receive glorified bodies (1 Corinthians 15), while John sees unbelievers receiving resurrected bodies prepared for eternal separation from God (Rev. 20:11-15).

6. We await final judgment. Christians will stand before the judgment seat of Christ (2 Cor. 5:10). Unbelievers will stand before the Great White Throne (Rev. 20:11-15).

7. Believers are destined for life with Christ in the new heavens and earth. The apostle John describes what it will be like when Jesus renovates our sinful and fallen world (Rev. 21-22).

8. Unbelievers are destined for eternal separation from God in hell. "Outer darkness" awaits those who reject Christ. Not that God is cruel. Unbelievers choose eternity on their own terms. As C.S. Lewis writes in

The Problem of Pain, "I willingly believe that the damned are, in one sense, successful, rebels to the end; that the gates of hell are locked on the inside."[5]

9. Our choices now have everlasting consequences. Jesus asks the question every person must answer: "Who do you say that I am?" (Matt. 16:15). And we must answer in this life, for there are no second chances beyond the grave (Heb. 9:27).

10. God has chosen not to reveal everything about the afterlife at this time. Paul is prevented from sharing his experiences in the "third heaven" (2 Cor. 12:4). John is forbidden from revealing some of what he hears in the Apocalypse (Rev. 10:4). For now, we should be content with what God has revealed in Scripture.

THINK *Questions for personal or group study*

Why do you think so many stories of near-death experiences are at odds with Scripture?

How does our understanding of the afterlife progress as we move from the Old Testament to the New Testament? Why is it important to understand the concept of "progressive revelation" – God's increased revelation of Himself and His will over time in Scripture?

What are some popular but unbiblical beliefs about life after death?

Why do you think final judgment for all people comes after their resurrection and not immediately after death?

Do you think the depictions of fiery judgment in Scripture should be taken literally? Why or why not?

SHARE *Talking points for discussing life after death*

Any reports of the afterlife must be measured against Scripture. God has chosen not to answer every question about life after death in His Word, but He gives us enough information to know many profound truths.

The Bible is clear that death is not the end of life; people retain conscious existence beyond the grave.

We also keep our identities after death and apparently have at least some memories of our lives on earth.

At death our souls / spirits separate from our bodies and we await resurrection and final judgment.

Those who have trusted in Christ are destined to enjoy eternity with Him in the new heavens and new earth. People who reject Christ have chosen to spend eternity apart from Him in hell.

Our choices now – on this side of the grave – have everlasting consequences.

DIVE *Go deeper in your study with these resources*

Heaven by Randy Alcorn

Life After Death: The Evidence by Dinesh D'Souza

What Happens After Life? 21 Amazing Revelations About Heaven and Hell by Ron Rhodes

48
SHEOL AND THE AFTERLIFE

While the doctrines pertaining to life beyond the grave are not fully developed in the Old Testament, there is ample evidence in the Hebrew Scriptures that the souls of people survive death. A key term used to describe the intermediate destiny of the deceased is *Sheol*.

Old Testament writers use the Hebrew word *Sheol* 65 times to describe the abode of the dead. It communicates the reality of human mortality and the impact of one's life on his or her destiny.

Ancient Israelites believed in life beyond the grave, borne out in such passages as Isa. 14:9-12, where *Sheol* contains "the spirits of the departed;" and 1 Sam. 28:13, where the deceased prophet Samuel temporarily appears as "a spirit form coming up out of the earth."

It's important to note that while the Old Testament consistently refers to the body as going to the grave, it always refers to the soul or spirit of people as going to *Sheol*, according to Robert A. Morey in *Death and the Afterlife*.

One source of confusion is the manner in which the King James Version translates *Sheol*, according to Morey: "The KJV translates Sheol as 'hell' 31 times, 'grave' 31 times, and 'pit' three times. Because of this inconsistency of translation, such groups as the Adventists ... and Jehovah's Witnesses have taught that Sheol means the grave."[1]

Fortunately, he adds, lexicons and rabbinic literature consistently understand *Sheol* as the place where the souls or spirits of persons go at death.

Down to *Sheol*

In fact, the first occurrence of *Sheol* in the Old Testament (Gen. 37:35) cannot possibly mean "grave." As Jacob holds the bloodied remnants of Joseph's coat, he laments about his deceased boy, "I will go down to Sheol to my son, mourning."

Whatever else *Sheol* may mean, in this passage it cannot mean Joseph's grave, for Jacob believes his son has been devoured by wild animals and thus has no grave. Jacob could not be buried in a common grave with Joseph.

According to the context, Jacob anticipates being reunited with Joseph in the underworld. He speaks of going "down" because it is assumed that *Sheol* is the place of departed spirits, likely a hollow place in the center of the earth.

There are other factors about *Sheol* to consider, among them:

1. When Old Testament writers want to identify the grave, they often use the Hebrew word *kever*, which is contrasted with *Sheol*. *Kever* is the fate of the body, while *Sheol* is the fate of the soul.

2. In the Septuagint, the Greek translation of the Old Testament, *Sheol* is never translated as *mneema*, the Greek word for grave.

3. *Sheol* is "under the earth" or "the underworld," while graves in Old Testament times tend to be built as sepulchers above the earth, in caves, or in holes in the earth.

4. While bodies are unconscious in the grave, those in *Sheol* are viewed as conscious.

Progressive revelation

Because God's revelation in Scripture is progressive, we see the concept of *Sheol* develop throughout the Old Testament. While it is described as dark (Lam. 3:6) and a place of helplessness (Ps. 88:4), trouble and sorrow (Ps. 116:3), God is both present in *Sheol* (Ps. 139:8) and able to deliver from it (Ps. 16:10; 49:15).

This leads some commentators to argue that there are two compartments in *Sheol*, one for the wicked and another for the righteous. Later Jewish literature describes these divisions, in which people experience a foretaste of their final destiny (see Enoch 22:1-14, an ancient Jewish work not part of the biblical canon).

Jesus' story of Lazarus and the rich man (Luke 16:19-31) seems to expand on this depiction, applying the Greek word *Hades* to the realm of the dead.

Other scholars contend, however, that *Sheol* is only for the wicked, while God rescues the spirits of the righteous from *Sheol* and takes them to a place of blessedness.

The ascension of Enoch and Elijah to heaven, for example, is cited to support the belief that the righteous under the old covenant could be taken directly into God's presence at the end of their earthly lives.

Today, we know that the souls/spirits of Christians enter heaven immediately upon death (2 Cor. 5:6-8). Evidently, the souls of unbelievers remain in *Sheol* where they await resurrection and final judgment.

THINK *Questions for personal or group study*

In what ways are *Sheol* and the grave different?

How might you respond to the person who argues that the Old Testament says nothing about life after death?

Why is it not possible for *Sheol* to mean a burial place?

Why do you think the Holy Spirit gives us such a limited view of life after death in the Scriptures – leaving us with so many unanswered questions?

What are the dangers of seeking to communicate with the deceased?

SHARE *Talking points for discussing Sheol and the afterlife*

While the doctrines pertaining to life beyond the grave are not fully developed in the Old Testament, there is ample evidence in the Hebrew Scriptures that the souls of people survive death.

Old Testament writers use the Hebrew word *Sheol* 65 times to describe the abode of the dead.

While the Old Testament consistently refers to the body as going to the grave, it always refers to the soul or spirit of people as going to *Sheol*.

Some Bible commentators contend that there are two compartments in *Sheol*, one for the wicked and another for the righteous.

Other scholars say that *Sheol* is only for the wicked, while God rescues the spirits of the righteous from *Sheol* and takes them to a place of blessedness.

In either case, the Old Testament testifies to the reality of life beyond the grave.

DIVE *Go deeper in your study with these resources*

Death and the Afterlife by Robert A. Morey

Sense & Nonsense about Heaven & Hell by Kenneth D. Boa and Robert M. Bowman Jr.

49
HADES AND THE AFTERLIFE

Hades is a Greek god whose name means "The Unseen." He is depicted as lord of the underworld, or the abode of the dead. So it should come as no surprise that Jesus and the New Testament writers borrow from the familiar term *Hades* to describe the realm of departed spirits.

What's more, they cut through the mythology to present a more accurate picture of the afterlife.

The word *Hades* appears 10 times in the New Testament, forming a linguistic bridge that takes us from the Old Testament view of life beyond the grave (in *Sheol*) to the New Testament position.

In coming to a biblically faithful understanding of *Hades*, it's important to state what the word does not mean.

It does not mean death, because the Greek word *thanatos* is used for death in the New Testament. Further, death (*thanatos*) and *Hades* appear together in Rev. 1:18, so they cannot mean the same thing.

Second, it cannot mean grave, because the Greek work *mneema* depicts the place where the bodies of the deceased are buried.

Third, it cannot mean hell, the place of final punishment for the wicked, because the Greek word *gehenna* is used for hell in the New Testament, along with other terms like "outer darkness," "eternal fire," and "lake of fire." Further, *Hades* is cast into the lake of fire in Rev. 20:14.

Fourth, *Hades* is not heaven, the intermediate state of Christians between death and resurrection, because the Greek word *ouranos* depicts heaven.

Progressive revelation

While *Hades* is consistently used in the Septuagint as the Greek equivalent of the Hebrew term *Sheol*, this does not mean *Hades* should be limited to the Old Testament understanding of the afterlife.

As we move through the Scriptures, God reveals more truths so that His revelation in Scripture may be described as progressive.

Put another way, the New Testament picks up where the Old Testament leaves off by further developing our understanding of what happens to a person after death.

During the period between the Old and New Testaments, the Jewish concept of *Sheol* progressed to the point where it was believed that *Sheol* had two distinct compartments: Torment, and Abraham's bosom or paradise.

This rabbinic understanding of *Sheol* is the basis for Jesus' story of Lazarus and the rich man (Luke 16:19-31). The rich man dies and finds himself in torment in *Hades*. Angels, on the other hand, carry Lazarus to Abraham's bosom, presumably the other compartment of *Hades*.

The conversation between Abraham and the rich man, the description of the rich man's consciousness and suffering, and the impassable gulf between the two compartments provide further details about *Hades* that build on the Old Testament understanding of life beyond the grave.

Context and *Hades*

Nevertheless, we should acknowledge that *Hades* is a somewhat flexible term whose precise meaning depends on context. Consider:

In Matthew 11:23-24 and Luke 10:15, Jesus uses *Hades* to depict the destruction of Capernaum.

In Matthew 16:18, He assures His followers that the shadowy afterlife (*Hades*) cannot overpower His church because He has come to conquer sin and death.

In Luke 16:19-31, He describes the torment suffered by the rich man in *Hades*, where a great chasm separates him from Lazarus and Abraham.

In Acts 2:27-31, Peter quotes from Psalm 16:8-11 to make it clear that Jesus, unlike David, did not remain among the dead in *Hades* but rose from the dead without His flesh suffering corruption.

In Revelation 1:18, Jesus holds the keys of death and *Hades*, meaning He has authority over death and its consequences.

Finally, in Revelation 20:13-14, Death and *Hades* are personified as giving up their dead, then they are thrown into the lake of fire. There is no more physical death, and no more temporary abode for the wicked dead in *Hades*.

Absent from the body

Some New Testament commentators believe Jesus escorted the Old Testament saints from *Hades* into heaven between His death and resurrection, citing Eph. 4:8-9 and 1 Peter 3:18-22; others dispute this, arguing that saints under the old covenant entered heaven immediately after death.

In any case, the New Testament describes believers after Christ's resurrection as entering heaven directly upon death (Phil. 1:23). There, they are present with the Lord (2 Cor. 5:6-8), worshiping with the angelic hosts of heaven (Heb. 12:22-23) at the altar of God (Rev. 6:9-11).

Meanwhile, the souls of deceased unbelievers continue to populate *Hades*, awaiting resurrection and final judgment, at which time they stand before the great white throne and are cast into *gehenna*, which is the focus of the next chapter.

THINK *Questions for personal or group study*

How are *Hades* and *Sheol* similar?

Why is *Hades* not the same as hell?

What does Jesus reveal about *Hades* in the parable of Lazarus and the rich man (Luke 16:19-31)? And what are the potential dangers of taking every detail literally?

Read Eph. 4:8-9 and 1 Peter 3:18-22. Do you think these passages support the belief that Jesus escorted Old Testament saints to heaven between His death and resurrection? What are some other possible interpretations of these verses?

Where do followers of Jesus go immediately upon death? Where do unbelievers go today when they die?

SHARE *Talking points for discussing Hades and the afterlife*

The word *Hades* appears 10 times in the New Testament, forming a linguistic bridge that takes us from the Old Testament view of life beyond the grave (in *Sheol*) to the New Testament position.

Hades is the abode of the dead, similar to *Sheol* in the Old Testament.

Hades is not death, the grave, hell, or heaven; the New Testament uses different Greek words to describe these realities.

The New Testament picks up where the Old Testament leaves off by further developing our understanding of what happens to the soul after death.

Hades, along with Death, is destined for the lake of fire. There will be no more physical death, and no more temporary abode for the wicked dead.

DIVE *Go deeper in your study with these resources*

Knowing the Truth about Heaven & Hell: Our Choices and Where They Lead Us by Harry Blamires; general editors J.I. Packer and Peter Kreeft

Afterlife: What You Need to Know about Heaven, the Hereafter & Near-death Experiences by Hank Hanegraaff

50
GEHENNA AND THE AFTERLIFE

The ultimate destiny of the wicked is the same habitation created for Satan and his demons – a place in English we call "hell," and a place Jesus and the New Testament writers describe variously as *Gehenna*, "outer darkness," "eternal fire," "eternal punishment," "lake of fire," and "the second death."

While *Sheol* and *Hades* generally depict the temporary abode of the dead, *Gehenna* and its associated terms describe the place of everlasting future punishment for those whose names are not written in the book of life (Rev. 20:15).

The term *Gehenna* is derived from the Valley of Hinnom. Located southwest of Jerusalem, this steep, rocky valley is the scene of human sacrifices to pagan deities (2 Kings 23:10; 2 Chron. 28:3; 33:6); is declared the "Valley of Slaughter" by Jeremiah (Jer. 7:31-34); and in Jesus' day is a trash dump with continuously burning fires.

The picture of a garbage heap where fires are never quenched and worms never stop feasting became to the Jewish mind an appropriate representation of the ultimate fate of idol worshipers.

How Jesus depicts *Gehenna*

Jesus seizes rabbinic language connected with *Gehenna*, such as "unquenchable fire" and "never-dying worms," to impress upon His listeners that their choices in this life have everlasting consequences. In fact, of the 12 uses of *Gehenna* in the New Testament, 11 come from the lips of the Messiah.

It's probable that Jesus uses *Gehenna* on only four occasions: In the Sermon on the Mount (Matt. 5:22, 29, 30); in warning the disciples not to fear men (Matt. 10:28; Luke 12:5); in a discourse on relationships (Matt. 18:9; Mark 9:43, 45, 47); and in His denunciation of the scribes and Pharisees (Matt. 23:15, 33).

Traditionally, these passages are understood to speak of final judgment, with Jesus using images from everyday life to warn about a place of everlasting separation from God.

However, some scholars see Jesus speaking in more limited terms. Steve Gregg, in *All You Want to Know About Hell: Three Christian Views of God's Final Solution to the Problem of Sin*, argues that Jesus may have used *Gehenna* literally to warn first-century Jews that they are about to suffer fiery judgment for their rejection of the Messiah at the hands of the Romans – a judgment that falls hard on Jerusalem and its inhabitants in A.D. 70.[1]

This is not to deny the existence of hell as a place of everlasting separation from God, since other texts speak of resurrection, final judgment, and fiery punishment for the wicked. But it is to encourage us to carefully consider the context so we do not glean more from a text than is warranted.

Is hell forever?

Anglican cleric John Stott, who wrote the influential book *Basic Christianity*, found the idea of eternal suffering in hell so repugnant he rejected it in favor of annihilationism.

Those who embrace the idea of body and soul ceasing to exist after spending some amount of time in hell point out that the "fire" and "worms" to which Jesus refers are indeed eternal, but the body and soul are destroyed. Two responses are offered.

First, the rabbinic understanding of these terms is that the bodies and souls of the wicked are eternal, not just the fires and worms, according to Robert Morey in *Death and the Afterlife*.

Second, the term "destroyed" in Matt. 10:28 does not mean annihilated. As *Thayer's Greek-English Lexicon* defines the word *apollumi*, it means "to be delivered up to eternal misery." In every instance where the word *apollumi* is found in the New Testament, something other than annihilation is described, writes Morey.[2]

For example, people do not pass into nonexistence when they become hungry (Luke 15:17), and wineskins don't vanish into thin air when they burst (Matt. 9:17). In each of these instances, the writers use the term *apollumi*.

While rejecting annihilationism, other Christian leaders favor a form of universalism that requires suffering in hell as a prerequisite for heaven.

But Jesus' teachings on "outer darkness," "eternal fire," and "eternal punishment" seem to support the concept of *Gehenna* as a place of conscious, everlasting separation from God.

Hell's inhabitants

It's important to note *who* and *what* are cast into the lake of fire: The beast and the false prophet (Rev. 19:20); Satan (20:10); anyone whose name is not found written in the book of life (20:15); cowards, unbelievers, the vile, murderers, the sexually immoral, sorcerers, idolaters, and all liars – meaning the unrepentant wicked (21:8); and ultimately Death and *Hades* (20:14).

The fires of hell devour all wicked humans and spirits, and even the consequences of sin, which are death and temporary disembodiment for the deceased. As the apostle Paul writes, those who don't know God and those who do not obey the gospel "will pay the penalty of eternal destruction, away from the Lord's presence ..." (2 Thess. 1:9).

Perhaps this divine act of taking out the trash is the first step in what Peter describes as God's work of creating new heavens and a new earth (2 Peter 3:10-13).

Fire and darkness

Finally, are we to take the lake of fire literally or figuratively? Godly scholars stand on both sides of the debate.

It may help to remember that the Bible uses fire metaphorically many times. Daniel sees the throne of God in heaven as "flaming fire, its wheels ... blazing fire" (Dan. 7:9). James describes the tongue as an appendage that "sets the course of life on fire, and is set on fire by hell" (James 3:6).

So, it may be that the Bible's depiction of hell in such graphic terms is God's way of explaining an indescribable place in language we can understand.

Whether literal or metaphorical, the fires of hell are to be avoided at all costs, and the blood of Jesus is to be pleaded for forgiveness of sins while there is yet time.

THINK *Questions for personal or group study*

What terms besides *Gehenna* do Jesus and the New Testament writers use to describe the eternal destiny of the wicked?

Do you think it's fair for God to punish someone eternally for sins committed in a single lifetime? Which passages of Scripture support your point of view?

Why do you think Jesus speaks so frequently about hell in the New Testament?

Who ultimately ends up in hell (see Revelation 19-21)? How does a person avoid hell?

What are the arguments in favor of annihilationism? Universalism? How might you respond biblically?

SHARE *Talking points for discussing Gehenna and the afterlife*

The ultimate destiny of the wicked is the same habitation created for Satan and his demons – a place in English we call "hell," and a place Jesus and the New Testament writers describe variously as *Gehenna*, "outer darkness," "eternal fire," "eternal punishment," "lake of fire," and "the second death."

The term *Gehenna* is derived from the Valley of Hinnom – the scene of human sacrifices to pagan deities in Old Testament times, and in Jesus' day a trash dump with continuously burning fires.

Jesus seizes rabbinic language connected with *Gehenna*, such as "unquenchable fire" and "never-dying worms," to impress upon His listeners that their choices in this life have everlasting consequences.

While some argue for annihilationism or universalism, Jesus' teachings on "outer darkness," "eternal fire," and "eternal punishment" seem to support the concept of *Gehenna* as a place of conscious, everlasting separation from God.

Whether literal or metaphorical, the fires of hell are to be avoided at all costs, and the blood of Jesus is to be pleaded for forgiveness of sins while there is yet time.

DIVE *Go deeper in your study with these resources*

All You Want to Know About Hell: Three Christian Views of God's Final Solution to the Problem of Sin by Steve Gregg

Erasing Hell: What God Said about Eternity, and the Things We've Made Up by Francis Chan and Preston Sprinkle

Four Views on Hell edited by William Crockett

51
A LOOK INTO TARTARUS

If *Sheol / Hades* is the temporary abode of deceased people, is there a transitory place of punishment for some demons?

It seems the answer is yes, in a place the New Testament refers to as *Tartarus.*

The New Testament mentions *Tartarus* only once, in 2 Peter 2:4. Many translations render it "hell," including the King James Version and the New American Standard Bible, while others, like the English Standard Version and the New International Version, provide footnotes linking the English word "hell" to the Greek name *Tartarus.*

The Holman Christian Standard Bible simply transliterates the Greek word in this passage, which reads: "For if God did not spare the angels who sinned, but threw them down into *Tartarus* and delivered them to be kept in chains of darkness until judgment ..."

A footnote in the HCSB reads: "*Tartarus* is a Greek name for a subterranean place of divine punishment lower than *Hades.*"[1]

In the apocryphal Book of Enoch (20:2), *Tartarus* is used as a place where fallen angels are punished, an interpretation Peter affirms.

So, *Tartarus* seems to be a place separate from *Sheol*, the Hebrew term for the abode of the dead; *Hades*, roughly the Greek equivalent of *Sheol*; and *Gehenna*, the lake of fire created for the Devil and his angels (Matt. 25:41) where wicked people also spend eternity (Rev. 20:15).

Ancient Greeks regarded *Tartarus* as a place where rebellious gods and other wicked ones are punished. Peter refers to *Tartarus* as the abode of certain fallen angels.

Pits of darkness

Peter reminds us that while Satan's ultimate destiny is hell, currently he is free, roaming the earth like a lion, looking for anyone he can devour (1 Peter 5:8). In a similar fashion, many of his demons are free – tempting, tormenting, and even possessing individuals.

At the same time, the New Testament teaches that some angels experience incarceration and conscious torment as they await the Day of Judgment.

Note first of all in 2 Peter 2:4 that God has cast some angels into *Tartarus*, committing them to "pits of darkness" or, as some translations render it, "chains of darkness." This Jewish apocalyptic phrase refers to a place of mental anguish and terror in the underworld.

Second, these angels are confined until the Day of Judgment. The word "confined" is in the present passive participle tense, meaning they are continually kept or reserved for judgment. No "soul sleep" for angels or humans, and no annihilation.

We find a similar passage in Jude 6, where we read God has "kept, with eternal chains in darkness for the judgment of the great day, angels who did not keep their own position ..."

We should note there may be other places of confinement for demons. For example, demons possessing the man called Legion beg Jesus not to banish them to the "abyss," an unfathomable pit mentioned nine times in the New Testament. In Revelation 9, 11, 17, and 20, we see that an angel called Destroyer rules over the abyss; that it is a fiery place kept under lock and key; that the beast is released from the abyss to foment great wickedness on the earth; and that Satan is temporarily imprisoned there.

Finally, in Rev. 9:14, an angel is commanded to release four demons confined at the Euphrates River.

A dark recess of hell?

We might ask: Is *Tartarus* an especially dark recess of hell, or a separate temporary abode until the final judgment of Satan and his demons?

If *Tartarus* is a compartment of hell, then why are demons kept there until judgment day, only to be returned? Why are some demons released from imprisonment in the abyss and at the Euphrates River, while those in *Tartarus* are offered no parole?

Finally, if there is no escape from *Tartarus*, how does this place of temporary confinement differ from the lake of fire?

While we may ponder these issues, it's always good to stick with what the Bible clearly teaches. First, Christ has defeated Satan, sin, and death for us; there is no redemption for the angels who rebelled. Second, Christ judges angels as well as people. And third, we may rest assured that Satan and all his demons have a place prepared for them – the lake of fire – where they will be cast one day and tormented forever.

If some especially vile fallen angels are kept in a temporary place called *Tartarus* and never allowed to carry out their evil intentions, so much the better for us.

THINK *Questions for personal or group study*

Why do you think some demons are free and others are confined?

What is the difference between *Tartarus* and the abyss?

If there is no reprieve from *Tartarus*, why didn't God just send the demons directly to hell? What difference do you think the Day of Judgment will make for them?

What are some ways the Bible describes the work of Satan and demons in the world today?

Why has God provided redemption for sinful people but not for Satan and demons?

Tartarus is a Greek name for a subterranean place of divine punishment lower than *Hades*. Peter and Jude write that it is a place where certain demons are confined until the Day of Judgment.

Today, Satan and many demons are free, while others are confined. But the ultimate destiny of all fallen angels is the lake of fire, which God created for them (Matt. 25:41).

In contrast to *Tartarus*, which is a place of permanent confinement, some demons are imprisoned temporarily in the abyss or at the Euphrates River, according to Scripture.

While there is no redemption for Satan and demons, Christ has conquered Satan, sin, and death for fallen human beings, and by His grace through faith we may receive everlasting life.

If some especially vile fallen angels are kept in a temporary place called *Tartarus* and never allowed to carry out their evil intentions, so much the better for us.

DIVE *Go deeper in your study with these resources*

Angels Elect & Evil by C. Fred Dickason

99 Answers to Questions about Angels, Demons & Spiritual Warfare by B.J. Oropeza

Angels Dark and Light by Gary Kinnaman

52
DOES THE BIBLE TEACH PURGATORY?

Do some Christians undergo purification from the stain of sin between death and entrance into heaven? Many who answer yes to that question embrace the doctrine of purgatory, which became official Roman Catholic dogma in A.D. 1438.

Simply stated, purgatory is a place or state of suffering where the dead bound for heaven achieve the holiness necessary to enter into the presence of God. It should be noted, according to Catholic teaching, that some saints go directly to heaven upon death, needing no purification, while those who die in the state of unrepented mortal sin find themselves at once, and eternally, in hell. All those in purgatory ultimately make it to heaven.

As the *Catechism of the Catholic Church* explains, "All who die in God's grace and friendship, but still imperfectly purified, are indeed assured of their eternal salvation; but after death they undergo purification, so as to achieve the holiness necessary to enter the joy of heaven."[1]

The *Pocket Catholic Dictionary* puts it this way: "The souls of those who have died in the state of grace suffer for a time in purging that prepares them to enter heaven. The purpose of purgatory is to cleanse one of imperfections, venial sins, and faults, and to remit or do away with the temporal punishment due to mortal sins that have been forgiven in the Sacrament of Penance. It is an intermediate state in which the departed souls can atone for unforgiven sins before receiving their final reward."[2]

The amount of time one spends in purgatory depends on the degree of purging needed. "Pope Gregory I taught that baptism absolves us of original sin but that we have to remit payment for our actual sins. This purging is a preparation of the soul for heaven," according to Chad Owen Brand in The Apologetics Study Bible.[3]

Some proponents of purgatory, however, argue that because the afterlife is experienced outside the element of time, purgatory should be seen as a state or dimension rather than as a place. Indeed, Catholic theologians speak of the great diversity of purgatorial suffering in both its intensity and its duration.[4]

Even so, the question for evangelical Christians is: Does the Bible support the doctrine of purgatory?

An escape through fire

Catholic apologists cite both the Apocrypha (a collection of writings found in the Catholic Bible but excluded from the 66 books of the Protestant canon) and the New Testament to support their belief in purgatory.

For example, the words of Jesus in Matt. 12:32 are cited to support the idea that sins may be forgiven in the age to come. But Jesus is not speaking of post-mortem suffering to atone for one's own sins; He is pointing out that there is no forgiveness available – ever – to the one who blasphemes the Holy Spirit.

Another oft-quoted passage is Matt. 5:26, where Jesus warns His followers to reach settlements quickly with adversaries lest they be thrown into prison until they pay the last penny. By extension, it is argued that souls with a sin debt must remit payment beyond the grave before entering heaven. But our Lord is not speaking about an after-death prison; He is providing practical advice for living peaceably among our neighbors in the here and now.

The most-often cited New Testament passage in favor of purgatory is 1 Cor. 3:10-15, in which Paul describes the judgment of believers' works. Verse 15 reads, "If anyone's work is burned up, it will be lost, but he will be saved; yet it will be like an escape through fire."

Even a cursory reading of this passage shows that Paul is speaking of believers' *works* being judged by fire, resulting in reward, not of their *sins* being purged through temporal punishment. In verse 14, Paul makes it clear that Christ's judgment of our works results in a reward, or a wage.

Believers' works, not their sins, are purged at the judgment seat of Christ. Paul uses figurative language to tell us the fire "discloses" or "tests" the quality of a Christian's works. Other New Testament passages speak of a time after resurrection when we give an account of our Christian stewardship, resulting in rewards or loss of rewards (see Rom. 14:10-12 and 2 Cor. 5:10).

Christ's sufficiency

Perhaps the strongest argument against the doctrine of purgatory is that it undermines the sufficiency of Christ. Just before His death on the cross, Jesus declares triumphantly, "It is finished!" (John 19:30). Among other things, this means the work of redemption is complete and that no more sacrifice for sins is required. The wrath of God has been satisfied as the One who knew no sin became sin for us, so that we might become the righteousness of God in Christ (2 Cor. 5:21).

The writer of Hebrews echoes this truth: "After making purification for sins, He [Jesus] sat down at the right hand of the Majesty on high" (1:3b). Further, "For by one offering He has perfected forever those who are sanctified" (10:14).

Jesus paid our sin debt in full on the cross. There is nothing we can do to be forgiven of sins except to believe on the Lord Jesus Christ, at which time the penalty for sins – past, present, and future – is removed. We have passed from spiritual death into spiritual life and no longer face condemnation (see John 5:24; Rom. 8:1).

Believers are declared in right standing with God (justified) and granted everlasting life. Then, through the lifelong process of sanctification, the indwelling Holy Spirit conforms believers to the image of Christ, completing the process in glorification, which occurs at the resurrection of the just.

Sins committed after justification affect our fellowship with Christ and should be confessed, but justification is never revoked and the purging of sins never falls on our shoulders. We may suffer *because* of our sins, but only Jesus suffered *for* our sins.

Treasury of merit

Another danger in the doctrine of purgatory is the idea of indulgences, which are believed to partially or fully cancel the debt of temporal punishment in purgatory. Once earned, these withdrawals from the Catholic Church's "treasury of merit," earned by the works and prayers of Jesus, Mary, and the saints of all ages, may be applied personally or applied to a deceased person believed now to be in purgatory.

Historically, this belief resulted in corrupt practices that spurred Martin Luther to post his 95 Theses to the door of All Saints' Church at Wittenberg, Germany, sparking the Reformation. The head of the Catholic Church in 1517, Pope Leo X, offered indulgences to finance the new St. Peter's Church in Rome. The proclamation by church officials – "as soon as the coin in the coffer rings, the soul from purgatory springs" – set Luther ablaze.[5]

Even so, the Catholic Church's first "pope" would have eschewed the very ideas of purgatory and indulgences. Peter writes that the gift of the new birth through the resurrection of Jesus from the dead gives us an "inheritance that is imperishable, uncorrupted, and unfading, kept in heaven for you, who are being protected by God's power through faith for a salvation that is ready to be revealed in the last time" (1 Peter 1:4-5).

He goes on to write of Jesus, "He Himself bore our sins in His body on the tree, so that, having died to sins, we might live for righteousness; by His wounding you have been healed" (1 Peter 2:24).

Heaven can't wait

The Bible describes heaven, not purgatory followed by heaven, as the intermediate state between death and resurrection for the follower of Jesus. In 2 Corinthians 5, the apostle Paul describes two different states of existence for the believer. While we are here on earth in our bodies, we are absent from the Lord. And when we are "out of the body" we are "at home with the Lord" (v. 8).

If there is an interim step between death and heaven, the Bible makes no mention of it, and we would do well to rest in the plainly stated promises of God's Word. For those who die in the Lord, heaven can't wait, nor should it.

One final thought: While evangelicals may disagree with our Catholic friends over the doctrine of purgatory, we share a common expectation of the return of the Lord, resurrection and final judgment, and new heavens and a new earth.

As the *Catechism of the Catholic Church* declares, "At the end of time, the Kingdom of God will come in its fullness. After the universal judgment, the righteous will reign for ever with Christ, glorified in body and soul. The universe itself will be renewed."[6]

THINK *Questions for personal or group study*

What is the connection between purgatory and indulgences?

Why should we be skeptical of doctrines drawn largely from Apocryphal writings?

While Catholics and evangelicals disagree about purgatory, what beliefs about the afterlife do we hold in common?

What does the doctrine of purgatory say about the sufficiency of Christ's sacrificial and substitutionary death?

What is the difference between purgatory and the judgment seat of Christ?

SHARE *Talking points for discussing purgatory*

In Catholic teaching, purgatory is a place or state of suffering where the dead bound for heaven achieve the holiness necessary to enter into the presence of God.

While proponents of purgatory cite several New Testament passages in support of this doctrine, these Scriptures in fact say nothing about an interim state between death and heaven for the righteous. Christians enter immediately into the presence of the Lord upon death.

Believers' works, not their sins, are purged at the judgment seat of Christ.

Perhaps the strongest argument against the doctrine of purgatory is that it denies the sufficiency of Christ.

We may suffer *because* of our sins, but only Jesus suffered *for* our sins.

DIVE *Go deeper in your study with these resources*

Reasoning from the Scriptures with Catholics by Ron Rhodes

Knowing the Truth About Heaven and Hell by Harry Blamires

Roman Catholics and Evangelicals: Agreements and Differences by Norman L. Geisler and Ralph E. MacKenzie

53
IS HEAVEN OUR FINAL HOME?

Is heaven the final destination of all who rest in Jesus? Or do we spend eternity someplace else?

In 2 Corinthians 5, the apostle Paul describes two different states of existence for the Christian. While we are "at home in the body we are away from the Lord." And when we are "out of the body" we are "at home with the Lord" (5:6, 8).

Let's unpack this marvelous truth. The New Testament teaches that upon death, believers' souls/spirits separate from our lifeless bodies and enter into the presence of God in heaven (see also Phil. 1:21-24). There we enjoy intimate fellowship with our Lord while awaiting the future resurrection and glorification of our bodies (John 5:28-29; 1 Cor. 15:51-58; 1 Thess. 4:13-18).

We see magnificent glimpses into the throne room of heaven through the visionary eyes of the apostle John in the Book of Revelation: the triune Godhead; an emerald-colored rainbow surrounding a glorious throne; living creatures; elders; angels; and redeemed people from every tribe, language, people, and nation. The combined voices of all creatures in heaven, on earth, under the earth, and in the sea proclaim, "Blessing and honor and glory and dominion to the One seated on the throne, and to the Lamb, forever and ever!" (Rev. 5:13).

We may be tempted to stop here, as if heaven is the final destination in life's long journey. It *is* breathtaking. But it gets better. Heaven, a place so awe-inspiring that Paul is not allowed to speak the inexpressible words he hears while visiting there, nevertheless is a temporary home for those who rest in the Lord until He returns to earth and brings us with Him.

As Randy Alcorn writes, "The intermediate Heaven is *not* our final destination. Though it will be a wonderful place, the intermediate Heaven is not the place we were made for – the place God promises to refashion on a resurrected Earth. We must not lose sight of our true destination. If we do, we'll be confused and disoriented in our thinking about where, and in what form, we will spend eternity."[1]

What should we know, then, about heaven?

VI. Other Apologetics Topics

Three heavens

While rabbis in ancient times envisioned as many as seven heavens, the Bible generally uses the Hebrew word *shamayim* and the Greek word *ouranos* in three ways:

1. The atmospheric heaven, or the sky (Gen. 1:8). It's where the birds fly (Mark 4:32), the clouds carry storms (Luke 12:56), and the rain falls (James 5:18).

2. The stellar heaven(s), where the moon and stars shine (Ps. 8:3; Heb. 11:12).

3. And the domain of God, or His dwelling place (1 Kings 22:19; Luke 20:4).

The Scriptures also speak of the "heavens" as a metaphor for where Christ reigns with His church (Eph. 2:6), as well as the unseen spiritual realm inhabited by evil beings (Eph. 6:12). The context determines the proper meaning of the word.

For the purposes of this brief study, we are concerning ourselves with what the apostle Paul calls the "third heaven" (2 Cor. 12:2), or the domain of God. It is the intermediate state between death and resurrection for Christians, giving way ultimately to everlasting life on a restored earth.

What about heaven?

The New Testament reveals many truths about this intermediate state for followers of Jesus:

- The Father, Son, and Holy Spirit reside in heaven, yet they have immediate access to earth (Matt. 3:16-17).

- God's will is done completely in heaven – and one day will be done on earth (Matt. 6:9-10).

- Angels surround the throne in heaven (Matt. 18:10), as do majestic heavenly creatures and redeemed people (Revelation 4-5).

- The heavenly throne is the heart of God's authority and majesty (Mark 16:19).

- Heaven is the place from which Satan fell and in which he has no future part (Luke 10:18; Rev. 20:10).

- Heaven is where believers' names are written down, providing assurance of everlasting life (Luke 10:20; Heb. 12:23).

- Christ is preparing a place for believers in heaven and will take us there one day (John 14:1-3), bringing us back to earth with Him when He returns (Rev. 19:11-16).

- Our citizenship is in heaven (Phil. 3:20-21).

- Our inheritance is in heaven – imperishable, uncorrupted, and unfading (1 Peter 1:4).

- Jesus came from heaven (John 3:31; 6:38, 42), ascended there after His finished work on the cross (Luke 24:51; Eph. 4:10; Heb. 4:14), and will descend from heaven one day to resurrect and glorify believers (1 Thess. 4:16-17; 1 Cor. 15:51-58).

- God brings heaven and earth together one day and dwells with us (Rev. 21:3-4).

- Nothing profane enters heaven – or the new heavens and new earth (Rev. 21:27 – 22:5).

Better by far

As wonderful as the intermediate heaven is, our ultimate destiny is the new heavens and new earth, which Peter and John describe as a place of righteousness and restored innocence (2 Peter 3:10-13; Revelation 21-22). Christ returns, resurrects and judges all people, establishes His kingdom in fullness, creates new heavens and a new earth, and gives us roles to play in the administration of His kingdom.

The Greek word John uses for "new" in Rev. 21:1 is *kainos*, which means "different from the usual, impressive, better than the old, superior in value or attraction."[2] In other words, God does not annihilate the old order of things and start again from scratch; He purges the sinful and fallen cosmos and restores it to its pristine beauty. Jesus calls this work "the regeneration" of the earth (Matt. 19:28), and Peter explains it as a cleansing and renewing by fire (2 Peter 3:10-13).

The new heavens and new earth stand in stark contrast to Eden after the Fall. God is fully revealed and we are glorified so that our natural desire is for the intimacy Adam and Eve experienced in the garden. God sets His throne among us, and we do not flee from His presence with the shame that drove Adam and Eve to hide among the trees. There is personal contact with our sovereign Creator. We call Him *Abba* – dearest Daddy – and He calls us His children. There is security, warmth, serenity, joy, and unending peace. God is with us and we never again experience the consequences of separation from the One who is our life.

While the intermediate heaven is the joyous aim of all who trust in Jesus, the new heavens and new earth are better by far. Satan, sin, and death – three enemies that Christ conquered through His finished work on the cross – are banished to the lake of fire, along with all those who reject God's provision for eternal life. God wipes the tears from our cheeks and declares that the former things – death, grief, crying, and pain – have passed away.

J.I. Packer writes, "As life in the 'intermediate' or 'interim' state between death and resurrection is better than life in this world that preceded it, so the life of resurrection will be better still. It will, in fact, be best. And this is what God has in store for all his children."[3]

Amen. Come, Lord Jesus.

THINK *Questions for personal or group study*

Why is heaven not the final destiny of Christians?

How does Revelation 4-5 give us a glimpse of what heaven is like?

What are the different ways the word "heaven" is used in the New Testament?

Where do you think heaven is? Is it a place, a state of being, or something different altogether?

Who and what have no place in heaven?

How does the intermediate heaven relate to the new heavens and new earth?

SHARE *Talking points for discussing heaven*

At death, believers' souls/spirits separate from our lifeless bodies and enter the presence of God in heaven, where we enjoy intimate fellowship with our Lord while awaiting the future resurrection and glorification of our bodies.

Heaven is not believers' final destination; when Christ returns to earth, we return with Him and serve Him in the new heavens and the new earth.

Generally, the Bible uses the term "heaven" in three ways: the atmospheric heaven (sky), the stellar heavens (space), and the domain of God (throne). The context determines the meaning.

To create the new heavens and the new earth, God does not annihilate the old order of things and start again from scratch; He purges the sinful and fallen cosmos and restores it to its pristine beauty.

While the intermediate heaven is the joyous aim of all who trust in Jesus, the new heavens and new earth are better by far.

DIVE *Go deeper in your study with these resources*

Heaven by Randy Alcorn

Sense & Nonsense about Heaven & Hell by Kenneth D. Boa and Robert M. Bowman Jr.

Heaven: An Eternal Place of Hope, Blessing, and Encouragement by Richard DeHaan

AfterLife: What You Need to Know About Heaven, the Hereafter & Near-death Experiences by Hank Hanegraaff

54

WHAT CHRISTIANITY WITHOUT HELL LOOKS LIKE

In late 2014 John Shore authored a commentary for *Patheos* entitled, "What Christianity Without Hell Looks Like." *Patheos* is a website providing information about various religions.

Reprinted in *TIME Ideas* and complete with a photo of a dove soaring in the sunlight, the article's main point is that Christianity without hell "would allow Christians to point upward to God's love."[1]

Shore is a popular Christian blogger and author, yet his column features a string of shockingly bad theological statements that nevertheless resonate well in today's relativistic culture.

Let's look at just four of his false statements.

1. Hell is not real

"The idea that the Bible declares hell a real and literal place is no more valid than the toxic lie that the Bible condemns homosexuality."[2]

If Shore's statement merely questions whether the fires and darkness of hell are literal, he might have a point. Many evangelical scholars argue that Jesus and the New Testament writers use figurative language to describe unbelievers' separation from God after resurrection and final judgment.

But clearly this is not Shore's point. He denies the very existence of hell.

Further, he sloughs off compelling Scriptures that place homosexuality in the same category as other sexual sins such as adultery. By tying homosexuality and hell together as alleged false doctrines, he commits a double fault.

2. Hell is a fear tactic

"Over the centuries those in positions of power within institutions of Christianity have methodically, relentlessly, and with great art used the doctrine of hell to exploit the innate fear of death that is harbored by one and all."[3]

Here, Shore commits the logical fallacy of false cause, presuming that a real or perceived relationship between things means that one is the cause of the other.

While it's true that some church leaders and institutions have used the fear of hell to extort money and favors from the faithful, these shameful deeds do not disprove the reality of hell. The reality of hell has nothing to do with one's opinion about it, or someone's abuse of its existence.

Hell exists because Jesus created it for the punishment of Satan and demons (Matt. 25:41) and then warned people not to take that same judgment upon themselves by rejecting Him (John 16:7-11).

3. Hell denies God's love

"A Christianity without hell would have nothing to recommend it but the constant and unending love of God. It would allow Christians to point upward to God's love – but never downward to His/Her wrath."[4]

This is a common mischaracterization of God – that because He is love, He cannot hate anything or express divine wrath.

But think about it: How loving is a God who does nothing about humanity's most monstrous sins?

Human beasts like Hitler, Stalin, and Pol Pot are responsible for the slaughter of millions of people whose lives ended in starvation, torture, human experimentation, or execution. How can the mere death of these tyrants by any means satisfy divine justice?

If we accept the doctrine of universalism as Shore seems to envision it, we must admit that Osama bin Laden and Mother Teresa are feasting at the same banquet table. Without the existence of hell, life indeed is cruel and life's Creator is eternally unjust.

4. Without hell we don't need salvation

"A Christianity without hell would be largely unevangelical, since there would be nothing to save anyone from."[5]

Shore assumes that an absence of evangelism is a good thing. But the "good news" of Jesus Christ must be placed in its proper context. The gospel is the wonderful story of God's redeeming grace. He rescues us from our lost state by sacrificing His own Son on the cross, satisfying His justice, and extending to us a restored relationship with Him by faith.

If God simply shrugs at our wickedness, He is neither holy nor truly loving. Worse, He is guilty of divine child abuse by sending His Son to die for no good reason.

The doctrine of Christ's finished work at Calvary stands or falls on the reality of hell. Christian author Edward Donnelly profoundly makes this case when he writes, "Let us be quite clear. If we lost hell, we will eventually lose the cross, for if there is no hell, there is no real point in the cross."[6]

THINK *Questions for personal or group study*

If the biblical depictions of a "lake of fire" are figurative, how might we explain hell to our lost friends who wonder whether hell exists at all?

Why do you think some people dismiss hell as merely a fear tactic?

If hell did not exist, how would that impact our view of God's justice?

How does the cross figure into our discussion of heaven and hell?

What questions could you ask your friends who say hell is a temporary place for the removal of sins? A place of annihilation?

SHARE *Talking points for discussing the reality of hell*

Many evangelical scholars argue that Jesus and the New Testament writers use figurative language to describe unbelievers' separation from God after resurrection and final judgment. This is not the same as denying the reality of hell.

Sadly, it's true that some church leaders and institutions have used the fear of hell to extort money and favors from the faithful, but these shameful deeds do not disprove the reality of hell.

The reality of hell has nothing to do with one's opinion about it, or someone's abuse of its existence.

Hell exists because Jesus created it for the punishment of Satan and demons, then warned people not to take that same judgment upon themselves by rejecting Him.

If we accept the doctrine of universalism, we must admit that Osama bin Laden and Mother Teresa are feasting at the same banquet table. Without the existence of hell, life indeed is cruel and life's Creator is eternally unjust.

If God simply shrugs at our wickedness, He is neither holy nor truly loving. Worse, He is guilty of divine child abuse by sending His Son to die for no good reason.

DIVE *Go deeper in your study with these resources*

All You Want to Know About Hell: Three Christian Views of God's Final Solution to the Problem of Sin by Steve Gregg

Erasing Hell: What God Said About Eternity, and the Things We've Made Up by Francis Chan and Preston Sprinkle

God Wins: Heaven, Hell, and Why the Good News is Better than Love Wins by Mark Galli and Randy Alcorn

55
THE GOODNESS OF HELL

One of the most disturbing truths of the Christian faith is the doctrine of hell. Atheists use it to deny the existence of a loving God. And Christians find themselves squeamishly defending the notion that a good God sends some people to a place of everlasting torment.

"Hell is of course the greatest evil of all, the realm of the greatest conceivable suffering," writes Christian author Dinesh D'Souza in *God Forsaken*. "Consequently, hell poses perhaps the deepest difficulty for Christian theodicy [an attempt to reconcile the goodness of God with the existence of evil]. Far from resolving the theodicy problem, hell seems to make it even worse."[1]

Atheist Robert Ingersoll asserted that hell "makes man an eternal victim and God an eternal fiend."[2]

Anglican cleric John Stott, who wrote the influential book *Basic Christianity*, found the idea of eternal suffering so repugnant he rejected it in favor of annihilationism.[3]

Even C.S. Lewis shuttered at the concept of hell. "There is no doctrine which I would more willingly remove from Christianity than this, if it lay in my power," he wrote.[4]

The goodness of hell

But let's consider for a moment that the notion of a loving God and the doctrine of hell are perfectly compatible. There is nothing of one that cancels out the other.

Jesus spoke frequently on hell and alluded to it in parables. He used the word *Gehenna*, derived from the Valley of Hinnom outside Jerusalem, where apostate Israelites in Old Testament times sacrificed their children to false gods. By Jesus' day it had become a fiery trash heap where unclaimed corpses were dumped. A nasty, unclean place that nevertheless served a utilitarian purpose.

Jesus told some religious leaders they were headed for hell. He warned his listeners against this place where the worm does not die and the fires are not quenched. He referred to hell as "outer darkness." And He said hell was created for Satan and demons, yet made it clear that many people will spend eternity there.

So in what possible way is hell good?

First, hell is good because it affirms God's justice. If God only had the qualities of benevolence and mercy, hell would be an unreasonable place. But God is infinitely holy and perfectly just. To sin against Him offends His very nature.

Human beasts like Hitler, Stalin, and Pol Pot are responsible for the slaughter of millions of people whose lives ended in starvation, torture, human experimentation, or execution. How can the mere death of these tyrants by any means satisfy justice?

If we accept the doctrine of universalism, we must admit that Osama bin Laden and Mother Teresa are feasting at the same banquet table. Without the existence of hell, life indeed is cruel and life's Creator is eternally unjust.

Second, hell is good because it affirms free will. While we may debate whether humans truly have free will, or simply make decisions within pre-determined boundaries, there is little question that God allows us to make choices for which we are held accountable. In a world where God refuses to grant humans real choices, there is no freedom to love God.

If we view life fatalistically, God is a cruel puppet master who manipulates us before discarding us like broken toys. But the biblical concept of hell carries with it the clear teaching that people choose to spend eternity apart from Christ. As C.S. Lewis so poignantly penned, "[T]he doors of Hell are locked on the inside."[5]

Without hell, our choices have no real meaning or lasting consequences.

Third, hell is good because it implies heaven. Many atheists attack the idea that a good God would send people to hell for eternity as payment for temporal sins. But they tend not to criticize the idea of a God who welcomes people into eternal bliss for being the recipients of His grace.

Freud argued that heaven is a product of wishful thinking. But if that's so, how does one explain the fact that religions embracing heaven also have clear doctrines of hell?

We are invited to join God in this life and the life to come by His grace through faith. We may reject Him and enter eternity on our own terms, but we cannot take God with us or it would cease to be hell.

Outer darkness

While it is troubling to consider eternity in "outer darkness," the Bible is clear that hell is a place people choose to live independently of God – forever.

We do not see the rich man repent of his sin in Luke 16, nor do we see those before the great white throne asking to be near Jesus (Revelation 20); indeed, the blasphemers and unrepentant in Revelation hide themselves from the presence of God, preferring death under a rock to life in the light of Christ.

A final caution: When we say hell is good, we do not mean to gloat over those who enter eternity without Christ, no matter how wicked they may be. The Lord Himself does not delight in the judgment of the ungodly but took the human condition so seriously He sent His Son to save us from ourselves.

THINK *Questions for personal or group study*

Why do you think people go to hell if Jesus said hell was created for Satan and his demons (Matt. 25:41)?

Do you think it's possible that hell is a place of temporary suffering rather than a place of everlasting conscious existence apart from God? How does Scripture support your point of view?

How might you reconcile the seemingly conflicting depiction of hell as a place of both fire and darkness?

Do you think it's possible for people in hell to repent of their sins and become truly remorseful over their rejection of God? Why or why not?

What problems do you see in Christian universalism (the belief that God ultimately redeems all people)? What are the strengths and weaknesses of annihilationism (the belief that the wicked cease to exist rather than suffer everlastingly in hell)?

SHARE *Talking points for discussing the goodness of hell*

The notion of a loving God and the doctrine of hell are perfectly compatible. There is nothing of one that cancels out the other.

Hell is good because it affirms God's justice. Without the existence of hell, life indeed is cruel and life's Creator is eternally unjust.

Hell is good because it affirms free will. Without hell, our choices have no real meaning or lasting consequences.

Hell is good because it implies heaven. If there is a place of eternal separation from God, there also must be a place of everlasting intimacy with Him.

The Lord does not delight in the judgment of the ungodly but took the human condition so seriously He sent His Son to save us from ourselves.

DIVE *Go deeper in your study with these resources*

Godforsaken: Bad Things Happen. Is there a God who cares? Yes. Here's proof by Dinesh D'Souza

The Problem of Pain by C.S. Lewis

The Justice of God in the Damnation of Sinners by Jonathan Edwards

Evil and the Justice of God by N.T. Wright

56
HOW THE WORLD WILL END

Remember December 21, 2012? If you believed doomsayers or John Cusack movies, the world was supposed to end that day. That was the date of the so-called Mayan Apocalypse, when an important cycle of the Maya Long Count Calendar drew to a close.

The date came and went, and we're still here. So much for end-of-days predictions that have made and broken pundits and self-proclaimed prophets for centuries. Not to be outdone by religious fanaticism, contemporary culture embraces the drama of a cataclysmic end to the world.

For example, in the 1979 film *Mad Max*, a shortage of fossil fuels drives the breakdown of society, prompting leather-clad motorcyclists to terrorize anyone with a full tank of gas.

In *Planet of the Apes*, astronaut George Taylor discovers he has traveled through space and time, returning to an earth where humans are mute and loud-mouthed armor-wearing apes are in charge.

In Ray Bradbury's frightening short story, *August 2026: There Will Come Soft Rains*, a robotic house continues to serve its human tenants long after they have become burnt silhouettes on the wall, presumably the victims of a nuclear holocaust.

And in *Hitchhiker's Guide to the Galaxy*, Arthur Dent wakes up to learn his home has been slated for demolition to make room for a new bypass; worse, the planet is set for destruction because officials from Earth never made it to Alpha Centauri to protest the demolition orders.

Whether frightening or funny, the end of the world is a topic of considerable interest and much debate. World religions and cults often contrive detailed apocalyptic views, including specific dates that, when missed, leave their leaders disgraced and their followers asking neighbors to return the cookware they thought they would never need again.

Seven biblical truths

In truth, Christians know that this sinful and fallen world – that is, the world order alienated from God, in rebellion against Him, and under the rule of Satan – will pass away. The Bible tells us so. And while evangelical Christians may debate the order of events yet to unfold, we can all agree on seven biblical truths about how the world will end.

First, the world will end when the Father says so. Jesus makes this clear in His narratives and parables. He tells His followers, "Now concerning that day and hour no one knows – neither the angels in heaven, nor the Son – except the Father only" (Matt. 24:36). The first-century Jew hearing the parable of the 10 virgins understands that no wedding begins until the father declares everything is ready. Meanwhile, Jesus cautions us to "be alert, because you don't know either the day or the hour" (Matt. 25:13).

Second, the world will end with the return of Jesus. It's important that we look for His physical and visible return. An unseen return in 1914, as Jehovah's Witnesses teach,[1] strips Jesus of His physical resurrection and thus His finished work of redemption. Remember what the angels tell the disciples as they witness Jesus' ascension: "This Jesus, who has been taken from you into heaven, will come in the same way that you have seen Him going into heaven" (Acts 1:11).

Third, the world will end with the resurrection of the dead. Christians are divided as to whether all people are resurrected at the same time, or whether there are multiple resurrections stretching across 1,000 years or more. But let's not allow our interpretations to get in the way of Jesus' plain teaching that "a time is coming when all who are in the graves will hear His voice and come out" (John 5:28-29).

Fourth, the world will end with the final judgment of all people. Believers will appear before the judgment seat of Christ and be rewarded for our faithfulness (2 Cor. 5:10). Unbelievers will stand before the great white throne and be punished for their works against the kingdom of God (Rev. 20:11-15).

Fifth, the world will end with a separation of God's people from those who have rejected Him. Jesus promises His followers, "I will come back and receive you to Myself, that where I am you may be also" (John 14:3). Unbelievers, however, are cast into hell, which Jesus describes as "outer darkness," a terrifying depiction of eternity far away from the Light of the world.

Sixth, the world will end with the creation of new heavens and a new earth. Peter gives us the image of a fiery purging in which our sinful and fallen world is refined into new heavens and a new earth (2 Peter 3:10-13). Revelation 21-22 provides further details of a restored creation.

Seventh, the world will end as human history began – with God dwelling with us. The restored earth will be our home and His throne. John hears a loud voice from God's throne declaring, "Look! God's dwelling is with men, and He will live with them. They will be His people, and God Himself will be with them and be their God" (Rev. 21:3).

So don't sweat the Hollywood hype or fanatical predictions. The end of the world, and its new beginning, are in the hands of its sovereign Creator.

THINK *Questions for personal or group study*

Why do you think so many people share a strange fascination with end-of-the-world predictions?

For something as important as the return of Christ, why isn't the Bible more specific about the exact order of events?

Christians have eagerly awaited the return of Jesus for nearly 2000 years. How might we respond to those who say we're waiting in vain – that He's not coming back?

How do we know Jesus hasn't already returned invisibly, as Jehovah's Witnesses claim?

In what ways will the return of Jesus set things right?

SHARE *Talking points for discussing the end of the world*

Religious fanatics and cultural icons often promote cataclysmic predictions of the end of the world. But the Bible is clear that the end of days is in the hands of our sovereign God.

Evangelical Christians may debate the order of events yet to unfold, but we can agree on clear biblical teachings about how the world will end.

Jesus said only the Father knows the day and hour of Christ's return; our task is not to predict, but to prepare.

Several events are to unfold surrounding the return of Christ, including the resurrection and final judgment of all people, a separation of the righteous from the wicked, and the creation of new heavens and a new earth.

The world will end as human history began – with God dwelling with us.

DIVE *Go deeper in your study with these resources*

Preparing for Jesus' Return: Daily Live the Blessed Hope by A.W. Tozer

Three Views on the Millennium and Beyond by Darrell L. Bock, editor

TOUGH QUESTIONS ABOUT GOD

57
A DIFFERENT GOD IN THE OLD AND NEW TESTAMENTS?

A common objection to the Bible is that it depicts a different God in the Old and New Testaments. The argument goes something like this: The God of Abraham, Isaac, and Jacob is distant, vain, and genocidal. The God of the New Covenant is softer, willing to send His Son to redeem a lost world.

This can't possibly be the same God, critics argue; therefore, the Bible cannot be true. But this objection reveals a basic misunderstanding of what the Old and New Testaments reveal about the nature of God.

The writers of Gotquestions.org put it well: "The fact that the Bible is God's progressive revelation of Himself to us through historical events and through His relationship with people throughout history might contribute to people's misconceptions about what God is like in the Old Testament as compared to the New Testament. However, when one reads both the Old and the New Testaments it quickly becomes evident that God is not different from one Testament to another and that God's wrath and His love are revealed in both Testaments."[1]

In many places, the Old Testament describes God as "a compassionate and gracious God, slow to anger and rich in faithful love and truth" (Ex. 34:6; see also Num. 14:18; Deut. 4:31; Neh. 9:17; Ps. 86:5, 15; 108:4; 145:8; Joel 2:13). In the New Testament, God's love for mankind is manifested more fully in the sending of His Son, Jesus Christ, who dies for us (John 3:16; Rom. 5:8; 1 Cor. 15:3-4).

In the Old Testament, God deals with the Israelites much as a loving father deals with his children, punishing them for their idolatry but delivering them when they repent of their sins. In much the same way, the New Testament tells us God chastens Christians for their own good. Hebrews 12:6, quoting Proverbs 3:11-12, says, "[f]or the Lord disciplines the one He loves, and punishes every son whom He receives."

God's wrath – and jealousy

But what about God's wrath – and jealousy? Both the Old and New

Testaments tell us that God delivers judgment on the unrepentant. He orders the Jews to destroy a number of people groups living in Canaan, but only after allowing them hundreds of years to repent (see, for example, Gen. 15:13-16). In addition, God's order to destroy these people has a divine purpose: "so they won't teach you to do all the detestable things they do for their gods, and you sin against the Lord your God" (Deut. 20:18).

When the Old Testament describes God as "jealous" (see Deut. 4:24), the word translated "jealous" (*qanna*) also means "zealous." God's jealousy "is an expression of His intense love and care for His people and His demand that they honor His unique and incomparable nature."[2] In the New Testament, Paul tells us "God's wrath is revealed from heaven against all godlessness and unrighteousness of people who by their unrighteousness suppress the truth" (Rom. 1:18).

Jesus often has harsh words for hypocrites (see Matthew 23) and even acts violently against them (John 2:15). He speaks more about hell than heaven, and He is depicted as a wrathful judge in verses foretelling His return (Rev. 19:11-16). Put simply, a God who loves what is good must necessarily hate what is evil.

A Redeemer for a wrecked human race

Throughout the Bible God patiently and lovingly calls people into a relationship with Him. Sin has wrecked the human race, resulting in spiritual and physical death and separation from our Creator (Rom. 3:10, 23; 6:23; Eph. 2:1). Paul writes that the whole world groans beneath the weight of sin (Rom. 8:22).

But from the moment Adam and Eve rebel against God, He provides a way for that broken fellowship to be restored. He begins with the promise of a Redeemer (Gen. 3:15); institutes a sacrificial system in which an innocent and spotless animal sheds its blood to atone for – or temporarily cover – man's sin; and then He sends His Son, the Lamb of God, to take away the sin of the world (John 1:29; 3:16).

When one reads the entire Bible, it becomes clear that the God of the Old and New Testaments does not change (Mal. 3:6; Heb. 13:8).

THINK *Questions for personal or group study*

Why do you think it's difficult for some people to accept that God is both wrathful and loving?

If God loves us so much that He sent His Son to die for us, why does He still send people to hell?

What good is an Old Testament sacrificial system that requires the death of a spotless animal to appease an angry God?

How might you explain the Old Testament sacrificial system in light of Jesus as the "Lamb of God, who takes away the sin of the world!" (John 1:29)?

In what ways does God's command to destroy wicked people demonstrate the loving aspects of His nature?

SHARE *Talking points for discussing the God of the Old and New Testaments*

The God of the Old Testament is the same as the God of the New Testament. While He deals with sinful people in different ways at different times, He is the same God yesterday, today, and forever (Mal. 3:6; Heb. 13:8).

The Old Testament in many places describes God as compassionate, gracious, slow to anger and rich in faithful love. In the New Testament, God's love for people is manifested more fully in the sending of His Son, Jesus Christ, who dies for us.

In both the Old and New Testaments, God deals with His people much as a loving father deals with His children, chastening them for their own good.

God's jealousy is not a petty human emotion but an expression of His intense love and care for His people.

We should remember that Jesus often has harsh words for hypocrites and even acts violently against them. He speaks more about hell than heaven, and the Book of Revelation depicts Him as a wrathful judge who is coming soon.

A God who loves what is good must necessarily hate what is evil.

DIVE *Go deeper in your study with these resources*

Is God a Moral Monster? Making Sense of the Old Testament God by Paul Copan

How Do You Know You're Not Wrong? Responding to Objections That Leave Christians Speechless by Paul Copan

God Behaving Badly: Is the God of the Old Testament Angry, Sexist, and Racist? by David T. Lamb

58
IS GOD GUILTY OF GENOCIDE?

In 1 Samuel 15:3 God commands King Saul: "Now go and attack the Amalekites and completely destroy everything they have. Do not spare them. Kill men and women, children and infants, oxen and sheep, camels and donkeys."

Bible stories like this are fodder for atheists like Richard Dawkins, who writes in *The God Delusion*, "The God of the Old Testament is arguably the most unpleasant character in all fiction: jealous and proud of it; a petty, unjust, unforgiving control-freak; a vindictive, bloodthirsty ethnic cleanser; a misogynistic, homophobic, racist, infanticidal, genocidal, filicidal, pestilential, megalomaniacal, sadomasochistic, capriciously malevolent bully."[1]

Though less strident than Dawkins, other cynics struggle to see God as loving and merciful in light of such Scriptures. So we must ask, "Is God a genocidal maniac?"

Hardly. God's love and wrath are not mutually exclusive. Rather, they are complementary qualities of His divine nature and His plan to rescue humanity.

God orders the destruction of the Amalekites and certain other groups for two primary reasons: to punish their accumulated sins, and to prevent their wicked influence from spreading.

The measure of sin

Scripture indicates that people and groups have a limit to the sins they commit unrepentantly before the Lord brings judgment upon them. For example, in Matthew 23 Jesus tells Israel's religious leaders they are filling up the measure of their fathers' sins; 40 years later, the temple is destroyed, Jerusalem is sacked, and the Jews are scattered.

The apostle Paul has a similar message for his fellow countrymen who prevent Christians from spreading the gospel to the Gentiles. "As a result, they are always completing the number of their sins, and wrath has overtaken them at last," he writes in 1 Thess. 2:16.

In the Old Testament, God tells Abraham his descendants will be exiled and abused for 400 years before God leads them into the Promised Land. The reason for the long delay is that the iniquity of the Amorites has not yet reached its full measure (Gen. 15:13-16). In other words, God plans to wait centuries while the Canaanite groups (including the Amalekites) slowly fill up their own cups of destruction. God never acts hastily or capriciously against them; His grace and mercy are longsuffering.

As stated in *Hard Sayings of the Bible*: "These nations are cut off to prevent the corruption of Israel and the rest of the world (Deut. 20:16-18). When a nation starts burning children as a gift to the gods (Lev. 18:21) and practices sodomy, beastiality and all sorts of loathsome vices (Lev. 18:25, 27-30), the day of God's grace and mercy has begun to run out."[2]

Unintended consequences

But why, specifically, the Amalekites? When the weary Israelites pass through the desert toward Canaan, the Amalekites pick off their weak, sickly, and elderly and brutally murder them. Moses reminds the Hebrews, "Remember what the Amalekites did to you on the journey after you left Egypt. They met you along the way and attacked all your stragglers from behind when you were tired and weary. They did not fear God" (Deut. 25:17-18).

Saul disobeys God by sparing some of the Amalekites, as well as their choice animals. As a result, there are consequences. Some commentators believe that Haman, who in the Book of Esther seeks the extermination of the Jews throughout the Persian Empire, is an Amalekite.

All right, but why punish "innocent" women and children? Individuals share in the life of their families and nations, participating in their rewards and punishments. But there is another consideration. If women and children bathed in idolatry and wickedness are spared, how long before a new generation of adults emerges like their pagan predecessors?

Finally, why kill the livestock? God does not want the Israelites to go to war in order to enrich themselves. Their solemn task is to carry out a death penalty, not line their pockets.

It is God's sovereign right to determine when people or groups have filled up their "measure of sin." When He decides that severe judgment must fall, we may rest assured that He is not forfeiting his grace and mercy; rather, the sinning party has rejected God and passed beyond the point of no return.

Stereotypical language

A few final comments may prove helpful in soothing any remaining squeamishness about the violent nature of the Israelites' conquest of Canaan. Paul Copan writes extensively on this issue in his book, *Is God a Moral Monster?* Among his observations:

- The language of commands to destroy certain Canaanite peoples includes stereotypical language – "all," "young and old," "men and women." This so-called consecrated ban (*herem*) could be carried out even if women and children are not present.
- The sweeping language of the biblical *herem* is directed at combatants.
- The ban language allows (and hopes for) exceptions; think of Rahab.
- The destruction language of ancient Near Eastern warfare (and the Old Testament) is exaggerated; groups of Canaanite people who supposedly are "totally destroyed" are still around later in Scripture.
- God's greater concern is to destroy Canaanite religion, not Canaanites per se.
- Many biblical texts speak of "driving out" the Canaanites, meaning expulsion from the land, not annihilation.

Copan summarizes, "We have many good reasons to rethink our paradigm regarding the destruction of the Canaanites. On closer analysis, the biblical text suggests that much more is going on beneath the surface than obliterating all the Canaanites. Taking the destruction of anything that breathes at face value needs much reexamination.[3]

What are some ways a nation may fill up its "measure of sin?" How can people know when they are approaching the limit?

Why do you think the innocent suffer when God brings judgment to bear on a nation? Couldn't He just "zap" the wicked?

What do you think would happen if God never intervened in the affairs of people?

How might you answer the charge that God is guilty of genocide?

In what ways is God's wrath compatible with His love? How is this illustrated in the driving out of the Canaanites?

SHARE *Talking points for discussing the justice of God*

God's love and wrath are not mutually exclusive. Rather, they are complementary qualities of His divine nature and His plan to rescue humanity.

God orders the destruction of the Amalekites and certain other groups for two primary reasons: to punish their accumulated sins, and to prevent their wicked influence from spreading.

Scripture indicates that people and groups have a limit to the sins they commit unrepentantly before the Lord brings judgment upon them. This sometimes is referred to as a "measure of sin."

God waits centuries while the Canaanite groups slowly fill up their own cups of destruction. God never acts hastily or capriciously against them; His grace and mercy are longsuffering.

When a nation starts burning children as a gift to the gods (Lev. 18:21) and practices sodomy, bestiality and all sorts of loathsome vices (Lev. 18:25, 27-30), the day of God's grace and mercy has begun to run out.

It is God's sovereign right to determine when people or groups have filled up their "measure of sin." When He decides that severe judgment must fall, we may rest assured that He is not forfeiting his grace and mercy; rather, the sinning party has rejected God and passed beyond the point of no return.

DIVE *Go deeper in your study with these resources*

Hard Sayings of the Bible by Walter C. Kaiser Jr., Peter H. Davids, F.F. Bruce, Manfred T. Brauch

Did God Really Command Genocide? Coming to Terms with the Justice of God by Paul Copan and Matt Flannagan

God at War: The Bible and Spiritual Conflict by Gregory Boyd

59

IS GOD TO BLAME FOR OUR MESSED-UP WORLD?

When my kids were young and complained about being on the wrong side of circumstances, my wife and I urged them to repeat this line: "When things go badly for me, it's usually my fault."

In other words, we challenged our son and daughter to own their part of a bad experience.

If a teacher singled them out from a group of misbehaving students, they were to understand that their behavior was wrong, whether done individually or in a group.

If they got into an argument with a friend, they were to review the conversation and see how their words contributed to the dust-up.

If someone stole a pair of gym shoes from their locker, they learned the wisdom of using the combination lock we provided for them while paying for new shoes out of their allowance.

Like us, many Christian parents swim against a strong cultural current of victimhood, which values freedom over responsibility and leads inevitably to an entitlement approach to life. The line between right and wrong is blurred. Good and evil are subjective realities, not objective standards. And when things go badly, there are always other people to blame.

Dear sir, I am

True, this frame of mind existed in Eden and has been handed down to succeeding generations through the sin nature, but victimhood seems especially strong in today's Western culture. It makes us long for the days of writer and Christian apologist C.K. Chesterton, who is credited with responding to a reporter's open question, "What's wrong with the world today?" with this simple response: "Dear sir, I am."[1]

Victimhood is a slippery slope. Once we are comfortable blaming others for our problems, it's easy to start blaming God, especially with respect to human suffering. In fact, this often is the first salvo of atheists who argue that if God exists and is good, He should eradicate suffering for all creatures. Let's look more closely at this argument.

The fact is that human suffering came about because people abused their ability to make choices, not because God wants to hurt us. As Christian author Lee Strobel writes, "God decided to give free will to men and women because this is the only way we can enjoy the highest value in the universe, which is love.... Without free will, we could never love, because in order to love we must have the choice not to love."[2]

Philosopher Peter Krceft, author of *Making Sense Out of Suffering*, writes, "Once God chose to create human beings with free will, then it was up to them, rather than to God, as to whether there was sin or not.... It's a self-contradiction – a meaningless nothing – to have a world where there's real choice while at the same time no possibility of choosing evil."[3]

A groaning creation

Consider this: The world produces enough food for each person to consume 3,000 calories a day. So why are people starving? Two main reasons are corrupt governments and selfish individuals – not God.

Even natural evil – earthquakes, floods, and the like – is rooted in sin. Adam's fall produced an immediate curse on the earth that continues today. As the apostle Paul notes: "We know that the whole creation has been groaning as in the pains of childbirth right up to the present time" (Rom. 8:22).

Cliffe Knechtle, an apologist focusing on college students, writes, "When we human beings told God to shove off, he partially honored our request.... We are born into a world made chaotic and unfair by a humanity in revolt against its Creator."[4]

The good news is that Christ has provided for our redemption, and for the regeneration of our planet, through His finished work on the cross. When He returns, the redeemed receive glorified bodies and the earth is purged of the effects of the Fall. Together, we are made new.

God has entrusted us with a great gift: the ability to make choices that have consequences. Therefore, when things go wrong for us, it's good to ask ourselves whether we had at least some role to play in the troubling turn of events.

THINK *Questions for personal or group study*

How can God maintain His sovereignty over all things if people have free will?

When God intervenes in the affairs of human beings – as He often does in the Bible – isn't He taking away free will in these instances?

How would you explain the love of God to a child whose parents were swept away in a flash flood?

What did the apostle Paul mean, in practical terms, when he wrote that the whole creation has been groaning as in the pains of childbirth right up to the present time?

How does the person and work of Christ answer the issue of pain and suffering in the world?

SHARE *Talking points for discussing our messed-up world*

Human suffering came about because people abused their ability to make choices, not because God wants to hurt us.

God gave us free will because this is the only way we can enjoy the highest value in the universe, which is love. Without free will, we could never love, because in order to love we must have the choice not to love (Lee Strobel).

It's a self-contradiction to have a world where there's real choice while at the same time no possibility of choosing evil.

Why does starvation exist in a world capable of producing enough food for everyone? Two primary reasons are corrupt governments and selfish people – not God.

Christ has provided for our redemption, and for the regeneration of our planet, through His finished work on the cross.

God has entrusted us with a great gift: the ability to make choices that have consequences. When things go wrong for us, it's good to ask ourselves whether we had at least some role to play in the troubling turn of events.

DIVE *Go deeper in your study with these resources*

Where is God When It Hurts? by Philip Yancey

The Case for Faith by Lee Strobel

Making Sense Out of Suffering by Peter Kreeft

60
WHY WE SUFFER

Horatio G. Spafford was a prominent attorney in Chicago in the 1800s and a friend of evangelist Dwight L. Moody. While Spafford was both respected and comfortable, he faced severe hardship.

First, he lost his four-year-old son to scarlet fever. Then his real estate investments along Lake Michigan literally went up in flames in the Great Chicago Fire of 1871. Not long after that, his four daughters drowned in a shipwreck, and his wife Anna survived the ordeal only because the ship's debris buoyed her as she floated, unconscious, in the Atlantic Ocean.

Crossing the sea to join his bereaved wife, Spafford was called to the captain's deck as the ship sailed past the foamy deep where his daughters were lost. The captain informed him that the waters there were three miles deep. Returning to his cabin, Spafford penned these words to the now-famous hymn:

When peace like a river attendeth my way,

When sorrows like sea billows roll;

Whatever my lot, Thou hast taught me to say,

It is well, it is well with my soul[1]

Why did such tragedy befall this godly man? Spafford may have wondered why, but ultimately he rested in the sovereignty of God.

We can better appreciate God's sovereignty, even in the darkest nights, by observing 10 reasons we suffer, according to Scripture.

1. We suffer because we sin. All of us are sinners (Rom. 3:10, 23). Unbelievers live lifestyles of independence from God, while believers experience moments, or seasons, of independence. Spiritual discipline is designed to target sin in a believer's life, and that discipline may be severe, including death (1 Cor. 11:29-32).

2. We suffer because others sin. Children suffer at the hands of an abusive parent. Citizens suffer at the hands of corrupt leaders. Rarely does our sin remain confined to us. King David numbered his troops, and

70,000 people suffered the consequences. Jesus suffered through no fault of His own but gave His life for our sins.

3. We suffer because we live in a sinful and fallen world. Accidents happen. Natural disasters take the lives of millions each year. The apostle Paul writes that the whole world is groaning beneath the weight of sin (Rom. 8:22).

4. We suffer because God allows us to make real choices. The sovereignty of God and the ability of people to make meaningful choices are two biblical truths. We are not robots; we actually can and do make choices for which God holds us accountable.

5. We suffer to make us long for eternity. This world is not our home; our citizenship is in heaven. The writer of Hebrews records, "These [heroes of the faith] all died in faith without having received the promises, but they saw them from a distance, greeted them, and confessed that they were foreigners and temporary residents on the earth (11:13)." When we suffer, it helps prevent us from clinging to this world, which is passing away.

6. We suffer to keep us from something worse. A fever sends us to the doctor, where our illness is diagnosed and a remedy prescribed. On a grander scale, suffering tells us there is something wrong with us, and with the world, and often leads us to the all-important search for Christ. Darkness, pain, suffering, loneliness, abandonment — all help us grasp the reality of life, now and eternally, without Christ.

7. We suffer to share in the suffering of Christ, and thus to be more like Him. Christians persecuted for their faith share in what Paul calls "the fellowship of His suffering" (Phil. 3:10). When we suffer, it also enables us to comfort others who suffer. Paul also writes, "For our momentary light affliction is producing for us an absolutely incomparable eternal weight of glory" (2 Cor. 4:17).

8. We suffer to honor God. Jesus tells us to take heart when we are persecuted for His sake (Matt. 5:10-11). And He warns us the world will hate us because it hated Him first. If Christians had easier lives it would make the gospel more attractive for the wrong reasons; God would become a means to an end rather than the end of all things Himself.

9. We suffer to grow spiritually. Jesus, who was perfect in His humanity, nevertheless "learned" obedience through suffering. Paul writes that he has "learned," in whatsoever state he is, to be content (Phil. 4:11). And Paul's "thorn in the flesh" is designed to keep him from boasting (2 Cor. 12:7).

10. We suffer to better anticipate the glories of heaven and the world to come. In Rev. 21:4 we read, "He will wipe away every tear from their eyes. Death will exist no longer; grief, crying, and pain will exist no longer, because the previous things have passed away." Paul writes, "For I consider that the sufferings of this present time are not worth comparing with the glory that is going to be revealed to us" (Rom. 8:18).

THINK *Questions for personal or group study*

What purpose do you believe suffering serves in the life of an atheist?

How can suffering advance the cause of Christ?

If God is good, and if Christians are His children, why do you think He allows – or causes – us to suffer? Couldn't He find other ways to teach us kingdom lessons?

How can anything good come from the evils of abortion, pediatric cancer, or child abuse?

How do you think God responds when we lash out at Him in anger because of suffering, or because He so often seems silent when we ask Him why?

SHARE *Talking points for discussing why we suffer*

We can better appreciate God's sovereignty by observing biblical reasons for our suffering.

Sin often is the root of suffering. We may suffer because we sin, because others sin, or because we live in a sinful and fallen world.

The sovereignty of God and the ability of people to make meaningful choices are two biblical truths. We are not robots; we actually can and do make choices for which God holds us accountable.

Sometimes we suffer to share in the suffering of Christ, and thus to be more like Him.

One day Jesus will wipe away every tear from our eyes. Death, grief, crying, and pain will exist no longer, fading into the past as former things that have passed away (Rev. 21:4).

DIVE *Go deeper in your study with these resources*

If God is Good by Randy Alcorn

Where is God When it Hurts? by Philip Yancey

Walking with God through Pain and Suffering by Tim Keller

God Forsaken: Bad Things Happen. Is there a God who cares? Yes. Here's proof by Dinesh D'Souza

SCIENCE AND RELIGION

61

ARE SCIENCE AND RELIGION CLOSER THAN WE THINK?

A Missouri pastor once sent me a *Huffington Post* article in which MIT Astrophysicist Max Tegmark assures us that religion and science are much closer than one might suspect, as evidenced by the results of a 2013 MIT Survey on Science, Religion and Origins.[1]

Tegmark and his colleagues present a detailed survey of how different U.S. faith communities view the science of origins, particularly evolution and Big Bang cosmology.

Their conclusion: "We find a striking gap between people's personal beliefs and the official views of the faiths to which they belong. Whereas Gallup reports that 46% of Americans believe that God created humans in their present form less than 10,000 years ago, we find that only 11% belong to religions openly rejecting evolution."[2]

For example, the Roman Catholic Church endorses evolution; yet only 58 percent of Catholics say evolution is the best explanation for life on earth.

Tegmark's conclusion: "The main divide in the origins debate is not between science and religion, but between a small fundamentalist minority and mainstream religious communities who embrace science."[3]

By the way, Southern Baptists are solidly in the "small fundamentalist minority" according to the survey and therefore stand accused of not embracing science.

Contributing to confusion

This is unfair for two reasons. First, it falsely paints many evangelical Christians as modern-day Neanderthals who still believe in a flat earth.

But more importantly, the MIT colleagues deliberately avoid defining their terms in the survey, resulting in much confusion.

For example, the first question reads: "What is the relationship between your religious beliefs and the theory of evolution/Big Bang cosmology?"

Nowhere does the survey provide a definition of "evolution" or "Big Bang cosmology."

So I sent an email to Tegmark, who graciously responded within 24 hours. "For the purpose of the survey, you can simply define those terms in whatever way you personally feel is reasonable," he wrote.[4]

Therein lies the problem. There are numerous and sometimes contradictory definitions of evolution and Big Bang cosmology. Getting scientists to agree on these terms is like asking John Calvin and Jacobus Arminius to draft a joint statement on TULIP.

Think of it this way: I might be in complete theological agreement with my pastor with respect to the doctrine of creation but answer the question differently than he does based on our separate understandings of evolution.

For example, I might be thinking of *microevolution*, which defines small-scale changes within species. This is not in conflict with God's creation of creatures "according to their kinds." Further, we can observe changes within species as a mechanism God built into His creatures to help them adapt to the rigors of surviving in a sinful and fallen world.

But suppose my pastor is thinking of *macroevolution*, which entails the descent of all life from a single living cell. Or he could be thinking in much broader terms of *atheistic evolution* or *theistic evolution*.

In any case, our presuppositions lead us to answer the question differently.

Tegmark notes, "The fact that the gap between personal and official beliefs is so large suggests that part of the controversy might be defused by people learning more about their own religious doctrine and the science it endorses, thereby bridging this belief gap."[5]

Agreed. But of equal value is for the scientific community to avoid using terms it is not willing to define.

In addition, it would help if many scientists did not cling so desperately to naturalism (the doctrine that the natural world is all there is) or materialism (the belief that material reality is the only reality). Certainly, many of our nation's leading scientific minds are more open to following the evidence wherever it leads than Harvard biologist Richard Lewontin, who wrote, "[M]aterialism is absolute, for we cannot allow a Divine Foot

61. Are Science and Religion Closer Than We Think?   **393**

in the door.... To appeal to an omnipotent deity is to allow that at any moment the regularities of nature may be ruptured, that miracles may happen."[6]

Three simple rules

So, how do we talk with our friends about the subject of origins? Here are three simple rules.

First, state our belief that God's revelation in Scripture is consistent with His revelation in nature. When there is an apparent conflict, it's likely due to an improper reading of the Bible or a misapplication of scientific principles.

Second, state that we are willing to go where the evidence leads, and ask if our friends are willing to do the same.

Third, talk less and listen more. Ask your friends to define evolution, the Big Bang, and other terms. Ask them how they came to their conclusions, and ask for their understanding of the biblical teachings of origins.

Perhaps our friends will come to the same conclusion as Astronomer Robert Jastrow, who writes, "For the scientist who has lived by his faith in the power of reason, the story ends like a bad dream. He has scaled the mountains of ignorance; he is about to conquer the highest peak. As he pulls himself over the final rock, he is greeted by a band of theologians who have been sitting there for centuries."[7]

THINK *Questions for personal or group study*

Why do you think so many people argue that science and belief are incompatible? How might you respond?

What are the advantages of defining our terms in a discussion of origins – and the dangers of not doing so?

What's the difference between microevolution and macroevolution? Does the Bible lend support to either of these processes?

What questions could you pose to a friend who embraces naturalism – the belief that the natural world is all that exists?

How might you engage a friend who believes God created the universe through the process of evolution?

SHARE *Talking points for discussing science and religion*

God's revelation in Scripture is consistent with His revelation in nature. When there is an apparent conflict, it's likely due to an improper reading of the Bible or a misapplication of scientific principles.

In discussing origins with friends who hold a naturalistic worldview, we should tell them we are willing to go where the evidence leads, and ask if they are willing to do the same.

We should talk less and listen more, asking our friends to define evolution, the Big Bang, and other terms, and then asking them how they came to their conclusions.

We might also ask about their understanding of the biblical teachings of origins. This leads to a better understanding of our friends and their views, and it may buy us the right to share a more fully orbed explanation of Scripture.

DIVE *Go deeper in your study with these resources*

God's Crime Scene: A Cold-case Detective Examines the Evidence for a Divinely Created Universe by J. Warner Wallace

Science & Belief: The Big Issues by Russell Stannard

God and the Astronomers / New and Expanded Edition 1992 by Robert Jastrow

62

THANK GOD FOR EARTHQUAKES

The Lisbon earthquake of 1755 changed everything. In minutes this thriving, affluent city was brought to its knees. Roughly 50,000 people died. The sky turned black. Fires raged. Then tidal waves washed over the port, drowning hundreds more.

Later, Voltaire wrote a poem challenging the prevailing view that this was a divine act of judgment. "Whilst you these facts replete with horror view, will you maintain death to their crimes was due?" he penned, adding, "Can you then impute a sinful deed, to babes who on their mother's bosoms feed?"[1]

Voltaire did not challenge the existence of God. He simply asked what kind of deity would create a world with such design flaws. It's a question other great thinkers of his day dared to ask as well – a question taken up by today's angry atheists and carried to the extreme conclusion that God does not exist.

The earthquake and tsunami that devastated Southeast Asia in 2004, and a similar disaster that struck Japan in 2011, are more recent examples of what may be described as natural evil. While many atheists concede that moral evil exists in the world, the idea of natural evil seems to prove either that God does not exist or, if He does, He is not a compassionate, all-powerful God worthy of worship.

Not so fast.

Plate tectonics

It is only in the last century that modern science has discovered the cause of earthquakes: plate tectonics, or the movement of giant masses of rock beneath the surface of the earth and the ocean floor.

As these colossal plates move and bump into each other, they sometimes rupture the surface of the earth, causing earthquakes. When these collisions take place beneath the ocean floor, the result is seaquakes followed by tsunamis.

In their book *Rare Earth*, Peter D. Ward and Donald Brownlee observe, "ours is still the only planet we know that has plate tectonics." They further show that plate tectonics is a "central requirement for life on a planet." It's also largely responsible for differences in land elevation that separate the land from the seas.[2]

But there's more. Plate tectonics recirculates carbon dioxide into the atmosphere, and without carbon dioxide we would not have life.

Dinesh D'Souza writes in *What's So Great About God*, "The whole tectonic system serves as a kind of 'planetary thermostat,' helping to regulate the earth's climate and preventing the onset of scorching or freezing temperatures that would make mammalian life, and possibly all life, impossible."[3]

Plate tectonics also aids the formation of minerals deep in the earth and their availability near the surface.

Finally, plate tectonics possibly is involved in the generation of the earth's magnetic field, without which earth's inhabitants would be exposed to cosmic radiation.

So, in a sense, we owe our existence to plate tectonics and the earthquakes it produces. Of course earthquakes often cause great destruction and claim the lives of many people. These are real tragedies that must not be minimized.

Creation's labor pains

However, to make the leap from tragic consequences of natural disasters to accusations that God is aloof, petulant, or non-existent isn't fair. People die of heatstroke and skin cancer but that doesn't make the sun – or its Creator – our enemy. Fires often devastate property and take innocent lives, but without fire many technological advances such as smelting metals would not be possible.

In addition, floods and hurricanes cause tragic death and destruction, but these natural disasters would be impossible without water, without which no living creature could survive.

The point here for Christians is not to concede the atheist's viewpoint, or to admit that God is fallible simply because natural disasters occur with great force and frequency.

It's true that something is wrong with the created order – and this has been the case ever since the Fall. Paul writes, "[T]he whole creation has been groaning together with labor pains until now" (Rom. 8:22).

But it's also reassuring to know that God works through our unbalanced world – and its tragic outbursts – to protect and preserve life. He may choose to use nature as an instrument of judgment, as with the sons of Korah (Num. 16:32). But mostly He works through the sinful and fallen world in which we live to keep it in check for our benefit.

THINK *Questions for personal or group study*

How would you describe plate tectonics to a friend? Then, how would you explain to that friend the necessity of the tectonics system to life on this planet?

In what ways do some atheists use natural disasters to "prove" God does not exist? How might you respond?

What is your response to the view that natural disasters occur because God either lacks the knowledge, will, or power to prevent them?

In Scripture, how does God sometimes use the natural elements to protect His people or to punish the wicked?

What changes do you think Jesus will bring to the natural order when He returns and creates new heavens and a new earth?

The earth's plate tectonics – discovered only in the last century – is a central requirement for life on a planet, and so far earth is the only planet we know that has plate tectonics.

The whole tectonic system serves as a kind of "planetary thermostat," helping to regulate the earth's climate and preventing the onset of scorching or freezing temperatures that would make mammalian life, and possibly all life, impossible (Dinesh D'Souza).

Plate tectonics causes earthquakes, which are essential to life on earth but also result in tragic loss of life. Even so, to make the leap from tragic consequences of natural disasters to accusations that God is aloof, petulant, or non-existent isn't fair.

People die of heatstroke and skin cancer but that doesn't make the sun – or its Creator – our enemy. Fires often devastate property and take innocent lives, but without fire many technological advances such as smelting metals would not be possible.

It's assuring to know that God works through our unbalanced world – and its tragic outbursts – to protect and preserve life. He may choose to use nature as an instrument of judgment, as with the sons of Korah (Num. 16:32). But mostly he works through the sinful and fallen world in which we live to keep it in check for our benefit.

DIVE *Go deeper in your study with these resources*

What's So Great About God: A Reasonable Defense of the Goodness of God in a World Filled with Suffering by Dinesh D'Souza

Rare Earth: Why Complex Life is Uncommon in the Universe by Peter D. Ward and Donald Brownlee

The Privileged Planet: How Our Place in the Cosmos is Designed for Discovery by Guillermo Gonzalez and Jay Wesley Richards

RELATIVISM AND UNBELIEF

63
ARE ALL RELIGIONS EQUAL?

In Cholula, Mexico, stands the Church of Our Lady of Remedies. It sits atop the largest archaeological site in the Americas – a pyramid laced with catacombs and filled with artifacts from pre-colonial days.

According to some accounts, the natives of Cholula refused to welcome Spanish Conquistador Hernan Cortes in the 16th century. So to teach them a lesson, Cortes massacred thousands and ordered the people to build 365 Catholic churches, one for each day of the year.

They never reached their goal, but Cortes made his point: The Aztecs were a conquered people, and their religion was subjugated to Roman Catholicism.

The Aztecs understood this – or they should have. Previously, they were the conquerors and had built their sacred sites atop those of other indigenous peoples.

An interesting side effect is that none of the religions remained pure. Rather, each incorporated some of the beliefs and practices of the previous peoples into their religious life.

As a result, in many parts of Latin America today Roman Catholicism is a skin stretched over the ancient bones of animistic and pagan practices that find open expression outside the Catholic Church in religions like Santeria and Voodoo.

The trend toward syncretism

This illustrates a modern tendency toward syncretism – the melding of many religious views. And this mindset affects the church.

Pastor, author, and syndicated radio host John MacArthur writes about a Christian broadcasting organization striving "to be a good neighbor to a variety of listeners." The network released a policy statement, part of which reads:

"When you are preparing your program for these stations, please avoid using the following: criticism of other religions and references to conversion, missionaries, believers, unbelievers, old covenant, new covenant, church, the cross, crucifixion, Calvary, Christ, the blood of Christ, salvation through Christ, redemption through Christ, the Son of God, Jehovah or the Christian life."

The statement continues, "These people listening are hungering for words of comfort. We ask you to adhere to these restrictions so that God's Word can continue to go forth. Please help us maintain our position of bringing comfort to suffering people."

How tragic, responds MacArthur, that an organization dedicated to bringing comfort refuses to so much as mention the elements essential to the only message that can bring true peace and comfort to a troubled soul.[1]

God is not one

The idea that all beliefs are equally valid isn't new, but it has come into sharper focus in more recent times.

Religious studies scholar Huston Smith writes, "It is possible to climb life's mountain from any side, but when the top is reached the trails converge. At base, in the foothills of theology, ritual, and organizational structure, the religions are distinct.... But beyond these differences, the same goal beckons."[2]

Fortunately, not everyone buys this. Stephen Prothero, professor of religion at Boston University, has written a best-selling book, *God is Not One: The Eight Rival Religions That Run the World – and Why Their Differences Matter.*

Prothero is not an evangelical Christian, but in some respects evangelicals owe him a debt of gratitude for venturing into a religious Thunderdome where political correctness meets the truth in a battle to the death.

Prothero writes that the tendency today is to say that all religions are true ... that we all worship the same God. But that view, says Prothero, is neither workable nor correct. A simple review of the world's great religions shows that there are distinctions that cannot be reconciled.

He writes, "One purpose of the 'all religions are one' mantra is to stop this fighting and this killing. And it is comforting to pretend that the great religions make up one big, happy family. But this sentiment, however well-intentioned, is neither accurate nor ethically responsible. God is not one. Faith in the unity of religions is just that – faith. And the leap that gets us there is an act of the hyperactive imagination."[3]

Doctrinal archaeologists

In Mexico, by the time Cortes built a Catholic Church atop the pyramid at Cholula, people in the community barely knew the significance of the pyramid. It had become overgrown.

Today, archaeologists combing the ruins are getting a clearer picture of the ancient peoples who first inhabited that part of Mexico, as well as who and how they worshiped.

In a sense, you and I must act as doctrinal archaeologists. We must strip away the overgrowth of biblical neglect and dig deeply through the layers of tradition, philosophy, and man-made rules.

When we do, we will rediscover the bedrock of true religion. As the apostle Paul writes, "No one can lay any other foundation than what has been laid – that is, Jesus Christ" (1 Cor. 3:11).

THINK *Questions for personal or group study*

What are some examples that disprove the claim that all religions are basically the same?

How is the God of the Bible different from the deities of Islam, Hinduism, and Daoism?

Why do you think it's attractive to blur the lines between religions?

How would you respond to the accusation that Christians – who say Jesus is the only way of salvation – are narrow-minded and judgmental?

What are some good, non-threatening questions you could ask a Muslim, Hindu, or Buddhist about his faith in order to start a conversation?

SHARE *Talking points for discussing whether all religions are equal*

The idea that all beliefs are equally valid isn't new, but it has come into sharper focus in more recent times.

A simple review of the world's great religions shows that there are distinctions that cannot be reconciled.

It may be comforting to pretend that the great religions make up one big, happy family. But this sentiment is neither accurate nor ethically responsible (Stephen Prothero).

Faith in the unity of religions is just that – faith. And the leap that gets us there is an act of the hyperactive imagination (Stephen Prothero).

Christians must act as doctrinal archaeologists, stripping away the overgrowth of biblical neglect, and digging deeply through the layers of tradition, philosophy, and man-made rules. What's to be unearthed? The bedrock of true religion: Jesus Christ (1 Cor. 3:11).

DIVE *Go deeper in your study with these resources*

God is Not One: The Eight Rival Religions That Run the World – and Why Their Differences Matter by Stephen Prothero

They Like Jesus but Not the Church: Insights from Emerging Generations by Dan Kimball

The God Who is There: Finding Your Place in God's Story by D.A. Carson

64
WHAT YOUNG ATHEISTS CAN TEACH US

Larry Alex Taunton directs the Fixed Point Foundation, which seeks innovative ways to defend and proclaim the gospel. A few years ago, his organization reached out to college-age atheists nationwide in a unique campaign. As Taunton contacted leaders of Secular Student Alliances and Freethought Societies, he had one simple request: Tell us your journey to unbelief.

Taunton did not dispute their stories or debate the merits of their views. He just listened. Many stepped forward – some reluctantly. Ultimately, Taunton found patterns emerging from the young atheists' stories, and he summarized them in an article in *The Atlantic*.[1]

There are common threads running through their stories:

The young atheists had attended church. Most participants didn't begin with a naturalistic worldview, but instead chose atheism as a reaction to Christianity, which they found lifeless, hypocritical, or uncompelling for a variety of reasons.

Their churches promoted vague missions and messages. The students heard plenty of messages on social justice, community involvement, and good deeds, but they failed to see a connection between these messages, Jesus, and the Bible. They knew intuitively that the church exists for more than social campaigns; it exists to proclaim the teachings of Jesus and His relevance to a sinful and fallen world.

Their churches fumbled the big questions. When asked what they found unconvincing about the Christian faith, the students mentioned a lack of satisfying answers to such issues as evolution vs. creation, sexuality, Jesus as the only way, and the reliability of the Bible. Not only was the church often ill equipped to delve into these issues; it lacked the stomach to tackle them at all.

They respect ministers who take the Bible seriously. The young atheists expressed grudging admiration for pastors and other Christians who embrace biblical teaching and are not ashamed to say so. As atheist, illusionist, and comedian Penn Jillette famously remarked, "I don't respect people who don't proselytize.... If you believe that there's a heaven and hell ... and you think that it's not really worth telling them this because it would make it socially awkward ... how much do you have to hate somebody to believe that everlasting life is possible and not tell them that?"[2]

Ages 14-17 are key. While some participants said they adopted atheism as early as eight years of age or as late as college, most admitted embracing unbelief in high school.

Emotions run deep. Most students said they lost their Christianity for purely rational reasons. However, the more they talked, the more they described a deeply emotional journey from belief to atheism. One young lady said she became an atheist after her father died – not because she blamed God for his death, but because he was abusive and she did not want to think her father was still alive somewhere.

Online is everything. When asked about the key influences in their conversion to atheism, not a single participant mentioned the "new atheists" like Christopher Hitchens, or their books or seminars. Rather, they mentioned YouTube or website forums.

Getting real

There's much we can do to engage our young atheist friends by listening to them, helping them wrestle with tough questions, and providing a connection between Christ and a broken world. But we also must address the doubts and fears of young people in our own churches.

If Christianity is not objectively true, rationally compelling, and personally engaging, then why should anyone – young or old – want to embrace it?

Scottish philosopher and skeptic, David Hume, once was spotted in a crowd listening to the preaching of George Whitefield, the noted evangelist of the First Great Awakening.

Someone said to Hume, "I thought you didn't believe in the gospel."

"I do not," Hume replied. Then, nodding toward Whitefield, he added, "But he does."[3]

THINK *Questions for personal or group study*

What are some reasons young atheists reject Christianity?

Why do you think the church so often is ill equipped to tackle the tough questions young atheists are asking?

In what ways does the social gospel – focusing on social justice, community involvement, and good deeds – fail to capture the hearts of young atheists?

Why is listening to the story of a young atheist's journey to unbelief so important in sharing the gospel with him or her?

How can the church improve its outreach to young atheists?

SHARE *Talking points for discussing the journey of young atheists*

Many young atheists did not begin that way. They chose atheism as a reaction to Christianity, which they found lifeless, hypocritical, or uncompelling for a variety of reasons.

The church often is ill equipped to delve into tough issues like evolution vs. creation, sexuality, Jesus as the only way, and the reliability of the Bible – a weakness that turns many students away.

Young atheists express grudging admiration for pastors and other Christians who embrace biblical teaching and are not ashamed to say so.

We should listen to our young atheist friends, help them wrestle with tough questions, and provide a connection between Christ and a broken world.

If Christianity is not objectively true, rationally compelling, and personally engaging, then why should anyone – young or old – want to embrace it?

DIVE *Go deeper in your study with these resources*

Stealing from God: Why Atheists Need God to Make Their Case by Frank Turek and Ravi Zacharias

unChristian: What a New Generation Really Thinks about Christianity ... and Why It Matters by David Kinnaman and Gabe Lyons

Who Made God? And Answers to Over 100 Other Tough Questions of Faith by Norman L. Geisler and Ravi Zacharias

HOMOSEXUALITY

65
WHAT EVERY CHRISTIAN SHOULD KNOW ABOUT SAME-SEX ATTRACTION

In the spring of 2015, Ireland became the first country to legalize gay marriage by popular vote after a referendum found that 62 percent of voters favored changing the constitution to allow gay and lesbian couples to marry.

Then in June the U.S. Supreme Court handed down its much-anticipated decision in *Obergefell v. Hodges*, making the United States the 20th nation to sanction same-sex marriage.

While reactions to the 5-4 decision ranged from euphoria to despair, the church already had found itself divided on the same-sex issue, with some denominations sanctioning gay marriage, others blessing same-sex unions, and still others remaining staunchly opposed to any sexual conduct outside the confines of lifelong, monogamous, heterosexual marriage.

A sense of inevitability

If polls were any indication prior to the Supreme Court decision, a majority of Americans already favored same-sex marriage. Now that it's the law of the land, momentum continues to build. The issue of gay rights, which is not restricted to same-sex marriage, has advanced with great speed to the point where many Americans are resigned to the belief that the public celebration of homosexuality is with us to stay. No doubt, many Christians share this sense of inevitability.

Indeed, leaders of the lesbian, gay, bisexual, and transgender (LGBT) community have done a masterful job of equating gay rights with civil rights. Therefore, to oppose homosexual behavior in general, or same-sex marriage in particular, is akin to being racist.

Through legal action, the media, educational initiatives, and other means, the LGBT community has sought to marginalize those who stand against the gay lifestyle on convictional, and particularly religious, grounds. Carry a biblical worldview into the public square and you risk being labeled a right-wing extremist engaged in "New McCarthyism."[1]

VI. Other Apologetics Topics

At the same time, through the way we live our lives, Christians to some degree have surrendered the moral high ground. Numerous surveys show that the sexual and marital behavior of Christians does not differ significantly from that of non-Christians, meaning our conduct stands in stark contrast to what the Bible teaches about God's intent for sexuality and marriage.

As the argument goes: If Christians engage in premarital sex, adultery, pornography, and divorce about as often as non-Christians, who are we to judge others?

God has spoken clearly

Thankfully, God has spoken clearly in His Word. His standards of sexual purity and marital fidelity apply to all people. They reflect both His holiness and His creative intent for pleasure, security, and procreation through life-long monogamous relationships between men and women created in His image.

It's to our benefit, therefore, to revisit the issue of homosexuality through a biblical lens – not just to know what the Bible says, but also to know what God has instructed the church to do about it.

Our appraisal of any belief or action must be grounded in the Word of God. Our response should be seasoned with equal doses of conviction and compassion.

As we look more closely at the issue in the following chapters, it's important to draw a distinction between the temptation known as unwanted same-sex attraction, which is not a sin, and same-sex desires and behaviors, which the Bible always characterizes as sinful.

Every human being struggles with what the apostle Paul calls the flesh – the tarnished image of God warring against God's Word and, for the believer, against God's indwelling Spirit.

We should explore what God has to say about sex and marriage; they're both good, by the way. We should rejoice in God's creative design, earnestly pursue personal holiness, vigorously contend for the faith, and love those who experience same-sex attractions, whether they celebrate these attractions or acknowledge them as foreign to the will of God.

The world is watching. And the world is judging our response to LGBT people. Rather than wring our hands over their stunning victories in our courts, especially the court of public opinion, the church should seize this divine opportunity to speak the truth in love (Eph. 4:15).

Too often we have spoken loveless truth, or surrendered truth in the name of love. Scripture calls us to embrace both truth and love.

THINK *Questions for personal or group study*

Why do you think the acceptance of homosexuality has grown so quickly in recent years?

How is the U.S. Supreme Court's decision to legalize gay marriage in all 50 states going to impact the American church? Your local church?

How might you respond to the person who equates opposing gay marriage with racism?

If you were invited to a gay wedding, would you attend? Why or why not?

What are some ways Christians could lovingly oppose homosexual activism?

SHARE *Talking points for discussing same-sex attraction*

The Bible speaks clearly against any sexual conduct outside the confines of lifelong, monogamous, heterosexual marriage.

God's standards of sexual purity and marital fidelity apply to all people. They reflect both His holiness and His creative intent for pleasure, security, and procreation through life-long monogamous relationships between men and women created in His image.

Every human being struggles with what the apostle Paul calls the flesh – the tarnished image of God warring against God's Word and, for the believer, against God's indwelling Spirit.

Our appraisal of any belief or action must be grounded in the Word of God. Our response should be seasoned with equal doses of conviction and compassion.

It's important to draw a distinction between unwanted same-sex attraction, which is not a sin, and same-sex desires and behaviors, which the Bible always characterizes as sinful.

DIVE *Go deeper in your study with these resources*

What Does the Bible Really Teach about Homosexuality? by Kevin DeYoung

The Same Sex Controversy by James R. White and Jeffrey D. Niell

What Every Christian Should Know about Same-sex Attraction by Rob Phillips

66

SEVEN BIBLICAL TRUTHS ABOUT SEX AND MARRIAGE

Scripture provides at least seven truths about sex and marriage. We'll explore key passages in detail in the next chapter.

1. The Bible condemns all forms of sexual behavior outside the bonds of heterosexual, monogamous, life-long marriage.

Homosexuality is not a special class of sin that makes it any more or less an act of rebellion against God than premarital sex, adultery, polygamy, pornography, or other sexual sins.

We do injustice to God's Word, and to those struggling with same-sex attraction, when we make homosexual conduct a special class of sin.

2. God has spoken clearly.

The Bible never speaks of homosexuality in a positive – or even a neutral – light. Sexual relations between members of the same gender always in Scripture are depicted as sinful.

God's Word describes such conduct as "an abomination," "degrading," "unnatural," "shameless," and a "perversion."

Those who commit same-sex acts, refuse to acknowledge them as sinful, and reject the call to repentance are outside the kingdom of God.

3. God's creative intent for sexual relations is good.

God created male and female, and He designed a unique, complementary sexual union between us in the bonds of heterosexual, monogamous, life-long marriage.

Summarizing the 2,000-year-old Christian narrative on sexuality and marriage, Pascal-Emmanuel Gobry writes, "The sexual act is meant to reflect God's love by fostering a union at once bodily and spiritual – and creates new life.... The fruitfulness of the marriage act reflects that God is a creator and has charged man to be an agent of his ongoing work of creation. And, finally, if God's love means total self-giving unto death on a Cross, then man and wife must give themselves to each other totally – no pettiness, no adultery, no polygamy, no divorce, and no nonmarital acts."[1]

Genesis 1-2 establishes at least seven norms for marriage: Marriage is covenantal, sexual, procreative, heterosexual, monogamous, non-incestuous, and symbolic of the gospel, according to Denny Burk in *What is the Meaning of Sex?*[2]

4. Jesus affirms Old Testament teachings about sexuality and marriage.

In Matthew 19 the Pharisees ask Jesus, "Is it lawful for a man to divorce his wife on any grounds?" (v. 3). Rather than debate the lawfulness of failed marriages, Jesus takes the religious leaders back to the Garden of Eden.

"Haven't you read," He replies, "that He who created them in the beginning made them male and female ... For this reason a man will leave his father and mother and be joined to his wife, and the two will become one flesh? So they are no longer two, but one flesh. Therefore, what God has joined together, man must not separate" (vv. 4-6).

The Pharisees respond, "Why then did Moses command us to give divorce papers and send her away?" Jesus tells them, "Moses permitted [not commanded] you to divorce your wives because of the hardness of your hearts. But it was not like that from the beginning" (vv. 7-8).

Clearly, the Lord has not changed His reasons for creating men and women, nor has His "divine accommodation" (allowing divorce under terms of the Mosaic Law) lowered His standards for sexual purity and marriage. There is no divine accommodation for homosexual conduct.

5. Christians share with our LGBT friends a struggle against sinful desires.

Everyone is born with "original sin" – a natural tendency to live independently of God. When we act upon fleshly desires, we violate God's holy standards and are in need of His saving grace.

The apostle Paul, quoting from the Psalms, reminds us, "There is no one righteous, not even one; there is no one who understands, there is no one who seeks God. All have turned away, together they have become useless; there is no one who does good, there is not even one" (Rom. 3:10-12). Paul further reminds us in Rom. 3:23, "For all have sinned and fall short of the glory of God," and then he points out both the consequences of our sin and the remedy, "For the wages of sin is death, but the gift of

God is eternal life in Christ Jesus our Lord" (Rom. 6:23). Paul even calls himself chief among sinners (1 Tim. 1:15).

Christians are far from perfect. We struggle with sins like lust, anger, lying, selfishness, arrogance, and other ways humanity rebels against our Creator. Remembering our sinful tendencies helps us see the sins of other people in a more accurate, and gracious, light.

6. People can change.

Paul makes this clear in 1 Cor. 6:9-11. He begins with a negative: "Do you not know that the unjust will not inherit God's kingdom? Do not be deceived: no sexually immoral people, idolaters, adulterers, male prostitutes, homosexuals, thieves, greedy people, drunkards, revilers, or swindlers will inherit God's kingdom."

Then, he reminds his fellow believers, "Some of you were like this; but you were washed, you were sanctified, you were justified in the name of the Lord Jesus Christ and by the Spirit of our God."

The evidence to date indicates that same-sex attraction typically is discovered early in life and involves a combination of biological, psychological, and environmental factors. Individuals with same-sex attraction likely will struggle with it their entire lives.[3] The difference is that the One who is in us is greater than the one who is in the world. God gives us the ability to overcome even the strongest sinful urges.

7. We should welcome into our churches those struggling with same-sex attraction.

This does not mean those living unrepentant, openly gay lifestyles should be received as members, or should play any role in the leadership of the church. But the church should be a safe place for anyone struggling with same-sex attraction to have a candid, caring conversation.

We should not deny church membership to those who confess same-sex attraction, and agree that same-sex lust and conduct are sinful, and who seek to overcome these sinful desires and behaviors by the power of God and the accountability of a community of fellow believers.

Would we not afford the same consideration to those who struggle with heterosexual lust, gossip, pride, or gluttony?

Summary

God has spoken clearly on the issue of same-sex conduct; the Scriptures never speak of it in a positive light – and further, describe it as sinful. God created us in His image and for relationships, and His creative intent for men and women is life-long, heterosexual, monogamous relationships in the confines of marriage, which pictures the relationship of Christ and His church. When tested about divorce, Jesus takes the Pharisees back to God's creative intent for marriage and proper sexual conduct.

Homosexuality is neither a special class of sin nor the unpardonable sin. All of us share fleshly desires, and all of us act on our natural-born tendency to live independently of God. But God did not leave us there. He did something about it. He sent His Son to earth, where He added to His deity sinless humanity, lived a perfect life, and on the cross took our sins upon Himself. Through His death, burial, and resurrection, He conquered Satan, sin, and death for us, and we may receive forgiveness of sins, everlasting life, and the presence of the Holy Spirit, who provides an avenue of escape from the most challenging sinful desires (see 1 Cor. 10:13).

The church should minister to people struggling with same-sex attraction, knowing that some of us were bound in sinful behaviors, but now we are washed, sanctified, and justified. Homosexuality is one form of sexual sin and is no greater or lesser sin than any other, although its bondage may cling more heavily and it may have graver physical, emotional, and relational consequences than other sins. Our Christian brothers and sisters may struggle with varying degrees of same-sex attraction their entire lives – and we should be there to struggle alongside them.

THINK *Questions for personal or group study*

Why do you think some Christians view homosexual behavior as a special class of sin? How might you respond biblically to that mindset?

If God is able to save us from the most grievous sins, why do some Christians saved out of the gay lifestyle still struggle with same-sex attraction?

If the apostle Paul writes in 1 Corinthians 6 that homosexuals cannot inherit the kingdom of God, how can they possibly be saved?

What questions should your church leaders ask a man who says he has same-sex attractions and wants to join the church?

What are some ways a local church can provide an effective ministry to those struggling with same-sex attraction?

SHARE *Talking points for discussing the Bible's perspective on sex and marriage*

The Bible condemns all forms of sexual behavior outside the bonds of heterosexual, monogamous, life-long marriage.

Scripture never speaks of homosexuality in a positive – or even a neutral – light. Sexual relations between members of the same gender always in Scripture are depicted as sinful.

Jesus affirms Old Testament teachings about sexuality and marriage.

Christians share with our LGBT friends a struggle against sinful desires.

The evidence to date indicates that same-sex attraction typically is discovered early in life and involves a combination of biological, psychological, and environmental factors. Individuals with same-sex attraction likely will struggle with it their entire lives.

Even so, people can change. The apostle Paul writes of the power of God to wash, sanctify, and justify sinners – including those who once engaged in same-sex behavior.

We should welcome into our churches those struggling with same-sex attraction.

DIVE *Go deeper in your study with these resources*

God and the Gay Christian? A Response to Matthew Vines edited by R. Albert Mohler Jr.

The Moral Vision of the New Testament: Contemporary Introduction to New Testament Ethics by Richard B. Hays

Same-sex Marriage: A Thoughtful Approach to God's Design for Marriage by Sean McDowell and John Stonestreet

67
SIX KEY PASSAGES - AND WHY THEY MATTER

While the whole of Scripture argues against all forms of sexual immorality, the following six passages speak directly to the issue of same-sex conduct. Several English versions are compared to highlight differences in translation.

Genesis 19:5

They [the men of Sodom] called out to Lot and said, "Where are the men who came to you tonight? Send them out to us so we can **have sex with them!**" (HCSB)

- "... that we may **know them.**" (KJV)

- "... that we may **have relations with them.**" (NASB)

- "... that we can **have sex with them.**" (NIV)

- ... that we may **know them.**" (ESV)

Summary

God destroys the ancient cities of Sodom and Gomorrah because of the people's wickedness, expressed most egregiously in their homosexual behavior. Jews and Christians traditionally have understood the story of Sodom and Gomorrah to speak directly to the issue of homosexuality – revisionist explanations of this passage notwithstanding.

Gen. 13:13 tells us, "Now the men of Sodom were evil, sinning greatly against the Lord." When two angels and the Lord Himself visit Abraham, the Lord says, "The outcry against Sodom and Gomorrah is immense, and their sin is extremely serious" (Gen. 18:20). Their sin clearly is homosexual behavior, for the men of Sodom surround Lot's house and demand that his angelic guests be given to them so they may "have sex with them" (Gen. 19:5). Lot implores the men, "Don't do this evil, my brothers" (v. 7), and he takes the extraordinary step of offering his two virgin daughters to them if they only abandon their intent for the guests under Lot's roof.

Other references to these two cities cast them in the light of grievous, unrepentant sin. Jude 7, for example, refers to their behavior as "sexual immorality" and "perversions," and 2 Peter 2:7 describes "the unrestrained behavior of the immoral." The depiction of the "men" of Sodom surrounding Lot's house shows that the entire populace is corrupt. The "whole population" – young and old, from every quarter – is engaged in this immoral practice (Gen. 19:4). For this sin, the Lord destroys the cities in an act of divine judgment.

Challenges

The most common objection to the plain reading of the text is the interpretation that the sin of Sodom is primarily inhospitality, not same-sex behavior. Proponents of this view often cite Ezek. 16:48-49 to say that the sin of the Sodomites is their refusal to take in needy travelers. No doubt the men of Sodom are an inhospitable bunch, but reading the next verse changes the perspective: "They were haughty and did detestable things before Me, so I removed them when I saw this" (v. 50). The word "detestable" – or "abomination" in other translations – brings us back to Leviticus, specifically Lev. 18:22 and Lev. 20:13, where homosexual conduct is in view.

Another challenge is that the use of the word *yada* – translated "know" in the KJV and ESV – does not refer to homosexual conduct. It's true that the word *yada* appears numerous times in the Bible and normally refers to knowing factual information, but at times *yada* plainly means to know someone intimately in a sexual fashion.

For example, in Gen. 4:1 Adam "knew Eve his wife; and she conceived …" (KJV). Further, a look at Judges 19:22-25 offers a close parallel to the story of Lot in Sodom. Certain "perverted men of the city" surround the home where a man and his concubine have been taken in as guests, demanding, "Bring out the man who came to your house so we can have sex (*yada*) with him!" (v. 22). The homeowner describes their intent as "evil" and "horrible" (v. 23), and he offers his virgin daughter and the guest's concubine in exchange. The men take the concubine, rape (*yada*) her and abuse her all night (v. 25).

The context determines the correct understanding of the word *yada*.

A third challenge is that Jesus mentions Sodom and Gomorrah but does not connect the cities with homosexuality. It's true that in Matt. 10:14-

15, as Jesus commissions the 12 disciples, He does not specifically refer to any sin for which the residents of the cities are guilty. His exact words are, "If anyone will not welcome you or listen to your words, shake the dust off your feet when you leave that house or town. I assure you: It will be more tolerable on the day of judgment for the land of Sodom and Gomorrah than for that town."

As James White and Jeffrey Niell explain, "Sodom's judgment had become axiomatic for the fullest outpouring of God's wrath throughout the Old Testament.... The issue is that these cities will be held accountable to God for their grievous sins. And the comparison is that it will be more tolerable for Sodom and Gomorrah in that day than for those cities that had experienced the visitation of the very apostles of the incarnate Lord, but refused their message of repentance and faith."[1]

A final challenge is that the story of Sodom and Gomorrah is not germane to the same-sex debate because it does not address loving, monogamous relationships. It only rails against homosexual gang rape and violence. Even if that were the case, it begs the question of what the Bible says, if anything, about loving, monogamous same-sex relationships. Again, White and Niell are helpful: "To call a relationship 'loving' in a biblical sense means it is in accordance with God's will and is fulfilling His purpose, resulting in His glory."[2] The Bible speaks positively of loving, monogamous, lifelong relationships between a man and a woman, but never of two women or two men.

Leviticus 18:22 and 20:13

Lev. 18:22 - You are not to sleep with **a man** as with **a woman;** it is **detestable**. (HCSB)

- Thou shalt not lie with **mankind,** as with **womankind**: it is **abomination**. (KJV)

- You shall not lie with a **male** as one lies with a **female**; it is **an abomination**. (NASB)

- Do not have sexual relations with a **man** as one does with a **woman**; that is **detestable**. (NIV)

- You shall not lie with a **male** as with a **woman**; it is **an abomination**. (ESV)

Lev. 20:13 - If a man **sleeps with a man as with a woman**, they have both committed **an abomination**. They must be put to death; their blood is on their own hands. (HCSB)

- If a man also **lie with mankind, as he lieth with a woman**, both of them have committed **an abomination** ... (KJV)

- If there is a **man who lies with a male as those who lie with a woman**, both of them have committed a **detestable act** ... (NASB)

- If a man has **sexual relations with a man as one does with a woman**, both of them have done what is **detestable** ... (NIV)

- If a man **lies with a male as with a woman**, both of them have committed **an abomination** ... (ESV)

Summary

These verses are part of the Holiness Code (Leviticus 17-26) dealing with laws, sacrifices, and purity regulations that distinguish the Hebrews from the idolatrous nations surrounding them. The code prohibits sowing a field with two kinds of seeds, wearing a garment made of two kinds of materials, and other activities that seem foreign to 21st century readers. This leads some critics to conclude that the passages on homosexual behavior also are meant only for Hebrews living in the ancient Near East.

However, there are good reasons to understand the prohibition of homosexual behavior as an expression of God's unchanging moral will. Kevin DeYoung offers six reasons not to set aside Lev. 18:22 and 20:13:

1. No disciple of Jesus should start with the presumption that the Mosaic commands are largely irrelevant. Jesus insisted that He did not come to abolish the tiniest speck from the law (Matt. 5:17-18).

2. There is no indication in the New Testament that Leviticus should be treated as particularly obscure or peripheral. The sexual ethic of the Old Testament was not abrogated like the sacrificial system, but carried forward into the early church. The law is good if one uses it lawfully (1 Tim. 1:8).

3. Paul's term for "men who practice homosexuality" (1 Cor. 6:9; 1 Tim.1:10) is derived from two words – *arsen* (man) and *koite* (bed) – found in Lev. 18:22 and 20:13 (Septuagint).

4. Leviticus uses strong language to denounce homosexual behavior, calling it "an abomination." Outside of Leviticus, the Hebrew word *to'ebah* appears 43 times in Ezekiel and 68 times in the rest of the Old Testament, usually with respect to grievous sins. We cannot reduce the word to a mere social taboo or ritual uncleanness.

5. The reference to a women's menstrual period (Lev. 18:19; 20:18) should not call into question the rest of the sexual ethic described in Leviticus 18 and 20. For starters, there is a clear progression in both chapters of sexual sin deviating in increasing measure from the design of male-female monogamy. Menstruation was not a sin but a matter of ritual uncleanness. But with the coming of Christ, the entire system that required ritual cleanness was removed.

6. Apart from the question of sex during menstruation, the New Testament affirms the sexual ethic of Leviticus 18 and 20.[3]

The prohibitions of Leviticus 18 and 20 are against behavior that is contrary to God's creative intent for sexuality. Further, the New Testament writers repeat the Levitical prohibitions against same-sex behavior (Rom. 1:26-27; 1 Cor. 6:9-11; 1 Tim. 1:8-11). Not a single passage in the Old or New Testaments depicts homosexual conduct in a positive light.

Challenges

One common objection is that these passages speak negatively of homosexual conduct that violates the gender roles appropriate to a patriarchal society because the act reduces the passive partner to the status of a woman. If this were the case, however, the active partner would be guiltier than the passive partner. Yet the Bible holds both parties equally to blame and subscribes the same punishment for both persons.

Another argument is that homosexual relations in the ancient Near East often occurred between social unequals – for example, a master and his slave or a man and a boy. Since this type of behavior is no longer considered appropriate in most cultures, the prohibition in Leviticus does not apply. However, Lev. 18:22 and Lev. 20:13 do not restrict the type of homosexual behavior that God considers an abomination; all forms of same-sex conduct are prohibited.

Yet another contention is that these verses decry violent behavior such as same-sex rape or homosexual behavior associated with idolatry like cult prostitution. They say nothing about same-sex conduct between "loving" and "committed" people. But the Hebrew word *zakar* always involves the male gender, whether translated "man," "male," or "mankind," thus meaning that all forms of male-male sexual activity are included in the prohibition. Further, Leviticus 18 condemns adultery, child sacrifice, and prostitution, which are wrong apart from any connection with cult prostitution. And Leviticus 20 places homosexuality between incest and bestiality, which have no direct link to idolatry. Finally, when the Lord wants to condemn cult prostitution, He does it clearly, as in Deut. 23:17.

Some, like Rabbi Jacob Milgrom, contend that the Levitical prohibitions against same-sex conduct applied only to the Jews, and only to non-Jews if they resided in the Holy Land. James White and Jeffrey Niell counter: "Essentially, Milgrom is arguing that homosexuality was wrong for an Egyptian if he resided in Judah, but it was not wrong if he lived in Egypt or Macedonia." Referring to this position as "geographical morality," the authors add, "Is it acceptable for a Jew to be a homosexual in New York, Denver, or Uganda, but not in Bethlehem?"[4]

Then, of course, come the arguments that Christians today selectively promote the portions of Leviticus that suit them – such as the commands against same-sex behavior – but ignore the parts dealing with dietary restrictions, agricultural practices, and the knitting of garments. In other words, if Christians today don't observe *all* of the Levitical prescriptions, they have no right to condemn homosexual behavior.

So, why don't we observe the dietary laws? Because Jesus removed them and declared all foods clean (Mark 7:19). Further, the laws about the separation of fabrics and seed were to distinguish the Hebrews from their neighbors; nowhere were the nations surrounding Israel punished for these behaviors, meaning they were specific to the Hebrews. In stark contrast, nowhere does Scripture set aside its prohibition against homosexual behavior.

Christian author Paul Copan goes further in helping us understand God's intentions behind the Bible's seeming "ubiquitous weirdness." While His laws for the Israelites appear to have covered every aspect of life – food laws, clothing laws, planting laws, civil laws, laws regarding marriage and sexual relations – these were not intended to be exhaustive, or necessarily permanent in all cases. Rather, "they were to be viewed first as visible reminders to live as God's holy people in every area of life. There wasn't any division between the sacred and the secular, between the holy and the profane. God was concerned about holiness in all things – the major and the minor, the significant and the mundane. In such legislation, Israel was being reminded that she was different, a holy people set apart to serve God."[5]

Copan notes that God gives the Israelites certain actions to carry out as a way of *symbolically* telling them not to get mixed in with the false ways of the nations: "Israel 'wore' certain badges of holy distinction that separated them from the morally and theologically corrupted nations surrounding them; they were not to get 'mixed in' with those nations' mind-set and behavior." For example, the prohibition against two kinds of seed in the same field "may refer to a Canaanite magical practice of the 'wedding' of different seeds to conjure up fertile crops."[6]

Rom. 1:26-27

This is why God delivered them over to **degrading passions.** For even their females exchanged natural sexual intercourse for what is **unnatural.** The males in the same way also left natural sexual intercourse with females and were inflamed in their lust for one another. Males committed **shameless acts** with males and received in their own persons the appropriate penalty for their **perversion.** (HCSB)

- For this cause God gave them up unto **vile affections**: for even their women did change the natural use into that which is **against nature**: And likewise also the men, leaving the natural use of the woman, burned in their lust one toward another; men with men **working that which is unseemly**, and receiving in themselves that recompense of their **error** which was meet. (KJV)

- For this reason God gave them over to **degrading passions**; for their women exchanged the natural function for that which is **unnatural**, and in the same way also the men abandoned the natural function of the woman and burned in their desire toward one another, men with men committing **indecent acts** and receiving in their own persons the due penalty of their **error.** (NASB)

- Because of this, God gave them over to **shameful lusts**. Even their women exchanged natural sexual relations for **unnatural** ones. In the same way the men also abandoned natural relations with women and were inflamed with lust for one another. Men committed **shameful acts** with other men, and received in themselves the due penalty for their **error**. (NIV)

- For this reason God gave them up to **dishonorable passions**. For their women exchanged natural relations for those that are **contrary to nature**; and the men likewise gave up natural relations with women and were consumed with passion for one another, men committing **shameless acts** with men and receiving in themselves the due penalty for their **error**. (ESV)

Summary

Of all biblical texts in the same-sex debate, Rom. 1:26-27 appears to be the most common and most-often cited. Before Paul may proclaim the good news of salvation by grace through faith, he must establish the human need for this divine gift, and he does so in the first two and a half chapters by laying out his case for the sinfulness of mankind.

The apostle singles out homosexuality in Rom. 1:26-27 to illustrate the descending spiral of depravity that befalls those who refuse to acknowledge God's lordship over their lives. God has revealed Himself to all people – including His eternal power and divine nature – in creation and conscience, leaving people without an excuse for rejecting Him in favor of idolatry and ungodly passions (Rom. 1:18-23). No one may stand before Christ on judgment day and proclaim he or she didn't know there was a divine designer or a divine moral lawgiver.

Meanwhile, as people reject the revelation of God and His holy standards, He allows them to descend a spiral staircase into outer darkness as they prefer other gods, profess themselves wiser than their Creator, and embrace the fleshly passions borne of unbelief. Three times in Romans 1 Paul writes that "God delivered them over" – in "the cravings of their hearts," "to degrading passions," and "to a worthless mind to do what is morally wrong." These are judicial acts on God's part in which essentially He says, "Have it your way, but take note that your sins will consume you."

Verses 26-27 form a single thought, connected by the introductory words, "This is why God delivered them over ..." These verses are not isolated from the rest of Romans 1 but fit perfectly within the context of Paul's theme of human depravity. God delivers them over to "degrading passions" (HCSB), "vile affections" (KJV), and "shameful lusts" (NIV). However the phrase is translated, it refers to desires and behaviors that dishonor God and degrade human dignity.

Paul then offers a fitting example of these behaviors, writing first about lesbianism and then male homosexuality. Females "exchanged natural sexual relations for unnatural ones," meaning they willfully sought same-sex relations in violation of God's revealed creative intent. Further, "males in the same way also left natural relations with females and were inflamed in their lust for one another," illustrating once again their conscious rebellion against God and His holy standards as revealed in nature.

Paul ends this verse by calling homosexual conduct "shameless acts" and pointing out that these acts result in "the appropriate penalty for their perversion." This penalty may include both temporal consequences of the gay lifestyle – higher than normal levels of certain physical illnesses, mental and emotional trauma, etc.[7] – and everlasting consequences for those who reject divine revelation and refuse to repent. Persons who land on Romans 1 are encouraged to read on, for Paul introduces the remedy for human depravity – the gift of God, which is eternal life in Christ Jesus our Lord (Rom. 6:23).

Challenges

One objection is that Paul is ignorant of the reality of sexual orientation. He has no idea that some people are naturally attracted to people of the same sex. Therefore, he misunderstands sexual orientation, which is widely understood and accepted today.

Responding to this appeal, it's important to understand that this argument implicates the Holy Spirit, who inspired Scripture. If Paul does not understand the subject about which he is writing, then the Spirit either is ignorant of modern concepts of sexuality or is lax by not enlightening Paul. If the modern concept of sexual orientation is to be taken as fact, then the Bible cannot be trusted to reveal what it means to be human, made in God's image, and guilty of sin as God defines it. If God does not know what it means to be gay in the 21st century, what else does He not know?

The assumption that Paul is unaware of "sexual orientation" is faulty. The American Psychological Association defines sexual orientation as "an enduring pattern of emotional, romantic and/or sexual attractions to men, women or both sexes."[8] Notice that orientation involves a person's enduring sexual attractions, and sexual attraction is virtually synonymous with desire. Thus sexual orientation is a person's persistent pattern of sexual attraction / desire toward either or both sexes.

There is no reason to believe that Paul is not fully aware of human attractions and desires, no matter how sinful they are. To expand on this a little, it's good to note that Paul hails from Tarsus, a major city in the Roman Empire. He is well trained, widely read, and familiar with Roman and Greek culture. Therefore, it's implausible to assert that he knew nothing of people who professed homosexuality as their "orientation." Plato's *Symposium*, written centuries before Paul's letter to the Romans, shows that those in ancient cultures are well aware of a wide range of homosexual behavior, even if they don't use the word "orientation."

Look at Paul's words: He refers to "degrading passions" or attractions/ desires, and he describes those who are "inflamed in their lust for one another." As Denny Burk writes, "Sexual desire that fixates on the same sex is sinful, and that is why God's judgment rightly falls on both desires and actions. Again, the issue Paul addresses is not merely sexual behavior but also same-sex attraction."[9]

A second argument is that Paul only condemns oppressive, pederastic, or socially mixed same-sex acts. This is what Paul means by "unnatural."

In response, we should point out numerous linguistic links between Rom. 1:26-27 and the creation narratives of Genesis 1-2. For example, Paul's use of the relatively unusual words *thelys* for females and *arsen* for males strongly suggests he is relying on the creation account of Genesis 1 where the same two words are employed in the Septuagint, the Greek translation of the Old Testament. These two terms highlight the sexual differences between males and females and suggest that homosexual relationships violate God's creative intent. For Paul, it seems clear that "unnatural" means homosexual conduct that goes against God's creative design.

A third argument is that "unnatural" refers to heterosexuals who go beyond their natural bounds and explore homosexuality. This is a subtle way of twisting Paul's words into an affirmation of homosexual behavior that is "natural to me." But to engage in *eisegesis* – reading a particular meaning into the text – is to place depraved human thinking above God's plainly revealed word. The entire context of Romans 1 argues against this sort of reasoning. In fact, to say homosexuality is "natural to me" and therefore good is to make Paul's point that rejecting God's revelation in creation and conscience results in nonsensical thinking and darkened reasoning.

There are other, less common, objections to the evangelical understanding of Rom. 1:26-27, including: (a) the view that the sinners mentioned in this passage are idolaters who engage in homosexual behavior as a way of denying the existence of God, therefore "Christian homosexuals" are not in view here; (b) the argument that Paul limits his remarks to the social and geographical context of his day; and (c) the contention that Paul is speaking only of Jewish purity laws, thus making the passage irrelevant in today's enlightened society.

We may respond by noting: (a) the whole of Scripture argues against the idea of a "Christian homosexual" – that is, one who embraces the mutually exclusive concepts of faith in Christ and unrepentant behavior that Scripture always calls sinful; (b) the context of Romans 1 makes it clear that Paul is writing about desires and behaviors that run contrary to God's revealed standards, which are unchanging; and (c) those who hold this view are acknowledging that the Hebrew Scriptures do indeed condemn homosexual behavior; further, Paul's repeated use of universal terms to describe humanity's rejection of God's self-revelation argue in favor of a wide application.

A final thought on this passage in Romans: As Richard B. Hays points out, we cannot read the judgments against unrighteous behavior apart from the rest of the letter of Romans with its message of grace and hope through the cross of Christ. The struggle may not be easy, but Christians have been set free from the power of sin through Christ's death, and we must continue to struggle to live faithfully in the present.[10]

1 Corinthians 6:9-10 and 1 Timothy 1:9-11

1 Cor. 6:9-10 - Do you not know that the unjust will not inherit God's kingdom? Do not be deceived: no sexually immoral people, idolaters, adulterers, male prostitutes, homosexuals, thieves, greedy people, drunkards, revilers, or swindlers will inherit God's kingdom. (HCSB)

- Know ye not that the unrighteous shall not inherit the kingdom of God? Be not deceived: neither fornicators, nor idolaters, nor adulterers, nor **effeminate**, nor **abusers of themselves with mankind** ... (KJV)

- Or do you not know that the unrighteous will not inherit the kingdom of God? Do not be deceived; neither fornicators, nor idolaters, nor adulterers, nor **effeminate**, nor **homosexuals** ... (NASB)

- Or do you not know that wrongdoers will not inherit the kingdom of God? Do not be deceived: Neither the sexually immoral nor idolaters nor adulterers nor **men who have sex with men** ... (NIV)

- Or do you not know that the unrighteous will not inherit the kingdom of God? Do not be deceived: neither the sexually immoral, nor idolaters, nor adulterers, nor **men who practice homosexuality** ... (ESV)

1 Tim. 1:9-11 - We know that the law is not meant for a righteous person, but for the lawless and rebellious, for the ungodly and sinful, for the unholy and irreverent, for those who kill their fathers and mothers, for murderers, for **the sexually immoral and homosexuals**, for kidnappers, liars, perjurers, and for whatever else is contrary to the sound teaching based on the glorious gospel of the blessed God that was entrusted to me. (HCSB)

- ... For **whoremongers, for them that defile themselves with mankind**... (KJV)

- ... and **immoral men and homosexuals** ... (NASB)

- ... for **the sexually immoral**, for **those practicing homosexuality** ... (NIV)

- ... for ... **the sexually immoral, men who practice homosexuality** ... (ESV)

Summary

These two passages address moral issues facing the congregation at Corinth and in Timothy's ministry. Corinth in particular is known for its sexual sins and gross immorality, due in part to the presence of pagan worship that features temple prostitution. Paul, who spent 18 months in Corinth, begins 1 Cor. 6:9 with the words, "Do you not know …" And he follows up with, "Do not be deceived …"

The apostle is restating what he has taught them before: The kingdom of God is a kingdom of righteousness. Seated on the throne is a righteous King. Those who remain in opposition to the righteous King have excluded themselves from citizenship in His kingdom. Paul also warns of the danger of false teachers who come into the church and deceive the followers of Jesus into believing that certain sinful behaviors should be accepted – perhaps even celebrated.

It's important to note that the only sin listed in 1 Cor. 6:9-10 that is not also listed in Leviticus chapters 18-20 is drunkenness. This supports the idea that Paul is linking this passage to Leviticus. This becomes even clearer when we look at the Greek word *arsenokoites*, a word not found in Greek literature prior to Paul's writings. Paul, the apostle to the Gentiles, is well familiar with the Septuagint (also known as the LXX), the Greek translation of the Old Testament. Where the LXX differs from the Hebrew text, Paul goes with the LXX, quite possibly because he knows his audience is more familiar with that version.

Why is this important? Because when we get to the terms used in the LXX at Lev. 18:22 and Lev. 20:13, we find the words *arsenos* (male) and *koiten* (to lie with sexually, have intercourse). The term "homosexuals" in 1 Cor. 6:9 is made up of these two terms: *arsenos* and *koiten*, thus *arsenokoites*. Paul may have picked up this word from rabbinic discussions of homosexuality, or he may have coined it himself. In any case, Paul's use of this unique word ties 1 Cor. 6:9-10 and 1 Tim. 1:9-11 with the commands against homosexual behavior found in Leviticus 18 and 20. Further, we should remember that the prohibition of homosexual behavior in Leviticus is not restricted to prostitution, pederasty, or any other category of homosexuality. It condemns all forms of same-sex immorality.

And yet there is good news. Some at Corinth have been rescued from immoral behavior by the saving power of Jesus Christ. 1 Cor. 6:11 reads, "Some of you were like this; but you were washed, you were sanctified, you were justified in the name of the Lord Jesus Christ and by the Spirit of our God." Paul is not writing to "gay Christians;" he is addressing those once trapped in homosexual lust and conduct but now transformed through the regenerating, justifying, and sanctifying work of God.

Change is possible – not necessarily instantaneous or easy. But when a person entrusts his life to Jesus, he is washed – regenerated, or born of the Spirit, given a new life. He also is *declared* righteous through the sovereign act of justification – and thereby acquitted of the penalty of all sins – and then *made* righteous over the course of his life as the indwelling Spirit sanctifies him, or conforms him to the image of Christ.

In writing to Timothy and Titus, Paul expresses his deep concern for the next generation of Christian leaders. He has invested himself deeply in their lives and writes to exhort them to remain faithful in the face of withering opposition. In his first letter to Timothy, Paul reminds his beloved young friend that while salvation is not attained through the law, the law nevertheless serves a proper purpose in exposing human sinfulness.

In 1 Tim. 1:9-11, Paul identifies three categories of sinners: the lawless and rebellious, the ungodly and sinful, and the unholy and irreverent. He then lists specific types of sinners that fall under these headings, including "the sexually immoral and homosexuals." The word "homosexuals" in Greek is *arsenokoites*, which we encountered in 1 Cor. 6:9-10. Paul refers to homosexuals as those for whom the law is intended, thereby tying this passage to Leviticus. Since the prohibitions in Leviticus are well known, and because Timothy no doubt is aware of Paul's previous teachings on the subject, there is no need for Paul to elaborate in this passage.

In short, Paul's writings to the church at Corinth and to Timothy address the issue of homosexual conduct. Paul links these passages to Leviticus and thus condemns all forms of same-sex behavior. He also leaves us with hope: Through His finished work on the cross, Jesus has paid the debt for these sins and invites us to repent and believe in Him for forgiveness and life-changing transformation. Because of Jesus, some who formerly engaged in same-sex behavior may now joyously declare that they have been washed, sanctified, and justified in the name of the Lord Jesus Christ and by the Spirit of our God.

Challenges

One argument is that English translations fail to rightly capture the meaning of the Greek term *arsenokoites*, normally translated "homosexuals" or "those who practice homosexuality." A more accurate understanding, it is said, is excessive lust and pederasty (same-sex relations between a man and a boy), or male prostitution. These sexual activities dominate the Greco-Roman context in which Paul lives.

In response, we should note that the term *arsenokoites* appears nowhere else in Greek literature until Paul coins the term here, according to Denny Burk, professor of Biblical studies at Boyce College and author of *What Is the Meaning of Sex?*[11] There are other words for homosexual behavior, but Paul chooses not to use them. Rather, he coins a term that derives from the Greek translation of Lev. 20:13, *arsenos koiten*, thus tying 1 Cor. 6:9-10 and 1 Tim. 1:9-11 with Leviticus.

Another argument is that Paul condemns abuses of homosexuality, not same-sex activity altogether. Since he lists homosexuality along with other abuses of legitimate activities – for example, sexual immorality as an abuse of loving, monogamous relationships – it is the *misuse* of homosexuality, not homosexuality itself, that is the issue.

In response, it should first be noted that the objection assumes there is some form of acceptable same-sex behavior; but as we've seen throughout this study, the Bible nowhere condones same-sex conduct of any kind. Further, we should point out that Paul offers a list of behaviors that are sinful in themselves – sexual immorality, idolatry, adultery, etc. – and homosexuality is part of that list.

Finally, we should ask: Is there some degree of sexual immorality that God finds acceptable? Certain kinds of idolatry? Adultery? May I excuse theft if I argue that I was born with a natural tendency to take things that don't belong to me? When we carry this argument to its logical conclusion, we see that Paul makes no exceptions for any form of homosexual conduct.

THINK *Questions for personal or group study*

How might you respond to the person who points out that the entire Bible addresses homosexuality *only* six times?

In what ways could it be argued that same-sex conduct is a form of idolatry?

What are weaknesses in the argument that the sin of Sodom is an absence of hospitality, not homosexuality?

Why are the prohibitions of homosexuality in Leviticus still valid today if the laws against eating shellfish or sowing a field with two kinds of seed are not?

Is there any biblical support for loving, monogamous, lifelong homosexual relationships? Why or why not?

How would you respond to the charge that the apostle Paul is unaware of sexual "orientation" and therefore writes his epistles in ignorance?

SHARE *Talking points for discussing the Bible and homosexuality*

Although only six passages in the Bible speak directly to the issue of same-sex conduct, the whole of Scripture argues against all forms of sexual immorality.

Not a single passage in the Old or New Testaments depicts homosexual conduct in a positive light.

God destroys the ancient cities of Sodom and Gomorrah because of the people's wickedness, expressed most egregiously in their homosexual behavior.

There is no indication in the New Testament that Leviticus should be treated as obscure or peripheral. The sexual ethic of the Old Testament – including its condemnation of homosexuality – was not abrogated like the sacrificial system, but carried forward into the early church.

The apostle Paul singles out homosexuality in Rom. 1:26-27 to illustrate the descending spiral of depravity that befalls those who refuse to acknowledge God's lordship over their lives.

Paul further makes it clear that God can deliver those struggling with same-sex attraction and free them from the bonds of the gay lifestyle (1 Cor. 6:11).

DIVE *Go deeper in your study with these resources*

Homosexuality and the Politics of Truth by Jeffrey Satinover

The Bible and Homosexual Practice: Texts and Hermeneutics by Robert A.J. Gagnon

Why Not Same-Sex Marriage? by Daniel Heimbach

68
BUT WHAT ABOUT...

Here are some commonly raised objections to the biblical view of same-sex conduct.

I was born this way

If homosexuality is genetically determined, then we may view it in the same light as race and gender, placing homosexuals in the same protected class as racial minorities and women. This also enables same-sex advocates to paint those who stand against homosexual behavior as oppressors who oppose civil rights. This is a winning strategy, as a Pew Research Center poll discovered, finding a direct correlation between the belief that homosexuality is inborn and support for same-sex marriage.[1]

We may legitimately question the validity of research that concludes the inborn nature of homosexuality, asking whether it has been authenticated and peer reviewed. At the same time, we should understand that the studies address only homosexuality's *origins*, not its normality or morality, according to Joe Dallas, Christian counselor, speaker, and author. Finally, we should be prepared to respond graciously and clearly if studies ever successfully link biology and homosexuality.

The "born gay" argument is based on the belief that what we are is what we were meant to be. But there is much that argues against this. We are imperfect from conception. All of us share in original sin and its consequences. Some of us have birth defects, or seem naturally inclined to antisocial behavior. Our human natures are fallen and therefore our tendencies only tell us what is, not what ought to be.

Incidentally, the contention that "I was born this way" is not limited to same-sex attraction with respect to human sexuality. A 2015 *New York Times* article by Richard A. Friedman cites new research showing that some women, like men, are "biologically inclined to wander." Women who carry certain variants of the vasopressin receptor gene are much more likely to engage in "extra pair bonding," the scientific euphemism for sexual infidelity.

While reporting the scientific findings, Friedman is quick to point out two caveats: "Correlation is not the same as causation; there are undoubtedly many unmeasured factors that contribute to infidelity. And rarely does a simple genetic variant determine behavior." And, he asks, "So do we get a moral pass if we happen to carry one of these 'infidelity' genes? Hardly. We don't choose our genes and can't control them (yet), but we can usually decide what we do with the emotions and impulses they help create."[2]

Joe Dallas writes, "David laments that he was born in sin (Ps. 51:5) and Paul confirms both the inborn nature of sin and our ongoing struggle with it (Rom. 6-7). The first human tragedy we see in Scripture speaks to this, as God informs Adam that sin's impact on him and his race will be both spiritual and physical (Gen. 3:17-19; see also Rom. 5:12-20). The sin nature manifests itself from birth and we wrestle with it until death."[3]

Our gay friends may tell us, "I can't help my same-sex attraction; I didn't ask to be this way." This is a wonderful opportunity for us to affirm them as precious people made in the image of God while acknowledging the pervasiveness of sin. Same-sex attraction is one of many manifestations of our fallen nature. At the same time, deliberate, immoral responses to our "natural" desires are acts of rebellion against God and thus are both sinful and harmful.

We might also encourage our Christian friends struggling with same-sex attraction by pointing out the beauty of suffering in the Christian life. Though He is God's Son, Jesus "learned obedience through what He suffered" (Heb. 5:8). The apostle Paul writes that his goal is "to know Him and the power of His resurrection and the fellowship of His suffering, being conformed to His death" (Phil. 3:10). After being stoned and left for dead outside Lystra, Paul returns with Barnabus, "strengthening the disciples by encouraging them to continue in the faith and by telling them, 'It is necessary to pass through many troubles on our way into the kingdom of God'" (Acts 14:22). Lastly, Paul writes this to the Romans: "[W]e also rejoice in our afflictions, because we know that affliction produces endurance, endurance produces proven character, and proven character produces hope. This hope does not disappoint, because God's love has been poured out in our hearts through the Holy Spirit who was given to us" (Rom. 5:3-5).

The American Psychological Association defines sexual orientation as "an enduring pattern of emotional, romantic, and/or sexual attractions to men, women, or both sexes." When describing where this attraction comes from, the APA is honest that "although much research has examined the possible genetic, hormonal, developmental, social, and cultural influences on sexual orientation, no findings have emerged that permit scientists to conclude that sexual orientation is determined by any particular factor or factors."[4]

"The bulk of evidence regarding the origin of homosexuality," writes Joe Dallas, "still points to a combination of biological, psychological, and environmental factors as its root.... Whatever its cause, though, homosexual orientation is usually discovered, not chosen."[5]

Desires may be involuntary, but acts are chosen. Dallas notes:

1. Homosexuality, like many sexual or emotional tendencies, seems to appear early in life and remain deeply ingrained over a lifetime; however, although homosexual orientation may not be chosen, homosexual behavior clearly is chosen; thus, those who choose it are morally culpable.

2. "Unchosen" and "unchangeable" do not necessarily mean "inborn." It still is unclear what role genetic, biological, or other factors play in the formation of homosexual desires.

3. "Inborn" does not mean "normal" or "God ordained." Many conditions are inborn, but their origin does not determine their normality or morality. Such determinations require a more substantive standard then the explanation of being "born that way."[6]

Sexual behavior sometimes is relegated to a secondary issue. "I'm not hurting anyone," we might hear. "What I do in the privacy of my home is my business and doesn't affect anything else I do." But behavior – public or private – is important, and sexual behavior is no less so.

God's creation of men and women includes His design for pleasure and procreation in sexual union, which later appears as a "type" of God's intimate, passionate commitment to His people (see Isa. 54:5-6; Hos. 2:19-20; Eph. 5:22-33). Homosexual behavior, however, is never mentioned positively in Scripture, while monogamous, life-long unity between a man and a woman is the highest expression of God's intention for intimacy in His people.

Stop judging me

Because Christians believe the Bible condemns same-sex behavior, defenders of this behavior charge us with "judging" LGBT people in violation of Jesus' words, "Do not judge, so that you won't be judged" (Matt. 7:1). Why are Christians so eager to condemn those engaged in same-sex conduct, yet remain virtually silent on the issue of adultery, or two people living together out of wedlock, or any number of other behaviors contrary to Scripture? Shouldn't we clean up our own act before judging others?

In response, perhaps we should begin by agreeing that many Christians impose double standards when condemning certain types of sins. And we should apologize for any real or perceived vitriol toward our LGBT friends. At the same time, we should challenge our friends' misuse of Scripture. In Matthew 7 Jesus corrects, not all types of judgment, but hypocritical judgment. He gives the brilliantly absurd illustration of someone pointing to a speck of dust in his neighbor's eye, all the while sporting a plank in his own eye.

But we *are* to judge behavior by the Word of God – especially in the church. And we are to speak up on issues of eternal significance. Our speech and our actions, however, should be seasoned with gentleness and respect. Perhaps the following New Testament passages are good reminders to us:

Matt. 18:15-17: If your brother sins against you, go and rebuke him in private. If he listens to you, you have won your brother. But if he won't listen, take one or two more with you, so that by the testimony of two or three witnesses every fact may be established. If he pays no attention to them, tell the church. But if he doesn't pay attention even to the church, let him be like an unbeliever and a tax collector to you.

Gal. 6:1: Brothers, if someone is caught in any wrongdoing, you who are spiritual should restore such a person with a gentle spirit, watching out for yourselves so you won't be tempted also.

Col. 3:12-15: Therefore, God's chosen ones, holy and loved, put on heartfelt compassion, kindness, humility, gentleness, and patience, accepting one another and forgiving one another if anyone has a complaint against another. Just as the Lord has forgiven you, so also you must forgive. Above all, put on love – the perfect bond of unity. And let the peace of the Messiah, to which you were also called in one body, control your hearts. Be thankful.

2 Tim. 2:24-26: The Lord's slave must not quarrel, but must be gentle to everyone, able to teach, and patient, instructing his opponents with gentleness. Perhaps God will grant them repentance to know the truth. Then they may come to their senses and escape the Devil's trap, having been captured by him to do his will.

James 1:19: My dearly loved brothers, understand this: everyone must be quick to hear, slow to speak, and slow to anger.

This is the 21st century

As the argument goes, Christians are on the "wrong side of history." The Bible is outdated and needs to be brought up to modern times – or abandoned altogether. After all, the Bible endorses slavery, prohibits eating shellfish, and commands people not to sew two kinds of fabric together. We've advanced beyond these ancient commands, so let's bring Christianity into the 21st century and stop labeling same-sex orientation as sinful.

Responding, we should note that there are several issues raised here. First, that the Bible is fluid and adaptable to our times. In fact, the Bible expresses the heart of the unchangeable God as He speaks to the rebellious heart of people. While the times have changed, the human heart has not; it continues to be deceitful above all things and desperately wicked (Jer. 17:9). God's standards of holiness remain the same because He remains the same yesterday, today, and forever (Heb. 13:8). That is, His holiness, His divine nature, and His standards of right and wrong are eternally constant.

Second, the charge that the Bible endorses slavery suggests that the person raising this charge is unfamiliar with scriptural context. The Bible does not endorse slavery as we understand it today. Slavery in Bible times operated much more as indentured servanthood, although where slavery resulted from warfare or other issues, the Bible expresses God's "divine accommodation," recognizing the sinfulness of people and seeking His people to be a light that exposes the sinfulness of the institution. Equally important, passages of Scripture encourage the freeing of slaves (Philemon 15-16) and condemn capturing another human being and selling him into slavery (Ex. 21:16; 1 Tim. 1:10). As Kevin DeYoung notes, "To make it sound like the Word of God is plainly for slavery in the same way it is plainly against homosexual practice is biblically indefensible."[7]

Finally, the argument about shellfish, sewing two kinds of garments together, etc., is addressed in the discussion of Lev. 18:22 and Lev. 20:13. As a brief recap, God gives the Israelites certain actions to carry out as a way of *symbolically* telling them not to get mixed in with the false ways of the nations around them. Israel "wears" certain badges of holy distinction that separate them from the morally and theologically corrupted nations surrounding them. These prohibitions are neither exhaustive nor necessarily permanent in all cases.

That's just your interpretation

Some argue that the Bible passages addressing same-sex behavior are subject to interpretation. Of recent note is Matthew Vines' book, *God and the Gay Christian*. The author attempts to argue that being a gay Christian in a committed same-sex relationship – and eventually marriage – is compatible with biblical Christianity. Other self-identified Christian authors have attempted to show that the Bible condemns homosexuality only in certain historic, geographic, or cultural contexts.

We already have dealt with alternative understandings of the Bible passages in question. At the same time, we should note that if *any* interpretation of a text can be true, then no interpretation is true. The goal of interpretation is to understand the author's meaning, not to read our meaning into the text. Studying the text in its original language; taking careful note of context; understanding the author's purpose and seeing what he has written elsewhere; comparing Scripture with Scripture – all of these are responsible approaches to any ancient text. The primary flaw of those promoting alternative interpretations of the biblical texts on homosexuality is known as *eisegesis* – imposing bias into a text rather than seeking to let the text speak for itself.

As an example of *eisegesis*, Matthew Vines argues that "Christians who affirm the full authority of Scripture can also affirm committed, monogamous same-sex relationships."[8] Vines' main argument is that the

Bible has no category for sexual orientation. So, when the Bible condemns same-sex acts, it is actually condemning "sexual excess," oppression, or abuse, not the possibility of permanent, monogamous, same-sex unions. This view begins with the conclusion that "committed, monogamous same-sex relationships" are part of God's creative intent for men and women, and are therefore good, and then seeks to inflict that view upon the biblical texts.

But in fact, the Bible nowhere limits its rejection of same-sex conduct to exploitative forms. The prohibitions of Lev. 18:22 and 20:13 are unqualified. Any male who lies with another male has committed an abomination. If homosexual actions were wrong because they were exploitative, why does Lev. 20:13 specify the death penalty for both participants?

Paul is equally unambiguous in Rom. 1:26-27. The reference to lesbianism in verse 26 describes behavior in the ancient Mediterranean world that is not confined to exploitative, abusive roles, or active vs. passive roles. Paul's transition to male homosexuality in verse 27 appears to cast all forms of male homosexuality in the same light. "Had Paul wanted to limit his remarks to pederasty he could have used Greek words that refer specifically to such activity," writes Robert A.J. Gagnon.[9]

Further, Gagnon reports that it is misleading to argue as if Jewish Christian writers had nothing but negative images from which to base their judgment of homosexuality. He cites several ancient Greco-Roman documents that tout the compassionate and beautiful character of same-sex love, including Plato's *Symposium*.[10]

I can't change

A popular view promoted today by gay activists is that people either are born gay or not, and they cannot change their orientation. Homosexuality has a genetic component that the writers of the Bible did not realize. So, the argument goes, if the uninformed writers of the Old and New Testament documents had only known about this, they would have changed their tune.

Much has been written in response to this view, some of which has been mentioned earlier in this book. Gagnon summarizes various scientific studies in *The Bible and Homosexual Practice: Texts and Hermeneutics*.[11] Here's a brief synopsis:

- Three studies in the 1990s sought to find a difference in the brains of homosexual and heterosexual people. While some differences were discovered, Neil and Briar Whitehead write, "Science has not yet discovered any genetically dictated behavior in humans."[12] In short, genetic influence on homosexuality is, if existent at all, relatively weak in comparison with family, societal, and other environmental influences.

- In the U.S. the odds of a given child becoming homosexual increase dramatically depending on the social environment. Two cultural markers are urban/rural and level of education. Homosexuality is more prevalent in urban areas, where there are increased opportunities to engage in homosexual behavior and where there are fewer sanctions against it. As for education, men and women who are more highly educated show a higher percentage of homosexual and lesbian behavior, perhaps in part because educators often encourage them to explore their "true" sexuality. Among those whose level of education does not extend beyond high school, only 1.8 percent of men and 0.4 percent of women identify themselves as homosexual/bisexual. Among college graduates the rates are 3.3 percent of men and 3.6 percent of women.

- Further studies indicate the elasticity of sexual behavior, with some who engage in homosexual behavior early in life transitioning to heterosexual later in life, and vice versa. Gagnon notes, "People who at one time or another experience homosexual impulses do so at different levels of intensity at different times of life, and for periods of different duration.... None of this corresponds to a doctrine of biological determinism."[13]

Can homosexuals change? Yes. Change can take different forms: a reduction or elimination of homosexual behavior; a reduction in the intensity and frequency of homosexual impulses; the experience of heterosexual arousal and marriage; or reorientation from exclusive or predominant homosexuality to exclusive or predominant heterosexuality.

"It is evident, then, that the genetic or intrauterine component of homosexual orientation is indirect and not dominant," concludes Gagnon. "Indeed, the latest scientific research on homosexuality simply reinforces what Scripture and common sense already told us: human behavior results from a complex mixture of biologically related desires (genetic, intrauterine, post-natal brain development), familial and environmental influences, human psychology, and repeated choices. Whatever predisposition to homosexuality may exist is a far cry from predestination or determinism and easy to harmonize with Paul's understanding of homosexuality."[14]

It's not a big deal

Self-identified Christians who support same-sex conduct may say something like this, "There are only a handful of Bible verses that even mention homosexuality. So, it's not that big a deal."

However, if we believe God's Word is inspired, inerrant, infallible, and sufficient, then every word *is* a big deal. For the Holy Spirit to inspire a single passage makes that passage true, meaningful, and relevant. The importance of a biblical doctrine is not necessarily tied to the number of times Scripture addresses it. For example, the phrase "1,000 years" is mentioned only six times in Scripture and limited to a single chapter (Revelation 20). Yet volumes have been written about the "millennium," and regardless of one's view of its ultimate fulfillment, all Christians look forward to the day when Christ returns and sets things right.

Further, even though there are only six passages that speak specifically of homosexuality, many other passages complement these verses. Consider, for example, these texts, which include the six primary passages addressed earlier: Gen. 9:20-27; 19:4-11; Lev. 18:22; 20:13; Judges 19:22-25; Ezek. 16:50 (possibly also 18:12 and 33:26); Rom. 1:26-27; 1 Cor. 6-9-11; 1 Tim. 1:9-11; and probably Jude 7 and 2 Peter 2:7. Add to these the texts on cult prostitution: Deut. 23:17-18; 1 Kings 14:24; 15:12; 22:46; 2 Kings 23:7; Job 36:14; and Rev. 21:8 and 22:15.

God has spoken clearly on the issue of same-sex behavior, and His perspective on our response to His creative intent is, well, a big deal. It's also good to keep in mind that when any narrative like the Bible is shared, it's not necessary to retell something that already has been clearly established. As James M. Hamilton Jr., writes, "In other words, as a writer introduces his audience to the world in which his story is set, if he tells them that world includes the earth's gravitational force pulling objects toward itself, he does not have to reiterate that explanation when he shows a plane crash. The author does not need to interrupt the narrative and remind his audience about gravity."[15]

Lastly, when it comes to believers, the biblical injunctions toward healthy sexuality (and against unhealthy sexuality) are not merely concerned with the private morality of individuals but for the health, wholeness, and purity of the Christian community. Israel is called to be a holy nation for the sake of all nations. Paul's injunction to "glorify God in your body" (1 Cor. 6:20) grows out of his passionate concern for the unity and sanctification of the community as a whole.

As we look at an injunction against prostitution (1 Cor. 6:15), we see that to engage in sexual immorality defiles the body of Christ. Through baptism, Christians have entered a corporate whole whose health is at stake in the conduct of all its members. The New Testament never considers sexual conduct a matter of purely private concern between consenting adults. According to Paul, everything we do as Christians, including our sexual practices, affects the whole body of Christ.[16]

THINK *Questions for personal or group study*

How might you respond to a gay friend who argues that he or she was born this way?

What are some of the causes of same-sex attraction? Why are these causes insufficient reasons for engaging in homosexual behavior?

How do some people abuse Scripture in defending their immoral behavior? And how might you respond to people who justify their gay lifestyle by quoting Jesus' command to "judge not?"

Do you think speaking out against same-sex behavior is equivalent to being a racist? How should you respond to the charge of "homophobia?"

How might you answer the person who says, "Well, that's just your interpretation of the Bible?"

Why do you think the gay community promotes the message that homosexuals cannot change? And how could you show them that message is not true?

Why is same-sex attraction a big deal, despite arguments to the contrary?

SHARE *Talking points for addressing objections to the biblical view of homosexuality*

Same-sex attraction is one of many manifestations of our fallen nature. At the same time, deliberate, immoral responses to our "natural" desires are acts of rebellion against God and thus are both sinful and harmful.

Homosexual behavior is never mentioned positively in Scripture, while monogamous, life-long unity between a man and a woman is the highest expression of God's intention for intimacy in His people.

While Jesus warns us not to judge hypocritically, Christians *are* to judge all things by the Word of God. And we are to speak up on issues of eternal significance. Our speech and our actions, however, should be seasoned with gentleness and respect.

Times have changed, but the human heart has not; it continues to be deceitful above all things and desperately wicked (Jer. 17:9). God's standards of holiness stay the same because He remains the same yesterday, today, and forever (Heb. 13:8). That is, His holiness, His divine nature, and His standards of right and wrong are forever constant.

If *any* interpretation of a text can be true, then no interpretation is true. The goal of interpretation is to understand the author's meaning, not to read our meaning into the text. Not a single passage in the Old or New Testaments depicts homosexual conduct in a positive light.

Can homosexuals change? Yes. Change can take different forms: a reduction or elimination of homosexual behavior; a reduction in the intensity and frequency of homosexual impulses; the experience of heterosexual arousal and marriage; or reorientation from exclusive or predominant homosexuality to exclusive or predominant heterosexuality. The apostle Paul reminds the Corinthians, "Some of you *were* like this ..."

DIVE *Go deeper in your study with these resources*

The Gay Gospel? How Pro-Gay Advocates Misread the Bible by Joe Dallas

Is God anti-gay? And other questions about homosexuality, the Bible and same-sex attraction by Sam Allberry

101 Frequently Asked Questions About Homosexuality by Mike Haley

Restoring Sexual Identity: Hope for Women Who Struggle with Same-Sex Attraction by Anne Paulk

STEWARDSHIP

69
WILL A MAN ROB GOD?

Consider the following questions:

- Does the Bible command tithing – that is, giving 10 percent of our income to God?

- If we don't tithe ... are we robbing God?

- Doesn't the Old Testament teach tithing, while the New Testament teaches giving?

- Isn't the whole issue one of law vs. grace?

These are important questions, and every sincere Christian wants to get the answers right. We all agree the Bible is our authority – and the last word on this issue. So let's look at what the Old and New Testaments have to say about tithing and giving.

Old Testament passages

Note the commands under the Mosaic Law, which required Israelites to pay tithes totaling more than 22 percent of their income each year – usually in the form of crops or animals:

Levitical tithe. Supported those who offered daily sacrifices on behalf of the people (Lev. 27:30-33; Num. 18:21).

Festival tithe. The Israelites were to bring food for themselves and the Levites on special feast days (Deut. 14:22-27).

Welfare tithe. Offered every third year for the Levite, foreigner, orphan, and widow (Deut. 14:28-29).

These tithes might be likened to taxes that funded Israel's national budget.

In addition, there were *freewill offerings* in which people gave whatever was in their hearts to give (Ex. 25:2-7; 1 Chron. 29:6-9).

A broader perspective

Stepping back to a broader perspective, Abraham and Jacob offered tithes prior to the giving of the law – Abraham, in a voluntary act, sharing the spoils of war; and Jacob, in a faithless effort to guarantee much of what God already had promised him (see Genesis 14 and 28).

The prophets, too, wrote about tithing as they called Israel back to faithfulness. For example, Malachi delivered God's charge to the Israelites to bring their full 10 percent into the storehouse so the Levites' work of leading corporate worship could continue. By withholding what God required, the Israelites robbed God and missed out on His blessings (see Malachi 3).

When all of these passages are studied carefully, it is clear that God commanded His people under the Old Covenant to tithe. But it is equally clear that the requirements of Israelites under the law do not automatically carry forward as commands for Christians under grace (see Rom. 6:14; 7:4, 6; 2 Cor. 3:7-11; Gal. 5:18; Col. 2:13-15; Heb. 8:13; 10:8-10).

Think about it: If we impose the Old Testament model on the church, each of us would be required to give upwards of 22 percent of our income to the church each year, with goodwill offerings over and above that.

Plus, we would still have to obey Christ's command to render unto Caesar … and as you well know, taxes typically take another 20 to 30 percent of our income.

New Testament passages

Does the New Testament teach tithing? Search as you might, you will not find a single verse in the New Testament that states, "Thou shalt tithe," although proponents point to a few passages that we should address.

In Matthew and Luke (Matt. 23:23; Luke 11:42) Jesus commends the scribes and Pharisees – who are under the Old Covenant – for tithing, but He condemns their wrong attitudes and motives. No command here for the church.

In Luke 18:9-14, Jesus commends a tax collector for his humility in the temple, while implying that a Pharisee who boasts publicly about his tithing already has received his reward. Nothing here for Christians, either.

Finally, the writer of Hebrews (Hebrews 7) argues that Melchizedek's priesthood is superior to the Levitical priesthood and, by extension, Jesus' priesthood is greater than all. The fact that Abraham paid tithes one time to Melchizedek cannot be used to support the idea that the New Testament requires church members to tithe.

A careful study of the New Testament, however, shows that first-century believers probably gave more than 10 percent – not because they were commanded to do so, but because they wanted to do so (see Luke 19:8; Acts 2:44-45; 4:34-37; 2 Cor. 8:1-5).

How Christians should give

The New Testament writers instructed believers to give in a number of ways:

1. Locally. Paul instructs the believers at Corinth the same way he instructed the churches of Galatia – to set in store a collection for safe keeping (1 Cor. 16:1-4). While this offering is to help the saints in Jerusalem, it is given through the church in Corinth.

The benefit of giving locally is that it shows you are committed to what God is doing through the local church.

2. Consistently. Paul exhorts the Corinthian believers to take up a weekly collection for their brothers and sisters in Jerusalem (1 Cor. 16:2).

The benefits of consistent giving are personal self-discipline and church budgeting.

3. Proportionately. Paul says each one should give as he or she has prospered (1 Cor. 16:2), suggesting a percentage, so that as a person's income grows, so does his or her giving. We also should give in proportion to need.

The benefit of proportionate giving is that everyone can be involved.

4. Sacrificially. Jesus praises the poor widow who gave two small coins, a fraction of the amount deposited that same day by men of more comfortable means (Luke 21:1-4). Paul tells the church at Corinth that the Macedonians have given to the saints in Jerusalem out of their deep poverty (2 Cor. 8:2).

The benefits of sacrificial giving are seeing God as the owner of all; humility; and the blessing of others.

5. Liberally. Jesus says and Paul writes that we reap in proportion to what we sow (Luke 6:38; 2 Cor. 9:6). This is not the prosperity gospel; it is God's promise to meet our needs and multiply our gifts in His kingdom work. God has a way of honoring good stewardship in many areas of our lives.

The benefit of liberal giving is knowing that we can't out give God.

6. Cheerfully. Too often, we write checks or make our gifts online to the local church with the same enthusiasm we pay our utility bills. Paul writes that God loves those who give cheerfully – literally, in a hilarious spirit (2 Cor. 9:7). Believers in Macedonia and Achaia were pleased to contribute to the saints in Jerusalem (Rom. 15:26-27).

The benefits of cheerful giving are a proper attitude and a truly unique response to the blessings of God.

A cause for concern?

But if we don't require Christians to tithe, how will we raise enough money to support our pastor, pay our church's bills, and fund worldwide missions?

Think about it this way: Making a tithe – or any fixed amount of giving – mandatory may in fact cap what God wants to do through us. Do you remember in the Book of Exodus, when God decided to fund the tabernacle through freewill offerings? The people responded by giving so much, Moses had to tell them to stop.

When the people of God catch a vision of God, you won't be able to stop them from giving to the work of God. After all, everything we have belongs to Him. The degree to which we give sacrificially and joyfully proves the degree to which our hearts are surrendered to the One who gave Himself for us.

Does the New Testament command us to give a legalistic amount? No. But the principles of stewardship Jesus and the apostles set forth show that when we give locally, consistently, proportionately, sacrificially, liberally, and cheerfully, we are fulfilling Scripture's highest commands: to love God and love others.

THINK *Questions for personal or group study*

What important principles of stewardship does the Old Testament establish that apply to Christians today?

Why do you think God required Israelites under the law to pay tithes totaling 22 percent or more of their annual income?

Even though the New Testament stresses giving rather than tithing, do you think a tithe is the minimum a Christian should give back to the Lord? Why or why not?

What do you see as the fundamental differences between Israel under the law and the church under grace? What are the key similarities? How should these similarities and differences impact our approach to stewardship today, if at all?

In your opinion, should the sacrificial giving of most Christians be focused on the local church? Why or why not?

SHARE *Talking points for discussing stewardship*

The Mosaic Law required Israelites to pay tithes totaling more than 22 percent of their income each year – usually in the form of crops or animals.

If we impose the Old Testament model on the church, each of us would be required to give upwards of 22 percent of our income to the church each year, with goodwill offerings over and above that. Plus, we would still have to obey Christ's command to render unto Caesar … and as you well know, taxes typically take another 20 to 30 percent of our income.

A careful study of the New Testament shows that first-century believers probably gave more than 10 percent – not because they were commanded to do so, but because they wanted to do so.

The New Testament writers instructed Christians to give locally, consistently, proportionately, sacrificially, liberally, and cheerfully.

When the people of God catch a vision of God, you won't be able to stop them from giving to the work of God. After all, everything we have belongs to Him.

DIVE *Go deeper in your study with these resources*

Managing God's Money: A Biblical Guide by Randy Alcorn

Christians in an Age of Wealth: A Biblical Theology of Stewardship by Craig L. Blomberg and Jonathan Lunde

Counterfeit Gods: The Empty Promises of Money, Sex, and Power, and the Only Hope that Matters by Timothy Keller

NOTES

Chapter 1: What Is Christian Apologetics?

1. William Dembski, "Foreword," Rick Cornish, *5 Minute Apologist: Maximum Truth in Minimum Time* (Colorado Springs, CO: NavPress, 2005), 11.

2. Douglas Groothuis, *Christian Apologetics: A Comprehensive Case for Biblical Faith* (Downers Grove, IL: IVP Academic, 2011), 16.

Chapter 2: What Good Is Christian Apologetics?

1. Gregory Koukl, *Tactics: A Game Plan for Discussing Your Christian Convictions* (Grand Rapids, MI: Zondervan, 2009), 38.

2. Douglas Groothuis, *Christian Apologetics: A Comprehensive Case for Biblical Faith* (Downers Grove, IL: IVP Academic, 2011), 31-33.

Chapter 3: What's Your Worldview?

1. Alex Rosenberg, *The Atheist's Guide to Reality: Enjoying Life without Illusions* (New York, W.W. Norton & Company, Inc.: 2011), 3.

2. Freddy Davis, "The Seven Questions That Define A Worldview," found at marketfaith.org.

3. James N. Anderson, *What's Your Worldview: An Interactive Approach to Life's Big Questions* (Wheaton, IL: Crossway, 2014), 12.

4. Some observers, like Richard G. Howe, contend that a worldview can be naturalistic even if it accepts the reality of an immaterial realm. Wicca, which acknowledges the existence of gods and goddesses, is one such example, according to Howe. See "Modern Witchcraft: It May Not Be What You Think," *Christian Research Journal*, Vol. 28, No. 1, 2005.

5. James W. Sire, *The Universe Next Door: A Basic Worldview Catalogue, 5ᵗʰ Edition* (Downers Grove, IL: InterVarsity Press, 2009), 22-23.

6. C. Fred Smith, *Developing a Biblical Worldview: Seeing Things God's Way* (Nashville, TN: B&H Publishing Group, 2015), 10.

Chapter 4: How Do I Know God Exists?

1. Harold L. Willmington, *Willmington's Guide to the Bible* (Carol Stream, IL: Tyndale House, 1981), 447.

2. W.W. Wiersbe, *The Bible Exposition Commentary, Vol. 1* (Wheaton, IL: Victor Books, 1996), 518.

3. Kenneth Wuest, "Romans in the Greek New Testament," *Word Studies in the Greek New Testament*, Vol. 1 (Grand Rapids, MI: Wm. B. Eerdmans Publishing Company, 1973), 30-31.

Chapter 5: The Arguments for God's Existence

1. Doug Powell, *Holman QuickSource Guide to Christian Apologetics* (Nashville, TN: Holman Reference, 2006), 27.

2. Norman Geisler, *Baker Encyclopedia of Christian Apologetics* (Grand Rapids, MI: Baker Academic, 2006), 276.

3. Douglas Groothuis, *Christian Apologetics: A Comprehensive Case for Biblical Faith* (Downers Grove, IL: IVP Academic, 2011), 207.

4. C.S. Lewis, *Mere Christianity* (New York: Collier Books / Macmillan Publishing Company, 1943), 17-39.

5. Powell, 82.

6. William Lane Craig, "Does God Exist?" found at http://www.reasonablefaith.org.

Chapter 6: How Do I Know the Bible Is True?

1. Norman L. Geisler and Frank Turek, *I Don't Have Enough Faith to Be an Atheist* (Wheaton, IL: Crossway, 2004), 228.

2. Tacitus, Annals 15.44, quoted in Lee Strobel, *The Case for Christ* (Grand Rapids, MI: Zondervan Publishing House, 1988), 82.

3. Michael Gleghorn, "Ancient Evidence for Jesus from Non-Christian Sources," found at http://probe.org.

4. Josephus, *Antiquities xx. 200*, cited in F.F. Bruce, *Jesus and Christian Origins Outside the New Testament* (Grand Rapids, MI: William B. Eerdmans Publishing Company, 1974), 13.

5. Josephus, *Antiquities 18.63-64*, cited in Edwin Yamauchi, "Jesus Outside the New Testament: What is the Evidence?" in *Jesus Under Fire*, ed. By Michael J. Wilkins and J.P. Moreland (Grand Rapids, MI: Zondervan Publishing House, 1995), 227, note 66.

6. *The Babylonian Talmud*, translated by I. Epstein (London: Soncino, 1935), vol. III, Sanhedrin 43a, 281, cited in Gary R. Habermas, *The Historical Jesus* (Joplin, MO: College Press Publishing Company, 1996), 203.

7. Lucian, *The Death of Peregrine, 11-13*, in *The Works of Lucian of Samosata*, translated by H.W. Fowler and F.G. Fowler, 4 vols. (Oxford: Clarendon, 1949), vol. 4, cited in Habermas, 206.

8. Various sources were consulted including John Foxe, *Foxe's Book of Martyrs* (Springdale, PA: Whitaker House, 1981); "What happened to the Twelve Apostles? How Do Their Deaths Prove Easter?" found at https://credohouse. org/blog/what-happened-to-the-twelve-apostles-how-do-their-deaths-prove-easter; and Ken Curtis, Ph.D., "Whatever Happened to the Twelve Apostles?" found at http://www.christianity.com/church/church-history/timeline/1-300/whatever-happened-to-the-twelve-apostles-11629558.

9. Paul Marshall, Lela Gilbert, Nina Shea, *Persecuted: The Global Assault on Christians* (Nashville: Thomas Nelson, 2013), 4.

10. Cited in *ibid.*, 9.

11. Cited in Cath Martin, "'70 million Christians' martyred for their faith since Jesus walked the earth," http://www.christiantoday.com/article/70.million. christians.martyred.faith.since.jesus.walked.earth/38403.htm, June 25, 2014.

Chapter 7: Seven Reasons to Trust the Scriptures

1. Norman L. Geisler and Frank Turek, *I Don't Have Enough Faith to Be an Atheist* (Wheaton, IL: Crossway, 2004), 228.

2. Nelson Glueck, *Rivers in the Desert: A History of the Negev* (New York: Farrar, Strauss & Cudahay, 1959), 31, cited in Norman L. Geisler, *Systematic Theology*, vol. 1 (Minneapolis, MN: Bethany House, 2002), 557.

3. Geisler, 559.

Chapter 8: Addressing Eight Common Objections

n/a

Chapter 9: Is the New Testament Canon Closed?

1. Craig L. Blomberg, *Can We Still Believe the Bible? An Evangelical Engagement with Contemporary Questions* (Grand Rapids, MI: BrazosPress, 2014), 76.

2. For a concise overview of the development of the Old Testament canon, including a discussion of the *Apocrypha* and *Pseudepigrapha*, see Blomberg, *Can We Still Believe the Bible?* 45-54.

3. *Ibid.*, 58-61.

4. *Ibid.*, 59.

Chapter 10: Which Translation of the Bible Should I Use?

1. *The Apologetics Study Bible* (Nashville: Holman Bible Publishers, 2007), xviii.

2. Many thanks to E. Ray Clendenen of B&H Publishing Group for help in completing this chapter.

3. Several sources were consulted including, "How Do They Stack Up?" from Holman Bible Publishers; "The Holy Bible: Translations & Versions," from Zondervan Bibles; and "A Guide to Popular Bible Translations," found at https://www.cokesbury.com/FreeDownloads/BibleTransGuide.pdf. While these sources varied from one another in some details, there was general agreement on the type of translation and reading level.

Chapter 11: Who Is the Real Jesus?

n/a

Chapter 12: Seven Keys to Unlocking the Real Jesus

n/a

Chapter 13: Did Jesus Ever Claim to Be God?

n/a

Chapter 14: What Have We Done with the Christmas Story?

1. Kenneth E. Bailey: *Jesus Through Middle Eastern Eyes: Cultural Studies in the Gospels* (Downers Grove, IL: IVP Academic, 2008), 26.

Chapter 15: What Do False Prophets Have in Common?

1. Walter Martin, *The Kingdom of the Cults* (Minneapolis: Bethany House Publishers, 1985), 16-17.

Chapter 16: Islam: An Overview

1. "The Future of World Religions: Population Growth Projections, 2010-2050," found at http://www.pewforum.org/2015/04/02/religious-projections-2010-2050/.

2. Surah 9:29, Maulana Muhammad Ali.

3. *The Illustrated Guide to World Religions*, Dean Halverson, general editor (Bloomington, MN: Bethany House, 2003), 111-112.

Chapter 17: Comparing Christianity and Islam

n/a

Chapter 18: Do Christians and Muslims Worship the Same God?

1. "Do Christians and Muslims Worship the Same God?" Oct. 23, 2007, found at http://chuckbaldwinlive.com/Articles/tabid/109/ID/491/Do-Christians-And-Muslims-Worship-The-Same-God.aspx.

Chapter 19: The Real Tragedy of Jihad

1. Bill Warner, *The Life of Mohammed: The Sira* (Nashville, TN: CSPI, LLC, 2010), 61.

2. N.S.R.K. Ravi, from an interview with the author in September 2003 at Ridgecrest Conference Center, N.C.

Chapter 20: The Ultimate Role Model: Jesus or Muhammad?

1. David Wood, "Muhammad and the Messiah: Comparing the Central Figures of Islam and Christianity," found in http://www.equip.org/article/muhammad-messiah-comparing-central-figures-islam-christianity/.

2. *Ibid.*

Chapter 21: Seven Words That Reveal Islam's Worldview

1. Bill Warner, *The Islamic Doctrine of Christians and Jews* (Nashville, TN: CSPI, LLC, 2010), 2.

2. Bill Warner, "The Muslim as Dhimmi," video found at http://www.politicalislam.com/muslim-dhimmi/.

3. Abu Ja'far Muhammad bin Jarir al-Tabari, quoted in Robert Spencer, *The Complete Infidel's Guide to the Koran* (Washington, D.C.: Regency Publishing, Inc., 2009), 202.

Chapter 22: Christianity Comes to Qatar

1. Quoted in Paul Marshall, Lela Gilbert, and Nina Shea, *Persecuted: The Global Assault on Christians* (Nashville, TN: Thomas Nelson, 2013), 165.

2. *Ibid.*, 4.

3. *Ibid.*, 9.

4. *Ibid.*, 168.

5. *Ibid.*, 168.

Chapter 23: Mormonism: An Overview

1. "Joseph Smith – History 1:19," *The Pearl of Great Price* (Salt Lake City, UT: Church of Jesus Christ of Latter-day Saints, 1982), 49. For an abbreviated testimony of Joseph Smith, see "Introduction," *The Book of Mormon: Another Testament of Jesus Christ.*

2. Fritz Ridenour, *So What's the Difference: A Look at 20 Worldviews, Faiths and Religions and How They Compare to Christianity* (Bloomington, MN: Bethany House Publishers, 2001), 130.

3. *Ibid.*, 131.

4. Bruce McConkie, *A New Witness for the Articles of Faith* (Salt Lake City, UT: Deseret Book Company, 1985), 67.

Chapter 24: Comparing Christianity and Mormonism

(Sources cited in table)

Chapter 25: Does the Bible Prove Preexistence?

1. Found at https://www.mormon.org/beliefs/plan-of-salvation.

2. Ron Rhodes, *The 10 Most Important Things You Can Say to a Mormon* (Eugene, OR: Harvest House Publishers, 2001), 70.

Chapter 26: Is Mormonism Necessary?

1. "Joseph Smith – History 1:19," *The Pearl of Great Price* (Salt Lake City, UT: Church of Jesus Christ of Latter-day Saints, 1982), 49. For an abbreviated testimony of Joseph Smith, see "Introduction," *The Book of Mormon: Another Testament of Jesus Christ.*

2. Joseph F. Smith, *Teachings of the Prophet Joseph Smith*, 327, found at http://blog.mrm.org/2014/07/ignorant-translators-careless-transcribers-or-designing-and-corrupt-priests/.

Chapter 27: Joseph Smith and Polygamy: A Teachable Moment

1. "Plural Marriage in Kirtland and Nauvoo," found at https://www.lds.org/topics/plural-marriage-in-kirtland-and-nauvoo?lang=eng.

2. Paul Copan, *Is God a Moral Monster? Making Sense of the Old Testament God* (Grand Rapids, MI: Baker Books, 2011), 68.

Chapter 28: When the Bible Speaks to Mormons

1. Lynn Wilder, "How I escaped the Mormon Temple," *Christianity Today* digital, Nov. 22, 2013.

2. *Ibid.*

3. *Ibid.*

4. *Ibid.*

5. "Articles of Faith: Thirteen basic points of belief to which Mormons subscribe," found at https://www.mormon.org/beliefs/articles-of-faith.

Chapter 29: Jehovah's Witnesses: An Overview

1. *2015 Yearbook of Jehovah's Witnesses* (Brooklyn, NY: Watch Tower Bible and Tract Society, 2014), 185–186.

2. *Ibid.*, 176.

3. "The Watchtower And Awake! - The 'Most Widely Circulated,' 'Most Widely Read' and 'Most Popular' Magazines in the World." found at http://defendingjehovahswitnesses.blogspot.com/2013/09/the-watchtower-and-awake-most-widely.html.

4. "Who was the Founder of Jehovah's Witnesses?" found at http://www.jw.org/en/jehovahs-witnesses/faq/founder/.

5. *Insight on the Scriptures*, vol. 1 (Brooklyn, NY: Watch Tower Bible and Tract Society, 1988), 969-970.

6. *Knowledge that Leads to Everlasting Life* (Brooklyn, NY: Watch Tower Bible and Tract Society, 1995), 41.

Chapter 30: Comparing Christianity and the Jehovah's Witnesses

(Sources cited in table)

Chapter 31: Did Jesus Die on a Torture Stake?

1. *Awake!*, Nov. 8, 1972, 28, quoted in Ron Rhodes, *Reasoning from the Scriptures with the Jehovah's Witnesses* (Eugene, OR: Harvest House Publishers, 1993), 395.

2. Robert M. Bowman, Jr., *Understanding Jehovah's Witnesses* (Grand Rapids, MI: Zondervan, 1995), 143.

Chapter 32: Is the Holy Spirit Like Electricity?

1. Matt Capps, "Why Theology Matters," *Facts & Trends*, August/September 2015, 30.

2. *Aid to Bible Understanding* (Brooklyn, NY: Watch Tower Bible and Tract Society, 1971), 1543.

Chapter 33: What Is the New World Translation?

1. Found at http://www.jw.org/en/publications/bible/.

2. Ron Rhodes, *Reasoning from the Scriptures with Jehovah's Witnesses* (Eugene, OR: Harvest House Publishers, 1993), 96.

3. *Ibid.*, 97.

4. *Ibid.*

5. *Ibid.*

6. Tal Davis, "The Revised 2013 Jehovah's Witnesses' Bible," found at http://www.marketfaith.org/2015/08/the-2013-revised-jehovahs-witnesses-bible/.

Chapter 34: Sharing Your Faith with Mormons and Jehovah's Witnesses

1. Gregory Koukl, *Tactics: A Game Plan for Discussing Your Christian Convictions* (Grand Rapids, MI: Zondervan, 2009), 37.

Chapter 35: Roman Catholicism: An Overview

1. Kenneth R. Samples, "What Think Ye of Rome? (Part One): An Evangelical Appraisal of Contemporary Catholicism," found at http://www.equip.org/PDF/DC170-1.pdf.

2. Ron Rhodes, *Reasoning from the Scriptures with Catholics*, (Eugene, OR: Harvest House Publishers, 2000), 19.

3. Harold O.J. Brown, *Heresies* (Garden City, N.Y.: Doubleday & Company, 1984), 310.

4. *Catechism of the Catholic Church* (New York: Doubleday, 1995), 254, par. 882.

5. *Creeds of Christendom*, Council of Trent.

6. *Catechism of the Catholic Church*, 319, par. 1129.

7. *Ibid.*, 358, par. 1285.

8. *Ibid.*, 291, par. 1030.

9. Ron Rhodes, 235.

Chapter 36: Was Saint Peter the First Pope?

1. *Catechism of the Catholic Church* (New York: Doubleday, 1995), 254, par. 881-882.

2. Michael F. Ross, "Was Saint Peter the First Pope?" *Christian Research Journal*, Vol. 36, No. 01, 10-11.

Chapter 37: The Word of Faith Movement: An Overview

1. Hank Hanegraaff, "The Counterfeit Revival (Part Four)," found at http://www.equip.org/article/the-counterfeit-revival-part-four/.

2. E.W. Kenyon, *The Father and His Family* (Lynnwood, WA: Kenyon's Gospel Publishing Society, 1964), 118, cited in Hank Hanegraaff, *Christianity in Crisis 21st Century* (Nashville, TN: Thomas Nelson, 2009), 19.

3. D.R. McConnell, *A Different Gospel* (Peabody, MA: Hendrickson Publishers, Inc., 1988), 23, 33, cited in Hanegraaff, *Christianity in Crisis 21st Century*, 18.

4. Kenneth Hagin, *Zoe: The God-Kind of Life, 1989, 35-36, 41,* found in https://preachersaidwhat.wordpress.com/2011/11/06/kenneth-hagin-said-what/.

5. Kenneth Copeland, *Following the Faith of Abraham I* (Fort Worth, TX: Kenneth Copeland Ministries, 1989), audiotape #01-3001, side 1, cited in Hanegraaff, *Christianity in Crisis 21ˢᵗ Century*, 25.

6. Copeland, quoted in "What's Wrong with the Faith Movement? Part Two: The Teachings of Kenneth Copeland," *Christian Research Journal*, June 30, 1994.

7. Copeland, *Holy Bible: Kenneth Copeland Reference Edition* (Fort Worth, TX: Kenneth Copeland Ministries, 1991), 129, cited in Hanegraaff, *Christianity in Crisis 21ˢᵗ Century*, 25.

8. Copeland, *Believer's Voice of Victory*, Trinity Broadcasting Network, April 21, 1991, cited in Hanegraaff, *Christianity in Crisis 21ˢᵗ Century*, 25.

9. Gloria Copeland, "Paul's Thorn in the Flesh," *Believer's Voice of Victory*, November 1983, cited in Hanegraaff, *Christianity in Crisis 21ˢᵗ Century*, 26.

10. Randy Frame, "Best-Selling Author Admits Mistakes, Vows Changes, *Christianity Today*, Oct. 28, 1991, 44-45, cited in Hanegraaff, *Christianity in Crisis 21ˢᵗ Century*, 31.

11. Benny Hinn, *Our Position in Christ #2: The Word Made Flesh* (Orlando, FL: Orlando Christian Center, 1991), audiotape #A031190-2, side 2, cited in Hanegraaff, *Christianity in Crisis 21ˢᵗ Century*, 26.

12. Hinn, *Double Portion Anointing*, part 3 (Orlando, FL: Orlando Christian Center, n.d.), audiotape #A031791-3, sides 1 and 2; aired on TBN, April 7, 1991, cited in Hanegraaff, *Christianity in Crisis 21ˢᵗ Century*, 29.

13. Hinn, *Prophecy for the '90s* (Orlando Christian Center, Jan. 1, 1990), audiotape cited in Hanegraaff, *Christianity in Crisis 21ˢᵗ Century*, 32.

14. Joel Osteen, *Your Best Life Now: 7 Steps to Living at Your Full Potential* (New York: Warner Faith, 2004), 129.

15. Osteen, Easter service messages in 2000 and 2004, cited in Hanegraaff, *Christianity in Crisis 21ˢᵗ Century*, 35.

16. Osteen, *Become a Better You: 7 Keys to Improving Your Life Every Day* (New York: Howard Books, 2007), 63.

17. Joyce Meyer, *The Most Important Decision You Will Ever Make: A Complete and Thorough Understanding of What It Means to Be Born Again* (Fenton, MO: Life in the Word, 1991), 37.

18. Meyer, *Eight Ways to Keep the Devil Under Your Feet* (New York: Warner Faith, 2002), 87-88.

19. Meyer adds, "And the religious world thinks that's heresy and they want to hang you for it. But the Bible says that I'm righteous, and I can't be righteous and a sinner at the same time." *From the Cross to the Throne*, audiocassette (St. Louis: Life Christian Center, n.d.), cited in Hanegraaff, *Christianity in Crisis 21ˢᵗ Century*, 43.

20. Creflo Dollar, *Creflo Dollar Ministries: World Changers*, Trinity Broadcasting Network, Sept. 15, 2002, cited in Hanegraaff, *Christianity in Crisis 21ˢᵗ Century*, 48, 50.

21. Dollar, *The Miracle of Debt Release*, audiotape series, copyrighted 2000; *Bible Answer Man*, July 5, 2002, cited in Hanegraaff, *Christianity in Crisis 21ˢᵗ Century*, 51.

22. T.D. Jakes, *The Potter's House*, Trinity Broadcasting Network, June 20, 1999, cited in Hanegraaff, *Christianity in Crisis 21ˢᵗ Century*, 54.

23. Jakes, *The Potter's House*, Trinity Broadcasting Network, June 7, 2004, cited in *ibid.*, 53.

24. Rod Parsley, *Praise the Lord*, Trinity Broadcasting Network, Aug. 7, 2003, cited in *ibid.*, 55.

25. Parsley, *Praise the Lord: Praise-a Thon*, Trinity Broadcasting Network, Nov. 9, 2000, cited in *ibid.*, 56.

26. Parsley, *Praise the Lord: Dominion Camp Meeting*, Trinity Broadcasting Network, July 6, 1999, cited in *ibid.*, 56-57.

27. Frederick K.C. Price, "Name It and Claim It! What Saith the WORD?" *Ever Increasing Faith Messenger* 10, 3 (Summer 1989); and *Ever Increasing Faith*, Trinity Broadcasting Network, Dec. 9, 1990, both cited in *ibid.*, 58.

28. Price further mocks the sufficiency of Jesus' atonement on the cross; see Hanegraaff, *Christianity in Crisis 21ˢᵗ Century*, 59.

29. Price, *Ever Increasing Faith*, Trinity Broadcasting Network, Nov. 23, 1990, cited in *ibid.*, 59-60.

30. Charles Capps, *Dynamics of Faith & Confession* (Tulsa, OK: Harrison House, 1987), 86-87.

31. *Ibid.*

32. Morris Cerullo, *The Miracle Book* (San Diego, CA: Morris Cerullo World Evangelism, 1984), xi.

33. *Ibid.*

34. Cerullo, *The Endtime Manifestation of the Sons of God* (San Diego: Morris Cerullo World Evangelism, Inc., n.d.), audiotape 1, sides 1 and 2; cited in Hanegraaff, *Christianity in Crisis 21ˢᵗ Century*, 69.

35. Paula White, "Follow God's Principles 'To Have it All,'" http://www.paulawhite.org/content/view/172/88888897, June 19, 2008, cited in Hanegraaff, *Christianity in Crisis 21ˢᵗ Century*, 73.

36. White, "Understanding the Power of Words over Your Money," http://www.paulawhite.org/content/view/172/88888897, June 19, 2008; *Praise the Lord*, Trinity Broadcasting Network, Feb. 6, 2004, cited in Hanegraaff, *Christianity in Crisis 21ˢᵗ Century*, 74.

37. Robert M. Bowman Jr., *The Word-Faith Controversy: Understanding the Health and Wealth Gospel* (Grand Rapids, MI: Baker Books, 2001).

38. R. Laird Harris, Gleason L. Archer Jr., and Bruce K. Waltke, eds., *Theological Wordbook of the Old Testament,* 2 vols. (Chicago: Moody Press, 1981), 1:192.

39. Matthew Henry, found at http://www.biblestudytools.com/commentaries/matthew-henry-complete/proverbs/18.html.

40. Meyer, *Approval Addiction: Overcoming Your Need to Please Everyone* (New York: Faith Words, 2005), 9-10.

41. Dollar, "The Just Shall Live by Faith," *Changing the World*, Trinity Broadcasting Network, Sept. 20, 1998, cited in Hanegraaff, *Christianity in Crisis 21st Century*, 122.

42. A.T. Robertson and W. Hersey Davis, *A New Short Grammar of the Greek Testament*, 10th Revised Edition (Grand Rapids, MI: Baker Book House, 1979), 227-28.

43. Osteen, quoted in Hank Hanegraaff, *Christianity in Crisis 21st Century*, 231.

44. Osteen, *Discover the Champion in You*, Trinity Broadcasting Network, May 3, 2004, cited in *The OSTEENification of American Christianity*, Christian Research Institute / Hank Hanegraaff (Charlotte, NC: Christian Research Institute, 2014), 9.

45. Copeland, *Authority of the Believer II* (Fort Worth, TX: Kenneth Copeland Ministries, 1987), audiotape #10-0302, side 1, cited in Hanegraaff, *Christianity in Crisis 21st Century*, 98.

46. *Hebrew-Greek Key Word Study Bible: Key Insights into God's Word*, ESV (Chattanooga, TN: AMG Publishers, 1984), 2311.

47. Copeland, *Praise the Lord*, Trinity Broadcasting Network, Feb. 5, 1986, cited in Hanegraaff, *Christianity in Crisis 21st Century*, 138.

48. John MacArthur, "What is the Secret to Contentment?" found at http://www.gty.org/resources/questions/QA149/what-is-the-secret-to-contentment.

49. Gordon D. Fee, *The Disease of the Health and Wealth Gospels* (Vancouver, British Columbia: Regent College Publishing, 1985, 2006), 28.

Chapter 38: Does God Have a Body?

1. Kenneth Copeland, *Following the Faith of Abraham I*, 1989 audiotape, #01-3001, side 1, found at http://www.rapidnet.com/~jbeard/bdm/exposes/copeland/general.htm.

2. Robert M. Bowman, Jr., *The Word-Faith Controversy: Understanding the Health and Wealth Gospel* (Grand Rapids, MI: Baker Books: 2001), 119.

Chapter 39: Was That a Miracle?

1. Norman L. Geisler and Frank Turek, *I Don't Have Enough Faith to Be an Atheist* (Wheaton, IL: Crossway, 2004).

2. *Ibid.*, 212.

3. *Ibid.*, 213.

Chapter 40: There's Death in That Box

1. Attributed to Lorenzo Snow, the fifth president of the Latter-day Saints.

2. Bob Smietana, "Snake-handling believers find joy in test of faith," *The Tennessean*, June 3, 2012, found at http://archive.tennessean.com/article/20120603/NEWS06/306030069/Snake-handling-believers-find-joy-test-faith.

3. *HCSB Study Bible* (Nashville, TN: Holman Bible Publishers, 2010), 1720, note 16:9-20.

4. Smietana, "Snake-handling believers find joy in test of faith," *The Tennessean*, June 3, 2012.

Chapter 41: What About Those Who Haven't Heard?

n/a

Chapter 42: When Words Lose Their Meaning

1. Lynne Truss, *Eats, Shoots & Leaves: The Zero Tolerance Approach to Punctuation* (New York: Gotham Books, a division of Penguin Group [USA] Inc., 2004).

2. Gregory Koukl, *Tactics: A Game Plan for Discussing Your Christian Convictions* (Grand Rapids, MI: Zondervan, 2009), 38.

Chapter 43: When a Question Is Better Than an Answer

1. Randy Newman, *Questioning Evangelism: Engaging People's Hearts the Way Jesus Did* (Grand Rapids, MI: Kregel Publications, 2004), 14.

2. *Ibid.*, 15.

3. *Ibid.*, 116.

4. *Ibid.*, 65.

Chapter 44: Why Many Non-Westerners Reject the Gospel

1. Ronald Muller, *Honor & Shame: Unlocking the Door* (USA: Xlibris Corporation, 2000), 19.

Chapter 45: How Can 5 Billion People Be Wrong?

1. http://www.adherents.com/Religions_By_Adherents.html, accessed Oct. 10, 2015.

Chapter 46: Should You Believe in Ghosts?

1. Hank Hanegraaff, *Afterlife: What You Need to Know about Heaven, the Hereafter & Near-death Experiences* (Brentwood, TN: Worthy Publishing, 2013), 115.

Chapter 47: Ten Biblical Truths About the Afterlife

1. Todd Burpo, found at http://www.oneplace.com/ministries/ask-hank/download-buy/books/life-after-life-after-life.html, accessed Oct. 12, 2015.

2. *Heaven is for Real: A Little Boy's Astounding Story of His Trip to Heaven and Back* by Colton Burpo and Lynn Vincent (Nashville, TN: Thomas Nelson, 2010).

3. *To Hell and Back: Life After Death – Startling New Evidence* by Maurice S. Rollins (Nashville, TN: Thomas Nelson, 1993).

4. Hank Hanegraaff, found at http://www.oneplace.com/ministries/ask-hank/download-buy/books/life-after-life-after-life.html.

5. C.S. Lewis, *The Problem of Pain* (Kindle Edition, HarperCollins e-books, 2009).

Chapter 48: Sheol and the Afterlife

1. Robert A. Morey, *Death and the Afterlife* (Minneapolis, MN: Bethany House Publishers, 1984), 74-75.

Chapter 49: Hades and the Afterlife

n/a

Chapter 50: Gehenna and the Afterlife

1. Steve Gregg, *All You Want to Know About Hell: Three Christian Views of God's Final Solution to the Problem of Sin* (Nashville, TN: Thomas Nelson, 2013), 86-98.

2. Robert A. Morey, *Death and the Afterlife* (Minneapolis, MN: Bethany House Publishers, 1984), 90.

Chapter 51: A Look into Tartarus

1. *The Apologetics Study Bible* (Nashville, TN: Holman Bible Publishers, 2007), 1859.

Chapter 52: Does the Bible Teach Purgatory?

1. *Catechism of the Catholic Church* (New York: Doubleday, 1995), 291.

2. John A. Hardon, *Pocket Catholic Dictionary* (New York: Image Books, 1985), 93.

3. Chad Owen Brand, *The Apologetics Study Bible* (Nashville, TN: Holman Bible Publishers, 2007), 1541.

4. Harry Blamires, *Knowing the Truth About Heaven & Hell: Our Choices and Where They Lead Us* (Ann Arbor, MI: Servant Books, 1988), 85.

5. Joseph Loconte, "When Luther Shook Up Christianity," *Wall St. Journal*, Oct. 30, 2015, A11.

6. *Catechism of the Catholic Church*, 295.

Chapter 53: Is Heaven Our Final Home?

1. Randy Alcorn, *Heaven* (Wheaton, IL: Tyndale House Publishers, 2004), 42.

2. *Theological Dictionary of the New Testament*, Gerhard Kittel and Gerhard Friedrich, editors (Grand Rapids, MI: William B. Eerdmans Publishing Company, 1985), 388.

3. J.I. Packer, quoted in Hank Hanegraaff, *AfterLife: What You Need to Know About Heaven, the Hereafter & Near-death Experiences* (Brentwood, TN: Worthy Publishing, 2013), 16.

Chapter 54: What Christianity without Hell Looks Like

1. John Shore, "What Christianity without hell looks like," *Patheos*, Oct. 28, 2014, found at http://www.patheos.com/blogs/johnshore/2014/10/what-christianity-without-hell-looks-like/.

2. *Ibid.*

3. *Ibid.*

4. *Ibid.*

5. *Ibid.*

6. Edward A. Donnelly, *Heaven and Hell* (Banner of Truth, 2002), 27, cited in "A Calvinist's Response to Talbott's Universalism" by Daniel Strange, *Universal Salvation?: The Current Debate*, edited by Robin A. Parry and Christopher H. Partridge (Grand Rapids, MI: William B. Eerdmans Publishing Company, 2003), 154.

Chapter 55: The Goodness of Hell

1. Dinesh D'Souza, *Godforsaken: Bad Things Happen. Is there a God who cares? Yes. Here's proof* (U.S.A.: Tyndale House Publishers, Inc., Reprint edition 2012), 224.

2. Robert Ingersoll, cited in Martin Gardner, *The Whys of a Philosophical Scrivener* (New York: St. Martin's Press, 1999), 301.

3. John Stott, cited in D'Souza, *Godforsaken*, 226.

4. C.S. Lewis, *The Problem of Pain*, cited in "Banished from Humanity: C.S. Lewis and the Doctrine of Hell" by Randy Alcorn, March 18, 2015, http://www.desiringgod.org/articles/banished-from-humanity.

5. Lewis, *The Problem of Pain*, cited in "Seeing Hell through the Reason and Imagination of C.S. Lewis" by Douglas Beyer, Jan. 1, 1998, http://www.discovery.org/a/507.

Chapter 56: How the World Will End

1. *The Greatest Man Who Ever Lived* (New York: Watch Tower Bible & Tract Society, 1991), 132.

Chapter 57: A Different God in the Old and New Testaments?

1. "Why is God so different in the Old Testament than He is in the New Testament?" found at http://www.gotquestions.org/God-different.html, accessed Oct. 18, 2015.

2. *Apologetics Study Bible* (Nashville, TN: Holman Bible Publishers, 2007), 273.

Chapter 58: Is God Guilty of Genocide?

1. Richard Dawkins, *The God Delusion* (Boston / New York: Houghton Mifflin Company, 2008), 51.

2. *Hard Sayings of the Bible*, Walter C. Kaiser Jr., Peter H. Davids, F.F. Bruce, Manfred T. Brauch (Downers Grove, IL: InterVarsity Press, 1996), 206-207.

3. Paul Copan, *Is God a Moral Monster? Making Sense of the Old Testament God* (Grand Rapids, MI: Baker Books, 2011), 184-185.

Chapter 59: Is God to Blame for Our Messed-up World?

1. "What's Wrong with the World?" The American Chesterton Society, found in https://www.chesterton.org/wrong-with-world/.

2. Lee Strobel, "Why Does God Allow Suffering?" *Christian Research Journal*, Vol. 24, No. 1, 2001, found at http://www.equip.org/article/why-does-god-allow-suffering/.

3. Peter Kreeft, quoted in *ibid*.

4. Cliffe Knechtle, quoted in *ibid.*

Chapter 60: Why We Suffer

1. "It is Well with My Soul" by Horatio Spafford and Philip Bliss, first published in 1876.

Chapter 61: Are Science and Religion Closer Than We Think?

1. You can read the results and view the survey questions at http://space.mit.edu/home/tegmark/survey.html (last accessed Oct. 20, 2015).

2. *Ibid.*

3. *Ibid.*

4. Max Tegmark, email to Rob Phillips received Feb. 13, 2013.

5. The MIT Survey on Science, Religion and Origins: the Belief Gap, http://space.mit.edu/home/tegmark/survey.html.

6. Richard C. Lewontin, "Billions and Billions of Demons," New York Review of Books, Jan. 9, 1997, found at http://www.nybooks.com/articles/archives/1997/jan/09/billions-and-billions-of-demons/.

7. Robert Jastrow, *God and the Astronomers* (New York: W.W. Norton & Company, Inc., 1992), 107.

Chapter 62: Thank God for Earthquakes

1. Voltaire, "The Lisbon Earthquake," in *Toleration and Other Essays* (New York: G.P. Putnam's Sons, 1912), 204-206.

2. Peter D. Ward and Donald Brownlee, *Rare Earth* (New York: Copernicus Books, 2004), cited in Dinesh D'Souza, *Godforsaken* (Carol Stream, IL: Tyndale House Publishers, Inc., 2012), 124-125.

3. Dinesh D'Souza, *What's So Great About God?* (Carol Stream, IL: Tyndale House Publishers, Inc., 2013), 125.

Chapter 63: Are All Religions Equal?

1. John MacArthur, *The MacArthur New Testament Commentary: Matthew 8-15* (Chicago: Moody Press, 1987), 400-401.

2. Huston Smith, *The World's Religions: Our Great Wisdom Traditions* (New York: Harper San Francisco, 1991), 73.

3. Stephen Prothero, *God is Not One: The Eight Rival Religions That Run the World – and Why Their Differences Matter* (New York: HarperOne, 2010), 3.

Chapter 64: What Young Atheists Can Teach Us

1. Larry Alex Taunton, "Listening to Young Atheists: Lessons for a Stronger Christianity," *The Atlantic*, June 6, 2013, found at http://www.theatlantic.com/national/archive/2013/06/listening-to-young-atheists-lessons-for-a-stronger-christianity/276584/.

2. Penn Jillette, video and transcript posted on The Gospel Coalition, http://blogs.thegospelcoalition.org/justintaylor/2009/11/17/how-much-do-you-have-to-hate-somebody-to-not-proselytize/.

3. Cited in Taunton, "Listening to Young Atheists."

Chapter 65: What Every Christian Should Know About Same-sex Attraction

1. For two views of New McCarthyism see "Rise of the New McCarthyism," http://www.pfaw.org/rww-in-focus/rise-of-the-new-mccarthyism-how-right-wing-extremists-try-to-paralyze-government-throug; and "The New 'McCarthyism' Exists, but It Has Nothing to Do with Ted Cruz," http://www.nationalreview.com/article/415932/new-mccarthyism-exists-it-has-nothing-do-ted-cruz-charles-c-w-cooke.

Chapter 66: Seven Biblical Truths About Sex and Marriage

1. Pascal-Emmanuel Gobry, "Why so many Christians won't back down on gay marriage," *The Week*, online edition, Sept. 3, 2014.

2. Denny Burk, *What Is the Meaning of Sex?* (Wheaton, IL: Crossway, 2013), 88-106.

3. For a fuller discussion of the scientific evidence, see Joe Dallas, "Speaking of Homosexuality," *Christian Research Journal*, Vol. 29, No. 06, 2006; and Robert A.J. Gagnon, *The Bible and Homosexual Practice: Texts and Hermeneutics* (Nashville: Abington Press, 2001), 395-432.

Chapter 67: Six Key Passages – and Why They Matter

1. James R. White and Jeffrey D. Niell, *The Same Sex Controversy: Defending and Clarifying the Bible's Message About Homosexuality* (Minneapolis: Bethany House, 2002), 46.

2. *Ibid.*, 51.

3. Kevin DeYoung, *What Does the Bible Really Teach about Homosexuality?* (Wheaton, IL: Crossway, 2015), 42-47.

4. White and Niell, 65.

5. Paul Copan, *Is God a Moral Monster? Making Sense of the Old Testament God* (Grand Rapids, MI: Baker Books, 2011), 74. See also Gordon J. Wenham, *Leviticus*, New International Commentary on the Old Testament (Grand Rapids, MI: Eerdans, 1979), 270.

6. *Ibid.*, 77.

7. See "The Negative Effects of Societal Endorsement of Homosexuality," Robert A.J. Gagnon, *The Bible and Homosexual Practice: Texts and Hermeneutics* (Nashville: Abington Press, 2001), 471-484.

8. apa.org/topics/light/orientation.pdf.

9. Denny Burk, *God and the Gay Christian? A Response to Matthew Vines* (Louisville: SBTS Press, 2014), 48.

10. Richard B. Hays, *The Moral Vision of the New Testament: Contemporary Introduction to New Testament Ethics* (New York: Harper Collins, 1996), 393.

11. Burk, 51.

Chapter 68: But What About …

1. "Public Opinion Trends of Gay Marriage," The Pew Forum on Religion and Public Life, cited in Joe Dallas, "Speaking of Homosexuality," *Christian Research Journal*, Vol. 29, No. 06, 2006.

2. Richard A. Friedman, "Infidelity Lurks in Your Genes," http://www.nytimes.com/2015/05/24/opinion/sunday/infidelity-lurks-in-your-genes.html?rref=collection%2Fcolumn%2Frichard-a-friedman.

3. Joe Dallas, "Speaking of Homosexuality," *Christian Research Journal*, Vol. 29, No. 06, 2006.

4. apa.org/topics/light/orientation.pdf.

5. Dallas, "Speaking of Homosexuality."

6. *Ibid.*

7. Kevin DeYoung, *What Does the Bible Really Teach about Homosexuality?* (Wheaton, IL: Crossway, 2015), 107.

8. Matthew Vines, *God and the Gay Christian* (New York: Convergent Books, 2014), 3.

9. Robert A.J. Gagnon, *The Bible and Homosexual Practice: Texts and Hermeneutics* (Nashville: Abington Press, 2001), 349.

10. *Ibid.*, 350-361.

11. *Ibid.*, 395-432.

12. Neil and Briar Whitehead, *My Genes Made Me Do It! A Scientific Look at Sexual Orientation* (Lafayette, LA: Huntington House, 1999), 209.

13. Gagnon, 418. The author cites numerous studies supporting the elasticity of sexual behavior and the possibility of change on pp. 418-429.

14. *Ibid.*, 430. The author expands on these comments in a section entitled, "Relation of the Scientific Data to Paul's Views," 430-432.

15. James M. Hamilton Jr., *God and the Gay Christian? A Response to Matthew Vines*, 29.

16. Richard B. Hays, *The Moral Vision of the New Testament: Contemporary Introduction to New Testament Ethics* (New York: Harper Collins, 1996), 391-392.

Chapter 69: Will a Man Rob God?

n/a

HOST AN APOLOGETICS WORKSHOP AT YOUR CHURCH

Hosting an apologetics workshop at your church is simple. Here's how:

Choose a format

Select from a:

- One-day workshop
- Two-day workshop (typically Saturday – Sunday)
- Three-day workshop (typically Friday – Sunday)

Pick a date

Go online to **OnceDelivered.net/upcoming/** and see available dates. Then contact Rob Phillips to confirm your workshop date(s):

Phone: 573.636.0400 ext. 304

Email: rphillips@mobaptist.org

Select your topics

Visit **OnceDelivered.net/topics/** and see the variety of workshop topics available, or contact Rob Phillips to discuss.

Popular formats and topics:

1. One-day workshops (cover three topics)
- What is Christian apologetics?
- Who is the real Jesus?
- What do false religions have in common?

Or 3-5 hours on a single topic:
- How do I know the Bible is true?
- What every Christian should know about Islam
- What every Christian should know about same-sex attraction

2. Two-day workshops

- What is Christian apologetics?
- How do I know the Bible is true?
- Who is the real Jesus?
- What do false religions have in common?
- What do Mormons, Jehovah's Witnesses, and Muslims believe?

Or one day on each of two topics:

- How do I know the Bible is true?
- What every Christian should know about Islam
- What every Christian should know about same-sex attraction
- An overview of world religions and cults

3. Three-day workshops

- What is Christian apologetics?
- What's your worldview?
- How do I know the Bible is true?
- Who is the real Jesus?
- What do false religions have in common?
- What do Mormons believe?
- What do Jehovah's Witnesses believe?
- Do Muslims and Christians worship the same God?

Or one day on each of three topics:

- How do I know the Bible is true?
- What every Christian should know about Islam
- What every Christian should know about same-sex attraction
- An overview of world religions and cults

Tell your church

Promote the workshop from the pulpit, through your Sunday school classes and small groups, in your bulletins and newsletters, and on your website.

Remember

Copies of *The Apologist's Tool Kit 3rd Edition* are made available at the workshop at a discounted price.

Your church's gifts through the Cooperative Program cover all travel expenses.

An honorarium is appreciated but not required.

ADDITIONAL RESOURCES

Other apologetics resources from the MBC:

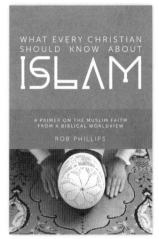

What Every Christian Should Know about Islam: A Primer on the Muslim Faith from a Biblical Worldview by Rob Phillips

The world's 1.6 billion Muslims are precious people for whom Christ died. At the same time, Islam is a false religion that strives for global conquest. *What Every Christian Should Know about Islam* offers a brief overview of this 1400-year-old religion and answers key questions about the religion of Muhammad from a biblical perspective.

Order the print edition at mobaptist.org/apologetics
Kindle edition available from Amazon

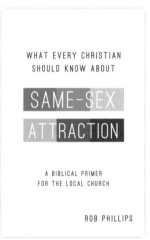

What Every Christian Should Know about Same-sex Attraction: A Biblical Primer for the Local Church by Rob Phillips

Christians are in the crosshairs of today's culture, which celebrates the gay lifestyle and accuses those who stand on biblical convictions of engaging in a new brand of McCarthyism. We should not despair, however. This is a God-ordained opportunity for followers of Jesus to love our lesbian, gay, bisexual, and transgender friends, and for the church to minister to those struggling with unwanted same-sex attraction. *What Every Christian Should Know about Same-sex Attraction* offers a brief overview of the Bible's clear teachings on homosexuality, and how Christians can express Christ-like love for our LGBT friends.

Order the print edition at mobaptist.org/apologetics
Kindle edition available from Amazon